Protecting the European ...orcing
EC Environmental Law

P. Kunzll

Law in its Social Setting

Protecting the European Environment: Enforcing EC Environmental Law

Edited by
Han Somsen
School of Law, University of Warwick

BLACKSTONE
PRESS LIMITED

First published in Great Britain 1996 by Blackstone Press Limited,
9–15 Aldine Street, London W12 8AW.   Telephone 0181-740 2277

© Legal Research Institute 1996

ISBN: 1 85431 604 4

British Library Cataloguing in Publication Data
A CIP catalogue record for this book is available from the British Library.

Printed by Bell & Bain Ltd, Glasgow

Contents

General Editor's Preface

Law in its Social Setting aims to foster the established commitment of Warwick to the contextual study of law. The series will bring together authors from other research centres in Britain and abroad to enrich debates on issues of contemporary importance in the area of socio-legal studies.

This collection of essays addresses what is the achilles heel of the Union's environmental policy: the effective enforcement of EC environmental law. Responding to proven flaws in the Community's machinery for the enforcement of EC environmental laws as well as to more recent developments such as the adoption of the Fifth Environmental Action Programme and the principle of subsidiarity, this book undertakes a welcome and original re-assessment of Community enforcement processes and instruments. Acknowledging the changed perceptions as to the desirability of centralized enforcement of Community environmental law, this timely collection of essays provides invaluable insights into the prospects for mobilizing the vigilance of individuals to enforce EC environmental law and to protect the European environment.

Mike McConville
University of Warwick

Editor's Preface

From its inception, the ideal of European integration through the establishment of supranational institutions, capable of adopting binding majority-decisions and which are enforceable by independent institutions, has enjoyed varying degrees of political and popular support. Although the final destination of this voyage of discovery remains unknown, it is clear even to the casual observer that the signing of the Treaty on European Union in 1992 represented a major change of direction, mirroring changed perceptions as to the desired nature and form of European integration. To equate this change with the notion of 'subsidiarity' would be a crude simplification, the Maastricht Treaty brought about numerous changes, increasing the Union's powers in existing and new fields and having varied impacts on different policy fields. Be this as it may, it is difficult to deny that the principle of subsidiarity, as formulated in Article 3b of the Treaty, rather accurately reflects the changing political tide in Europe, particularly in the United Kingdom.

As it is the most important tool for European integration, European Community law is necessarily profoundly affected by this change. This equally applies to European Community environmental law and one might therefore be tempted to argue that any demise of the Community's involvement in this sphere ought to be accepted as a matter of political reality. Indeed, it is difficult to argue against the proposition that the Community should only address those environmental problems it can tackle better than when the Member States act individually. A principle to this effect is in fact found in the first environmental action programme of 1973 and which is unlikely to meet with opposition from even the staunchest believer in a federal Europe.

However, there remain crucial differences between the environment and other areas of human concern, a fact which is becoming increasingly clouded by the subsidiarity debate. It is one thing to allow a Member State to adopt lower social standards than other Member States in a quest to secure competitiveness of national industry but quite another to sanction relaxed national environmental standards affecting the survival of a common heritage. The environmental lawyer ought to make it his/her responsibility continuously to remind policy-makers of established principles of international and Community law which acknowledge the environment's special status.

However, to concentrate exclusively on the Union's involvement in environmental standard-setting would be to deny the wider impact of the recent changes on subsequent stages of the policy-process such as the implementation and enforcement of EC environmental law. The enforcement of environmental directives, in particular, is traditionally regarded as the achilles' heel of the Community's environmental policy. It has been observed that the relative lack of industrial competitors with a strong interest in ensuring compliance with environmental directives means that additional responsibilities are placed on the Commission as guardian of the Treaties under Article 169 of the Treaty (*Macrory*). Yet, legal, practical and – perhaps most importantly – political constraints clearly have undermined the effectiveness and hence credibility of the infringement procedure as a means to protect the European environment (see in particular the chapters by *Macrory* and *Faulks and Rose*). Given the confrontational nature of the Court's newly acquired powers under Article 171 EC to impose a lump sum or penalty payment on defaulting Member States, it is doubtful whether this innovation will significantly improve the effectiveness of the infringement procedure.

The question therefore arises whether the failures of the infringement procedure are likely to be exacerbated by the recent political changes, or whether the trend to place greater responsibilities with Member States in carrying out Community objectives resulting in a more decentralized enforcement of Community environmental law could compensate for some of these shortcomings. In this regard it should be recalled that the Court, as early as in 1962, predicted that 'the vigilance of individuals to uphold their rights' would amount to an effective supervision of Community law additional to that entrusted to the Commission and the Member States under Articles 169 and 170 of the Treaty. Initially, the main beneficiaries of the Court's case law endowing individuals with rights they can uphold in their national courts, appeared largely confined to participants in the market, in particular traders and workers and their families. However, with the evolution of the Court's case law regarding direct effect and the emergence of notions of 'indirect effect', and more recently also State liability for breaches of Community law, the prospects for the national enforcement of European Community environmental law needs to be re-assessed.

The changed climate appears to favour increased involvement of national courts and administrations in the enforcement of Community environmental law. It is striking in this respect that all contributors, representing widely varied interests, agree on the desirability of greater decentralized enforcement albeit for different reasons. *Rehbinder* suggests the establishment of national complaint boards as a means to de-politicize and streamline the infringement procedure for breaches of EC environmental law, a proposition also echoed by representatives of the RSPB (*Faulks and Rose*) and the Department of the Environment (*Noble*). This idea would be particularly valuable in the context of dealing with practical breaches of Community standards, which the Commission is clearly less well placed to address. Another reason for seriously contemplating the creation of an additional strand at national level for dealing with complaints rests in the fact that the alternative – endowing DG XI with powers analogous to those enjoyed by the Competition Directorate General to carry out on the spot investigations – is unlikely to be acted upon in the foreseeable future (*Clinton-Davis*).

In the absence of such initiatives, however, it becomes even more vital to explore fully the opportunities afforded by the existing legal framework for individuals to uphold EC environmental law. *Krämer* and *Jans* convincingly show that, strictly speaking, in legal terms, these opportunities are legion. Direct effect, indirect effect and the supremacy of EC environmental directives are potent vehicles at the disposal of individuals to ensure that the administration gives precedence to Community environmental law over conflicting national provisions. The *Francovich* judgment, too, opens up significant opportunities for the indirect enforcement of Community environmental law.

However, there remain striking differences in the extent to which national courts and administrations have been sympathetic to arguments based on Community law. Jans' survey of Dutch experience relating to the implementation and enforcement of the directive on environmental impact assessment, in particular the role played by the Dutch courts and administration in choosing the most appropriate way of giving precedence to the directive in its application – by way of abstract or concrete review – contrasts sharply with experience in the United Kingdom. In so far as these differences are embedded in national laws relating to standing and access to legal aid, recourse to harmonization might be considered but remains extremely complex (*Rehbinder*). The European Court of Justice, too, can be expected to continue its contribution to the establishment of minimum national standards of access to justice (*Sands*).

Yet, disparities in national procedural laws only partly explain these national variations. In particular, social attitudes of lawyers and administrators appear to play at least as significant a role, something not always sufficiently appreciated by the academic community. *Tromans* observes in his contribution that:

> Whilst judicial awareness of EC law has increased by leaps and bounds, it may sometimes be a daunting prospect to embark upon a complex explanation of the relevance of a particular [EC] measure to a judge, planning inspector or lay bench of magistrates; particularly when it is uncertain how such submissions will be received.

It is therefore hoped that this collection of essays not only clarifies some of the legal issues surrounding the decentralized enforcement of EC environmental law, but also will make a positive contribution to changing some of the perceptions of those national actors most directly involved in the day-to-day enforcement of Community environmental law.

Han Somsen
Earlsdon, Coventry

Acknowledgements

This volume arose out of a Conference held at Warwick University on Thursday and Friday, 7 and 8 July 1994, at which these papers were presented and discussed for the first time.

I am grateful to Directorate General XI of the Commission of the European Communities for its generous financial contribution towards the costs of the Conference, to the Director of the Legal Research Institute, Professor Mike McConville, for his encouragement and also to Annemarie Sprokkereef, for her translation and moral support throughout the year. I thank John McEldowney for introducing me to the intricacies of UK environmental law, Gavin Anderson for his help at the preparation stage of the Conference programme and Harrie Temmink for always keeping me informed of the latest developments.

I should like to record my gratitude especially to Joseph McCahery, for his invaluable and professional advice during the most crucial stages of the project.

I am extremely fortunate to have been in a position to draw upon the vast experience of Bernadette Royall, Conference Organiser of the Legal Research Institute, who frequently worked late hours, and single-handedly took care of arrangements for speakers and the Conference, and prepared the papers for publication. I am deeply indebted to her and her family who have graciously accepted the consequences of her commitment. I also am indebted to Jennifer Mabbett, Aileen Stockham, Lesley Morris and Valerie Innes, for their practical assistance, patience and good humour.

Finally, I am only too well aware that the ultimate success of the conference and this volume is owed entirely to the expertise and enthusiasm of the contributors.

Han Somsen
August 1996

List of Contributors

Dr. Peter Bird's responsibility in the National Rivers Authority is that UK law complies with the requirements of European and other international legislation affecting water quality. This includes interpretation of legislation, determining data collection programmes and reporting the results to appropriate bodies. He has worked with the NRA for the last five years and before that for Anglian Water.

Lord Clinton-Davis is House of Lords Opposition Frontbench Spokesman on Transport and former Environment Commissioner (1985–9). He is a consultant on European affairs and law with S.J. Berwin & Co.

John Faulks is European Community Liaison Officer at the Royal Society for the Protection of Birds. He qualified as a Solicitor in 1990 and joined the RSPB in 1993 having worked with Clifford Chance in London and Brussels and the Foundation for International Environmental Law and Development.

Professor David Freestone is the Legal Advisor of the Environment Department of the World Bank and Professor of Law at the University of Hull. From 1987 to 1989 he was Advisor to the Ministry of Foreign Affairs, Antigua and Barbuda. He is Managing Editor of the *International Journal of Estuarine and Coastal Law* and Advisory Board member of *Water Law* and European Advisor of the *European Environmental Law Review.*

Professor Jan Jans is Professor of European Law at the University of Amsterdam; PhD 1987 State University of Groningen (Netherlands); 1987–8 Leverhulme Fellow University of Edinburgh (Europa Institute, Faculty of Law); Advisor to the Commission on Environmental Impact Assessment.

Dr. Ludwig Krämer is Head of the Waste Management Unit in DG XI of the European Commission, the Directorate General responsible for environmental matters.

Professor Richard Macrory is a barrister and Denton Hall Professor of Environmental Law at Imperial College, London. He is editor of the Journal of Environmental Law and was first Chairman of the UK Environmental Law Association.

David Noble was formerly attached to DG XI and is presently with the Solicitor's Office, Department of the Environment.

Professor Eckard Rehbinder is Professor of Law and Co-Director of the Institute for Foreign and International Law, Frankfurt am Main.

Ian Rose leads Allen & Overy's EC Environmental Law Unit, based in Brussels. He served a period of in-service training for five months, from October 1993, with the waste management policy unit of DG XI of the Commission of the European Communities.

Laurence Rose is Head of the European Programmes Department of the Royal Society for the Protection of Birds. He joined the RSPB in 1983 after a period in industrial production management.

Philippe Sands is a practising English barrister and founder of the Foundation for International Environmental Law and Development (FIELD), now based at SOAS, London. Since 1990 he has also been Visiting Professor at New York University. He has provided legal advice and assistance on international environmental law to numerous governments, inter-governmental organizations and the private sector.

Han Somsen lectures evironmental law at the University of Warwick. He is European Advisor of *Water Law* and case editor of the *European Environmental Law Review*, (Graham & Trotman) and editor in chief of the *Yearbook of European Environmental Law* (Oxford University Press)

Lord Slynn of Hadley is Lord of Appeal in Ordinary (1992–). He served as an Advocate General (1981–8) and was a judge at the European Court of Justice (1988–92). He has been a Visiting Professor at various prestigious institutions throughout the world.

Stephen Tromans is a partner at Simmons & Simmons which he joined in 1990. He heads the firm's Environmental Law Department. He is Vice-Chairman of the UK Environmental Law Association and an Editor of the *Journal of Environmental Law* (OUP) and Chairman of the Law Society's Environmental Law Sub-Committee.

Jamie Woolley has worked in commercial practice in the city of London, in legal aid practice, in community law centres and is currently a Principal Solicitor with Sheffield City Council. He is legal advisor to the Association of Metropolitan Authorities' Environment Forum, is a council member of UKELA and a founder member of the Environmental Law Centre.

Table of Abbreviations

AC	Appeal Cases
AG	Advocate General
All ER	All England Law Reports
BEUC	Bureau Européen Union de Consumateurs
BHS	British Herpetological Society
CEMR	Council of European Municipalities and Regions
COMAH	Council Directive on the control of Major Accident Hazards
DG	Directorate General
DoE	Department of the Environment
DoE NI	Department of the Environment Northern Ireland
EC	European Community
ECJ	European Court of Justice
EEC	European Economic Community
EIA	Environmental Impact Assessment
EOC	Equal Opportunities Commission
EPA	Environmental Protection Act
ERDF	European Regional Development Fund
EU	European Union
FOE	Friends of the Earth
GATT	General Agreement on Tariffs and Trade
HMIP	Her Majesty's Inspectorate for Pollution
ICJ	International Court of Justice
IRLR	Irish Law Review
LBTC	London Boroughs Transport Committee
MAFF	Ministry for Agriculture Fisheries and Food
MEP	Member of the European Parliament
MNR	Marine Nature Reserve
NGO	Non Governmental Organisation
NRA	National Rivers Authority
NYU	New York University
RPB	River Purification Board
RSPB	Royal Society for the Protection of Birds
SAC	Special Areas of Conservation
SO	Scottish Office
SPA	Special Protection Area
SSSI	Site of Special Scientific Interest
TA	Technische Anweisung
TEU	Treaty on European Union
UK	United Kingdom
UNCED	United Nations Conference on Environment and Development

VAT   Value Added Tax
VNO   Verening Nederlandse Ondernemingen
WLR   Weekly Law Reports
WWF   Worldwide Fund for Nature

List of EC Cases

Case 26/62, *Van Gend & Loos*, [1963] ECR 1.
Case 106–107/1963, *Alfred Topfer and Getreide-Import Gesellshaft v Commission*, [1965] ECR 405.
Case 6/64, *Costa v ENEL*, [1964] ECR 585.
Case 57/65, *Lütticke*, [1966] ECR 258.
Case 13/68, *Salgoil*, [1968] ECR 661.
Case 14/68, *Wilhelm*, [1969] ECR 1.
Case 11/70, *Internationale Handelsgesellschaft*, [1970] ECR 1125.
Case 33/70, *SACE*, [1970] ECR 1213.
Case 18/71, *Di Porro*, [1971] ECR 811.
Case 39/72, *Commission v Italy*, [1973] ECR 1.
Case 2/74, *Reyners*, [1974] ECR 631.
Case 33/74, *Van Binsbergen*, [1974] ECR 1299.
Case 41/74, *Van Duyn*, [1974] ECR 1337.
Case 43/75, *Defrenne*, [1976] ECR 455.
Case 52/75, *Commission v Italy*, [1976] ECR 277.
Case 111/75, *Haaga*, [1974] ECR 1201.
Case 13/76, *Dona*, [1976] ECR 1333.
Case 21/76, *Handelskwekerij Bier v Mines de Potasse d'Alsace*, [1976] ECR 1735.
Case 45/76, *Comet*, [1976] ECR 2043.
Case 51/76, *Nederlandse Ondernemingen*, [1977] ECR 113.
Case 74/76, *Volpi*, [1977] ECR 1213.
Case 106/77, *Simmenthal*, [1978] ECR 629.
Case 83/78, *Pigs Marketing Board*, [1978] ECR 2347.
Case 120/78, *Cassis de Dijon*, [1979] ECR 649.
Case 148/78, *Ratti*, [1979] ECR 1629.
Case 265/78, *Ferwerda*, [1980] ECR 617.
Case 21/79, *Commission v Italy*, [1980] ECR 1.
Case 91/79, *Commission v Italy*, [1980] ECR 1099.
Case 92/79, *Commission v Italy*, [1980] ECR 1099.
Case 102/79, *Commission v Belgium*, [1980] ECR 1473.
Case 171/79, *Commission v Italy*, [1981] ECR 465.
Case 272/80, *Criminal Proceedings against Frans-Nederlandse Maatschappij voor Biologische Produkten*, [1981] ECR 3277.
Case 8/81, *Becker*, [1982] ECR 53.
Case 30–41/81, *Commission v Italy*, [1981] ECR 3379.
Case 68/81, *Commission v Belgium*, [1982] ECR 153.
Case 69/81, *Commission v Belgium*, [1982] ECR 163.
Case 96–97/81, *Commission v Netherlands*, [1982] ECR 1791 and 1819.
Case 172/81, *Fabricants Raffineurs d'Huiles de Graissage v Inter-Huile*, [1983] ECR 555.
Case 249/81, *Commission v Ireland*, [1982] ECR 4005.

List of EC Legislation

Directive 67/548 on the approximation of the laws, regulations and administrative provisions relating to the classification, packaging and labelling of dangerous substances, OJ 1967 No. L 196/1.

Directive 68/151 on coordination of safeguards which are required by Member States of companies within the meaning of the second paragraph of Article 58 of the Treaty, with a view of making such safeguards equivalent throughout the Community, OJ 1969 No. L 65/8.

Directive 70/157 on the approximation of the laws in the Member States relating to the permissible sound level and the exhaust system of motor vehicles, OJ 1970 No. L 42/16.

Directive 70/220 on the approximation of the laws of the Member States on measures to be taken against air pollution by emissions from motor vehicles, OJ 1970 No. L 76/1.

Directive 71/144 extending the time limit laid down in article 10 of Directive 67/548, OJ Special English Edition No. L 1/15.

Directive 71/305 on award procedures for public construction projects, OJ 1971 No. L 185/5.

Directive 72/306 on the approximation of the laws of the Member States relating to the measures to be taken against the emission of pollutants from diesel engines, OJ 1972 No. L 190/1.

Directive 73/173 relating to the classification, packaging and labelling of dangerous preparations (solvents), OJ 1973 No. L 189/7.

Directive 73/404 on the approximation of the laws of the Member States relating to detergents, OJ 1973 No. L 347/1.

Directive 74/290 adapting to technical progress Council Directive 70/220, OJ 1974 No. L 159/61.

Directive 75/439 on the disposal of waste oils, OJ 1975 No. L 194/23.

Directive 75/440 on the quality of surface water intended for the abstraction of drinking water, OJ 1975 No. L 194/26.

Directive 75/442 on waste, OJ 1975 No. L 194/39.

Directive 75/716 on the approximation of the laws of the Member States relating to the sulphur content of certain liquid fuels, OJ 1975 No. L 307/22.

Directive 76/160 on the quality of bathing waters, OJ 1976 No. L 30/1.

Directive 76/207 on the implementation of the principle of equal treatment for men and women as regards access to employment, vocational training and promotion, and working conditions, OJ 1976 No. L 39/40.

Directive 76/403 on the disposal of polychlorinated biphenyls and polychlorinated terphenyls, OJ 1976 No. L 108/41.

Directive 76/464 on pollution caused by certain dangerous substances discharged into the aquatic environment, OJ 1976 No. L 129/33.

Directive 76/769 on the approximation of the laws, regulations and administrative provisions of the Member States relating to restrictions on the marketing and use of certain dangerous substances and preparations, OJ 1976 No. L 262/12.

Directive 77/102 adapting to technical progress Directive 70/220, OJ 1978 No. L 32/32.

Directive 78/1015 on the approximation of the laws of the Member States on the permissible sound level and exhaust system of motorcycles, OJ 1978 No. L 349/21.

Directive 78/176 on waste from the titanium dioxide industry, OJ 1978 No. L 54/19.

Directive 78/319 on toxic and dangerous waste, OJ 1978 No. L 84/43.

Directive 78/659 on the quality of fresh waters needing protection or improvement in order to support fish life, OJ 1978 No. L 222/1.

Directive 78/665 adapting to technical progress Directive 70/220, OJ 1978 No. L 223/48.

Directive 79/113 on the approximation of the laws of the Member States relating to the determination of the noise emission of construction plant and equipment, OJ 1979 No. L 33/15.

Directive 79/409 on the conservation of wild birds, OJ 1979 No. L 103/1.

Directive 79/869 concerning the methods of measurement and frequencies of sampling and analysis of surface water intended for the abstraction of drinking water in the Member States, OJ 1979 No. L 271/26.

Directive 79/923 on the quality required of shellfish waters, OJ 1979 No. L 281/47.

Directive 80/51 on the limitation of noise emissions from subsonic aircraft, OJ 1980 No. L 18/26.

Directive 80/68 on the protection of groundwater against pollution caused by certain dangerous substances, OJ 1980 No. L 20/43.

Directive 80/777 relating to the exploitation and marketing of natural mineral waters, OJ 1980 No. L 229/1.

Directive 80/778 relating to the quality of water intended for human consumption, OJ 1980 No. L 229/11.

Directive 80/779 on air quality limit values and guide values for sulphur dioxide and suspended particulates, OJ 1980 No. L 229/30.

Directive 81/334 adapting to technical progress Directive 70/157, OJ 1984 No. L 196/47.

Directive 82/176 on limit values and quality objectives for mercury discharges by the chlor-alkali electrolysis industry, OJ 1982 No. L 81/29.

Directive 82/242 on the approximation of the laws of the Member States relating to methods of testing the biodegradability of non-ionic surfactants and amending Directive 73/404, OJ 1982 No. L 109/1.

Directive 82/501 on the major-accident hazards of certain industrial activities, OJ 1982 No. L 230/1.

Directive 82/883 on procedures for the surveillance and monitoring of environments concerned by waste from the titanium dioxide industry, OJ 1982 No. L 378/1.

Directive 82/884 on limit values for lead in the air, OJ 1982 No. L 378/15.

Directive 83/129 concerning importation into Member States of skins of certain seal pups and products derived therefrom, OJ 1983 No. L 91/30.

Directive 83/189 laying down a procedure for the provision of information in the field of technical standard and regulations, OJ 1983 No. L 109/8.

Directive 83/29 amending Directive 78/176 on waste from the titanium dioxide industry, OJ 1982 No. L 32/28.

Directive 83/513 on limit values and quality objectives for cadmium discharges, OJ 1983 No. L 291/1.

Directive 84/156 on limit values and quality objectives for mercury discharges by sectors other than the chlor-alkali electrolysis industry, OJ 1984 No. L 74/49.

Directive 84/360 on the combating of air pollution from industrial plants, OJ 1984 No. L 188/20.

Directive 84/491 on limit values and quality objectives for discharges of hexachlorocyclohexane, OJ 1984 No. L 274/11.

Directive 84/533 on the approximation of the laws of the Member States relating to the permissible sound level of compressors, OJ 1984 No. L 300/123.

Directive 84/534 on the approximation of the laws of Member States relating to the permissible sound level of tower cranes 1984, OJ 300 No. L 130/

Directive 84/535 on the approximation of the laws of the Member States relating to the permissible sound level of welding generators, OJ 1984 No. L 300/142.

Directive 84/537 on the approximation of the laws of the laws of the Member States relating to the permissible sound level of powered hand-held concrete breakers and picks, OJ 1984 No. L 300/156.

Directive 84/631 on the supervision and control within the Community of the transfrontier shipment of hazardous waste, OJ 1984 No. L 326/31.

Directive 85/203 on air quality standards for nitrogen dioxide, OJ 1985 No. L 87/1.

Directive 85/203 on air quality standards for nitrogen dioxide, OJ 1985 No. L 87/1.

Directive 85/210 on the lead content of petrol, OJ 1985 No. L 96/25.

Directive 85/337 on the assessment of the effects of certain public and private projects on the environment, OJ 1985 No. L 175/40.

Directive 85/339 on containers of liquids for human consumption, OJ 1985 No. L 176/18.

Directive 85/405 adapting to technical progress Directive 79/113, OJ 1985 No. L 223/9.

Directive 85/406 adapting to technical progress Directive 84/533, OJ 1985 No. L 233/11.

Directive 85/407 adapting to technical progress Directive 84/535, OJ 1985 No. L 233/16.

Directive 85/408 adapting to technical progress Directive 84/536, OJ 1985 No. L 233/18.

Directive 85/409 adapting to technical progress Directive 84/537, OJ 1985 No. L 233/20.

Directive 85/469 adapting to technical progress Directive 84/631 on the supervision and control within the Community of the transfrontier shipment of hazardous waste, OJ 1985 No. L 272/1.

Directive 85/536 on the approximation of the laws of the Member States relating to the permissible sound level of power generators, OJ 1984 No. L 300/149.

Directive 85/538 on the approximation of the laws of Member States relating to the permissible sound level of lawnmowers, OJ 1984 No. L 300/171.

Directive 85/577 to protect the consumer in respect of contracts negotiated away from business premises, OJ 1985 No. L 372/31.

Directive 86/278 on the protection of the environment, and in particular of the soil, when sewage sludge is used in agriculture, OJ 1985 No. L 272/1.

Directive 86/279 amending Directive 84/631 on the supervision and control within the European Community of the transfrontier shipment of hazardous waste, OJ 1986 No. L 181/13.

Directive 86/280 on limit values and quality objectives of certain dangerous substances included in list I of the Annex to Directive 76/464, OJ 1986 No. L 181/16.

Directive 86/594 on airborne noise emitted by household appliances, OJ 1986 No. L 344/24.

Directive 86/609 on the approximation of laws, regulations and administrative provisions of the Member States regarding the protection of animals used for experimental and other scientific purposes, OJ 1986 No. L 358/1.

Directive 86/662 on the limitation of noise emitted by hydraulic excavators, rope-operated excavators, dozers, loaders and excavator-loaders, OJ 1986 No. L 384/1.

Directive 87/101 amending Directive 75/439 on the disposal of waste oils, OJ 1987 No. L 42/43.

Directive 87/112 adapting to technical progress for the second time Directive 84/631 on the supervision and control within the European Community of the transfrontier shipment of hazardous waste, OJ 1987 No. L 48/31.

Directive 87/18 on the harmonization of laws, regulations and administrative provisions relating to the application of the principles of good laboratory practice and the verification of their applications to tests on chemical substances, OJ 1987 No. L 15/29.

Directive 87/217 on the prevention and reduction of environmental pollution by asbestos, OJ 1987 No. L 85/40.

Directive 87/252 adapting to technical progress Directive 84/539, OJ 1987 No. L 117/22.

Directive 87/354 amending certain directives on the approximation of the laws of the Member States relating to industrial products with respect to the distinctive numbers and letters indicating the Member States, OJ 1987 No. L 192/43.

Directive 88/77 on the approximation of the laws of the Member States relating to the measures to be taken against the emission of gaseous pollutants from diesel engines for use in vehicles, OJ 1988 No. L 36/33.

Directive 88/180 amending Directive 84/538 on the approximation of the laws of the Member States relating to the permissible sound level of lawnmowers, OJ 1988 No. L 81/69.

Directive 88/189 laying down a procedure for the provision of information in the field of technical standards and regulations, OJ 1983 No. L 109/8.

Directive 88/320 on the inspection and verification of good laboratory practice, OJ 1988 No. L 145/35.

Directive 88/379 on the approximation of the laws, regulations and administrative provisions of the Member States relating to the classification, packaging and labelling of dangerous preparations, OJ 1988 No. L 187/14.

Directive 88/609 on the limitation of emissions of certain pollutants into the air from large combustion plants, OJ 1988 No. L 336/1.

Directive 89/235 amending Directive 78/1015 on the approximation of the laws of the Member States on the permissible sound level and exhaust system of motorcycles, OJ 1989 No. L 98/1.

Directive 89/369 on the prevention of air pollution from new municipal waste incineration plants, OJ 1989 No. L 163/32.

Directive 89/429 on the reduction of air pollution from existing municipal waste incineration plants, OJ 1989 No. L 163/32.

Directive 89/458 amending with regard to European emission standards for cars below 1.4 litres, Directive 70/220, OJ 1989 No. L 226/1.

Directive 89/491 adapting to technical progress Directives 70/157, 70/220, 72/245, 72/306, 80/1268 and 80/1269 relating to motor vehicles, OJ 1989 No. L 238/43.

Directive 89/514 adapting to technical progress Directive 86/662, OJ 1989 No. L 253/35.

Directive 89/629 on the limitation of noise emission from civil subsonic jet aeroplanes, OJ 1989 No. L 363/27.

Directive 90/219 on the contained use of genetically modified micro-organisms, OJ 1990 No. L 117/1.

Directive 90/220 on the deliberate release into the environment of genetically modified organisms, OJ 1990 No. L 117/15.

Directive 90/313 on the freedom of access to information on the environment, OJ 1990 No. L 158/56.

Directive 90/656 on the transitional measures applicable in Germany with regard to certain Community provisions relating to the protection of the environment, OJ 1990 No. L 353/59.

Directive 90/660 on the transitional measures applicable in Germany with regard to certain Community provisions relating to the protection of the environment, in connection with the internal market, OJ 1990 No. L 353/79.

Directive 91/155 laying down detailed arrangements for the system of specific information relating to dangerous preparations in implementation of Article 10 of Directive 88/379, OJ 1991 No. L 76/35.

Directive 91/157 on batteries and accumulators containing certain dangerous substances, OJ 1991 No. L 78/38.

Directive 91/271 concerning urban waste water treatment, OJ 1991 No. L 135/40.

Directive 91/448 concerning the guidelines for classification referred to in Article 4 of Directive 90/219, OJ 1991 No. L 239/23.

Directive 91/692 on standardizing and rationalizing reports on the implementation of certain environmental directives, OJ 1991 No. L 377.

Directive 92/43 on the conservation of natural habitats and of wild fauna and flora, OJ 1992 No. L 206.

Decision 82/795 on the consolidation of precautionary measures concerning chlorofluorcarbons in the environment, OJ 1982 No. L 329/29.

Decision 75/437 concluding the Convention for the prevention of marine pollution from land based sources, OJ 1975 No. L 194/5.

Decision 77/585 concluding the Convention for the protection of the Mediterranean Sea against pollution and the Protocol for the prevention of pollution of the Mediterranean Sea by dumping from ships and aircraft, OJ 1977 No. L 240/1.

Decision 77/586 concluding the Convention for the protection of the Rhine against chemical pollution and an additional agreement, signed in Berne on 29 April 1963, concerning the International Commission for the protection of the Rhine against pollution, OJ 1977 No. L 240/35.

Decision 77/795 establishing a common procedure for the exchange of information on the quality of surface fresh water in the Community, OJ 1977 No. L 334/29.

Decision 80/372 concerning chlorofluorcarbons in the environment, OJ 1980 No. L 90/45.

Decision 81/420 on the conclusion of the protocol concerning cooperation in combating pollution of the Mediterranean Sea by oil and other harmful substances in cases of emergency, OJ 1981 No. L 162/4.

Decision 81/462 on the conclusion of the Convention on long-range transboundary air pollution, OJ 1981 No. L 181/11.

Decision 81/691 on the conclusion of the Convention on the conservation of Antarctic marine living resources, OJ 1981 No. L 252/26.

Decision 81/856 of 19 October 1981, OJ 1981 No. L 319/17.

Decision 82/459 establishing a reciprocal exchange of information and data from networks and individual stations measuring air pollution within Member States, OJ 1982 No. L 210/1.

Decision 82/461 on the conclusion of the Convention on the conservation of migratory species of wild animals, OJ 1982 No. L 210/10.

Decision 82/72 concerning the conclusion of the Convention on the conservation of European wildlife and natural habitats, OJ 1982 No. L 38/1.

Decision 83/101 concluding the protocol for the protection of the Mediterranean Sea against pollution from land-based sources, OJ 1981 No. L 67/1.

Decision 84/132 on the conclusion of the protocol concerning Mediterranean specially protected areas, OJ 1984 No. L 78/36.

Decision 84/358 on the agreement for cooperation in dealing with pollution of the North Sea by oil and other harmful substances (Bonn Agreement), OJ 1984 No. L 188/7.

Decision 85/613 concerning the adoption, on behalf of the Community, of programmes and measures relating to mercury and cadmium discharges under the Convention for the prevention of marine pollution from land-based sources, OJ 1985 No. L 375/20.

Decision 85/71 concerning the list of chemical substances notified pursuant to Directive 67/548 on the approximation of laws, regulations and administrative provisions relating to the classification, packaging and labelling of dangerous substances, OJ 1985 No. L 30/33.

Decision 86/277 on the conclusion of the protocol to the 1979 Convention on long-range transboundary air pollution on long-term financing of the cooperative programme for monitoring and evaluation of the long-range transmission of air pollutants in Europe (EMEP), OJ 1986 No. L 181/1.

Decision 86/85 establishing a Community information system for the control and reduction of pollution caused by the spillage of hydrocarbons and other harmful substances at sea, OJ 1986 No. L 77/33.

Decision 87/57 concluding the protocol amending the Convention for the prevention of marine pollution from land-based sources.

Decision 88/540 concerning the conclusion of the Vienna Convention for the protection of the ozone layer and the Montreal Protocol on substances that deplete the ozone layer, OJ 1988 No. L 297/8.

Decision 89/569 on the acceptance by the European Economic Community of an OECD decision/recommendation on compliance with principles of good laboratory practice, OJ 1989 No. L 315/1.

Decision 90/170 on the acceptance by the European Economic Community of an OECD Decision/recommendation on the control of transfrontier movements of hazardous waste, OJ 1990 No. L 92/52.

Decision 90/230 amending the lists of standardization institutions set out in the annex to Directive 83/189, OJ 1990 No. L 128/15.

Decision 91/274 concerning a list of Community legislation referred to in Article 10 of Directive 90/220, OJ 1991 No. L 135/56.

Decision 91/359 allocating import quotas for chlorofluorocarbons for the period 1 July 1991 to 31 December 1992, OJ 1991 No. L 193/42.

Decision 91/400 on the conclusion of the fourth ACP-EEC Convention, OJ 1991 No. L 229/1.

Recommendation 75/436 regarding cost allocation and action by public authorities on environmental matters, OJ 1975 No. L 194/1.

Recommendation 79/3 to the Member States regarding methods of evaluating the cost of pollution control to industry, OJ 1979 No. L 5/29.

Regulation 1210/90 on the establishment of the European Environment Agency and the European environment information and observation network, OJ 1990 No. L 120/1.

Regulation 1734/88 concerning export from and import into the Community of dangerous chemicals, OJ 1988 No. L 155/2.

Regulation 2496/89 on a prohibition on importing raw and worked ivory derived from the African elephant into the Community, OJ 1989 No. L 240/5.

Regulation 348/81 on common rules for imports of whales or other cetacean products, OJ 1981 No. L 39/1.

Regulation 3626/82 on the implementation in the Community of the Convention on international trade in endangered species of wild fauna and flora, OJ 1982 No. L 384/1.

Foreword

When I went to the University of Warwick's Environmental Law Conference at the invitation of Mr. Han Somsen to chair part of the programme I expected the speakers to be, as they were, highly qualified to talk about their chosen allotted subjects. I had not appreciated how numerous, how enthusiastic and how well-informed those who enrolled for the conference would be. The questions asked were not the faltering sort which politeness requires that someone should ask in order to rescue the chairman during the ten minutes before a session is due to close. They were lively, penetrating and perceptive.

Perhaps I should have appreciated that this would be so. The importance of protecting the environment is now realized not only by the self-avowed Green, the economist, the lawyer, the industrialist (unless in some cases it clashes with his economic interest) but much more widely – we now have over a thousand members of the United Kingdom Environmental Law Association – and in retrospect it was evident that this high-powered conference would attract many knowledgeable participants.

Recollection of lectures and the answers to questions, however, inevitably fades. It would have been a great waste if these lectures had not been preserved. Mr. Somsen has done a great service in persuading each of the speakers to produce a text, and in collating and editing them in this book.

It is now obvious that enforcing environmental standards, and thereby protecting the environment, cannot be left to traditional national court remedies; it is no less clear that many of the threats to our planet and our lives have to be tackled on an international or at the very least on a regional basis. The European Community is in the van of such action and has a unique opportunity to develop it further. In earlier days there may have been much debate about the Community's powers to act in such matters – even derision about how the protection of wild birds could possibly aid the achievement of the Common Market – but that is long since past. The Advocate General's opinion (mine) and judgment in the *Danish Beer Bottle* case made it plain that environmental considerations could constitute mandatory requirements to override the prohibition of restrictions on imports; the Single European Act in Article 130 and now the Maastricht Treaty recognize to a considerable degree the interaction of environmental and economic issues and the importance of giving full weight to the former. At the same time the limits of the Community's ability to act became increasingly of concern; in the German *Leybucht* case we realized how difficult it was for the Commission to keep any eye on what was happening in the Community and to apply to the European Court of Justice for interim relief in sufficient time. Whatever the validity of arguments now advanced to curb the Community's activities in other areas it seems inevitable that where the protection of the environment is concerned the Community must itself act with the full support of the Member States.

The articles which follow tackle in depth many aspects of these problems – identifying issues, defining standards, effectively enforcing them. How can the Commission be effective, how far does the Environmental Agency need further powers to compel the giving of information and powers of inspection to enable it to produce the kind of intelligence which the Community needs; is the court in a real sense and environmental law tribunal – should individuals or, even more, environmental interest groups have the power to go to the court without detailed investigations as to whether they are directly and individually concerned? Are directives the best instruments for laying down standards, or should there be more regulations, and is it right that so much should depend on an analysis of the precise rule adopted in the directive should an individual seek to bring an action against a Member State in reliance on the terms of a directive which has not been implemented.

There is a wealth of material concerned with environmental law cases in this book which is at the same time of wider relevance. The discussions by Mr. Jans and Mr. Krämer on direct effect and by Mr. Somsen on *Francovich* (which is only at the beginning of its journey) are striking but not the only striking examples. Those who are interested in the working out of, dare I say it even those who appear to attach overriding importance to, the principle of subsidiarity will find the discussion of the role of the Commission, of national government and agencies such as the National Rivers Authority and local government of great value. For those more interested in what happens on the ground than in the substantive and procedural law the detailed accounts of the *Leybucht* and the *Marisma de Santoña* cases, the experience of the Royal Society for the Protection of Birds, the importance of access to information on environmental matters will all prove valuable reading.

This book contains a remarkable range and depth of material on the importance of ensuring that Environmental Law is sufficient for the demands of our time but even more on the importance of ensuring that we devise adequate methods to enforce it. I have no doubt that the book will be widely appreciated and studied.

Slynn of Hadley

1. Enforcing EC Environmental Law: A Personal Perspective

Lord Clinton-Davis

Implementation and enforcement of European Union – and in this context environmental – legislation is absolutely essential to Union policy. In many ways its environmental policy has been one of the great success stories of the Union. This is despite the politicization of the process at all levels by Member States working all too often to neutralize Commission proposals; within the Commission itself in response to pressures usually emanating from the Member States; and within the European Parliament in response to extensive lobbying from one end of the political and/or industrial spectrum to the other. Even before the Single European Act provided a legal basis for environmental legislation for the first time – and I like to think that DG XI (the Environment Directorate-General) and my own Cabinet played a not insignificant role in ensuring this – something like 100 separate pieces of legislation affecting the environment had been enacted.

Yet, the inclusion of Title VII on environment in the EC Treaty was of enormous significance. Notably in its provision that environmental protection requirements would be a component of all the Community's other policies (Article 130r(2)); in making specific provision that the Community and the Member States should cooperate with third countries in pursuing environmental objectives (Article 130r(5)); and in enabling a Member State to maintain or introduce more stringent protective measures, providing that these are compatible with the Treaty (Article 130t).

Moreover, the principal provision for facilitating the establishment and functioning of the internal market (Article 100a) buttressed the value of Title VII by providing that the Commission in its proposals under Article 100a, when dealing with measures relating to health, safety, environmental protection, and consumer protection is obliged to take as a base a high level of protection (Article 100a(3)), and by the further recognition in Article l00a(4) that, providing a Member State notifies the Commission of its intention to apply national provisions on grounds of major needs, as set out in Article 36 of the EC Treaty, or in relation to the protection of the environment or the working environment, it can rely upon such national legislation.

Article 36 itself has important environmental implications, enabling the prohibitions or restrictions on imports, exports or goods in transit to be justified on grounds of public morality, public policy or public security; the protection of health and life of humans, animals or plants; the protection of national treasures possessing artistic, historic or archaeological value; or the protection of industrial and commercial property. Such prohibitions or restrictions shall not, however, constitute a means for arbitrary discrimination or a disguised restriction on trade between Member States.

The EU has been and will continue to be critically important as a forum for environmental policy-making, notwithstanding recent discussions which preceded the signing of the Maastricht Treaty and which may suggest that environmental policy should in effect be repatriated.

Enacting EU legislation is one thing, implementing and enforcing it is quite another. There are simply too many instances of Member States failing to transpose or to transpose properly EU directives into their national legal orders, least of all within the time limits prescribed. A salient example of this occurred a few years ago when a pariah ship carrying toxic cargo attempted to unload its cargo in a number of ports of European Member States. It was then discovered that Member States had failed to transpose the relevant directive relating to the transport of toxic substances into their national laws for periods far beyond that prescribed in the directive itself.

Enforcement is also far too patchy. DG XI has no powers to undertake the monitoring or policing of compliance with EU legislation in any way comparable to the powers possessed by DG IV, the Competition Directorate-General. Yet, it is worth remembering that within the compass of the Single Market, equivalent standards of implementation and enforcement of EU environmental law are of critical importance.

The greatest corpus of EU environmental legislation has been enacted on the basis of unanimity by the Member States themselves. Of course this has followed rigorous discussion in the working groups or in the Committee of Permanent Representatives (COREPER) and in the Council itself. Frequently, Member States, or some of them, seek to emasculate Commission proposals. The law is not imposed by faceless bureaucrats sitting in Brussels. It is the Member States themselves who are the authors of legislation. Yet when attacked for non-compliance, they more often than not round on the Commission for taking too harsh a view of the enforcement of EU law and go on to suggest that they are being discriminated against unfairly. Striking in this context is the suggestion made by the former British Foreign Secretary, Douglas Hurd, when Britain was facing infraction proceedings over questions affecting the environmental impact assessment directive and the water directives, that the Commission was invading every nook and cranny of British life. Then there was the suggestion that Britain, despite its less than flawless record on implementation of environment law, should be less diligent in its observance of these matters. Even more recently, there was a dispute as to the cost of the implementation the urban waste water directive of 1991. The Department of the Environment had estimated its cost as being £2bn. The Treasury, anxious to avoid or delay its application, suggested just months later a miraculous rise to £10bn.

An even earlier instance of such attempts to avoid compliance with the law resulted in the case of a provision in the bathing water directive which required Member States to identify bathing waters which fell within the scope of the directive. The information, to the best of my recollection, was something like the following:

France identified 1400 bathing beaches, Italy 1100, lovely little land-locked Luxembourg, 37 and the United Kingdom, with the longest coastline of all Member States in Europe, identified 27.

Despite all this, the issue of defaults in implementation has been afforded a high profile at the Dublin Summit of the European Council in June 1990. In the Final Declaration it was stated that:

> Community environmental legislation will only be effective if it is fully implemented and enforced by Member States. We therefore renew our commitment in this respect. To ensure transparency, comparability of effort and full information for the public, we invite the Commission to conduct regular reviews and to publish detailed reports on its findings. There should also be periodic evaluations of existing directives to ensure that they are adapted to scientific and technical progress and to resolve persistent difficulties in implementation; such reviews should not, of course, lead to a reduced standard of environmental protection in any case.

This theme was further developed in the 5th Environmental Action Programme and at the Maastricht Summit a Declaration was agreed which stressed the need for community legislation to be accurately transposed into national law and effectively applied. The Treaty on European Union contains new powers for the European Court of Justice to fine Member States which fail to comply with its judgments. However, the Treaty has failed to give powers to the Commission to enforce environmental law on a basis comparable to that of competition law. While the Commission, and DG XI in particular, would have to enjoy considerably extended powers, would this not have a far more direct and immediate effect in dealing with or mitigating the damaging consequences of breaches of environmental law? In addition, unlike the new provisions in the Treaty, would this not also have the effect of making the polluter pay?

In fact I made a written submission to the House of Lords Select Committee on the Enforcement of Environmental Legislation,[1] elaborating the case for the Commission to be able to take action against an aberrant undertaking, rather than against an offending Member State; to possess a small inspectorate, comparable to that in DG IV; to be able to carry out dawn raids to avoid the destruction of relevant evidence; to impose fines against the undertaking in question; and to provide, of course, a right of appeal to the undertaking in question against the finding and/or the penalty to the European Court of Justice. My colleagues in the House of Lords did not warm to this proposal. Of course it is right that it could not take effect without further legislation consequent upon the review of the Maastricht Treaty by the Inter-Governmental Conference in 1996. Unquestionably however, it would have great value in arresting the mischief being done in environmental cases, it would ensure that the European Court of Justice would not be caught up in political controversy and, perhaps above all, it would have been a case of making the polluter rather than Member States pay for the damage done to our environment.

I have to concede, much to my regret, that this proposal is unlikely to see the light of day.

New potential for enforcement may have arisen in the case of *Francovich*, in which the Court laid down principles by which individuals who have suffered as a result of a Member State's failure to implement a directive should be able to seek financial compensation from the State, providing that they can show identifiable rights and a causal link between non-implementation and the damage sustained. The effects of this case in the environmental field have yet to be explored. Moreover, the *Factortame* case suggests that national courts must consider applications for injunctions in cases where they have referred issues of compliance to the European Court of Justice for decision.

The role of the European Environment Agency (EEA) should prove to be extremely important in helping to improve the quality and comparability of environmental information and in developing methodologies to enable data

---

[1]   House of Lords Select Committee on the European Communities (1992).

collection and analysis to be improved. However, many questions remain. Is it likely or desirable that a Community Environmental Inspectorate under the aegis of the EEA or of DG XI should emerge? If so, what form should it take? Simply to inspect the national inspectors or to take on a role comparable to that in DG IV? What powers should they have? What should be the respective roles of the European Parliament and national Parliaments in monitoring environmental legislation, its implementation and enforcement? Should there also be a role for Non Governmental Organizations? Assisted by the coming into force of the directive on freedom of access to environmental information, pressure from NGOs has been of considerable importance in highlighting failures to implement and enforce environmental law. The question whether the structural funds and other forms of Community funding could be used to play a part in implementation and enforcement of environmental law has been considered, but would the withholding of such aid be compatible with the wider interests of ensuring that the poorer members of the EU are not relatively more handicapped than others?

The final topic that I wish to mention relates to that of subsidiarity – and they talk of little else in the public houses of Coventry – and whether this concept is likely further to constrain not only the development of EU environmental law in the future but also the enforcement and implementation of existing law. Will some Member States, perhaps even the majority, seek to utilize the notion of subsidiarity to restrict the emergence of new environmental law at EU level and intimidate the Commission into taking a far lower profile as far as its enforcement is concerned? It is as well to recall that the doctrine of subsidiarity was introduced at the instance of the European Commission into the Single European Act. Article 130r(4) provided the Community shall take action relating to the environment to the extent to which the objectives referred to in paragraph 1 can be attained better at Community level than at the level of the individual Member States. This led to few, if any, problems until the debates on Maastricht began to develop and it was suggested by some, particularly the United Kingdom, that this was a novel concept despite the evidence to the contrary which I have just cited.

There was a major difference of approach over the construction of the concept of subsidiarity between the Commission and those Member States who wished to confine the development of environmental policy. The latter engaged in much talk before and during the Edinburgh Summit of repealing a great body of environmental legislation; repatriating environmental legislation was the great trumpet call of the time, reflecting the nooks and crannies intellectual approach of the Foreign Secretary. The Commission's approach was essentially to pose the question how and at what level the environment can be best protected. It was a difference between those who thought positively about the environment and those who sought to obstruct the further development of european environmental law.

To be realistic – and one can only hope that it will be in the short term – this national approach has assumed undue prominence. It has been reflected by something of a malaise within the Commission explicable in part by the fact that the current Commission has only had a two year mandate and by the fact that some Member States have set about being deliberately provocative and obstructionist. On the other hand, I am reasonably confident that the European Court of Justice will side with the Commission in its construction of the role of subsidiarity in the future development of European environmental law.

Perhaps I can now set out some of my principal conclusions:

1. Member States must afford much more attention to the implementation and enforcement of EU environmental law. This will require a change of attitude and greater transparency as far as the Member States are concerned. If they fail to do this, I believe that the people of Europe, for whom European environmental law has been one of the most popular policies, will exert pressure for a transfer of competences, in this field at least, to the European Union;
2. Member States must not view directives as allowing undue flexibility in terms of their transposition or as being 'the easy way out';
3. the European Environment Agency should be enabled to ensure that information provided by Member States is accurate. It may be necessary, therefore, to verify data directly by visiting Member States themselves;
4. an environmental audit inspectorate should be set up to examine policies and the performance of authorities in Member States, to carry out spot checks on the data collected and to seek to obtain greater harmonization of standards of inspection;
5. there must be greater openness at meetings of the Environment Council. The public is entitled to know what their own Ministers have said and how they have voted. As Commissioner I used to hand out confidential letters to each Environment Minister indicating breaches of environmental law allegedly committed by their own governments. One has to go much further than that. It is really completely unsatisfactory for a Minister to hold a press conference or to make statements on

television or radio which are in flat contradiction to what (s)he has said in the Council itself;

6. more staff are urgently required by DG XI to investigate complaints. Contrary to the assertion made in the House of Lords' Report to which I have already referred, priorities have long been established by DG XI in dealing with the vastly inflated number of cases which have come their way over the course of the last eight to nine years. Another weapon in DG XI's armoury, despite strong opposition from the Member States, is to publish compliance letters, reasoned opinions and replies from the Member States. Again this goes to the heart of enabling people to be informed about what is happening to their environment;

7. the House of Lords Select Committee made a very strong plea to the Commission to make greater use of interim measures. I wholly agree. However, the effectiveness of this proposal will largely depend on the response by the European Court of Justice itself. So far this process does not appear to have been too much encouraged.

Firm enforcement of the law is of vital importance in ensuring that the law does not fall into disrepute. It is critical, too, in establishing the credibility of the European Union to protecting the environment which governments merely hold in trust for their 340 million people.

2. Community Supervision in the Field of the Environment

Richard Macrory

I THE NATURE OF COMMUNITY ENVIRONMENTAL LEGISLATION

The purpose of this contribution is to present an overview of the European Commission's role in ensuring that Community environmental law is implemented within Member States, and to consider what conclusions, if any, can be drawn from recent statistical trends relating to the Commission's activities. The difficulties of ensuring effective enforcement can be viewed as the achilles heel in the development of a truly international environmental order despite the rapid growth in conventions and treaties concerning environmental protection[1] From this perspective the Community and the distinctive powers given to the European Commission can be seen as something of a laboratory or experiment in the development of a new form of supra-national legal system. It is certainly not a perfect role model, but one that raises the intensity of international supervision to a new level. New mechanisms are being introduced into more recent international environmental agreements which attempt to secure improved implementation, and consciously or unconsciously draw on devices already employed within the Community legal order.[2] Aside from its innovative

---

[1] The 1992 study for the United Nations Conference on Environment and Development (UNCED) revealed the extent to which countries fail to comply even with reporting obligations under international environmental treaties: *The Effectiveness of International Environmental Agreements* (Sand 1992). See also Freestone 1994.

[2] See in respect to the Vienna Convention for the Protection of the Ozone Layer the mechanism agreed by the 1992 Meeting of the Parties under which a party may make a complaint concerning non-compliance by another party, and thereby initiate an investigation by a special

role on the international stage, the procedures are as least as important from an internal perspective: for the practitioner or individual within a Member State the machinery of Community enforcement powers now provides a distinctive dimension over and above existing national procedures and remedies.

Any discussion on the implementation and enforcement of law should begin by considering the nature of the legal obligations in question. Community environmental legislation presents a wide variety of differing types of obligations, and their character can have a powerful influence on both the ease with which the laws are implemented and enforced within Member States and on the extent to which monitoring of implementation can be carried out effectively. Most Community laws to date are in the forms of directives rather than regulations, although the level of detail contained in some directives suggest that the content might be equally appropriate for a regulation. Certainly, the rationale for adopting a directive as opposed to a regulation is not always clear, and in its 1992 study of implementation and enforcement, the House of Lords Select Committee was concerned that neither the Commission nor the Council of Ministers had clearly articulated or developed principles concerning the choice of legal instruments.[3] Regulations are by definition self-executing and impose direct obligations within Member States without the need for national transposing legislation.[4] The extent to which there is a failure to implement obligations contained with regulations within a Member State is therefore largely a reflection of defects within that country's legal and administrative structure which are applicable both to national and Community law alike. These defects may, of course, be considerable, and while it is tempting to argue all Community environmental laws should be in the form of regulations rather than directives it does not follow that this would necessarily resolve implementation issues; rather it would shift the nature of the problem.[5]

Implementation Committee. Quoted in Freestone, *op. cit.,* note 1 and see Gehring and Oberthur 1993.

[3] House of Lords Select Committee 1992.

[4] The European Court of Justice has long held the direct applicability of regulations would be jeopardized where a Member State attempts to transpose its content into national legislation: see *Commission v Italy* [1973] ECR 101. Nevertheless, obligations under some regulations may require national measures to be taken before effect can be given to them; see for example the establishment of national competent authorities under the Eco-Labelling Regulation 880/92, OJ 1992 No. L 99.

[5] The House of Lords (note 3 supra) concluded that the wholesale use of regulations was neither appropriate nor would it solve many problems of implementation.

Whatever the form of legal instrument adopted, it is equally important to consider its structure and content. For those Community laws dealing explicitly with environmental standards for tradeable products (e.g. emissions from motor vehicles, lead content of paint), the pressures of the market and the more visible means of verifying compliance means that implementation failure does not appear to be a major issue. This may not be true of all sectors, especially, say, where product manufacture is dominated by a large number of small and medium sized enterprises, or where opportunities and the economic incentives for avoidance are powerful. But the presence of industrial competitors with a strong interest in ensuring compliance across the sector provides a significant pressure for in securing implementation.

Probably the major difficulty occurs with those Community policies which are dependent largely on national action taken within the confines of Member States, and do not involve products or services which are sold or traded across national boundaries. Examples would include the protection of groundwaters, the carrying out of environmental assessment procedures in connection with a construction project, or the prohibition of hunting of protected species of birds (which, of course, may migrate across other countries). In such cases, information concerning implementation or the lack of it does not so readily come to light. These types of obligations, which form the majority of Community environmental measures, have generally take the form of directives, implying that Member States are obliged to achieve the stated policy goals but are left with considerable administrative discretion as to how to achieve them.[6] Within this broad range of types of environmental directives, there are considerable differences in the nature of obligations placed on Member States. These distinctions, often derived from subtle differences in drafting, compound the problem of monitoring and securing implementation. To take some examples, some directives prescribe explicit and precise goals that must be achieved in a given sector which in theory are at least more readily susceptible to monitoring and enforcement.[7] Another class contains similarly precise goals in specific sectors or areas but the relevant articles leave a large element of discretion to Member States in determining where they are to apply.[8] Depending on the precise provisions of the legislation in

---

6 Article 189 Treaty Establishing the European Community: 'A directive shall be binding, as to the result to be achieved, upon each Member State to which it is addressed, but shall leave to the national authorities the choice of forms and methods'.

7 For example, Directive 80/779, OJ 1980 No. L 219, on air quality limits values and guide values for sulphur dioxide and suspended particulates; Directive 80/778, OJ 1980 No. L 229, relating to the quality of water intended for human consumption.

8 For example the designation of Shellfish waters under Directive 79/923, OJ 1979 No. L 281.

question, the discretion involved may by no means be wholly unfettered and in a number of recent cases the European Court of Justice appears to have adopted what is essentially an objective approach towards review, and well beyond the *Wednesbury* reasonableness test familiar to British administrative lawyers. In the bathing water case against the United Kingdom[9] the European Court considered that the definition of a bathing water under the directive was a matter of objective fact:

> The bathing areas of Blackpool and of Southport have for a long time been bathing resorts meeting the criteria [of the directive]. Accordingly, as from notification of the directive they should have been considered bathing areas within the meaning of the directive.[10]

We also have examples in recent years of Community environmental legislation which are not confined to particular sectors such as water or waste, but cut across conventional administrative boundaries and areas of responsibility, imposing obligations that reach deep into national decision-making at many levels. This type of 'horizontal' directive, exemplified by the 1985 Environmental Assessment Directive[11] and the 1990 Access to Environmental Information Directive[12] can raise quite distinct challenges and difficulties for both Member States and the Community institutions when it comes to ensuring full implementation. These latter directives, in particular, are centred on procedural obligations rather than the attainment of precise or measurable goals and are therefore more readily susceptible to abuse.

Given the range of environmental policy issues, the fundamentally differing characteristics of the obligations contained within Community environmental legislation are hardly surprising. But it also needs to be said that Community legislation often does not appear to have been drafted or designed with enforcement issues in mind. No doubt in the first decade or so of the development of Community environmental legislation many Member States assumed that the obligations contained in directives were little more than policy intentions or aspirations rather than distinct legal

---

9   C–56/90, *Commission v United Kingdom*, [1994] 1 CMLR 769. For an analysis of the case see Geddes 1994.

10 *Ibid*, para. 35. See also C–355/90, *Commission v Kingdom of Spain*, [1993] ECR I–4221, concerning the classification of special protection areas under the wild birds directive where the Court was prepared to be equally interventionist.

11 Directive 85/337, OJ 1985 No. L 175, on the assessment of the effects of certain public and private projects on the environment.

12 Directive 90/313, OJ 1990 No. L 158, on the freedom on access to information on the environment. The Eleventh Annual Report by the Commission on monitoring the application of Community law (OJ 1994 No. C 154) notes that three Member States had yet to notify any national implementing measures even though the date for transposition was 1 January 1993.

obligations. Directives were very inconsistent as to the requirements on Member States concerning the provision of situation reports to the Commission, a glaring omission only begun to be rationalized in 1991.[13] Whether a provision was drafted in 'objective' or 'subjective' terms – a choice that has a critical effect on the ability of the Commission and others to review implementation – seems almost a matter of chance.[14] Even in a contemporary climate where at least the more binding nature of directives is widely appreciated and the problems of implementation recognized, the exigencies of late-night voting and compromise politics still lead to drafting that can readily be predicted to raise problems of implementation.[15]

II ARTICLE 169 PROCEDURES

Since the foundation of the Community the European Commission has had an institutional duty to 'ensure that the provisions of this Treaty and the measures taken by the institutions pursuant thereof are applied'.[16] Galvanized by the criticism of the European Parliament following the Seveso incident in the early 1980s,[17] the Commission began a more intense effort in monitoring the implementation of Community environmental legislation and commencing infringement proceedings where appropriate, largely through the legal unit of Directorate General XI. Various informal mechanisms such as the provision of advice to Member States on drafts of national legislation and the development of 'package' meetings with representative authorities from different Member States have been developed as means of reinforcing and supplementing the more formal provisions for enforcement under Article. 169. And while the legal unit within Directorate General XI remains of critical importance, the approach of individual policy units within the Directorate General towards the question of implementation is highly significant. In some fields, such as

---

[13] Directive 91/692, OJ 1991 No. L 337, which standardizes and rationalizes the reports that must be made by Member States for a number of environmental directives. Before the amendments introduced by this directive, the Bathing Water Directive, for example, required regular reports to be made to the Commission by Member States on the state of bathing waters while the Drinking Water Directive 80/778, OJ 1980 No. L 229, contained no equivalent obligation.

[14] For example the definition of 'bathing water' in the Bathing Water Directive was drafted in objective terms – supra note 9. In contrast, the obligation to designate shellfish waters under the 1979 Shellfish Waters Directive leaves more discretion to Member States.

[15] See, for example, Article 6 of the 1990 Access to Environmental Information Directive which extends its ambit to 'bodies with public responsibilities for the environment and under the control of public authorities'.

[16] Article 155 EC Treaty.

[17] European Parliament Resolution of 11 April 1984 OJ 1984 No. C 127.

chemical regulation, there appears a strong tradition in ensuring that Member States reveal and exchange information on implementation problems at an early stage. In other areas there appears to have been more emphasis on policy making at the expense of policy implementation.

Nevertheless, the Article 169 procedures are at the heart of the process. Article 169 is expressed in fairly broad terms, permitting the Commission or Member States to bring proceedings against a Member State for failure to fulfil a Treaty obligation. The Commission is not obliged to commence proceedings,[18] but if it does so it must first give the Member State the opportunity to provide observations on the issue. If the Commission still considers the Member State to be in breach – and Article 169 provides no time-table details for this stage of the process – then it is obliged to deliver a Reasoned Opinion. If the Member State fails to comply with the Reason Opinion within a period specified by the Commission, then the Commission may bring the matter before the European Court of Justice, though it is not obliged to do so.[19] A ruling by the European Court does not itself ensure implementation. The Commission has recently identified eighty-six judgments of the European Court which had not been complied with by Member States as at 31 December 1993, and no less than twenty of these related to environmental matters.[20] Before Maastricht, the European Court, like any other international tribunal, had no direct sanctions to ensure that its judgments were followed by a Member State, and had relied largely upon its moral authority within the Community, and the mutual self-interest of Member States in seeing the rule of law respected. As the figures from the Commission illustrate, this was not sufficient, and new procedures introduced into the Treaty follow Maastricht introduce the possibility of direct sanctions against a defaulting Member State. Article 171 of the Treaty, as amended, provides a similar procedure to the Article 169 powers where a Member State fails to comply with a judgment of the European Court, and can culminate in a Reasoned Opinion specifying a time-limit for compliance with the judgment, followed by new powers given to the Court to order the Member State to pay a lump sum or penalty payment.

---

18 *Commission v Italy*, [1968] ECR 323, *Commission v France*, [1971] ECR 1003.

19 Member States may also bring infringement proceedings against another Member State but the procedures are somewhat modified – see Article 170 EC Treaty. The complaining State must first bring the matter to the attention of the Commission which must provide an opportunity for both Member States to make written and oral observations before it delivers a Reasoned Opinion. If the Commission fails to deliver such an Opinion within three months, the complaining Member State may go directly before the Court. As far as is known, these procedures have not yet been invoked in any environmental matter.

20 Twelfth Annual Report on the Application of Community Law, OJ 1995 No. C 254.

The Treaty therefore provides for a number of formal or pre-litigation steps before a matter can be brought before the Court, and in practice the vast majority of proceedings never reach the Court.[21] Figures of the total number of proceedings in the environmental sector for the years 1981–1994[22] indicate that following a peak of 108 Reasoned Opinions in 1988 and 19 cases before the European Court in 1989 there has been a falling back of these stages although the number for 1994 has more than doubled in comparison with 1993. The number of initial Article 169 letters, though, appears further to have fallen from 90 in 1993 to a lower unspecified number in 1994.[23] The Commission suggests that the reason for this drop relates almost entirely to the decrease of infringement proceedings for failure to notify national measures implementing directives. Since the Commission did not drop its guard, and the number of new directives which fell due for transposal in 1994 was comparable to the number for 1993, the explanation lies in improvements in the conduct of Member States as regards adopting transposal measures. An increase in the number of Reasoned Opinions for 1993 was put down to a large number of directives which required transposal in 1992, and the reduced number of cases going before the Court:

...highlights the effectiveness of action by the Commission which succeeds in most cases persuading Member States to observe Community law without having to go so far as a referral to the Court.[24]

Equally, of course, the Commission may also be choosing sounder cases to take against Member States, and Member States are increasingly aware of the developing jurisprudence of the European Court which generally has showed remarkably little sympathy for defences raised by Member States where questions of non-implementation are concerned. It should also be stressed that according to the Commission's own procedural rules, each stage of the process – issuing an Article 169 letter, sending a Reasoned Opinion, and referring the matter before the European Court – requires a

---

[21] Direct intervention before the Court without the need for the Commission to go through such pre-litigation procedures is provided in three cases under the Treaty: Article 93(2) (state aids), Article 225 (state restrictions on free movement) and, of most relevance in the environmental field, At. 100(4)(a) (stricter national environmental standards).

[22] Due to a different break-down of statistical material and the lack of detail adopted in the Twelfth Report in general not all relevant data for 1994 are available.

[23] *Op. cit.* note 20.

[24] Eleventh Annual Report to the European Parliament on monitoring the application of Community Law, OJ 1994 No. C 154.

collective decision of the whole Commission.[25] This means that the process carries considerable political authority, and cannot be merely put down to the actions of a single, over-zealous official, or even an over-interventionist Department. But it also makes it an administratively complex and time-consuming procedure, and one which can be open to fairly crude lobbying and blocking manoeuvres by Commissioners based in other Directorates and with their own special interests. It is difficult to pin down with any precision the extent and significance of such interference, and it is clearly an area which will not be revealed by the Commission in its Annual Reports. Nevertheless, apocryphal stories abound, and the procedures clearly have a political as well as legal dimension.

III FORMS OF NON-COMPLIANCE

The Treaty does not define when a Member State fails to fulfil its obligations under Community law, but the Commission has categorized three main forms:

   (i) a failure by a Member State to communicate to the Commission national laws and other national measures implementing the Community instruments in question; each directive prescribes a time-limit (normally two or three years) by which date Member States must notify their national laws used or passed to implement the directive.

   (ii) incomplete or incorrect transposition of Community obligations into national law, implying that a Member State has communicated the text of national implementing measures but that these fail to reflect fully the obligations under the relevant directive.

   (iii) the failure to apply the Community obligations in practice, whatever the state of the national law.

I have argued elsewhere that the dividing line between these categories is not always as conceptually easy as might first appear, particularly between (ii) and (iii).[26] But since it is these categories which are used for statistical purposes up to the twelfth report, and clearly they do place rather different

---

[25] The exception is for an Article 169 letter concerned with a simple failure by the Member State to notify national legislation within the prescribed time-limit; no full decision of the Commission is required.

[26] Macrory 1992. The descriptive account here of the procedures is based on material contained in this article.

demands on the Commission, I will maintain the distinctions for the purpose of this analysis.

The failure to communicate is by definition confined to implementation of directives, and in enforcement terms requires little or no legal judgment. Communication has taken place within the time-limit or it has not, and by the early 1980s, the Commission introduced standardized, speedier procedures which avoided the need for a decision of the whole Commission to initiate Article 169 proceedings. The judgment and discretion for the Commission comes in deciding whether to pursue further action against the Member State especially where it has promised the Commission that relevant national laws will be passed, albeit late. The rise in the volume of legal proceedings for non-communication has been dramatic: under thirty in 1988 and 1989 in the environmental sector rising to 79 in 1990 and 95 in 1992, with a drop to 42 in 1994. In 1992, the figure represented almost 70 per cent of all DG XI Article 169 letters, easily the highest proportion over the last five years. It is always difficult to judge to what extent this is due to the expedited administrative procedures, or due to an increase in the quantity and complexity legislation agreed in recent years. As already indicated, though, the figures suggest that Member States are increasingly unlikely to resist such proceedings, and given the rigorous approach shown by the European Court to this type of non-implementation, it sometimes remains surprising that Member States still often fail to address problems of national implementation of complex measures until well into the two or three year period prescribed in directives. Figures provided by the Commission for environmentally related directives suggests a reasonably high level of compliance in the long run and the country by country figures are consistent with the country by country pattern for all types of directives. Such accumulated figures, though have limited use. They are based solely on numbers of directives, and give no qualitative reflection of the environmental significance of individual directives – a figure of 90 per cent or 95 per cent may sound impressive but the outstanding remaining 5 per cent or 10 per cent may include directives of critical importance to the protection of the environment.

Partial implementation, the second type of infringement, clearly involves more challenging enforcement skills. Both the legal meaning of the directive itself must be understood – in the absence of case-law, this is not necessarily a straightforward task in itself, and there may well not be consistent internal agreement within the Commission itself. The implications of the national laws communicated must be fully judged against the directive, requiring a sensitivity to national styles of legislative drafting and the complexities of national legal systems. The position is made more complex where Member States have relied upon pre-existing legislation to meet their obligations in which case its detailed terminology is unlikely to be closely aligned with that of the directive, but the State will claim that the objectives are the same. As a contrasting approach – and one that is causing some degree of unease – there is an emerging tendency both in Britain and elsewhere to adopt a drafting policy known as 'copy-out' where the terms of the directive are transposed into national law word for word in an attempt to avoid any argument of miscongruence. This policy may itself be vulnerable to challenge if the Member State appears to be failing to respect the spirit of the directive, and indeed the fundamental purpose for adopting the instrument of a directive rather than a regulation in the first place.

The need to ensure that laws are implemented in practice as well as in formal terms has been endorsed by Member States, and the Commission has not shirked from considering this to be as an important type of non-implementation as the more formalistic categories outlined. This category represents the most difficult and controversial area of enforcement for the Commission, yet the numbers have increased significantly in recent years. Single figures before 1987 to a peak of 62 in 1990 and 33 and 37 respectively in 1991 and 1992. These cases are often extremely controversial, raise complex questions of fact and law, and may attract considerable local press attention. The issues are likely to be politically sensitive, imply heavy financial costs, and may involve direct private interests. To make the enforcement procedure more problematical, the failure to implement in practice may frequently be due to action or inaction on behalf of local or regional bodies over which Central Government has little control, while it is Central Government which must respond and answer to the Commission on behalf of the Member State. It is these types of cases where one is most likely to encounter other parts of the European Commission exercising their influence and power to block infringement procedures or to suspend their operation.

IV INFORMATION GAPS

In the environmental sector, the Commission has no real powers of investigation comparable in any way to those it possesses in the competition field.[27] There are as yet no Community environmental inspectors, and as yet

---

[27] Council Regulation No 17 of 6 February 1962, OJ Special Edition 1959–62, 87.

the European Environmental Agency[28] possesses no direct power of enforcement. The Commission is therefore peculiarly dependent on receiving information from external sources, and the complaint system developed by the Commission and governed by the Commission's internal rules of administration, is intended to fill this information gap. It is particularly important where questions of non-implementation in practice are concerned, although complaints on partial implementation are also received; a detailed analysis by a national environmental law expert of what are often subtle discrepancies between Community law and national implementation measures may prove an invaluable pointer for the Commission. The whole system in many ways represents a remarkably creative piece of institutional development which can add a distinctive political and legal dimension to local environmental disputes. No legal interest in the matter complained of need be shown, and no costs are involved beyond those voluntarily incurred by the complainant.

The system is common to all areas of Community law, and was first developed in the 1960s in the context of the internal market. But it is the environmental field that have given rise to a spectacular growth in the numbers of complaints received. The number of complaints jumped from 37 in 1985 to 165 in 1986, rising to 480 in 1990 when they represented over one third of all complaints received annually by the Commission.[29] In the Tenth Report on Implementation (1992)[30] the Commission noted that the number of complaints had risen by more than one-third since 1991, though the Eleventh Report is less specific.[31] There, the Commission notes generally that the total number of complaints in all sectors was slightly down in 1993 as compared to 1992 (from 1185 to 1040), while in the section relating to the Environment (initially drafted by DG XI, it must be presumed) there is a dry comment that if the number of complaints received by the Commission appears to have fallen, 'this is partly because the Commission is now merging cases for treatment together where the nature of the problem or the legal instrument infringed is identical.'[32] In 1994 the total number of complaints rose again to 1145.[33]

The system is open to criticism as well as praise, and many within the Commission are alive to negative aspects of the procedures. Investigating the types of issues raised in complaints can be intensely resource-intensive,

---

[28] Regulation 1210/90 OJ 1990 No. L 120.

[29] Macrory 1992 *op. cit.* note 26.

[30] Tenth Annual Report to the European Parliament on Commission monitoring of the application of Community law OJ 1993 No. C233.

[31] *Op. cit.* note 21.

[32] *Ibid.*, Section G, para. 1.1.

[33] Twelfth Annual Report, *Op. cit.* note 20.

and assuming that *prima facie* the complaint raises a question on non-implementation of Community law the Commission is reluctant to prioritize particular types of complaints for a higher or lower level of investigation. The process is largely reactive, with the Commission's own priorities being shaped and perhaps manipulated by external forces. A country by country comparison of complaint numbers (the United Kingdom has long been in the lead in the environmental sector, but now closely followed by Spain) may tell one something about each country's level of compliance with Community law. But equally, if not more so, it reflects traditions of political activism within each country, current environmental priorities of lead non-governmental organizations who make use of the process, and the adequacy of national procedures to provide satisfactory remedies in the environment field.

Various suggestions have been made to improve the efficiency of the system, including the establishment of Commission offices within Member States to act as a first point of referral, or the requirement that complaints are initially made and filtered through Members of the European Parliament. Yet the ability and right of citizens to by-pass national governments and bodies and make representations direct to a supra-national enforcement body marks a bold institutional initiative, particularly for those countries where access to domestic courts and tribunals is not easy, or where traditions in open and responsive administrations are not well developed. Certainly, in its comprehensive study of the implementation and enforcement of Community legislation, the UK House of Lords Select Committee recommended against introducing radical new filter or other similar mechanisms:

> ...the complaints procedure remains a vital means for individual citizens to bring pressure on regulatory authorities to comply with Community law. The sheer numbers of complaints made and of consequent referrals to the Court of Justice are sufficient testament to the need for such a mechanism.[34]

The Committee went on to suggest a number of administrative reforms to improve the handling of complaint investigations, including increased staffing level within DGXI, a clearer sense of priorities, greater powers of direct inspection, speeding up of decision-making, and more openness in the procedures – the initial stages, at least until the sending of a Reasoned Opinion, are still dominated by conventions of confidentiality associated with international diplomacy. In contrast to national Government, the Commission is not obliged under any constitutional convention to respond

---

[34] *Op. cit.* note 3.

to such a report by a national Parliament body but a number of the suggestions are being considered actively.

V SOME CONCLUSIONS

For the lawyer, the question that perhaps should now faced is the extent to which Article 169 proceedings should no longer be viewed as largely an administrative device coloured by discretion and diplomatic convention and negotiations which may or may not culminate in more formal legal proceedings before the Court. The initial procedures, including the complaint process, are dominated by the Commission's own internal rules of procedures which are not publicly available. Parties other than the complainant and the relevant Member State have no right to make representations to the Commission, even where, as may often be the case of non-implementation in practice, their own interests may be directly affected by the outcome of the decision. The European Court has provided little comfort to those who attempt to question the Commission's decisions not to initiate proceedings. Article 169 letters and their responses by Member States are not yet published. A more mature legal system should begin to address these issues, while being alive to the dangers of frustrating what is already a complex process with an excess of legalistic checks and restraints. More available information is certainly a key start. In 1990, the Commission caused considerable concern among Member States when, in a deliberately provocative step, it first released a country by country comparison of Article 169 letters in the environmental sector.[35] As this contribution has tried to demonstrate, drawing realistic conclusions from statistical tables is a delicate exercise, yet the base information is important. In this context it is regrettable that the level of detail, particularly on a sector by sector and country by country basis, in the Commission's Eleventh Report of the Commission contains far less detail than the Report for the previous year a trend which, as has been seen, has continued in the Twelfth Report.

At the end of the day, the Commission's powers of supervision and enforcement cannot hope to deal with all implementation failures within Member States, particularly in such a diverse field as the environment. Nor should they. Nevertheless, the initiatives taken by the Commission in recent years have done much to bring home the binding nature of Community obligations to Member States, and to raise public awareness of the distinctive supra-national system of law that has been created within the Community.

---

[35] European Commission Press Release, 8 February 1990.

3. The European Court of Justice: An Environmental Tribunal?

Philippe Sands

I INTRODUCTION

In considering the development of the European Community's rules on environmental protection it is appropriate to assess the role of the Court of Justice (by which term I include the European Court of Justice and now the Court of First Instance). Given the large body of the Court's case law which relates to environmental matters it is now possible to assess preliminarily whether it has contributed to the development of rules of environmental protection, or limited their scope. In other words, can the Court of Justice be considered an environmental tribunal?

In my view the question can be answered in the affirmative. In this paper I try to explain why. Apart from the fact that the Court has had an opportunity to address a broad range of environmental issues in an extensive jurisprudence of more than 100 cases, it has also demonstrated a willingness to recognize the place which environmental protection has in the Community legal order. The Court has (on occasion) granted to environmental protection objectives an equal (or occasionally greater) weight over entrenched economic and trade objectives. And it has indicated a willingness to recognize and act upon some of the special characteristics of environmental issues.

It is in relation to the last mentioned aspect that the Court really has an opportunity to establish a claim to characterize itself as the first international environmental tribunal. The Court of First Instance has currently before it a case in which it is being asked by 18 plaintiffs to rule that Article 173 of the EC Treaty should be interpreted and applied to take into account the particular characteristics of EU citizens' environmental interests, as opposed to economic interests.[1] As counsel in that case I have had ample opportunity to consider whether the Court is indeed an 'environmental' tribunal! Not unexpectedly, the Commission has invoked a traditional, economic approach to *locus standi* to deny that any of the applicants are 'directly' and 'individually' concerned by the relevant decision. The manner in which the Court deals with the admissibility stage of the case will provide a good indication of whether, and if so to what extent, the Court is an 'environmental tribunal'.

At one, straightforward level there can be no doubt that the Court of Justice *is* an environmental tribunal. As the judicial institution of the EC the Court is required to ensure that in the interpretation and application of the EC Treaty 'the law is observed':[2] since 1976, when the Court first addressed an explicitly environmental issue[3] more than 100 cases involving explicit environmental issues have been brought to the Court.

II JURISDICTION OF THE EUROPEAN COURT

1. Articles 169 and 170

Environmental cases reach the European Court in a number of ways. The most frequent route is via Article 169 of the EC Treaty. Since 1980 the EC Commission has brought more than sixty cases to the ECJ alleging the failure of a Member State to comply with its EC environmental obligations. The Commission is almost always successful. Most of these cases are relatively straightforward and do not indicate one way or another how seriously the Court takes environmental obligations. However, its judgments have been useful to determine, *inter alia*, that Member States may not plead provisions, practices or circumstances existing in their internal legal system to justify a failure to comply with an environmental obligation;[4] that mere administrative practices which may be altered at the whim of the administration do not constitute the proper fulfilment of an

---

[1] Case T–585/93–13, *Stichting Greenpeace Council v EC Commission*, order of the Court of First Instance of 9 August 1995 (not yet reported). See generally Lininger 1995.

[2] EC Treaty, Article 164. The ECJ also has competence in relation to the interpretation and application of the 1950 ECSC Treaty and the 1957 Euratom Treaty.

[3] See Case 21/76, *Handelskwekerij Bier v Mines de Potasse d'Alsace*, [1976] ECR 1735. *Op. cit.* note 37.

[4] Cases 30 to 41/81, *EC Commission v Italian Republic*, [1981] ECR 3379; Case 134/86, *EC Commission v Belgium*, [1987] ECR 2415.

environmental obligation under a directive;[5] and that the legal obligations imposed on a Member States environmental directive pursuing total harmonization are limited to those dangerous substances specifically listed in the directive and not to other unlisted dangerous substances as well.[6] More recently, the European Court has considered the legality of measures taken in the context of environmental trade obligations[7] and the failure to execute one of its own judgments (under Article 171 of the EC Treaty).[8]

Under Article 170 of the EC Treaty a Member State which believes another Member State has breached its obligations has a similar right to bring a matter before the ECJ, but to the best of my knowledge only one case concerning alleged breaches of environmental obligations has been brought under this provision.[9]

Under Article 171, as amended by the Treaty on European Union, the Court of Justice may impose a lump sum or penalty payment on a Member State that has failed to comply with one of its judgments. In such circumstances it will first be for the Commission to specify the amount of the lump sum or payment which it considers appropriate in the circumstances. Although this new provision has not, at the time of this paper, been utilized, one can well imagine that a failure to comply with a judgment of the Court of Justice which results in an environmental injury could provide a basis for its being invoked.

2. Article 173

Under Article 173 of the EC Treaty the Court of Justice (and the Court of First Instance) is competent to review the legality of certain acts of the EC Council and Commission. There are four grounds for review: lack of competence, infringement of an essential procedural requirement, infringement of the EEC Treaty or any rule relating to its application, or misuse of powers. Actions may be brought by privileged applicants (a

---

5   Cases 96 and 97/81, *Commission of the European Communities v Netherlands*, [1982] ECR 1791 and 1819.

6   Case 291/84, *Commission of the European Communities v Netherlands*, [1989] 1 CMLR 479 (concerning the failure to implement into national law Directive 80/68/EEC on the protection of groundwater against pollution by certain dangerous substances).

7   Case 182/89, *Commission of the European Communities v France*, [ECR] 1990 I–4337 where the ECJ held that France had infringed Article 10(1)(b) of Council Regulation 3626/82/EEC (on the implementation of CITES) by granting import licenses for skins of certain feline animals originating in Bolivia.

8   Case C–75/91, *Commission v Netherlands*, (wild birds).

9   Case 141/78, *France v United Kingdom*, [1979] ECR 2923, where France successfully brought proceedings against the United Kingdom for unlawfully having enforced domestic legislation setting a minimum mesh size for prawn fisheries.

Member State, the Council or the Commission) in most cases, by the European Parliament and the European Central Bank for the purposes of protecting their prerogatives, and by any natural or legal person provided that the act concerned is a decision addressed to that person or is of 'direct and individual concern' to that person.

Under Article 173 the Court of Justice has considered, *inter alia*, the legality of the treaty basis of EC and EURATOM environmental legislation.[10] As indicated above, the Court of First Instance is now being asked under Article 173 to decide cases brought by environmental groups and individuals alleging violations by the EC Commission of its legal obligations under the EEC Treaty.

The Court of Justice also has jurisdiction under Article 175, under similar conditions as Article 173, to challenge the failure of the EC Council or Commission to have acted in pursuance of its environmental obligations under the EEC Treaty. To date no environmental case appears to have been brought under this provision.

3. Article 177

The ECJ has also considered environmental questions on the basis of its jurisdiction under Article 177, the 'preliminary reference procedure'. Under this provision the national courts of the Member States may refer to the ECJ questions concerning, *inter alia*, the interpretation of the EC Treaty and the validity and interpretation of acts of the EC institutions, provided that a decision on the question is necessary to enable the national court to give a ruling on the question. Preliminary references from national courts to the European Court of Justice are used when a dispute before the national courts raises a complex question or questions of EC law or where the dispute turns on the EC point and no appeal lies against the decision of the national court. The Article 177 procedure has been used on several occasions to allow the EC to rule on matters of an environmental nature, such as questions concerning the disposal of waste from a nuclear power plant,[11] and the compatibility with EEC law of the ban by an Italian municipality on the sale and distribution of plastic bags and other non-biodegradable packaging material.[12]

---

[10] Case C–62/88, *Greece v Council*, [1990] ECR 1527; Case C–300/89, *Commission v Council*, [1991] ECR I –2867; Case C–70/88, *Parliament v Council*, [1991] I ECR 4335.

[11] Case 187/87, *Saarland and Others v Minister for Industry, Post and Telecommunications and Tourism and others*, [1988] ECR 5013.

[12] Case 380/87, *Enichem Base et al v Commune of Cinisello Balsamo*, [1989] ECR 2491.

4. Interim Measures

The EC Commission can also apply to the Court of Justice for interim measures under Article 186 of the Treaty – a form of interlocutory relief well established in Community jurisprudence and quite often employed, for example, in competition and anti-trust cases. The Commission has to show a good arguable case, that the need for relief is urgent and that irreparable damage to the Community interest will be done if the order is not granted. The Member State can defend itself by establishing that it will suffer irreparable harm if the order is made. The Commission is in the fortunate position of not having to give a cross-undertaking in damages in the event that it ultimately loses the case.

The Court of Justice has indicated that interim measures may be prescribed in environmental cases. In *EC Commission v Germany,* the European Court considered the circumstances in which it would be prepared to prescribe necessary interim measures in environmental cases.[13] The case concerned the construction in Germany of a reservoir and related site, and the Commission sought a:

(a) declaration that the construction violated Article 4(1) of the 1979 wild birds directive; and

(b) the adoption of interim measures to suspend the work until the Court had given its decision on the main application.

The Court held that for a measure of this type to be ordered the application must state the circumstances giving rise to the urgency and the factual and legal grounds establishing a *prima facie* case for the interim measures.[14] The Court rejected the application on the grounds that the Commission had failed to prove urgency: the application had been submitted after the project was well under way and the interim measures had not been sought until 'a large part of the work had already been completed', and it could not be shown that it was 'precisely the next stage in the construction work ... which will cause serious harm to the protection of birds ...'[15]

---

[13] Case 57R/89, *EC Commission v Germany*, [1989] ECR 2849. See also Freestone's contribution in Chapter 12.

[14] *Ibid.* para. 15.

[15] *Ibid.* paras. 17 and 18.

III EVALUATION

The Court has developed a rich body of case-law on environmental issues, as this brief and non-exhaustive list indicates. Indeed, it is fair to say that the Court is pre-eminent as an international tribunal in dealing with legal aspects of environmental protection, and as such its jurisprudence will no doubt provide useful guidance to other international courts and bodies which face legal issues, in particular the delicate and difficult task of balancing environmental concerns with competing social objectives, particularly those of an economic nature. Notable recent developments include the establishment by the ICJ of an Environmental Chamber;[16] the consideration of international environmental issues by various human rights courts around the world;[17] and the decisions of various GATT Panels.[18] The recent creation by the World Bank of an Inspection Panel is noteworthy, in particular because it allows groups to file complaints directly.[19]

The ECJ therefore stands at the forefront of an emerging global trend. In the limited sense that it has in this body of case law addressed a wide range of legal issues relating to the protection of the environment there can be little doubt that the Court is an environmental tribunal. However, the question of whether the Court is an environmental tribunal must also be asked at a deeper level.

Full consideration of the criteria for deciding whether a court or tribunal may be considered to be 'environmental' lies beyond the scope of this introductory paper. In preparing this paper, I have however found it helpful to ask three questions:

- has the Court demonstrated a willingness to recognize the place of environmental objectives in the Community legal order?
- has the Court given environmental objectives equal weight to, or even precedence over, the trade and other economic objectives which the EC was originally designed to promote? and
- has the Court recognized and acted upon the particular characteristics of environmental issues?

---

[16] Sands 1995 pp. 148–63.
[17] *Ibid.* pp. 220–30.
[18] *Ibid.* pp. 687–717.
[19] *Ibid.* pp. 148–63.

1. The Court's Willingness to Recognize the Place of Environmental Objectives in the EC Legal Order

There can be little doubt that the answer to the first question is generally affirmative, even if the case law is not absolutely consistent (history suggests that the Court's tendencies will depend on the particular facts of each case and who is sitting on the bench). If anything, of all the Community institutions the Court has played a pre-eminent role in recognizing and further developing environmental objectives in the Community legal order.

As early as 1985 the Court of Justice had ruled that environmental protection was 'one of the Community's essential objectives'.[20] That the Court could reach such a conclusion before the Single European Act had amended the EEC Treaty to include specific provisions on environmental protection may have been a welcome finding from an environmental perspective, but it was a surprising one for many common lawyers. It was also surprising in the sense that the Court was willing to recognize that environmental protection measures might also limit free trade rules.[21] Nevertheless, the ruling followed the Court's general approach to interpretation and application of the EEC Treaty, and was not unexpected in light of its ruling five years earlier that 'provisions on the environment may be based upon Article 100 of the [EEC] Treaty'.[22]

More recently the Court has indicated further support for its early commitment to formalizing the place of environmental protection in the Community legal order. In 1991 the Court relied on a provision of Article 130r(2) of the EEC Treaty ('[e]nvironmental protection requirements shall be a component of the Community's other policies') to support its conclusion that environmental protection measures could be adopted under Article 100a of the EEC Treaty rather than Article 130s: 'a Community measure cannot be covered by Article 130s merely because it pursues environmental protection objectives'.[23] In deciding that a directive could be

---

[20] Case 240/83, *Procureur de la République v Association de Défence des Bruleurs de l'Huiles Usagées*, [1985] ECR 531, para. 13

[21] See notes 30 and 31 and accompanying text.

[22] Case 92/79, *EC Commission v Italy*, [1980] ECR 1099, para. 8. Article 100 allows the Council to issue directives for the approximation of such laws in member states as 'directly affect the establishment or functioning of the common market'.

[23] Case C–300/89, *EC Commission v EC Council*, [1991] I ECR 2867, para. 22. Article 100a allows the Council, acting by qualified majority, to adopt measures for the approximation of the laws in member states which 'have as their object the establishment or functioning of the internal market'; Article 130s allows the Council, acting unanimously, to decide what action is to beaten by the Community relating to the environment.

based on Article 100a where it was concerned both with the protection of the environment and the elimination of disparities in conditions of competition, the Court gave a significant boost to the Commission's legislative programme for environmental protection by bringing much of it within the qualified majority decision-making process.[24]

The Court has also frequently affirmed the importance of proper transposition into domestic law of environmental directives, recognizing that certain environmental provisions are intended to create rights and obligations for individuals. In 1991 the Court stated that '[i]n order to guarantee complete and effective protection of groundwater it is vital that the prohibitions set out in the directive be expressly embodied in national law'.[25] One of the reasons for this was that 'procedural rules ... are intended to create rights and obligations for individuals [and] they must be incorporated into German law with the precision and clarity necessary to satisfy fully the requirements of legal certainty'.[26] A further justification indicates the Court's appreciation of the particular characteristics of environmental issues: 'a faithful transposition becomes particularly important in a case where the management of the common heritage is entrusted to the Member States in their respective territories'.[27]

On the other hand, there are also indications that the Court will on occasion interpret environmental directives in such a way as to lead to a result which will not afford absolute protection to environmental resources. By way of example: *Gourmetterie Van den Burg* again interpreting the 1979 birds directive, the Court held that a Member State had no right to afford a given species which was neither migratory nor endangered stricter protection (by way of trade restrictions) than that afforded to it by the legislation of the Member State on whose territory the species occurred, where such legislation is in accordance with the directive – a conclusion

---

[24] But cf. Case C–155/91, *EC Commission v EC Council*, Judgment of 17 March 1993, where the Court held that Article 130s and not Article 100a was the appropriate legal basis 'where harmonization of the conditions of the market within the Community are only ancillary to the act to be adopted': (para. 17). By the time the of this second judgment the point was, in a practical sense at least, somewhat moot since the Treaty of European Union had amended Article 130s to introduce qualified majority decision-making by the Council on most environmental issues. The importance of the legal basis, and the proper characterization of a Community measure, nevertheless remains since Article 130s nevertheless retains unanimity voting (without prejudice to Article 100a) on certain types of environmental measures, including those which are primarily of a fiscal nature, or concerning town and country planning, or significantly affecting a member State's choice between different energy sources.

[25] Case 131/88, *EC Commission v Germany*, [1991] ECR 825, para. 19 (groundwater protection).

[26] *Ibid.* para. 61.

[27] Case 339/87, *EC Commission v Netherlands*, [1990] I ECR 851, para. 28.

whose justification is hard to understand given the actual wording of the directive.[28]

Similarly, in Case 252/85 the Court upheld the right of France to apply national provisions allowing the use of lines and horizontal nets ('pantoles' or 'matoles') to catch thrushes or skylarks even though use of such techniques was expressly prohibited by Article 8(1) in conjunction with Annex IV(a) of the 1979 birds directive.[29] The justification for its conclusions (that the technique only captures a small number of birds, that they are captured in a judicious manner, and that France approached the EC Commission to try to reach agreement) is hardly designed to signal the Court's commitment to environmental protection.

2. The Court's Willingness to Give Environmental Protection Objectives Precedence over Economic Objectives

The Court has certainly demonstrated a willingness to recognize that environmental limitations might limit full effect being given to the trade and economic objectives which are enshrined in the EC Treaty. One question which now arises is whether this is slowly being whittled away as the full implications of earlier case-law becomes apparent.

Particularly in relation to the balance between free trade and environmental protection objectives the Court has developed a jurisprudence which distinguishes it from its counterpart GATT dispute-settlement panels. In relation to environmental protection requirements, the Court first held in 1983 that 'the principle of freedom of trade is not to be viewed in absolute terms but is subject to certain limits justified by the objectives of general interest pursued by the Community provided that the rights in question are not substantively impaired', and that environmental protection requirements could justify limits on free trade.[30]

In the *Danish Bottles* case the Court went even further, stating unequivocally that 'the protection of the environment is a mandatory requirement which may limit the application of Article 30 of the Treaty'.[31] The Court reached its conclusion on the basis of the law as it stood before the entry into force of the Single European Act, nevertheless invoking the

---

[28] Case C–169/89, *Criminal proceedings against Gourmetterie van Den Burg*, [1990] ECR I–2143.

[29] Case 252/85, *EC Commission v France*, [1988] ECR 2243.

[30] Case 240/83, *op. cit.* note 20, para. 12.

[31] Case 302/86, *EC Commission v Denmark*, [1988] ECR 4607, para. 9. Article 30 provides, *inter alia*, that 'measures having equivalent effect [to quantitative restrictions] shall, without prejudice to the following provisions, be prohibited between Member States'. Article 36, which sets forth exceptions to Article 36, does not list environmental protection.

Act to justify its prior conclusion that the protection of the environment was 'one of the Community's essential objectives'.[32]

By 1993 the Court was prepared to go further still, ruling that the principle enunciated in Article 130r that 'environmental damage should as a priority be rectified at source' could be invoked to allow the conclusion that movements of waste could be limited between and even within Member States (in the absence of Community legislation on the waste in question) the Court stated: 'it is for each region, commune or other local entity to take appropriate measures to receive, process and dispose of its own waste'.[33] In reaching this rather dramatic (from an environmental perspective) conclusion, the Court rather surprisingly invoked the principles of self-sufficiency and proximity set out in the 1989 Basle Convention on the Control of Transboundary Movements of Hazardous Wastes and their Disposal.[34] This was surprising because the Convention had not been adopted at the time the dispute originally arose and had been in force for barely three months even at the time of judgment, because even at that later date the Community was a signatory but not a party to the Convention, and because the Convention only implicitly (and even then subject to important caveats) invokes the principles identified by the Court only in its preamble! Each of these reasons serves to underscore the Court's willingness to give significant weight to environmental principles and objectives, even where they might be considered to be in an emergent state.

In a similar vein (and again in the context of the 1979 wild birds directive), the Court has ruled that the power of a Member State to reduce the size of a special protection area can only be justified on exceptional grounds which must 'correspond to a general interest which is superior to the general interest represented by the ecological objective of the directive', and that economic and recreational requirements do not constitute such exceptional grounds.[35]

To my mind these cases illustrate the Court's willingness to give environmental protection objectives precedence over economic objectives in appropriate circumstances.[36] They also reflect the significant role played by the Court in the development of EC environmental law, to the point that it will place certain limits on free trade rules.

---

[32] *Op. cit.* note 20.

[33] Case C–2/90, *EC Commission v Belgium*, [1993] 1 CMLR 365, para. 34.

[34] Basle, 22 March 1989, in force 5 May 1992, 28 ILM 649 (1989).

[35] Case C–57/89, *EC Commission v Germany*, [1991] ECR 883 (paras. 21 and 23–4).

[36] Cf. Case 252/85, *Op. cit.* note 29.

3. The Willingness of the Court to Recognize Particular Characteristics of Environmental Issues

Finally, it may be useful to consider whether the Court can be considered an environmental tribunal by reference to its willingness to recognize (and act upon) the particular characteristics of environmental issues and problems. This concluding part of this paper necessarily is somewhat speculative, since I am not sure agreement would be possible on what those characteristics might be. However, what I have in mind, largely as a result of preparation for this volume, are the following sorts of characteristics:
- that environmental resources and the pollution which harms them do not, for the most part, respect national boundaries and are therefore part of a common heritage, ownership and responsibility;
- that harm to the environment can affect a large number of natural or legal persons irrespective of their economic status, or their economic rights or interests;
- that environmental and aesthetic well-being may differ from economic well-being in several respects, including the fact that environmental interests will generally be shared by the many rather than the few and that it will consequently often be difficult to identify an individual with a particular environmental interest.

At this point it is unclear to me whether the Court has really grappled with this aspect of my criteria, although it may be possible to discern some, limited signs that the Court might be inclined to recognize the particular nature of environmental interests.

Thus, as early as 1976, in a case under the 1968 Brussels Convention on the recognition and Enforcement of Judgments, the Court upheld the right of victims of transboundary pollution to choose the national court before which they could commence legal proceedings for damages. The Court ruled that Article 5(3) of the 1968 Brussels Convention must be interpreted 'in such a way as to acknowledge that the plaintiff has an option to commence proceedings either at the place where the damage occurred or the place of the event giving rise to it'.[37] The Court is implicitly recognizing that environmental harms can be transboundary in nature and that the law should recognize that feature by introducing flexibility into the applicable conflicts rules. And, as indicated earlier, the Court's willingness to invoke the 'common heritage' principle as an aid to interpreting and applying the law illustrates that it will, on occasion, rely upon the underlying rationale of

---

[37] See Case 21/76, *Op. cit.* note 3.

certain EC environmental legislation to allow it to reach a conclusion which it might not otherwise have reached, or to fortify it in reaching that conclusion.[38] A similar willingness might be thought evident in the *Wallonian Waste Case*. Having found that waste should be regarded as a product within the meaning of Article 30 of the EEC Treaty and that its movement should not in principle be impeded, the Court found that waste has 'a special characteristic' since its accumulation 'even before it becomes a health hazard, constitutes a threat to the environment'.[39]

In *Greenpeace* the Court is being asked by the applicants to recognize that environmental harm raises a completely new kind of problem in the field of remedies under the Community legal order. Specifically, the applicants argue that the Court's prior Article 173 jurisprudence relates solely to economic interests, and that 'individual concern' should be construed to ensure that individuals whose environmental rights established by an act of EC legislation (such as Directive 85/337 on environmental impact assessment) should have effective access to the Community courts in order to obtain effective protection of those rights and to ensure that 'in the interpretation and application of the treaties the law is observed'.[40]

I recognize that the Court's acceptance of the applicants' basic argument on 'individual concern' would take Community law on *locus standi* beyond the principles which it has so far followed. Nevertheless, I think it is fair to say that if the Court addresses the applicants' argument on individual concern and rejects it as a matter of principle, it will in effect be saying that environmental interests are no different from economic interests. It will also be suggesting that, for all practical purposes, there are no circumstances in which the Commission could be judicially reviewed under Article 173 in respect of alleged violations of EC environmental laws (since it is hard to imagine circumstances in which victims of environmental harms might be considered to be part of a 'fixed and ascertainable' class).[41] According to the applicants' the Court's reliance upon a traditional approach would be doubly damaging for the Community legal order: it would limit the application of the rule of law, and it would signal the Court's unwillingness to recognize an equal place for environmental values in the Community legal order.

---

[38] Case 339/87, *Op. cit.* note 27.

[39] Case C–2/90, *Op. cit.* note 33, para. 30.

[40] Case C–70/88, *Parliament v Council*, [1990] ECR I–2041, para. 23.

[41] See e.g., Cases 106–107/1963, *Alfred Topfer and Getreide-Import Gesellschaft v Commission*, [1965] ECR 405.

IV CONCLUSIONS

In answer to the questions posed at the beginning of this paper, I consider that the Court's jurisprudence indicates a readiness to give a considerable degree of support to environmental arguments. It's approach clearly must be considered on a case-by-case basis, but the general tendency is to extend the weight of environmental arguments and limit the extent of economic arguments. Therefore even in this deeper sense the Court has demonstrated an awareness of environmental issues and a willingness to act in the interests of environmental protection. How far it is prepared to go may well be revealed by its approach to the arguments in the *Greenpeace* case.

4. Enforcing EC Environmental Law: The National Dimension

David Noble

I INTRODUCTION

In the established tradition of the University of Warwick Law School, this paper seeks to place some of the legal and procedural questions and arguments surrounding enforcement of European Community environmental law into their political and institutional context. The purpose of so doing is to examine the deficiencies present in the systems of enforcement which currently exist and to consider possible future developments.

II TRANSPOSITION OF EUROPEAN COMMUNITY ENVIRONMENTAL DIRECTIVES

There exist four main operational constraints (as distinct from policy restraints) on the timely and adequate transposition of Community environment legislation in the United Kingdom. These are:

1. the manner in which European Community directives are transposed into UK law taken together with the institutional constraints arising from the need for Parliamentary time to transpose directives either into statute or statutory instrument form and the available administrative and legal resources for the task;
2. a lack of understanding in the European Commission of the particular features of the Anglo-Irish legal system and as part of that, the different drafting traditions as distinct from those of continental Europe in

conjunction with the complexity of existing legislation and common
law in the environment field in the UK;

3. the unequal weighting of resources in favour of new law-making
   against enforcement of existing rules (the traditional problem for
   enforcers of laws);

4. an absence of intellectual and legal rigour in the assessment of
   transposing legislation by the European Commission coupled with an
   unresolved tension between the rule of law and the role of politics in
   that institution.

Taking these in turn, there are three main vehicles for the UK Government
to use for the transposition of EC environmental directives; primary
legislation, secondary or subordinate legislation and directions to public
bodies. Primary legislation for the transposition of directives, whilst
attractive in many respects since it gives Parliament the full opportunity to
discuss the details of the transposing measures and ensures the most
publicity to the transposition activity, provides a relatively lengthy period
for drafting and redrafting, often involves an extensive consultation period
before the introduction of a Bill and has considerable disadvantages. The
pressure on the legislative programme for almost any Government is such
that most Departments and Ministries cannot expect to have more than one
legislative vehicle in any one session of Parliament and there is little
guarantee that its purposes naturally coincide with the transposition of
environmental directives. Timing and availability of relevant statutory
vehicles can therefore never be predicted with certainty and this can be of
critical importance in relation to the dates set in the directives for the
coming into force of the provisions of the directive. Infrequently therefore,
will primary legislation be the main or sole method of transposition of
Community directives on the environment although elements of recent
legislation such as the Water Act 1989 and the Environmental Protection
Act 1990 contain important transposing provisions and powers for further
transposition by subordinate legislation.

Increasingly, transposition of environmental directives falls to be carried
out by statutory instrument made under specific provisions in environmental
legislation, solely or combined with the powers contained in section 2 of the
European Communities Act 1972. The advantages of this approach are that
the amount of Parliamentary time involved is considerably reduced, often in
the case of statutory instruments which are subject to the negative resolution
procedure in Parliament to little more than an examination by the Joint
Committee on Statutory Instruments. In the case of instruments which
substantially affect provisions of Acts of Parliament however, the

affirmative resolution procedure[1] requires debates in, and approval of the instrument by both the House of Commons and the House of Lords. Even this amount of Parliamentary time can be difficult to secure given the pressure of other business. Against this advantage of relative speed and greater control of the timetable have to be set the restrictions contained in Schedule 2 to the 1972 Act which limit the power for implementing Community obligations via subordinate legislation.

Finally, recent environmental legislation has seen the growth in powers for the executive to direct other elements of the executive or free-standing administrative and regulatory agencies to give effect to Community obligations.[2] Although some debate has taken place as to the adequacy of directions as transposing measures, it is to be hoped that the details in clause 66 of the Environment and Countryside Bill 1994 will remove all doubt from them. Their advantage clearly is the speed and ease with which they can be made, equating them almost to the typical form of Presidential decree common in republican administrations in continental Europe. Against this, the use of directions harbours a number of limitations. They can only be addressed to other elements of the state administration, their existence is less immediately apparent than is the case with either primary or secondary legislation (although the reforms introduced by the 1994 Bill will improve this considerably) and finally, the general directions have tended to merely direct a body to exercise some or all of its powers and the process of giving effect to a particular directive so the trace of transposition becomes less transparent than when legislative vehicles are used.

The second difficulty which faces those responsible for implementing Community legislation in the sphere of the environment in the UK is the lack of understanding at the European level of the differences which exist between the Anglo-Irish drafting tradition and that employed in continental European countries and more particularly the Community itself. Despite its particular position in UK law, the legislation of the European Communities remains in style at least, largely similar to conventional international legal texts. Traditionally, to give effect to international obligations in conventions and protocols, the UK has introduced legislation transposing into domestic law the obligations and rights under the particular international instrument. The same approach has been adopted in relation to the transposition of Community directives. However, the desire for legislative precision, for the avoidance, as far as possible, of doubt and contradiction in the UK drafting

---

[1] As recommended by the Joint Committee on Statutory Instruments - second special report 1977-78 HL 236, HC 579.
[2] See for example section 7(2)(b) of the Environment Protection Act 1990 and section 5(2)(a) of the Water Resources Act 1991.

tradition has caused difficulties in relation to transposition of Community directives. First, the use of language different from that used in the Community text has led to enforcement action under Article 169 of the EC Treaty by the Commission for incorrect transposition. In response to the developing jurisprudence of the European Court of Justice in relation to direct effect and *Francovich* related damages[3] there has been a tendency towards the 'copy-out' school of transposition even in cases where this simply transfers the question of clarification from the draftsman to the courts.

It has been said that environmental law is a young branch of the law.[4] Whereas this may be true of such legislation at a Community level, the existence of environmental legislation in the UK from the late 19th century together with the common law of nuisance makes the application of a further layer of regulatory controls on an already complicated legislative and jurisprudential tableau particularly difficult. Those at the centre involved with a relatively limited number of legislative provisions drafted in wide supra-national terms have shown little appreciation for the difficulties encountered at the Member State level. Against this it has to be noted that there has been little realization at the time when environmental directives have been adopted by the Council of Ministers of the legislative changes needed to give effect to the new rights and obligations agreed to. The example of the transposition of directive 85/337 on environmental impact assessment in the UK via more than a dozen statutory instruments is salutary in this respect.

This lack of understanding between the two levels of law-making, the Community and Member State, persists in relation to the broad misunderstandings of remedies available to aggrieved citizens in the Anglo-Irish legal system. The absence of an administrative tribunal or court system as is to be found in the continental systems such as in France and Germany and the contrast between those and the administrative law remedies available under the system of judicial review in the UK have always proved difficult for the UK to explain and defend.

There is, as a third constraint on the effective transposition of Community environmental legislation, the common institutional and organizational phenomenon of the 'cinderella' nature of enforcement of existing legislation as distinct from the attractions of new legislation. This has infected the Commission in relation to environmental legislation, certainly in the early days before the creation of a specific unit with responsibility for

---

3 For a detailed analysis of the *Francovich* remedy in European environmental law see the contribution by Somsen in Chapter 7.
4 See Krämer in his contribution in Chapter 6.

the application of Community law in Directorate General XI. Partly as a consequence of this and partly regardless of this the Commission has shown itself to be reluctant to participate in the detail of the transposition problems set by its own drafting and the problems caused by amendments to legislation introduced through the Council of Ministers and Parliament's consideration of draft texts. The absence of authoritative interpretations of contradictory or unclear parts of directives and the distinct difficulties Member States have encountered in securing a single view from different parts of the same Directorate General, the Legal Service of the Commission or the College of Commissioners itself has made transposition problems far more extensive and long-running than needs to be the case. Whilst it is appreciated that it is the European Court of Justice which, in the end, has the final responsibility for interpretation of Community legislation, an authoritative view from the Commission of what its interpretation of a particular provision is going to be would help Member State legislators enormously in the drafting of transposing measures since it is the Commission under Article 169 of the Treaty which has the primary responsibility for the supervision of the correct application of Community law. Indeed the experience of Member States in recent years as recipients of many hundreds of pre-article 169 and Article 169 correspondence emphasizes the fact that the Commission has been largely reactive and not pro-active in its approach to ensuring correct application of Community environment law.

This, in turn, leads to the fourth and final constraint on the full transposition of Community environmental legislation. As part of the reactive approach adopted by the Commission in this field, enforcement has tended to be haphazard, spasmodic and largely complaint-led. As the report on the implementation of Directive 85/337 reveals there has, for that directive at least, been a considerable patchwork of transposition across the Community and yet there has been little concerted comprehensive attempts by the Commission to check all Member State transposing measures and issue proceedings for non-transposition or inadequate transposition. Too much of the enforcement activity has been in response to individual complaints made directly to the Commission often about individual projects. In any logical system of enforcement, the institution with such responsibilities is better served by concentrating on ensuring appropriate transposition of the legislation into Member State law and then moving to the next level (if indeed such activity is appropriate at the supra national level) of ensuring that the transposing legislation is producing the correct results in practice. Commission enforcement of environmental legislation has tended to jumble the two activities together in an incoherent ensemble and, in many cases, to concentrate on the latter at the expense of the former.

Add to this the inherently political nature of the Commission, the influence that individual Member States may have through their appointed Commissioners or by virtue of the importance to the Commission of a particular policy area (such as regional development) and one sees that the role of politics is often, in the end, triumphant over the rule of law in relation to enforcement activity in the hands of the Commission. This is a point which has not gone without notice amongst environmental organizations which in the early part of the 1980s used the Commission complaints procedure extensively in the belief that that way effective enforcement lay.[5] Whilst it is still possible to secure a change to national legislation for the price of a first class letter of complaint to the Commission it is less certain, prone to delay, open to extensive political bargaining and far less publicly open than pursuit of remedies through the domestic courts.

III APPLICATION OF EUROPEAN COMMUNITY LAW IN PRACTICE

The last constraint on the full transposition of Community environment legislation recurs as a further limitation on the effective application of that law in the United Kingdom in practice. Reliance upon the Commission as the enforcing authority with respect to individual breaches of Community directives using its powers under Article 169 of the Treaty is inherently unsatisfactory. If the Commission has proved to be a relatively unsuccessful vehicle for the enforcement of transposing legislation in the Member States, the experience in relation to individual projects covered by Directive 85/337 on environmental impact assessment magnifies these limitations in relation to individual breaches starkly.

The absence of technically qualified staff to provide the necessary evidence concerning the inadequacy of the assessments carried out in respect of certain projects in purported satisfaction of the requirements of that directive; the distance of the Commission in Brussels from, say, a local authority in the north of Scotland and the associated lack of local knowledge; the fact that correspondence on the individual complaint is routed through the central Government authorities via the permanent representation for the UK in Brussels all contribute to the delays and the tendency to pursue poor cases which has typified the enforcement of individual breaches by the Commission.

---

5 See the contribution by Faulks and Rose in Chapter 10.

Add to this again the inherently political nature of the Commission as mentioned before and the value of the Commission as an agency for enforcing the correct application of the provisions in directives in the Member States is brought into true focus. A remote, politically influenced unwieldy bureaucracy without the necessary technical and legal resources (and often skills) is not the best vehicle for the task of ensuring the practical application of Community environmental legislation at the level of individual decision-making in the Member States. Arguably, Article 169 as originally drafted was never designed for the use to which it has been put in the field of Community environment policy for these very reasons. Enforcement of the application of a directive's provisions (assuming adequate transposition or direct effect) is a classic case where the principle of subsidiarity should operate, that is that this task is better done at the local level, Member State, region, locality using the appropriate administrative and judicial systems.

What then of the enforcement of Community environmental legislation by the administrative and judicial systems in the United Kingdom? Until perhaps last year the assessment one would have been forced to give would have been that progress on this front had been slow and patchy in that it appeared few cases alleging the breach of a transposed directives' provisions had been brought, fewer still had been mounted in relation to non-transposed provisions where the argument was made that those provisions were of direct effect and in those cases where the requirements of environmental directives had been considered the courts had not shown themselves to be particularly competent in their handling of the issues. Regardless of the results on which I make no comment, few lawyers can have been impressed by the way in which issues of Community law were handled by the UK courts in *R v Secretary of State for the Environment ex parte Twyford Parish Council*[6], *R v Swale Borough Council ex parte the RSPB*[7], *Kincardine and Deeside District Council v Forestry Commission*[8] and *Wychavon District Council v Secretary of State for the Environment.*[9] Indeed this line of cases which consider the details of the EIA directive could qualify for the title of 'The strange mystery of the missing Article 177 reference' since not one of them led any domestic court to refer any question of interpretation to the ECJ under the procedure provided for under

[6] *R v Secretary of State for the Environment ex parte Twyford Parish Council* [1991] JPL 643.
[7] *R v Swale Borough Council ex parte the RSPB* [1991] 1 PLR 6.
[8] *Kincardine and Deeside District Council v Forestry Commission* [1991] SCLR 729.
[9] *Wychavon District Council v Secretary of State for the Environment*, The Times, 7 January 1994.

Article 177 of the Treaty. This had to await a case from Bavaria which raised questions of what is a 'project' for the purposes of the directive and whether Member States can, as the UK has done, make provision for transitional cases going through the consent process at the time when the directive was to have been transposed.[10]

In short, confidence in the Commission as the appropriate and effective institution for enforcement of the application in practice of Community environment provisions has been proved to be misplaced and the vacuum created by that experience did not appear to have been filled by domestic institutions and jurisprudence.

However, I believe that in recent months we have witnessed the beginning of a turning of the tide in respect of domestic courts of the involvement in this field. Following, as so often in Community environmental matters, developments in other policy areas such as the Community's fishing, employment and social security policies, the domestic courts have begun to consider questions of interpretation of Community environmental directives (even in cases where there has been no transposing legislation) and developing adequate, indeed powerful, remedies.

It is perhaps possible to identify the *Factortame* litigation[11] as the genesis of this willingness of advocates and the judiciary to consider these issues and to develop remedies against the State and its agents. There, the House of Lords accepted the argument that the court could make a declaration against the State as to the existence of public rights conferred under Community legislation and was prepared to suspend the operation of domestic legislation which had the effect of breaching Community provisions pending final judgment following a reference to the ECJ under Article 177.

However, for environmental law the cases which may well come to be seen to have revolutionized local enforcement of the proper transposition and application of Community legislation are *R v Secretary of State for Employment ex parte Equal Opportunities Commission*[12] and *R v Secretary of State for the Environment ex parte the RSPB* House of Lords.[13] In the

---

[10] Case C-362/92, *Bund Naturschutz in Bayern eV, Richard Stahndorf and 40 others and Freistaat Bayern*, 9 August 1994 (not yet reported).

[11] *R v Secretary of State for Transport ex parte Factortame (No.2)* [1991] 1 AC 603 and *R v Secretary of State for Transport ex parte Factortame*, [1990] 2 AC 85 and *R v Secretary of State for Transport ex parte Factortame (No. 3)* 26.3.96 (not yet reported).

[12] *R v Secretary of State for Employment ex parte Equal Opportunities Commission* [1994] 2 WLR 409.

[13] *R v Secretary of State for the Environment ex parte the RSPB*, House of Lords, The Independent, 10 February 1995.

former the House of Lords concluded that the High Court had jurisdiction under Order 52 rule 1(2) of the Rules of the Supreme Court to declare that primary legislation was incompatible with Community law despite the absence of a decision against which one of the prerogative orders under Order 53 rule 1 would be appropriate. This case, the judgment of Otton J. in *R v Secretary of State for the Environment and others ex parte Greenpeace Ltd. and another*[14] and *R v Secretary of State for Foreign Affairs ex parte the World Development Movement Limited*[15] also established the very generous *locus standi* rules for statutory bodies and non governmental organizations to mount these types of judicial reviews. In ex parte the RSPB the applicants sought to challenge the administrative implementation by the Government of provisions of Directive 79/409 on the conservation of wild birds in the absence of domestic legislation transposing the relevant provisions in the directive on the basis that the result of this application in practice was in breach of the provisions of the directive. No argument of direct effect of the provisions of the directive was made by the applicants and the courts were prepared to review the actions of the Secretary of State in purporting to give effect by administrative means to the requirements under the directive to classify the most appropriate areas for bird conservation purposes in specified cases. In deciding to refer to the ECJ under Article 177 the question of whether a Member State is entitled to take account of the considerations mentioned in Article 2 of Directive 79/409 (economic and recreational factors) in classifying an area as a Special Protection Area for wild birds, Lord Jauncey of Tullichettle giving the judgment of the Court refused the RSPB's application for interim declaratory relief having assumed that such a remedy was available in law. In doing so he stated that:

> A declaration that the Secretary of State acts unlawfully if ... he fails to act in a certain way is tantamount to an instruction to the Secretary of State to act in a particular way. It is not declaratory of anyone's rights but a mandatory order which, if it were to be granted by way of relief, would usually be granted in the form of a interim injunction

It seems that the tide has turned in favour of domestic enforcement by the courts of Community environmental law in respect of incompatible domestic law, incorrect application in practice of Community law and possibly the non-transposition of Community law. This latter category is the subject matter of another application for judicial review brought by the Royal Society for the Protection of Birds where, in seeking a judicial review

---

[14] *R v Secretary of State for the Environment and others ex parte Greenpeace Ltd. and another* [1994] 4 All ER 352.

[15] *R v Secretary of State for Foreign Affairs ex parte the World Development Movement Limited*, The Independent, 11 January 1995.

of the decision by the Minister of Agriculture to grant licences for the killing of fish-eating birds, the applicants have amended their application (granted by Latham J on 19 October 1994) to seek a declaration that provisions in the Wildlife and Countryside Act 1981 are inconsistent with the provisions in the wild birds directive. At present the action is stayed pending consultation by the Government on proposals to amend the domestic legislation to reflect the directive.

IV SIGNS FOR THE FUTURE OF ENFORCEMENT OF EC ENVIRONMENTAL LAW

There are a number of developments and trends which will, in time produce further changes in the pattern of enforcement as described in the preceding sections of this paper.

First, in the light of the recent domestic jurisprudence there will be a continuing development of judicial review of the State and emanations of the State (on which the decision of Blackburne J. in *Unison v South West Water plc*[16] will be of significance in the environmental field, if upheld on appeal) for failure to respect whether in primary or secondary legislation or administrative action the provisions of EC directives on the environment. Undoubtedly, this type of immediate, direct and local judicial enforcement is the most effective method of securing compliance.

Enforcement by the Commission under Article 169 *may* become more focused upon its primary role of securing full and adequate transposition rather than being reactive to external complaints on individual cases and thereby largely failing to check transposing legislation. In this the Commission may be influenced by the continuing interest shown by the Parliament, most particularly by its Environment, Public Health and Consumer Protection Committee, in 'auditing' the enforcement by the Commission of transposition of environmental legislation by the Member States. The Parliament itself has already displayed considerable interest in the enforcement of existing environmental legislation, most particularly through the *Jackson report on implementation of environmental directives*. Institutional reform following the 1996 Inter Governmental Conference may also radically alter the roles and responsibilities of these institutions in respect of enforcement of environmental law.

Greater awareness of what is happening in practice in the Member States as a result of information flowing into and published by the European

---

[16] *Unison v South West Water plc* [1995] IRLR 15

Environment Agency, by greater cooperation and co-ordination of national enforcement agencies through the 'Chester Network' and greater public access to information arising from the directive on freedom of access to environmental information[17] will also serve to reveal inadequacies of transposition and application in practice. This will strengthen enforcement activity both at Commission and Member State levels.

Finally, it is to be hoped that there will be greater effort among the Member States in establishing formal and informal links between themselves and together with the Commission to discuss matters arising during the period for transposition of new directives to ensure that common positions can be adopted on questions of interpretation, scientific data and application in practice. A change of emphasis and, probably resources, at both Commission and Member State level from creating new legislation to ensuring the complete transposition and satisfactory practical operation of existing Community legislation on the environment is required. As for new legislation itself, if enforcement of those new provisions is to be markedly easier to achieve than was the case for earlier legislation, greater attention will have to be given to questions of drafting prior to adoption by the Council (where inevitably last minute compromise amendments may often lead to obscurity of drafting), to addressing transitional issues (since in many Member States Community legislation on the environment is not building on a clean sheet but is being laid across an already regulated area) and to greater consistency in style and approach.

---

[17] Directive 90/313 on freedom of access to environmental information, OJ 1990 No. L 158.

5. Legal Protection in European Environmental Law: An Overview

J. H. Jans[1]

I THE DIRECT EFFECT OF EC ENVIRONMENTAL LAW

1. General Observations

The European Court of Justice established the foundations for its case law concerning the direct effect of EC environmental law in the *Van Gend en Loos* case in 1963.[2] In this case, the Court ruled that EC law can create rights for private individuals, which are enforceable independent of the laws of Member States. In its subsequent case law the Court developed the following conditions for the direct effect of EC law:

1. the provision must establish a clear obligation on the part of Member States;
2. the obligation must be unconditional;
3. the obligation must not be dependent on further implementing measures by the institutions of the Community or the Member States;
4. Member States must not be left with any discretion in the implementation of the obligation.

In the Court's current case law these criteria are summarized as follows: provisions of Community law are directly effective if they are unconditional and sufficiently precise.[3] The initial rather restrictive criteria have been

---

[1] Translated from the Dutch by Annemarie Sprokkereef.

[2] Case 26/62 [1963] ECR 1.

[3] Case C–236/92, *Comitato di coordinamento per la difesa della Cava*, [1994] ECR I–485.

significantly relaxed in the course of time. The most important rule which can be extracted from the Court's case law is that any discretion granted to Member States in the implementation of a provision of EC law rules out its direct effect. Examples are provisions allowing national authorities a degree of freedom of choice or provisions leaving them discretion in the exercise of their powers. In those cases, in so far as fulfilment of the Community obligation is conditional upon the implementing measures, only once these competences have been exercised can they be relied upon. However, it should be recalled that for a provision of EC law to lack direct effect the discretion must be 'real'. The Court's case law also shows that vagueness or imprecision of a provision of Community law does not always need to be an obstacle for its direct effect.

The way in which the Court has extended the concept of direct effect in recent years justifies the thesis that according to Community law the crucial criterion is whether a provision provides a national court with sufficient guidance to apply it or use it for the purpose of review without exceeding the limits of its judicial powers. Thus seen, a provision of Community law is directly effective if the national court can apply the provision without interfering with national or EC authorities. This implies that even in cases where Member States enjoy real discretion some degree of direct effect may nevertheless exist. Thus, powers are never unfettered as the *rule of law* implies that the exercise of State competences is prescribed by legal rules. Hence, often the provision of Community law conferring discretionary competences at the same time establishes the conditions for their exercise in turn providing the national court – as long as the provision is 'sufficiently precise' (case C 236/92) – with numerous powers of control. In other words, the essence of direct effect is that it precludes the existence or adoption of national laws exceeding the discretion left by the directive. In the case law of the Court, too, indications can be found that the doctrine of direct effect of Community law is developing in that direction. By way of example, reference can be made to the *VNO* case where it was decided that a provision of a directive could be invoked before a national court so as to establish whether national implementing measures exceeded the limits of discretion left to Member States.[4] The judgment of the Court in *Marshall II* shows that the mere fact that, in fulfilling its Community obligations, a Member State enjoys discretion to choose between various *methods*, does not rule out its direct effect if in substance that Member State does not enjoy any real freedom.[5] In the light of this case law, it is suggested to adopt the following working definition of the concept direct effect of

---

[4]   Case 51/76 [1977] ECR 113.
[5]   Case C–271/91 [1993] ECR I–4367.

Community law: a provision of Community law is directly effective if it can be relied upon by individuals before a national court as against the State without that court having to exceed the limits of its judicial powers. We are concerned with so-called vertical direct effect, which refers to the relation of individuals *vis-à-vis* the State.

Direct effect of primary Community law, in as far as relevant for environmental law, has been accepted by the Court in respect of, *inter alia*, Articles 12, 30, 34, 36, 85, 86, 93(3) and 95 of the EC treaty. Thus, the validity of national environmental law incompatible with these provisions can be challenged before national courts.

2. Direct Effect of Provisions of Environmental Directives

Apart from the direct effect of provisions of primary Community law in the sphere of the environment, the possibility to invoke provisions of environmental directives after expiry of their deadline for implementation is particularly important. Thus, directives need to be implemented by way of national legislation, raising the significance of environmental directives in national legal orders where these were not, belatedly or otherwise incorrectly implemented.

Evidently it is not viable nor desirable here to examine the many individual environmental directives, which each in turn contain numerous provisions, for their direct effect. Instead, various more general categories of provisions frequently found in environmental directives will be examined.

a. Directly effective product standards

Environmental directives laying down precise and detailed conditions with which products harmful to the environment must conform before being placed on the market will normally produce direct effect, as is illustrated by the Court's judgment in *Ratti*.[6] The so-called solvents Directive 73/173 contains detailed provisions regarding packaging and labelling of varnish.[7] Italian legislation imposed additional conditions and required publication of certain information not demanded by the directive. Ratti, who complied with the directive but not with the additional requirements of the Italian legislation, was prosecuted. The Court considered in this respect:

> It follows that a national court requested by a person who has complied with the provisions of a directive not to apply a national provision incompatible with the

---

[6]   Case 148/78 [1979] ECR 1629.

[7]   OJ 1973 No. L 189.

directive not incorporated into the internal legal order of a defaulting Member State, must uphold that request if the obligation is unconditional and sufficiently precise.

Ratti was subsequently acquitted since the provisions of the directive could be considered unconditional and sufficiently precise.

In the light of this judgment, product standards such as those contained in the batteries Directive 91/157[8] can be considered to be directly effective. Thus, on the basis of this directive Member States must prohibit the marketing of alkaline manganese batteries containing more than 0.025 per cent of mercury by weight. National provisions which do not possess the required stringency and specify a value of for example 0.05 per cent can be challenged by invoking the directive, the standard of 0.025 per cent evidently being sufficiently precise.

The reverse is also true and a more stringent product standard can therefore be challenged. For this to be possible the directive, as in the *Ratti* case, needs to contain a so-called 'free movement' clause which indeed is found in the batteries Directive:

> Member states may not impede, prohibit or restrict the marketing of batteries and accumulators covered by this Directive and conforming to its provisions. (Article 9).

Such a clause is directly effective – as was confirmed in *Ratti* – and a more stringent national standard would be incompatible with such a provision.

b. Direct effect and minimum harmonization

As is well known, the vast majority of European Community environmental directives lay down minimum standards of protection but allow more stringent national standards (so-called minimum harmonization).[9] This applies in particular to emission standards and environmental quality objectives. Does the fact that a directive allows Member States to adopt more stringent environmental standards imply that such directives do not produce direct effects? Thus, the emission standard applying to existing municipal waste-incineration plants whose nominal capacity is less than six tonnes of waste but at least one tonne per hour is 100 mg/Nm3.[10] To what extent is such an emission standard directly effective?

The answer in respect of such emission standards is that they are directly effective in as far as the directive establishes a sufficiently precise minimum standard. In the present example, measures which would allow the emission of dust particles exceeding 100mg/Nm3 are in breach with the directive and can be challenged directly on the basis of the emission limit value of the

---

[8]   OJ 1991 No. L 78.
[9]   See Article 130t and for example case C–376/90, *Commission v Belgium*, [1993] CMLR 513.
[10] Directive 89/429, Article 3, OJ 1989 No. L 203.

directive. However, national measures containing more stringent standards, for example an emission limit value of 50 mg/Nm3, can not be challenged on the basis of the directive simply because in that case no provision of the directive would be breached.

c. Provisions requiring further implementing measures

Environmental directives requiring further national or European implementing action do not produce direct effects. Thus, the Court in case C–236/92 decided that Article 4 of the old waste directive 75/442[11] is not directly effective.[12] That provision generally provided that Member States should take the necessary measures to ensure that waste is recovered or disposed of without endangering human health and without using processes or methods which can harm the environment. According to the Court this provision does not fulfil the conditions (unconditional and sufficiently precise) for direct effect because it is a framework provision:

> which is a programme to be followed and sets out the objectives which the Member States must observe in their performance of the more specific obligations imposed on them by Articles 5 to 11 of the directive concerning planning, supervision and monitoring of waste disposal operations.

The Court therefore concluded that:

> the provision at issue must be regarded as defining the framework for the action to be taken by the Member States regarding the treatment of waste and not as requiring, in itself, the adoption of specific measures or a particular method of waste disposal. It is therefore neither unconditional nor sufficiently precise and thus is not capable of conferring rights which individuals may rely on as against the State.

Such framework provisions are a regular phenomenon in EC environmental directives and often take the form of a general obligation. For example, it is submitted that Article 2 of the waste oils Directive 75/439[13] is not directly effective. This provision contains the general obligation that Member States must take the necessary measures to ensure that waste oils are collected and disposed of without causing any avoidable damage to man and the environment. In this case, too, the directive further specifies this obligation. Hence these general obligations cannot be invoked independently in national courts. Specific provisions of a directive detailing general obligations, however, can be relied upon. In the Netherlands, a number of

---

[11] OJ 1975 No. L 194.

[12] Case C–236/92, *Comitato di coordinamento per la difesa della Cava*, [1994] ECR I–485.

[13] OJ 1975 No. L 194 and OJ 1991 No. L 377.

questions have arisen in respect of the direct effect of Article 1(1) of the old titanium dioxide Directive 78/176[14] which provided:

> The aim of this Directive is the prevention and progressive reduction, with a view to its elimination, of pollution caused by waste from the titanium dioxide industry.

This general provision was spelled out in more detail in a number of subsequent operative provisions. The Dutch court was asked to clarify whether, apart from the operative provisions of the directive, Article 1(1) should be afforded independent significance and, if so, whether this provision was directly effective. A number of environmental interest groups interpreted this provision as a 'stand-still' principle, against which the Dutch licensing system could be reviewed. In court it turned out that this provision could not be invoked in Dutch courts.[15] (13 May 1985.) In view of the European Court's decision in case C–236/92 this judgment would seem to be correct.[16]

The duty to conduct environmental impact assessments for so called 'Annex II projects' also requires further implementing rules. On the basis of Article 4(2) of the Environmental Impact Assessment (EIA) Directive[17] projects which have been listed in Annex II of the directive shall be made subject to an environmental impact assessment where Member States consider that their characteristics so require. For this purpose, Member States must establish the necessary criteria and/or thresholds to determine whether or not a certain type of project is to be made subject to the EIA procedure. One of the projects which are listed in Annex II 11(d) are waste water treatment plants. Under Dutch law the construction of a waste water treatment plant is not made subject to an EIA and in a Dutch court a number of interested parties sought to rely on the directive. The court decided that Article 4(2) of the EIA Directive leaves a margin of discretion to the competent authorities within the Member State to determine whether Annex II projects need to be subject to an environmental impact assessment. The activities listed in Annex II need not, according to the court, necessarily have considerable effects on the environment in all cases and need only be examined when Member States deem this necessary on the basis of their characteristics. Therefore more detailed rules by Member States are necessary and it can not be maintained that the directive puts Member States under an obligation to subject Annex II projects to an environmental impact assessment without any room for discretion.

---

[14] OJ 1978 No. L 54.

[15] KB 13 May 1985, No. 26. M en R 1986, 90–4, with note by J.H. Jans.

[16] Case C–236/92, *Comitato di coordinamento per la difesa della Cava*, [1994] ECR I–485.

[17] OJ 1985 No. L 175.

From this judgment it can be deduced that a margin of discretion, in conjunction with the necessity of more detailed national rules, rules out direct effect. The opposite conclusion would mean that a court would be required to determine the thresholds, thus exceeding its judicial powers. A related question is whether on the basis of the directive a directly effective obligation exists to examine whether a EIA should be carried out. If this were to be the case local planning authorities could be required to decide in a concrete case whether, in view of the likely environmental effects, an environmental impact assessment is required. On this question there exists as yet no case law.

Against the background of the case law referred to above it is not likely that courts will accept the direct effect of Article 2 of the EIA Directive. In this provision a general duty is imposed on Member States to ensure that, before consent is given, 'projects likely to have significant effects on the environment' are made subject to an environmental impact assessment.[18] In the above mentioned case concerning a waste water treatment plant it could be argued that, as waste water treatment plants are not covered by Dutch law, the court should have reviewed this legislation against Article 2 of the directive. In other words, the court should have examined whether that particular case concerned a project which could have considerable environmental effects.

For projects which do not fall within the scope of Annexes I or II of the directive, the direct effect of Article 2 seems to be even more problematic. Thus, Article 2 of the directive indicates, in the last sentence, that projects which could have considerable environmental effects are listed in Annexes I and II. To put it differently, only Annex I and Annex II projects must be made subject to an environmental impact assessment on the basis of the directive.

Another type of obligation arising out of environmental directives requiring further implementing rules and therefore apparently lacking direct effect, are provisions on the basis of which Member States have to classify geographical areas to be made subject to special protection measures. An example is the classification of special bird protection areas on the basis of the birds Directive.[19] For protected species of birds Member States 'classify in particular the most suitable territories in number and size as special protection areas for the conservation of these species, taking into account their protection requirements in the geographical sea and land area where this directive applies' (Article 4(1)). A failure to classify special protection areas in cases where protected species of birds and migrating birds do occur

---

[18] *Ibid.*
[19] OJ 1979 No. L 103.

in the territory of that Member State should clearly be considered to be in breach with the directive. This can result in an infringement procedure initiated by the Commission on the basis of Article 169 EC. In Case C–334/89 Italy was brought before the European Court because it had not classified special protection areas. The European Court considered in this case:

> The Italian Government has not, either during or before the proceedings before the Court, reported any special conservation measures adopted by it at national level of the species listed in that annex. Nor has it made any claim to the effect that none of the species in question occurs in Italian territory. *Accordingly, it should have established special protection areas and adopted special conservation measures in respect of the species present on its territory.*[20]

The European Court ruled that Italy had not fulfilled its obligations under the birds Directive. From this case it can be concluded that there exists an obligation to classify special protection areas when specific species of birds occur in the territory of the Member State. A much more difficult question is whether the directive also creates an obligation to classify, in a particular case, a certain clearly identified area as special protection area. In other words, does the birds Directive directly impose an obligation to classify for instance the *Oostvaardersplassen* (a Dutch nature conservation area) a special protection area because of its cormorant and spoonbill colonies? Or does the *Dollard* have to be classified because of the presence of large groups of avocets? From the case law of the European Court it appears that Member States enjoy a margin of discretion in the classification of special protection areas. In the German *Leybucht* case (57/89) the question was to what extent Member States can reduce or modify the geographical size of a special protection area.[21] The European Court considered:

> Member states do have a certain discretion with regard to the choice of territories which are most suitable for classification as special protection areas pursuant to Article 4 (1).

On the basis of this judgment the conclusion has been drawn that when Member States do enjoy a certain discretion, an obligation to classify a particular area would be difficult to establish. This would only be different if this discretion to act is restricted by the Member State itself, for example because the area in question had been given protected status on the basis of other, national or international laws or conventions such as the Ramsar Convention.

That a Member State's discretion could indeed be more limited than is suggested by the *Leybucht* case becomes clear from a more recent

---

[20] Case C–334/89, *Commission v Italy*, [1991] ECR I–93 (emphasis supplied).
[21] Case 57/89 [1991] ECR I–883.

judgment. In case C–355/90 judgment was passed against Spain for failing to classify the Marismas de Santoña as a special protection area.[22] The Spanish Government referred to the *Leybucht* case and argued to possess the discretion not to classify the area. The European Court stated:

> Although it is true that Member States retain a certain degree of discretion in respect of the choice of special protection areas, the classification of the areas nonetheless has to be based on ornithological criteria, determined by the directive, such as the presence of birds listed in Annex I and the qualification of a habitat as a wetland. In this respect, the Marismas de Santoña constitute one of the most important ecosystems of the Iberian peninsula for numerous water birds. In fact, various migratory birds hibernate in the swamp on their way to Africa. Amongst those birds are various species threatened with extinction, in particular the spoonbill. The area regularly harbours 19 species listed in Annex I of the directive as well as at least 15 species of migratory birds.[23]

Spain was subsequently found to have failed to fulfil its obligations under the birds directive. Although this case, like case C–334/89,[24] concerned a breach of Treaty procedure in which direct effect as such was not at issue, it seems to me that this case law is relevant in this respect. If the European Court has limited discretion in classifying special protection zones under the birds directive in such a way that a concrete obligation to classify a certain area can result, than it becomes very difficult to see why this obligation should not be directly effective.

Other environmental directives such as the bathing water Directive,[25] the freshwater fish Directive[26] and the shellfish water Directive contain similar obligations.[27] In the context of these directives too, it will have to be determined in each individual case whether on the basis of the criteria in the directive in question a particular area should be classified or not. As regards the bathing water directive, existing case law points to similar conclusions as the birds directive cases discussed above. On the basis of the former, for example, bathing water in bathing areas should satisfy minimum standards. In case C–56/90 one of the questions addressed was which waters had to be considered as bathing areas falling within the scope of the directive.[28] The European Court points out that the directive defines the term 'bathing water' as all running or fresh waters or parts thereof and sea water, in which bathing is either explicitly authorized by the competent authorities of the Member State or not prohibited and traditionally practised by a large

---

22 Case C–355/90 [1993[ECR I–4221.
23 Unofficial translation from the French.
24 Case C–334/89,*Commission v Italy*, [1991] ECR I–93.
25 OJ 1976 No. L 31.
26 OJ 1978 No. L 222.
27 OJ 1979 No. L 281.
28 Case C–56/90, *Commission v UK*, [1994] CMLR 765.

number of bathers. According to the United Kingdom it was unclear whether Blackpool and Southport fell within the scope of this directive. Again, in this case Member States appear to enjoy little discretion. From the presence of changing huts, toilets, markers and lifeguards it could be inferred that areas fall within the scope of the directive and therefore its quality objectives had to be adhered to.

On the other hand, however, if Member States do have considerable discretion in determining areas to which stringent environmental quality objectives apply, there can be no direct effect. For example, on the basis of certain air quality directives Member States can classify areas to which more stringent air quality objectives apply.[29] Such areas are classified when 'the Member State concerned considers' these zones should be afforded special environmental protection. Where a directive leaves Member States with such considerable discretion the provision is evidently not directly effective.

d. Derogation clauses and direct effect

Often environmental directives impose a certain obligation on Member States, whilst at the same allowing derogations subject to certain conditions. An illustrative example is the EIA Directive. Article 4(1) provides that projects listed in Annex I should always be made subject to an environmental impact assessment. Article 2(3) of the directive however, states that Member States may, 'in exceptional cases', exempt a specific project whole or in part from the provisions laid down in the directive. The question arises whether the discretionary powers in Article 2(3) rule out the direct effect of Article 4(1). In other words, does Article 2(3) endow Member States with a discretion to a degree that the obligation to carry out an environmental impact assessment for Annex I projects cannot be invoked? The answer to this question, it is submitted, is in the negative. From case law of the European Court outside the field of environmental law, such as case 41/74 *van Duyn*,[30] it becomes clear that when the derogation clause is subject to judicial review, this does not affect the direct effect of the principal provision.

Dutch case law conforms with this conclusion. Direct effect in those cases resides in the limits which the provision poses to the exercise of certain public competences. The exercise of these powers is subject to judicial review and such provisions therefore are directly effective. The power to derogate *as such*, in other words the question whether this power to derogate should be invoked, is not directly effective.

---

[29] E.g. Article 4(2) of directive 80/779, OJ 1980 No. L 229.
[30] [1974] ECR 1337.

In respect of the direct effect of the – limits of – the powers to derogate, another issue deserves consideration. Thus, when the principal provision is directly effective, but the power of derogation *as such* is not, this may produce results which are in conflict with the objective and the scope of the directive. From the case law of the European Court outside the field of environmental law it appears that in cases where a directive contains both directly effective and non-directly effective provisions, an individual can invoke directly effective provisions 'which owing to their particular subject-matter are capable of being severed from the general body of provisions and applied separately'.[31] *A contrario* it can be concluded that directly effective provisions in environmental directives cannot be invoked when they cannot be severed from the general body of provisions.

The following example may serve by way of illustration. Article 3(1) of Directive 90/313 concerning the freedom of access to environmental information[32] states that Member States shall ensure that public authorities are required to make available information relating to the environment to any natural or legal person at his request and without having to prove an interest. It would seem plausible that this provision is sufficiently precise and unconditionally formulated as to produce direct effect. Article 3(2) of the directive empowers Member States to refuse such a request for information where it affects public security, commercial and industrial confidentiality and a number of other public or private concerns. Article 3(2) concerns a power and not an obligation on the part of the Member State. Direct effect in the sense that Member State are obliged to refuse to make information relating to for example commercial and industrial confidentiality available is therefore out of the question. Does this mean that as long as Article 3(2) of the directive has not been implemented, on the basis of the direct effect of Article 3(1) all environmental information *has* to be made public?

All these questions, it is submitted, have to be answered in the light of the *Becker* case.[33] It therefore needs to be examined when it is possible, in the light of the context in which it has to be placed, to separate a particular provision from the provisions in a directive. This could be achieved by considering the effects of the direct effectiveness of one single provision and the compatibility of these effects with the objective and scope of the directive. In the case of the Directive on access to information, it seems that a general obligation to provide environmental information would go too far and produce results which are in conflict with the general context of the

---

[31] Case 8/81, *Becker*, [1982] ECR 53.
[32] OJ 1990 No. L 158.
[33] Case 8/81, *Becker*, [1982] ECR 53.

directive. Public authorities should be given the opportunity to consider, on an individual basis, whether any of the derogation clauses should apply and to deny a public authority this margin of discretion would be in conflict with the objective of the directive. Therefore, in this example, the direct effect of the directive can only be invoked when information is being denied on a ground other than those contained in Article 3(2).

e. Enforcement measures with direct effect

From the case law of the European Court it follows that obligations arising from environmental directives should be considered obligations to attain a certain result rather than mere obligations to take all necessary steps.[34]

An individual will be primarily interested in the question whether he can, by invoking the directive, force public authorities to take certain measures resulting in compliance with the standards contained in that directive. In general, national law provides a wide range of instruments which public authorities can use to attain the right level of environmental protection. Thus, a plant producing excessive emissions of dangerous substances can be closed down, be the subject of criminal sanctions etc. The question which needs to be addressed here is to what extent an individual can rely on the direct effect of environmental directives relating to enforcement mechanisms in cases of failure to comply with the standards set out in a directive.

It is submitted that, in respect of the question *how* standards contained in environmental directives are enforced, it must be assumed that Member States enjoy considerable discretion, albeit evidently within the limits of Article 5 EC (effective, preventive and proportional). As a result of this discretion, an individual does not have a (directly effective) right to demand *specific* enforcement action, unless this has been expressly specified in the directive itself. In this respect directives prescribing in detail the inspection, supervision and other enforcement mechanisms should be mentioned. When directly effective enforcement provisions exist they will have to be applied, a question which needs to be examined from directive to directive. An example of a directly effective enforcement provision is Article 5(4) of Directive 76/464.[35] This directive compels national authorities to establish emission standards in permits to prevent water pollution. The provision states:

> Should the emission standards not be complied with, the competent authority in the Member States concerned shall take all appropriate steps to ensure that the conditions of authorization are fulfilled and, if necessary, that the discharge is prohibited.

---

[34] Case C–56/90, *Commission v UK*, [1994] 1 CMLR 765.
[35] OJ 1976 No. L 129.

This provision implies that it is not permitted to tolerate discharges which violate the Community emission standards of Directive 76/464. Another example is offered by Article 12 of groundwater Directive 80/68.[36] When the conditions for an authorization are not respected the authorities need to withdraw the authorization if necessary. Other environmental directives similarly contain enforcement provisions.[37]

In the absence of concrete and specific provisions however, it is in the first place for Member States to determine how the factual situation must be brought in line with the situation legally required, although it appears from the relevant case law that the European Court can subject this decision to vigorous review.[38]

If discretionary competences exist this would appear to rule out the direct effect of the obligation to enforce Community values. In this respect, the conclusion of Advocate-General Mischo in the German *TA-Luft* cases deserves consideration.[39] In his opinion, Member States enjoy discretion as to the choice of the measures which are necessary to enforce air quality standards.[40] The institutions of the Community would only be able to challenge the approaches adopted by Member States if it appeared from the facts that these are not capable of achieving the intended goals.

In conclusion, for as long as the factual and legal situation have not been brought into line it must be assumed that although the obligations imposed by the directive are not fulfilled, individuals do not always have the right to invoke the directive by insisting that concrete enforcement measures are taken by the public authorities.

3. Consequences of Direct Effect: General Comments

a. Integral application of Community law

In the second *Simmenthal* case the European Court of Justice explained the implications of direct effect in combination with the principle of supremacy.[41] In the exercise of its jurisdiction, every court is obliged integrally to apply Community law and protect the rights of individuals granted by it, setting aside any conflicting provisions of national law, irrespective of the question whether these provisions were adopted prior or

---

[36] OJ 1980 No. L 20.

[37] E.g. Article 8(1) of Directive 89/369, OJ 1989 No. L 163.

[38] See outside the field of environmental law cases, Case 68/88, *Commission v Greece*, [1989] ECR 2965; C–326/88, *Hansen*, [1990] ECR I–2911; C–177/88, *Dekker*, [1990] ECR I–3941.

[39] Case C–361/88 [1991] ECR I–2567 and case C–59/89 [1991] ECR I–2607.

[40] Article 3(1) of directive 80/779, OJ 1980 No. L 229.

[41] Case 106/77 [1978] ECR 629.

subsequent to the Community rule. In other case law it is held that all directly effective provisions can be invoked against the State, emanations of the State included. A national court is required to give precedence to Community law over conflicting provisions of national law. In addition, the European Court has also drawn attention to the implications of direct effect for the national authorities responsible for implementation. In the *Fratelli Costanzo* case the Court decided that all national public authorities, including regional and local authorities, are under an obligation to apply directly effective provisions of Community law.[42]

In its case law the Court uses several formulations to describe the implications of direct effect. On the one hand, the Court considers that private individuals can invoke rights from directly effective provisions of Community law which the national court has to uphold and, on the other hand, that a directly effective provision of Community law can be invoked before a national court. Both formulations stress the role of national courts in enforcing direct effect. The second, more neutral formulation, appears preferable since the formulation focusing on rights of private individuals is misleading in so far as it gives the impression that directly effective provisions of Community law always involve the granting of subjective rights to private individuals. In reality, the way in which a directly effective provision can be invoked in the national legal system and the form in which this occurs, is to a large extent dependent on national law. Hence, private individuals are first and foremost dependent on the legal procedures established by national law. The form in which the direct effectiveness of a provision can be invoked is therefore determined by national law. To invoke a directly effective provision in the course of a summary procedure in a civil court will have a different result than when direct effect is invoked in an administrative or a criminal procedure. Depending on the procedure used, reliance on a directly effective provision of Community law can lead to full or partial annulment of a decision taken by the competent authority, it may be quashed, damages, an order of *certiorari*, a prohibition, an order for mandamus or an injunction may be awarded. In short, in principle it can result in anything a national court according to national law is empowered to impose on public authorities. In the case of environmental law the problem of direct effect will primarily arise in public law disputes before various administrative courts. When competent authorities take concrete decisions, for example by granting, withdrawing or changing environmental permits, it is the courts with jurisdiction over these matters that will predominantly be competent to rule on these conflicts. In respect of directly

---

[42] Case 103/88 [1989] ECR 1839.

effective provisions of Community law, this can, as we will see below, lead to non-application of the national law in conflict with the directive and/or annulment of the decision.

Civil courts will be competent in cases concerning actions as a result of unlawful acts by the State as a consequence of its failure to fulfil its obligations under environmental directives. In principle this can lead to the award of damages, injunctions, etc.

When the direct effect of Community law is invoked in criminal procedures, this will often concern a situation where national law prohibits something that should be allowed on the basis of a directive. Suspects who successfully invoke Community law will be discharged as the charge will be no criminal offence. Hence, in such a case the national provision on which the charge is based will be set aside or declared inapplicable.

b. The denial of the horizontal direct effect of directives

Directives do not produce horizontal or third-party effect in the sense that, in the absence of national implementing measures, they apply directly and as such can impose obligations on private individuals. Directives are, according to Article 189(3) EC, addressed at Member States and oblige them to take the necessary measures and therefore have *vertical* direct effect only. In principle therefore, direct effect can not be invoked to establish a breach of a provision of the directive in purely private legal relations.

Directly effective provisions of a directive will normally only be invoked as against emanations of the State. It is important to note that the term 'emanations of the State' must be interpreted broadly. As is made clear in *Foster v British Gas*, legal subjects can 'in any event' invoke directly effective provisions of directives against a body, whatever its legal form, which has been made responsible, pursuant to a measure adopted by the State:

> for providing a public service under the control of the State and has for that purpose special powers beyond those which result from the normal rules applicable in relations between individuals.[43]

Regional gas and electricity companies, privatized water companies, but probably also certain waste disposal companies possibly fall within this broad definition.

Apart from lacking horizontal effect, a directive *a fortiori* also lacks *inverse* vertical direct effect. Put differently, a public authority can not invoke the directive as against an individual and in this way force this person to act in accordance with the directive in a situation in which the

---

[43] Case C–188/89 [1990] ECR I–3313.

obligations under the directive have not yet been implemented in the national legal order. When a Member State fails to comply, this can not be held against an individual (principle of estoppel).

c. The duty of 'directive-conform interpretation'

National courts are under a duty to interpret national law in the light of a directive ('directive-conform interpretation'). The doctrine of directive-conform interpretation implies that where there is a conflict between national provisions and a directive, national courts are under a duty as much as possible to interpret national law in a way which conforms with the relevant directive. In the *Marleasing* case the Court observed as follows:

> In applying national law, whether the provisions in question were adopted before or after the directive, the national court called upon to interpret it is required to do so, as far as possible, in the light of the wording and the purpose of the directive in order to achieve the result pursued by the latter and thereby comply with the third paragraph of Article 189 of the Treaty.[44]

Directive-conform interpretation must hence be regarded as a means to prevent a national court from taking a decision which is in conflict with Community law. This duty does not only apply to legal procedures in respect of national authorities but also to procedures involving purely private legal relations. The Court finds the legal basis for the doctrine of directive-conform interpretation in Article 5 of the Treaty. Directive-conform interpretation of national laws which do not accord with the requirements of the directive, does not release the Member State of its obligation to amend those laws.[45] It is possible, however, to apply provisions of national law to maximize the impact of the directive.

4. Implications of the Direct Effect of Environmental Directives

a. Integral application of environmental directives

As has been seen, integral application of the directive, protection of the rights of individuals and non-application of conflicting national laws are the most important legal implications of the direct effect of directives. The question arises, however, what this means for environmental law in practice or, put differently, what it is that should be applied 'integrally'.

The answer to this question would appear to depend on what the environmental directive exactly *obliges*. In each instance it has to be borne in mind that the basis for direct effect resides in the obligations imposed on the Member States by the directive. In respect of each provision of each

---

[44] Case C–106/89 [1990] ECR I–4135.
[45] See Case C–338/91, *Steenhorst-Neerings*, [1993] ECR I–5475.

directive it therefore has to be examined what the obligations it imposes really are. The fact that directly effective provisions of environmental directives have to be applied integrally therefore results in a large diversity in application modalities.

In the case of environmental product standard directives which very often pursue complete harmonization, direct effect implies that a product which satisfies the environmental requirements of the directive is allowed on the market whilst products which do not meet the requirements have to be refused.

In environmental directives which are concerned with minimum harmonization, for example directives concerning water and air quality, direct effect can be found in the limits the directive establishes in respect of the maximum level of pollution. These minimum standards in those cases must be applied. Application of directly effective emission standards or quality objectives prevents the lawful application of national environmental law which is not sufficiently stringent in the light of Community environmental standards.

In some of the derogation clauses described above, for example the exemptions from the EIA obligation, direct effect resides in the limits within which these powers of exemption can be exercised. This implies that the power of exemption as such cannot be reviewed but only the extent to which the authorities have remained within the limits allowed by the directive.

The significance of this remark becomes clear when we examine the powers of exemption in the EIA Directive more closely. Earlier it was shown that the powers of exemption in Dutch EIA legislation are too broad compared to Article 2(3) of the directive. In a procedure before the competent administrative court this led to the setting aside of the Dutch exemption provisions on the ground that they were in conflict with the directly effective provision in the directive. Consequently, the exemption provisions contained in Dutch law could no longer be applied and *all* projects at issue had to be made subject to an EIA. In such a situation the question arises whether the competent authorities can directly invoke the powers of exemption in the directive since, if there is an element of direct effect here, this provision arguably should be applied. It is submitted, however, that this should not follow from the direct effect of Article 2(3) of the EIA Directive for a number of reasons. The EIA Directive does not impose a duty to grant an exemption when an exceptional case arises but merely creates the power to do so. Holders of a planning permission do, therefore, not obtain a right to be exempted as a result of the directive. The question whether an exemption should be granted in a particular instance is something which is not addressed by the directive and in that respect the directive is therefore not directly effective. Direct effect, and hence the obligations for Member States, resides in the limitation of the use of these powers to exceptional cases. Or, in other words, the directive obliges Member States to limit the exercise of their powers of exemption to exceptional cases. *This* limitation has direct effect and should be applied in the sense of *Fratelli Costanzo* alluded to earlier. 'Application' therefore means nothing else than 'fulfilling obligations'. Since the directive does not contain a duty to grant an exemption when an exceptional case occurs, a Secretary of State or Minister can not directly invoke the directive. Such a form of 'application' of environmental law would amount to what we have termed 'inverse vertical direct effect'; it would be the State invoking an unimplemented provision of a directive (and not the other way round as is usually the case where vertical direct effect is concerned). The same problem featured in the Netherlands in the case of Directive 84/631[46] concerning the supervision and control of the transfrontier shipment of hazardous waste. According to the Dutch Government the grounds of objections of Article 4(6) of Directive 84/631 were directly effective and could be applied in the sense that the competence to raise objections against the exports of waste could be based directly on the directive. However, here too it is not the grounds of the objections as such that possess direct effect, but the limits within which this derogation can be exercised. Furthermore, it did not appear from Directive 84/631 that an obligation to raise objections against the exports of waste exists in the cases described by the directive. Under such circumstances an obligation to raise objections can not be said to exist. This leads to the conclusion that it must be determined in each individual case what the obligations contained in a directive are and what rights the directive aims to protect.

It will not always be easy to determine which obligation the directive imposes and what rights the directive aims to protect. Examples are provided by the directives in the fields of water and air quality. The limit values in these directives are primarily aimed at protecting the environment. Authorizations which have been granted by the national authorities containing less stringent standards will have to be quashed by national courts. However, can the national authority then subsequently apply the directive's limit values and incorporate them in the authorization? In other words, does the directive create a duty to grant an authorization when limit values are not exceeded? On the one hand it could be argued, also in the light of Article 130t EC, that such a right to be granted an authorization

---

[46] OJ 1984 No. L 326.

does not exist. On the other hand, it is also difficult to perceive a situation in which the competent authority does not have to take the interests of those seeking authorization into account. If in such a situation the national authority would not have the power to apply the limit values the result could be that, against the spirit and objective of the directive, those seeking authorization would be burdened disproportionately. It is submitted, therefore, that the extent to which national authorities can apply provisions in directives which have not been implemented, depends on the question which obligations the directives imposes and which rights the directive aims to protect. This requires careful examination by the national court in each case and directive. However, no case law of the European Court exists on this issue and these remarks therefore remain somewhat speculative.

b. Denial of horizontal direct effect of environmental directives

It has already been observed that directives do not produce horizontal effect in that they can not impose obligations on individuals without national implementing measures and as such can not be invoked against private individuals. A directive can under those circumstances never impose obligations on private individuals as against a Member State itself, the Court concluded in the Italian fish water case.[47]

In Dutch case law this doctrine is applied consistently. In the *Drente Crows* case the problem was addressed to what extent the birds Directive, can impose obligations on private individuals.[48] In this case a society of hunters had called for a day of crow hunting. Dutch hunting laws still allow crow hunting whilst in principle the birds are granted protection by the directive. An environmental interest group argued that the hunters acted illegally because their behaviour breached the directive. The judge in the case dismissed the application and considered that directives create obligations for Member States, i.e. to amend national laws. It would go too far, according to the judge, to accept that in legal relations between private individuals one would have to act as if these amendments had already been made. Another example is provided by the decision of a Dutch court in short cause where the Belgian firm Cockerill Sambre was taken to court by several environmental interest groups in connection with discharges into the river Maas.[49] One of the arguments was that in particular the discharges of so called 'PACs' breached directive 76/464. Cockerill would, according to the applicants, have abused the fact that the Belgian State had failed to

---

[47] Case 14/86, *Pretore di Salò v X*, [1987] ECR 2545.
[48] President Rechtbank Assen 11 April 1989, M en R 1989, 372–4, with note by van Acht and Jans.
[49] President Rechtbank Maastricht 3 February 1993, MR 1993/17.

comply with its obligations under the directive. The court dismissed the application with the argument that the directive addresses Member States, and therefore does not have the effect of binding private individuals directly.

In short, an individual can invoke the directive *vis-à-vis* national authorities, but not another individual. This position is completely in line with the case law of the European Court of Justice on this problem. Individuals do therefore not act illegally when they act in breach with standards set in EC environmental directives if these standards have not been incorporated into national legislation. In addition, it appears difficult to argue that mere acts by private individuals which are in conflict with standards set in directives should be qualified as abuse of non-fulfilment by national authorities. Only in exceptional cases of intentional acts there may be some room for applying the doctrine of abuse of another party's non-fulfilment, in this case the State's.

c. Indirect horizontal direct effect of environmental directives in multi-lateral legal relations?

Although neither in the literature, nor in existing case law horizontal effect of environmental directives has been accepted, this does not mean that incorrectly implemented environmental directives produce no horizontal legal *effects* between individuals. Thus, an environmental directive can impose obligations on individuals in a more indirect way. When competent authorities grant a permit in breach with the terms of a directive a possible appeal by a third party affected can result in annulment of the permit. In such a case, acts by the individual which were permitted after annulment of the permit no longer will be which in turn may have several consequences in the sphere of civil liability. Clearly, in this way, horizontal effects can occur.

There are other ways in which environmental directives can produce indirect horizontal effects. Thus, when a third party invokes a directly effective provision in an environmental directive, for example in an appeal procedure against the grant of an environmental permit, a successful appeal would mean that the holder of the permit is brought in a difficult position because the permit will be void. This is not exceptional, as a permit contravening national environmental law can also be annulled. An interesting example is found in the case law concerning the compatibility of Dutch EIA legislation with the EIA Directive. The directive contains an unconditional EIA obligation for various projects listed in an Annex including waste incineration installations, chemical treatment plants or land fill of toxic and dangerous wastes. Dutch law, on the other hand, imposed an EIA-obligation only when the installation had a capacity exceeding 25,000 tonnes per year. In a number of decisions national courts have invalidated authorizations granted in those cases because no EIA had been carried out. The thresholds specified in Dutch law, since they clashed with the directive, were irrelevant. Characteristic was the consideration of the court that since *the developer* had not furnished the information required by the directive, *competent authorities* could not legally grant an authorization. In this case, the obligations of authorities and individuals merge. Competent authorities can, on the basis of the direct effect of the EIA Directive, no longer take a legal decision without a prior environmental impact assessment. In the context of Dutch EIA legislation this resulted in a situation where the developer, on sanction of dismissal of his application, must carry out an environmental impact assessment. As long as the developer has not submitted an environmental impact assessment report competent authorities cannot legally grant an authorization. The developer is therefore well-advised to prepare an EIA report. This example shows that if a third party successfully invokes the direct effect of the EIA Directive the directly affected party is put in a disadvantaged position as a result. In the present writer's view, however, it is misconceived to regard this an unacceptable horizontal effect. The effects for the directly affected party have to be seen as flowing from the rights which the third party has obtained on the basis of the directive *against the competent authorities*. The unfavourable implications of direct effect for the directly affected party do not stem from the directive itself, but from the fact that the authorities have failed to fulfil their obligations under the directive. Had the directive been correctly implemented, the authorities would not have granted the authorization in the first place. In as far as the additional obligations result from the authorities' failure to fulfil their obligations under the directive in respect of other individuals, this is not equivalent to horizontal effect. The example does show, however, that vertical direct effect may produce horizontal side-effects, in particular in tri- or multi- lateral legal relations. In tri-lateral environmental legal relations this means, almost necessarily, that honouring the rights of third parties implies additional obligations for the developer (and *vice versa*). If this were to be considered as a manifestation of horizontal direct effect, *quod non*, the doctrine of direct effect would lose all its significance in such cases. Such an interpretation, therefore, needs to be rejected.

d. The duty of directive-conform interpretation of environmental directives

It has been submitted above, that the doctrine of directive-conform interpretation is a judicial tool to avoid discrepancies between national and Community law.

i) Indirect horizontal effects   It follows from the Court's case law that the duty of national courts to interpret national law in conformity with EC law applies not only in vertical but also in purely horizontal relations, hence between individuals *inter se*.[50] In such cases, too, horizontal effects would seem to exist.[51] In order to illustrate the significance of this doctrine for environmental law the example of the above-mentioned case of the court in Maastricht in *Cockerill Sambre* is appropriate.[52] Although in this case the issue of the horizontal direct effect of the limit values of directive 76/464 did not arise as such, the question nevertheless arose to what extent the doctrine of directive-conform interpretation imposed an obligation on *Cockerill Sambre* to comply with the limit values. In this respect it should be remembered that following *Marleasing* the national court is obliged to interpret national law 'as much as possible' directive-conform. Although doctrinal differences exist as to the precise meaning of this phrase, presumably national law must be sufficiently flexible to enable such an interpretation to take place. When, as in the case of *Cockerill Sambre*, clear environmental legislation exists on the basis of which certain polluting activities are allowed to take place, the doctrine of directive-conform interpretation of directives offers few prospects. After all, the national court can hardly reverse an 'it is allowed' into a 'it is not allowed' as this would militate with the principle of legal certainty. Similarly, when the polluter acts in accordance with an authorization which has been recently granted it would seem difficult to defend that it is unlawful to act in accordance with its conditions because the limit values of the directive have been exceeded. This is despite the fact that according to Dutch liability law an action for damages is not automatically precluded if the defendant has acted in conformity with the permit. In these type of cases a direct action against the authorized discharge is unlikely to succeed and affected third parties would be better advised to challenge possible acts and decisions of the authorities concerned by invoking the (vertical) direct effect of limit values.

---

[50] Case C–106/89, *Marleasing*, [1990] ECR I–4135.
[51] See Opinion of Advocate General Darmon in Case C–236/92, *Comitato di coordinamento per la difesa della Cava*, [1994] ECR I–485 para. 28.
[52] President Rechtbank Maastricht 3 February 1993, MR 1993/17.

Direct action directed at the authorized discharger on the basis of Community law only offers possibilities in a legal situation which is open to various interpretations. In such a case directive-conform interpretation of directives can force the polluter to behave in accordance with the provisions and standards in the directive. In particular, it is submitted that the 'duty of care', which is central to liability law in many national legal systems, should be interpreted in the light of the limit values contained in the directive. The violation of limit values (or other obligations arising out of environmental directives) contained in unimplemented environmental directives would constitute a breach of the principle of 'duty of care', and hence be unlawful. As already noted, this kind of directive-conform interpretation is feasible only if a court has been left the necessary leeway to do this.

Directive-conform interpretation of national criminal environmental law will obviously have to be approached even more carefully than is the case with private and administrative law. Thus, as a result of directive-conform interpretation of provisions of criminal law an act could become an offence which would never have been punishable without the directive. The principle of legal certainty, as the Court has recognized, implies that a *de facto* retrospective criminalization should be avoided.

ii) Directive-conform interpretation of competences and obligations? An important question is when a court should apply directive-conform interpretation. In the Netherlands the extent to which too broadly formulated implementation rules have to be interpreted in the light of the directive has been subject to considerable debate. The issue surfaced for the first time in the *Brent Geese* case. This case concerned the compatibility of Dutch hunting legislation (Article 53 *Jachtwet*) with the birds directive, in particular the problem that the criteria listed in the directive had not been transformed into Dutch law. The competent public authority argued that even though the criteria for the grant of an authorization had been too broadly defined, they could still be applied by taking the standards of the directive into account as much as possible. The court dismissed this argument and set aside the law in question.[53] As will be seen, however, in a more recent decision in a similar case the same judge, without further explanation, opted for directive-conform interpretation of the birds directive[54]

---

[53] ARRS 6 March 1986, M en R 1987, 16–9, with case note by J.H. Jans.
[54] ARRS 10 September 1992, AB 1994, 79. tB/S 1992, nr. 111, with case note of RJGMW, AAe 1994, 600–5, with case note by Th.G. Drupsteen.

One of the criteria featuring in the birds directive is that of 'serious damage'. Article 53 of the *Jachtwet* does not contain this restricting condition. Instead of setting aside the *Vogelwet* because of the conflict with the directive (as in the decision in 1986) the court considered in a decision in 1992 that 'it had to be established whether the black crows, jackdaws and magpies had – as required by the directive – caused considerable damage'. In sections of the Dutch literature this example of directive-conform interpretation of the directive has been applauded. Setting aside the legislation would have meant that hunters who on the basis of the directive would have been eligible for a hunting permit, would not obtain one merely because Dutch authorities had not managed to implement the directive correctly. Directive-conform interpretation of the directive does not have this effect; hunters receive what they are entitled to, i.e. an examination of their application in accordance with the criteria of the directive.

The present writer finds it difficult to agree with this view on directive-conform interpretation of directives. The birds Directive does not endow hunters with the right to have their application for an authorization examined according to the criteria in the directive but provides Member States with the power to make such a grant possible, which is something completely different. The power to make that choice resides with national legislators. By opting for directive-conform interpretation the court takes this decision out of the hands of the national authorities and hence exceeds the limits of its powers.

This problem has also been addressed in Dutch case law on the compatibility of Dutch legislation of waste with Directive 84/631. Dutch courts had repeatedly decided that national law did not comply with the directly effective requirements of Article 4(6) of the directive and could therefore not be applied. Following these decisions, the Minister for the Environment defended the position that if Dutch legislation would be interpreted in the light of the directive, it would not be in conflict with the directive and could therefore be applied. In more recent decisions the courts have explicitly ruled against this argument. The Court has confirmed that directive-conform interpretation of directives as an instrument of implementation, to allow authorities to continue to exercise competences under a directive which have been wrongly implemented in national legislation, cannot be accepted.

The criticism which has been levelled against this approach can be summarized as follows. National courts turn things on their head. The court does reject directive-conform interpretation of directives as a method of interpretation, because there is nothing left to interpret after national legislation has been annulled because it does not comply with directly effective provisions of the directive. According to the critics this order has to be reversed: first it must be assessed whether directive-conform interpretation of a directive can make up for the shortcomings of national legislation and only if that is impossible it would be required to use direct effect as an emergency solution.

Drawing on my earlier arguments concerning the duty to integrally apply environmental directives the position taken by the Dutch courts in the waste export cases must be correct. The directive does not contain an obligation, but only powers of discretion to file an objection. In that situation there is no need for a directive-conform interpretation of the directive to prevent a court from having to contravene the directive. When conflicting national legislation is not applied, the court acts entirely in accordance with the objective and scope of the directive.

The situation is different when a directive obliges the competent authorities to act. An example would be a directive containing emission standards both aiming to protect rights of third parties (against pollution) and to protect rights of the party directly affected. The latter would be the case when activities which are detrimental to the environment are not illegal *per se*, but only if a particular limit has been exceeded. Put differently, when it follows from a directive that intends to confer a right on individuals to have their application for a permit examined in accordance with the directive, than an interpretation based on the indirect effect of the directive is justified. In such a case, in order to guarantee the rights of those directly affected it would even be *necessary* to apply a directive-conform interpretation. The too broadly defined emission standards from the national provisions of implementation will then be 'narrowed down' to those in the directive and they can subsequently be applied. (*Steenhorst-Neerings*, case C–338/91). Summarizing this argument, it can be concluded that in answering the question when a national court should apply directive-conform interpretation or when the direct effect of a provision of a directive should be applied, the substance of the obligations it imposes, seen in the light of its objectives and scope, are decisive.

Finally it should be reiterated that directive-conform interpretation does not release the Member State of their duty to ensure that proper legislation implementing directives are put into place. Likewise the direct effect of provisions of directives does not release the Member State from its obligation to implement. The argument of Member States that direct effect guarantees that the affected party, at least in his relation to the State, will obtain what he is entitled to anyway, has been dismissed by the Court on several occasions Improperly implemented directives cause uncertainty about the legal position of those to whom the directive applies which is why the Court insists on complete and correct implementation. Directive-conform interpretation occurs when a court squares provisions of a directive and national law where a 'normal' interpretation would have been in conflict with the directive. Directive-conform interpretation is therefore artificial and exceptional and only serves as a makeshift for poor implementation. Complete and correct implementation remain necessary to put an end to legal uncertainty.

5. The Requirement of National Remedies and the Personal Scope of Environmental Directives

In the English case of *Twyford Parish Council and others versus Secretary of State for the Environment and another* the question was raised who in fact can rely on the direct effect of the provisions of EIA Directive 85/337.[55] Two parish councils and three private individuals contested the validity of a decision of the Secretary of State concerning the construction of a six-lane motor way in the vicinity of Winchester. According to the applicants, no environmental impact statement of assessment had been prepared, and no opportunity had been given for public information and consultation as prescribed by the directive. The judge in the case felt that there was no doubt that the applicants were amongst those whom the directive was intended to benefit and that its provisions were unconditional and sufficiently precise. But, he said, the question arose whether this alone would entitle him to rely on the failure to implement the directive within the prescribed time. Would they, he wondered, in addition have to demonstrate that they had suffered in consequence of that failure? The answer to this question was in the affirmative. The High Court held that there is no ground for the view that, if the terms of a directive, which should have been implemented but had not were breached, an individual who had not thereby suffered could enforce it against the defaulting State. This case provides a striking illustration of the need for answering the question what requirements European Law imposes on national systems for the protection of rights under environmental law, in the event of alleged breaches European environmental law.

a. Legal protection and Article 5 of the EC Treaty
Increasingly, obligations in respect of the legal protection of private individuals who are confronted with a breach of their rights under

---

[55] High Court, Queen's Bench Division (Judge McCullough) 26 October 1990, *Twyford Parish Council and others v Secretary of State for the Environment and another*, CMLR 1992, 276–301.

Community law are based on Article 5 of the Treaty. European law has long avoided the question of legal protection at national level, in cases where essentially Community standards are at issue. Because there is no Community legislation on the subject, it is for the national legal order of each Member State to designate the competent courts and to lay down the procedural rules for proceedings designed to ensure the protection of the rights which individuals acquire through the direct effect of Community law.[56] The European Court of Justice, referring to Article 5 of the EC Treaty, requires only two conditions to be met by national procedural law. First, the rules relating to Community proceedings may not be less favourable than those governing the same right of action on an internal matter and, second, these rules must in no case be laid down in such a way as to render impossible in practice the exercise of the rights which the national courts must protect. Thus the first condition means that the prohibition against discrimination also extends to national procedures of judicial control. It should be remembered that offering access to courts in respect of the direct effect of Community standards not only has a function as far as the protection of the private individual's rights are concerned, but is also important as an objective instrument of control with a view to ensuring that the behaviour of Member States is in conformity with Community law.[57] As early as the *Van Gend en Loos* case the Court ruled that:

the vigilance of individuals concerned to protect their rights amounts to an effective supervision in addition to the supervision entrusted by Articles 169 and 170 to the diligence of the Commission and of the Member States.[58]

Legal protection in those fields of national administrative law, such as environmental law, on which Community law has a considerable impact, cannot be evaluated solely from the viewpoint of the protection of personal rights afforded by the law. The second condition in effect has set standards of effectiveness for national procedures for the protection of rights. It is this requirement of effectiveness that has above all been extended and developed in the Court's later decisions.[59]

From this case law it can be deduced that Community law contains a general obligation for Member States, essentially based on Article 5 of the EC Treaty, which obliges the State to ensure that efficient judicial protection exists which can guarantee the rights conferred on individuals by

---

[56] Case 45/76, *Comet*, [1976] ECR 2043; Case 265/78, *Ferwerda*, [1980] ECR 617.
[57] Case 26/62, *Van Gend en Loos*, [1963] ECR 1.
[58] *Ibid.*
[59] E.g. case C–340/89, *Vlassopoulou*, [1991] ECR I–2357.

the Treaty. National law should provide the necessary remedies to allow enforcement the directly effective provisions in the courts.

b. Legal protection and Article 30 of the Treaty

The importance the Court attaches to the availability of legal remedies for private individuals whose rights under Community law have been jeopardized is also evident in the context of judicial review of national measures in the light of the free movement of goods which is illustrated, for instance, by the decision of the Court in the case of the German *Reinheitsgebot*.[60] One aspect of this case was the incompatibility with the EC Treaty of the absolute prohibition on the marketing of beer containing additives. The Court considered that by virtue of the principle of proportionality, traders must also be able to apply, under a procedure which is easily accessible to them and can be concluded within a reasonable time, for the use of specific additives to be authorized by a measure of general application. Moreover, where traders are improperly refused access to the market, they must in the words of the Court be able 'to challenge before the courts' such refusal. Not providing a means of appeal can make a measure which curtails imports disproportional and therefore in breach of Article 30 of the EC Treaty, a decision which was recently confirmed by the Court.[61]

For environmental law, too, this case law is relevant. As is well-known, there exist a large number of environmental directives which regulate, prohibit, or impose conditions on the bringing on the market of products which are harmful to the environment. In general, these directives do not provide for legal remedies for directly affected or third parties. In the light of the body of case law just discussed it appears that decisions of competent authorities preventing products from entering the market can be challenged in the courts on the basis of Article 30 of the Treaty. In addition, similar possibilities would seem to exist for the legal protection of third parties; the incorrect admission on the market of environmentally damaging product should also be challengeable in the national courts.

c. Legal protection in secondary environmental law

An issue which deserves particular consideration here is the extent to which European environmental law affects the question which persons are to be regarded as interested parties by the national legal system and ought to be put in a position to be able to appeal against certain administrative decisions in the field of environmental law.

---

[60] Case 178/84 [1987] ECR 1227.
[61] Case C–18/88, *GB-Inno-BM*, [1991] ECR I–5941.

In the first place, Member States must create means of recourse to the courts where a specific directive expressly so requires. Directive 90/313 on freedom of access to information on the environment is an example where this is the case. Article 3 of the directive gives any natural or legal person a right to information relating to the environment, whilst Article 4 provides for judicial and administrative review where this person is refused the desired information. To some extent the EIA Directive provides another example. Article 6 of the directive requires that the application for a permit, and the information gathered in connection with the environmental impact assessment is 'made available to the public' and that 'the public concerned is given the opportunity to express an opinion before the project is initiated'.

Both the freedom of access to the environment Directive and the EIA Directive apply to large groups of interested third parties who fall within the scope of direct effect of the directives. From this it could be concluded that, when the content of a Community law standard relates to the protection of individuals, it would be contrary to the intention and purpose of this legal standard if it could not be relied upon in the courts.

Other directives which oblige Member States to make some means of recourse to the courts available that might be referred to here are Directive 84/532 relating to the common provisions for construction plants and equipment,[62] and Directive 92/53, relating to type approval of motor vehicles and their trailers.[63] A further example is provided by Article 39 of Euratom Directive 80/836 on basic safety standards for the health protection of the general public and workers against the dangers of ionising radiation.[64]

d. Access to justice and the personal scope of environmental directives
In addition there is the question as to whom Member States must offer a means of protecting their rights where a directive does not contain any express provisions on the matter. In this respect, reference needs to be made to the decisions of the European Court of Justice relating to the direct effect of environmental directives.

The Court has stated that it would be incompatible with the binding effect attributed to a directive by Article 189 to exclude, in principle, the possibility that the obligation which it imposes *may be invoked by those concerned*[65] In addition the Court held that the right to rely on the directive

---

[62] OJ 1984 No. L 300.
[63] OJ 1992 No. L 225.
[64] OJ 1980 No. L 246 and OJ 1984 No. L 265.
[65] Case 41/74, *Van Duyn*, [1974] ECR 1337.

'is not confined to individuals coming within the scope *ratione personae* of the directive '. After all, the Court observed, it cannot be ruled out that other persons might also have a direct interest.[66]

Whether there can be said to exist an interest is a matter which must, of course, be decided according to European law and not according to national law. In the light of these decisions, the decision of the High Court in the Twyford Down case above must be rejected. What is relevant is not whether loss has been suffered, but whether someone has a direct interest in compliance by the Government with obligations under the directive.

This raises the question as to who environmental directives intend to benefit and, furthermore, who has a direct interest in Member States' compliance with obligations of directives. To whom is EC environmental law addressed and what are the legal consequences of this personal scope of EC environmental law (which is used broadly as including those who have a direct interest) especially in respect of direct effect? Whose 'interests', or perhaps one should say 'rights', are protected by EC environmental law?

For many areas of European law it is relatively straightforward to determine this personal scope. The free movement of workers applies to people who are, actually or potentially, in paid employment; the free movement of services is concerned with those who want to offer their services across borders; the right of establishment applies to professionals who want to exercise their activities in another Member State. In other areas, likewise, it is immediately clear to whom the law applies: a taxable person has the right to have certain tax facilities, the beneficiaries of the principle of equal treatment are those who allege to have been violated in their rights. All these examples have in common that they are located within bi-lateral legal relationships: the authorities and the party directly involved who has obtained rights on the basis of Community law as against these authorities.

Environmental law on the other hand, national and European, is characterized by a tri-lateral relationship: authorities, party directly affected and the third party. The term 'directly affected party' signifies the polluter, the permit holder or applicant, developer or importer of goods or products which are dangerous for the environment. In short: he or she who undertakes or intends to undertake a certain activity which might have an impact on the environment. By third party is meant those who might object to certain activities having an impact on the environment: those living in the vicinity of an industrial plant, environmental interest groups etc. Broadly

---

66 Joined cases C–87/90, C–88/90 and C–89/90, *Verholen*, [1991] ECR I–3757.

speaking one could say that the connection between directly involved and third parties is that between market interests and environmental interests.

By means of State intervention, such as requirements of prior authorization, public authorities act as intermediaries between directly affected and third parties, but with exclusive responsibilities and tasks and powers in line with those responsibilities. The question about the personal scope of a directive, therefore, is indirectly also a question about the substantive scope of protection: who (and therefore also what!) is protected by European environmental law?

In general, the view is supported that the personal scope of European environmental law is related to the intensity with which environmental law has been harmonized. In the case of minimum harmonization it is mostly the third party who is protected. Thus, such environmental directives will precisely stipulate which types of pollution are unlawful in the context of European law. For directly affected parties these directives are less important because they leave the authorities' power to take more stringent measures than those laid down in the directive unaffected. For applicants of permits and permit holders, directives pursuing minimum harmonization only offer protection insofar as they prevent competitors from other Member States from producing under less stringent environmental conditions.

An example of Dutch case law where the EIA Directive was used to interpret the term 'party affected' is found in the decision regarding the production of an electricity plant.[67] In this case Texaco appealed against the decision by the Secretary of State for Economic Affairs not to use the coal gasification process. Texaco had been affected by this decision because it had specialized in this procedure and saw its chances of obtaining the contract to build the installation practically reduced to zero. The court in its decision pointed to the second recital to the directive which states that one of the aims of EIA Directive is the objective to remove unfavourable competitive conditions caused by disparities between the laws in force in the various Member States. The court considered subsequently, that 'interested' parties include those who, like Texaco, have an interest in unambiguous legislation as regards environmental impact assessment in the Member States of the Community.

When the personal scope of environmental directives is more closely examined, it appears that it is very rare for a particular person or group or persons to be named or indicated in the directive. One of the few exceptions

---

[67] VzCBB 4 January 1991, KG 1991, 26, AB 1991, 185, M en R 1991, 219–25, with case note by Jans and Uylenburg, Publiek Domein 1991, 143–51, with case note by H.G. Sevenster, AA 1991, 576–81, with case note by Th.G. Drupsteen.

are the aforementioned freedom of access to environmental information and EIA Directives. Both in the case of the access to information Directive and the EIA Directive large groups of people fall within its personal scope. It follows that when the substance of a provision of Community law relates to the protection of individuals, it would be incompatible with the spirit and objective of that provision if it could not be invoked before the courts.

Where environmental directives relate to the manufacture and distribution of products which may be dangerous or harmful to the environment, another clearly defined group of interested parties is introduced – the manufacturers and importers of the products regulated by the directives in question. Their interest is above all that, to the extent the directives impose limits on the powers of Member States to take more stringent environmental measures, these limits are observed. Provisions which are important to them are those such as Article 15 of Directive 90/220 on the deliberate release into the environment of genetically modified organisms.[68] This directive provides that Member States shall not prohibit, restrict or impede the placing on the market of products containing genetically modified organisms which comply with the requirements of this directive, on grounds relating to the notification and written consent of a deliberate release under this directive.

Where, as in the above examples, the directive itself indicates which persons fall under its operation, there is of course no problem deciding the extent of its direct effect. Manufacturers and importers can certainly be regarded as affected parties in cases such as those described above. Of course, it cannot therefore be said *ius dem generis* that third parties are not eligible for the protection of the law.

Much more difficult are those cases where a directive imposes an obligation on the national authorities to maintain environmental standards, particularly emission standards or quality standards which are almost by definition aimed at protecting the interest of the environment as such. The question arises whether this implies that any third party falls within the scope of the direct effect of the directive and must therefore be regarded as an interested party? This might imply the availability of a civil action which could serve as a test case on a matter affecting the public interest, where such directly applicable Community environmental standards are involved.

The European Court's decisions contain indications that this conclusion should indeed be drawn; the decisions in the German *TA-Luft* cases being of particular interest in this respect.[69] What was involved in case C–361/88 was the manner of implementation in Germany of Directive 80/779 on air quality limit values and guide values for sulphur dioxide and suspended

---

[68] OJ 1990 No. L 117.

[69] Case C–361/88 [1991] ECR I–2567 and case C–59/89 [1991] ECR I–2607.

particles.[70] Under this directive the Member States are obliged to ensure that concentrations of sulphur dioxide and of particles suspended in the air do not exceed the limit values in the directive. This is a form of minimum harmonization, establishing a lower limit for pollution which can still be regarded as acceptable. In Germany these limit values were converted by means of the so called T(echnische) A(nleitung) Luft, a legal instrument whose mandatory nature was disputed. The Court considered, referring to earlier decisions, that one of the things that is required of national implementing legislation is that it does indeed guarantee the full application of the directive in a sufficiently clear and precise manner so that, where the directive is intended to create rights for individuals, the persons concerned can ascertain the full extent of these rights and, where appropriate, rely on them before the national courts. The Court then applied this rule to the case in question and first of all analysed to what extent the directive did indeed confer rights on individuals. According to Article 1 of the directive, these limits were established to improve 'the protection of human health' and 'the protection of the environment'. The Court concluded from the first of these objectives that:

> whenever the exceeding of the limit values could endanger human health, the persons concerned must be in a position to rely on mandatory requirements in order to be able to assert their rights.

This demonstrates that rights can be bestowed on individuals by quality standards that have a very general protective aim. It would indeed seem that the Court desires a public interest civil action to be available in the event of a breach of directly effective environmental quality standards by Member States. In case C–59/89, which concerned Directive 82/884 on a limit value for lead in the air,[71] we find similar considerations to those in case C–361/88.

In view of the fact that individual rights can be acquired as a result of the general protective aim of an air quality directive, it is hard to see why a different conclusion should be reached in respect of other kinds of environmental standards, for example emission standards and product standards, which besides serving the purpose of market integration naturally also serve an environmental purpose. This view is supported in the Court's decision of 20 May 1992 in case 190/90,[72] *EC Commission v the Netherlands*, in respect of the alleged improper implementation of Directive 82/501 on the major-accident hazards of certain industrial activities.[73] This

---

[70] OJ 1980 No. L 229.
[71] OJ 1982 No. L 378.
[72] Case C–190/90,*Commission v the Netherlands*, [1991] ECR I–3265.
[73] OJ 1982 No. L 230 and OJ 1988 No. L 336.

directive too, in view of the Court's judgment, would seem to have created rights for individuals (see particularly consideration 17).

In the *Balsamo* case[74] the Court made clear that procedural rules do not always give individuals rights which they may enforce before national courts. Article 3(2) of the 'old' waste Directive 75/442 required the Member States to inform the Commission in good time of any draft rules concerning, *inter alia,* the use of products which might be a source of technical difficulties as regards disposal or lead to excessive disposal costs. The Italian Government did not notify the Commission the decision of the Mayor of Cinisello Balsamo which prohibited the supply to customers of non-biodegradable plastic bags. The competent Italian court submitted questions to the Court of Justice, *inter alia*, if Article 3(2) of the directive gives individuals a right which they may enforce before the national courts in order to obtain the annulment of suspension of national rules on the ground that those rules were adopted without having previously been communicated to the Commission. According to the Court Article 3(2) is intended to ensure that the Commission is informed of any plans for national measures regarding waste disposal so that it can consider whether Community harmonizing legislation is called for and whether the draft rules submitted to it are compatible with Community law. However, neither the wording nor the purpose of the provision in question concerned provides any support for the view that failure by the Member States to inform the Commission in itself renders unlawful the rules thus adopted. The Court made clear that Article 3(2) of the Waste Directive concerned *relations between the Member States and the Commission* and does not give rise to any right for individuals which might be infringed by a Member State's breach of its obligation to inform the Commission in advance of draft rules.

It is evident however from another decision of the Court that procedural rules can contain rights an obligations for private individuals.[75] The case concerned, *inter alia* the formal obligations flowing from Articles 7 to 11 and Article 13 of Directive 80/68 on the protection of groundwater against pollution caused by certain dangerous substances. Article 7 requires prior examination of the hydrogeological conditions and Articles 8 to 11 and Article 13 impose further requirements on the issuing of authorizations. The authorizations may not be issued until it has been checked that the groundwater, and in particular its quality will undergo the requisite surveillance (Article 8) which is why Articles 9 and 10 of the directive lay down the information to be specified in the authorizations. The authorizations may be granted for a limited period only, and are reviewed at

---

[74] Case 380/87 [1989] ECR 2491.
[75] Case 131/88, *Commission v Germany*, [1991] ECR 825.

least every four years (Article 11). Moreover, the directive imposes an obligation on the Member States to monitor compliance with the conditions laid down in the authorizations and the effects of discharges on groundwater (Article 13). The Court observed that the procedural provisions of the directive lay down, in order to guarantee effective protection of groundwater, precise and detailed rules 'which are intended to create rights for individuals'. In particular this decision shows that the term 'rights and obligations' should be understood not only to include he rights and obligations of individuals, but far more in terms of 'having an interest in' or 'being affected by'. The conclusion must therefore be that in such cases the Member State must offer interested parties adequate legal protection against breaches of obligations imposed by directives. The necessity of offering legal protection clearly does not depend on the presence of subjective rights (*recours subjectif*) but serves equally to safeguard the law (*recours objectif*). In this sense, Community law as expressed by the Court of Justice is developing along lines much closer to the French and Dutch systems of administrative law than those of Germany and the United Kingdom.

II THE SIGNIFICANCE OF THE *FRANCOVICH* CASE FOR THE ENVIRONMENT

In the well known *Francovich* case the European Court of Justice ruled that individuals may sue the State if their rights are breached by infringements of Community law attributable to a Member State.[76] The State is hence liable for damages suffered by individuals as a result of breaches of Community law attributable to it. For such liability to arise, the Court has formulated three conditions:

- the directive must create rights for individuals;
- the content of those rights can be identified on the basis of the directive;
- a causal link must exist between the Member State's breach of its obligations and the damage suffered by the individuals affected.

It is for the Member State, in the framework of national regimes governing liability, to indemnify the consequences of the damages caused. The procedural rules governing this Community inspired public authority liability are hence governed by national law. National liability law including its procedural rules therefore serve as a vehicle for the remedy of public

---

[76] Joined cases C–6/90 and C–9/90 [1991] ECR I–5357. For a detailed analysis see Han Somsen's contribution in Chapter 7.

authority liability based on Community law. However, national provisions which are more restrictive than the conditions formulated in *Francovich* must be ignored.[77] Since the direct effect of a provision of a directive is not a requirement, breaches of provisions which lack direct effect can also give rise to liability.

1. The Grant of Rights to Individuals

At this stage, the consequences of the judgment for the environment are not quite clear. In particular, differences of opinion are possible in respect of the question when an environmental directive entails the grant of rights to individuals. Are these rights limited to subjective property rights or is a more extensive interpretation to be preferred? In this respect, I refer once more to the remarks made above which showed that from the case law of the Court in respect of the implementation of environmental directives it appears that the Court is quick to accept rights for individuals. Initially therefore, it would seem that the notion of 'rights for individuals' should not be interpreted in the narrow, subjective sense. Breaches of environmental directives will often involve breaches of rights of individuals.

2. Attribution to the State

Another possible problem which is particularly important for environmental law is the following. From the Court's case law regarding the implementation of environmental directives it follows that it views the obligations contained in environmental directives as obligations of result rather than obligations 'to take all necessary steps'.[78] If the result is not achieved, the directive cannot be said to have been properly implemented in the national legal order which in turn may lead to a judgment in an infringement procedure. One of the conditions for liability in the *Francovich* case is that the breach of Community law can be *attributed* to the State. Conceptually, the following distinctions can be made:

- failure to implement by a Member State;
- incorrect implementation by a Member State, possibly involving concurrent liability of the Community legislator in cases of imprecise or ambiguous legislation;

---

[77] Cf. Case C–177/88, *Dekker*, [1990] ECR I–3941.
[78] Case C–56/90, *Commission v UK*, [1993] ECR I–4109.

- correct formal implementation, but erroneous application by local or regional authorities;
- correct formal implementation, subsequently followed by correct application by competent authorities, but where an individual acts in breach of the authorities' decision and hence in breach with the directive.

The case law relating to the implementation of environmental directives suggests that in all four cases the breach of Community law may result in a judgment for failure to fulfil a directive in an infringement procedure. If, for the purpose of the question of attribution, the same stringent approach is followed as in the context of questions of implementation, than each breach – including those by individuals – can in fact be attributed to the State. In that case, a form of strict liability would therefore in fact be introduced, imposing liability for own fault, acts of other State authorities and individuals. This could even be the case if the legislator at national level has introduced completely satisfactory the required implementing legislation.

When a Member State has not adopted the necessary implementing legislation and breaches by individuals can be attributed to the State, the absence of horizontal direct effect becomes less problematic. Thus, in such a case the State rather than the polluter can be held liable for the breach of the directive. There is Dutch case law supporting this view.[79] In a procedure initiated by a number of environmental interest groups against discharges by the Belgian company Sopar, the Court of Appeal in The Hague considered in respect of Directive 76/464 that the mere fact that a directive does not produce horizontal direct effect does not preclude the affected individual to start an action against the State failing to adhere to EC obligations.

Further case law by the Court will have to establish when a breach of an environmental directive can be attributed to the State and whether the Court will draw a parallel with its stringent case law in the context of infringement procedures. Another possibility would be to approach the question of attribution along similar lines as those relating to the non-contractual liability of the Community (Article 215 EC) In that case the liability of the State for breaches of Community law will be more limited in scope. Following its judgments in *Brasserie du Pêcheur* and *British Telecommunications*, it indeed appears that the Court has opted for the latter, more restrictive, approach.[80]

---

[79] Hof's-Gravenhage 19 November 1992, rolnr. 91/629.

[80] Joined cases C-46/93 and C-58/93, *Brasserie du Pêcheur SA* and *Federal Republic of Germany* and between *The Queen* and *Secretary of State for Transport ex parte: Factortame Ltd and Others,* 5 March 1996 (not yet reported) and Case C-323/93, *The*

Another area of confusion in this regard concerns the relationship between central and local Government. For example, local Government can act in breach of EC environmental law when it applies the national implementing provisions in good faith. It must be assumed that, at least on the basis of Dutch civil liability law, they are liable. According to Dutch liability law, fault or negligence are irrelevant in cases of public authority liability. It could be argued that these local and regional authorities in turn can exercise a right of redress on central Government which, after all, is responsible for correct implementation. If it is accepted that incorrect application of environmental law which in itself has been correctly implemented can give rise to liability on the basis of the *Francovich* case, the reverse situation may also arise. Thus, in that case the State may be held liable for breaches committed at local or regional level. Does the State, too, enjoy a possibility of redress? These and other questions may in future be brought to the attention of the Court of Justice.

3. Damage Suffered as a Result of Breaches of European Environmental Law

The *Francovich* case shows that an action for damages against the State is possible. It is unclear, however, to what extent this embraces environmental damage rather than mere pecuniary damage. Future case law will have to clarify this. In addition, for third affected parties a prohibition, an order for mandamus or an injunction will usually be more useful than compensation and the question arises to what extent the *Francovich* case accommodate these needs. In the present writer's opinion, in this respect the *Francovich* case should not be interpreted too restrictively. *Francovich* after all concerned the detrimental financial consequences of the State's failure to act. As a matter of principle, there appear to be few objections against extending the remedies at the disposal of adversely affected individuals if this means that the effect of directives in Member States is strengthened. Its significance would be that breaches of provisions of environmental directives lacking direct effect could also be challenged with an order of certiorari, a prohibition, an order for mandamus or an injunction. Apart from certain remedies for third affected parties, the *Francovich* case possibly also provides the possibility for directly affected parties to obtain compensation for certain damages resulting from incorrect implementation. For example, if the authorities have granted a permit on the basis of national

---

Queenn and H.M. Treasury ex parte: Britisch Telecommunications plc, 26 March 1996 (not yet reported). For a more detailed analysis of these recent cases see further Somsen's chapter in this volume.

legislation which has not yet been adapted to the directive, the permit can be revoked and ultimately the applicant will have to act in accordance with the more stringent requirements which in turn may involve additional investments in the production process. It appears that these costs, hence those necessary to comply with the more stringent Community standards, are not amenable for compensation because, had the directive been correctly implemented, these costs would also have been incurred. On the other hand, costs which have been incurred by an individual after relying in good faith on the correctness of national environmental law can be compensated. In this respect one could think about certain development costs.

4. Significance for National Liability Law

The impact of *Francovich* will be less profound for Dutch public authority liability law than for some other Member States since in Dutch law public authority liability is by no means unknown. On the basis of Dutch public authority liability it must already be assumed that acts of public authorities (and not only the State) breaching Community law are unlawful. Community law forms part of current national law and is supreme and the legality of State actions can therefore be judicially reviewed against Community law. As has become clear since the *Hofmann-La Roche* case, (26 September 1986) breaches of statutes, which is what we are concerned with here, *prima facie* involves public authority liability. In this context it must be noted that the *Francovich* case does not prevent a more stringent public authority liability regime than that which follows from the case itself. In this sense the case must be regarded as merely laying down minimum standards.

III DIRECT EFFECT IN NATIONAL ENVIRONMENTAL LAW

For national environmental law the doctrine of direct effect, as described above, has the following implications:

1. State action in breach of directly effective provisions of directives must in principle be considered, as a matter of liability law, unlawful;
2. permits granted in breach with provisions of directives are open to annulment by administrative courts;

3. individuals acting in accordance with provisions of environmental directives cannot be successfully criminally prosecuted on the basis of national legislation at variance with that directive.

1. Direct Effect in National Civil Procedures

Dutch civil courts have accepted that, as a matter of Dutch law, breaches of directly effective provisions of environmental directives are unlawful. The issue arose as early as the 1970s in the context of the case of the nuclear reactor at Borsele. The court in The Hague considered that if the State would allow the radiation levels of the Euratom directive to be exceeded, this would be illegal.[81] Environmental interest groups had advanced that the State had acted unlawfully because it had breached Euratom directives which prescribed maximum permissible radiation levels. The court ruled that these directives create rights enforceable against the State. Breaches of those values were unlawful under Dutch law. The court took into consideration the fact that the levels contained in the directive were of fundamental importance and represented a vital interest for the population. The application was rejected, however, because breaches of the levels had not been shown.

This judgment acknowledges that breaches of European environmental standards by the State under Dutch law should be considered unlawful. The question could be asked exactly *against whom* breaches of European environmental standards by national authorities is unlawful. It suffices to recall that from the case law of the European Court it appears that in respect of environmental directives it may often be presumed that these also aim to protect the rights of individuals.

2. Direct Effect in National Administrative Procedures

a. Concrete review of permits against directly effective provisions of environmental directives

Dutch administrative case law, in particular that of the Council of State, shows that permits violating provisions of environmental directives must be annulled by administrative courts and that permits can be directly reviewed against the provisions of the directive.

An illustrative example is provided by the *Urenco* case.[82] Permits had been granted to Urenco based on nuclear energy legislation allowing,

---

[81] Rb.'s-Gravenhage 23 Oktober 1974, NJ 1975, 115.

[82] AGRS 27 March 1991, M en R 1991, 424–8, with case note by Nijhoff, NJB 1991, 1204–5, AB 1991, 537, with case note by AFMB.

amongst others, the possession and disposal of fusionable material. In the course of legal proceedings, Article 6 of the Euratom directive concerning radiation levels was invoked to show that the permit violated this provision. The court considered that the public authorities should have reviewed the permit against the provisions of the directive. Since there was no proof that such a review had taken place, the court annulled the permit.

A second example is offered by case law of national courts concerning the relation between legislation regarding the prevention of water pollution and Article 3(4) of directive 76/464.[83] On the basis of that directive discharges into surface waters of so-called 'Black-List' substances such as mercury and cadmium are only permissible on the basis of temporary permits. Although in the Netherlands any discharge of such substances into surface waters is prohibited, this does not apply to substances which manifest themselves merely as traces in other substances. Yet, in cases where permits are granted for discharges of substances with traces of Black-List substances, Dutch law does not contain an obligation for the authorities to only temporarily grant the permit. The court ruled that permits which are not temporarily granted had to be annulled.

These examples show that courts require public authorities to examine whether their decisions accord with the directive. If it is shown that the public authorities have failed to take EC law into account in the exercise of their powers, the permit will be annulled.

b. Abstract review against directly effective provisions of environmental directives

Apart from concrete review of permits against a directive, the Dutch courts have also applied the abstract review method. This type of review does not involve direct review of a permit against a directive, but the interpretation of the national legislation on the basis of which the permit has been granted in the light of the directive. If the national legislation does not comply with the requirements of EC law it will not be applied. The permit will subsequently, more or less automatically, be quashed on the ground of breach of statutory requirements since, after setting aside the contravening provisions of national environmental law, the legal basis for the permit has disappeared.

A good illustration is provided by the previously mentioned *Brent Geese* case where a permit was annulled because of breach of the bird Directive.[84] Dutch hunting legislation prohibited the hunting of brent geese. On the basis of Article 53 of the *Jachtwet*, providing completely unfettered powers,

---

[83] AGRS 25 September 1992, MR 1992/46.
[84] ARRS 6 March 1986, M en R 1987, 16–9, with case note by J.H. Jans.

the Minister for Environment had granted a permit for hunting the birds. The brent goose is a protected bird in the birds Directive. The hunting of the birds is in principle prohibited by Article 7 of the directive, unless the conditions of Article 9 have been fulfilled. For example, hunting may be authorized if there are no other satisfactory solutions to prevent serious damage to crops. In its judgment the court concludes that the Dutch derogation is much more extensive than allowed by the directive.

The court ruled that under those circumstances the authority to grant permits contained in the Dutch legislation must be set aside and replaced by the unconditional prohibition as formulated in Article 7 of the directive. The result: the hunting of brent geese is prohibited because the Dutch criteria on the basis of which permits are granted are too relaxed in comparison to the directive, even when the permit in question itself *does* comply with the criteria in the directive.

In a later judgment the same judge opted for a different approach in an identical case.[85] In this case the judge chose for directive-conform interpretation of Article 53 *Jachtwet* and then reviewed the decision against the *Jachtwet* thus interpreted. In essence this amounts to abstract review of the permit against the directive. In the last case the court apparently considers it possible to grant a permit which conforms with the requirements of the birds directive. On this point the judgment of 1992 therefore fundamentally departs from the judgment of 1986.

A second example is provided by Dutch case law concerning transfrontier shipment of hazardous waste which has already been considered on numerous occasions above. In these cases, too, it was found that Dutch legislation was too liberally formulated in comparison with the Directive. For example, Dutch law allowed objections to be raised against the export of hazardous waste on grounds other than those mentioned in Article 4(6) of directive 84/631. The decision by the Minister for Environment not to allow the exportation was subsequently quashed on the ground of breach of statutory requirements. After all, the legal basis which is legally required for the grant of the permit after the provisions had been set aside had in a way disappeared.

Finally, a third example were abstract review has been applied is offered by the case law relating to the compatibility of Dutch EIA legislation with the grounds for exemption in Article 2(3) of the directive. In this case, too, the decision to exempt a project from an environmental impact assessment was not concretely reviewed against the provisions of the directive but the court ascertained whether Dutch legislation conformed with the

[85] ARRS 10 September 1992, AB 1994, 79. tB/S 1992, nr. 111, with case note by RJGMW, AAe 1994, 600–5, with case note by Drupsteen.

requirements of the directive. Since, after review, it appeared that the grounds of exemption in Dutch legislation were broader than the grant of exemptions in specific and exceptional cases, as required by the directive, the court judged the legislation to be inapplicable. The decision to exempt the project from an EIA was subsequently quashed.

c. The practical significance of concrete or abstract review

An important question which needs to be addressed is the practical significance of the different types of review carried out by Dutch courts. The answer to this question is that the consequences of abstract review are much more profound than those of concrete review.

The consequence of abstract review is that the national legal basis for the decision that has been quashed has disappeared. Hence, the legal basis has been set aside by the national court. This implies that, for as long as the incompatible legislation has not been amended, the national authorities are unable to act lawfully. This is even so when the national authorities in the particular case at hand have acted in accordance with the directive. This last point is well illustrated by the *Brent Geese* case already mentioned.[86] The defence by the Secretary of State that the hunting permit at issue *did* comply with the directive was rejected by the court. It is for this reason that in the cases concerning the transport of hazardous waste and exemptions to the EIA Directive the courts did not even get as far as to review the particular decision. These examples, once more, show that the question whether in a particular case the requirements of the directive have been fulfilled does not feature at all in cases of abstract review. In brief, as a consequence of abstract review the competent authorities are completely unable to grant permits until national law has been amended.

The consequences of concrete review are clearly less profound. Even when the implementing legislation does not comply with the directive, as long as the competent authorities ensure that the conditions in the individual permit accord with the conditions of the directive, the permit will have been lawfully granted. By way of example; if in the *Urenco* case discussed above[87] abstract review had taken place the decision would have been quashed on the ground of breach of statutory requirements and, until the legislation had been amended, it would have been impossible to grant a new improved permit. Although concrete review resulted in the permit being annulled, nothing precludes the competent authorities from granting permits which take into account the values and principles of the Euratom directive.

---

[86] ARRS 6 March 1986, M en R 1987, 16–9, with case note by J.H. Jans.
[87] AGRS 27 March 1991, M en R 1991, 424–8, with case note by Nijhoff, NJB 1991, 1204–5, AB 1991, 537, with case note by AFMB.

d. A Community law preference for abstract or concrete review?

It can be asked whether in Community law a preference exists for one of the above mentioned forms of review. In the present writer's opinion the answer is in the affirmative and two factors are important in this respect. First, in the case law of the European Court concerning the way in which directives must be implemented there are indications of a preference for abstract testing. As is well known, as regards the implementation by a Member State of obligations imposed by a directive, it does not suffice if in a Member State's territory no activities occur which are in conflict with the directive. It is also important that an adequate body of law is put into place which prohibits the activities which are in breach of the directive.[88] Also when in an individual case a State's actions comply with a directive's requirements, that State can still be acting in breach of the obligations imposed under that directive. Abstract review has in this respect the advantage that it puts pressure on national authorities to amend speedily national legislation. In the case of concrete review legislation will also have to be amended to meet the requirements of the directive, but the pressure which abstract review puts on the legislator is absent. In my view there therefore exists a Community preference for abstract review, which is partly inspired by Article 5 of the Treaty.

The second factor playing a role in the choice between abstract and concrete review is the objective of the directive. A method of review leading to a result which in itself does not accord with the objectives of the directive should be avoided . The results of the method of review applied will therefore have to be assessed in the light of the objectives of the directive. When abstract review leads to a result which is in conflict with the basic goals of the directive, its application should be refrained from. Abstract review in cases of regular air pollution, water pollution, nuisance, but also nuclear energy installations could hence ultimately lead to results which are in conflict with the basic objectives of the directive. When, for example, the powers of authorities responsible for granting authorizations have been too broadly formulated in the light of a directive, abstract review would result in a situation where authorizations can no longer be granted at all. The question can be asked whether this is intended since the system frequently occurring in environmental directives of 'prohibition + permit' arguably in most cases is not intended to prohibit certain activities *per se*, but to allow them only under certain conditions, regulated by a system of permits. From those directives it can often be inferred, albeit implicitly, that

---

[88] See for example case C–339/87, *Commission v Netherlands*, [1990] ECR I–851, para. 25.

applicants have a right to have their permit application dealt with in accordance with the conditions and criteria of the directive. In those cases abstract review would result in a breach of the rights which directly interested parties may have on the basis of the environmental directive.

Even although there may exist an *a priori* preference for abstract review, it still needs to be ascertained whether this does not lead to a result which is in conflict with the directive, for example because rights which other parties derive from the directive are breached. This requires close examination of each directive and possibly even each provision of what exactly the directive aims to protect.

When we apply these considerations to Dutch case law dealt with in this a paper, it seems that in most cases the correct method of review has been applied; in the birds cases, the power to exempt from the EIA obligation and the export of waste the abstract method of review has been justifiably used. The birds Directive does not aim to grant hunters a right to have permit applications dealt with in accordance with the criteria specified in the directive. The aim is to leave Member States the discretion whether or not an exception can be made to the general rule that no bird hunting is allowed. The EIA Directive's general principle is that all Annex I projects are made subject to an environmental impact assessment and that Member States have the choice whether or not to include an exemption clause in their legislation. No rights can be derived from the directive to be granted an exemption or to have an application for an exemption considered by the relevant authorities. As regards the export of waste falling within the scope of directive 84/631 it can also not be argued that it follows from the directive that export of waste *has* to be prohibited when the conditions of Article 4(6) are fulfilled. Member States have been left the discretion to adopt legislation prohibiting the export of waste in certain cases. It cannot be maintained that the obligation on the part of the authorities to object to exports of dangerous waste is directly effective and there is hence also no corresponding right for private individuals. In the cases mentioned Dutch courts have therefore correctly applied the abstract review method.

In the *Urenco* case[89] and the decision regarding the temporary permit to discharge Black List substances[90] on the other hand, concrete review has been rightly used. The relevant directives in these cases do not aim to prohibit certain activities dangerous to the environment *per se*. Abstract review would disproportionately disadvantage the applicant and lead to results which are in conflict with the objectives and spirit of the directive. In

[89] AGRS 27 March 1991, M en R 1991, 424–8, with case note by Nijhoff, NJB 1991, 1204–5, AB 1991, 537, with case note by AFMB.
[90] AGRS 25 September 1992, MR 1992/46.

these type of cases, abstract review therefore has to be refrained from. In such a case courts must limit review to the question whether the decision of the authorities in itself is in breach with the relevant directive.

3. Direct Effect in Criminal Procedures

Direct effect in criminal procedures arises in particular when the Prosecution Service decides to prosecute a criminal offence which on the basis of European environmental law is not punishable. The *Ratti* case is the European example.[91] For the Dutch legal order reference can be made to a decision of the court in the Hague. The court acquitted a vendor of grapefruits which according to Dutch pesticide legislation contained an excessive level of ethane, but which complied with the European standards fixed in a directive.[92] On the basis of Dutch law the quantity of ethane in fruit should not exceed 0.1 mg/kg. It had been proved that grapefruits had been sold which exceeded this standard. Directive 88/298 however, has set the maximum acceptable level of ethane in fruit at 2 mg/kg. According to the court in The Hague, the Dutch State is not free to decide to enforce legislation which has not been brought into line with the directive. These are provisions which in terms of their substance are unconditional and sufficiently precise which suspects can invoke in a criminal procedure. As a result, Dutch legislation which has not been amended has to be set aside. The court came to the conclusion that the facts which had been proven were not illegal, and therefore the suspect had to be acquitted

Similarly, in the *Scottish Red Grouse* case the European Court decided, regarding the infringement of some prohibitions in the Dutch '*Vogelwet*' concerning the sale of species threatened with extinction, that these prohibitions were at variance with the Treaty.[93] In this case a *gourmetterie* in The Hague had put the Scottish red grouse on its menu, a protected bird under the 'Vogelwet'. The owner argued that he had bought the birds in the United Kingdom, where this species is not protected. The European Court judged that the Dutch prohibition breached the rules on the free movement of goods. In this case direct effect was used as a private defence against the State; Dutch law prohibits something which should not have been prohibited on the basis of European law. Here too, the judgment of the

---

91 Case 148/78 [1979] ECR 1629.
92 Hof 's-Gravenhage 3 February 1989, NJ 1989, 541.
93 Case C–169/89, *Gourmetterie van Den Burg*, [1990] ECR I–2143.

European Court resulted therefore in acquittal in the national criminal procedure.[94]

IV LEGAL PROTECTION AGAINST ENVIRONMENTAL ACTS OF THE COUNCIL AND THE COMMISSION

Finally, it is important to devote some attention to another aspect of judicial protection in this chapter. The legal protection of individuals against breaches of EC environmental law by public authorities or other individuals, through the doctrines of direct effect and supremacy, to a large extent takes place through national procedures. However, where individuals object to the substance of EC environmental law itself, there are few options at national level to seek review.[95] Although the legality of an environmental directive can be challenged in a national procedure, according to EC law the national court is not competent to pronounce on its validity.[96] In these cases, the Treaty does not provide for any direct legal protection and the national court will make use of the preliminary ruling procedure of Article 177 and refer a question to the Court of Justice.

Neither does recourse to an action for annulment under Article 173 offer a solution. Actions for annulment of directives or regulations brought by individuals will undoubtedly be ruled inadmissible.[97]

In the framework of the Article 173 procedure actions by individuals against *decisions* by the Council and the Commission are admissible. Although the implementation of EC environmental law largely takes place in the Member States, the Commission increasingly seems to possess decision-making powers in the sphere of the environment. At times these powers are provided by the Treaty, in other cases it is secondary Community law providing the Commission with powers to adopt decisions. An example of powers to adopt decisions derived from the Treaty is provided by the provisions relating to State aid (Articles 92 and 93). In the meantime it appears that these provisions are also relevant for decision-making concerning national State aids in the sphere of the environment. On the basis of these provisions, the Commission has the power to approve national environmental aids, not to approve them or to make aid subject to certain conditions, whilst other, more procedural decisions can also be

---

[94] HR 20 November 1990, NJB 1991, 617–8, NJ 1991, 241, DD 91.103, M en R 1991, 497–8, with case note by Jans.

[95] For a detailed account of this issue see Chapter 3 by Philippe Sands.

[96] Case 314/85, *Foto Frost*, [1987] ECR 4199.

[97] Case T–475/93, *Buralux*, order of 17.5.94, not yet reported.

taken. Recently the new policy of the Commission in this field has been published.[98]

Another example is provided by the Treaty provisions concerning undistorted competition (Articles 85 and 86). In practice, it has become clear that certain practices of undertakings, also when they concern environmental protection, can be in conflict with Treaty provisions. Here too, the Commission possesses powers to take decisions.[99]

In respect of the Commission's powers to take decisions derived from secondary Community law particular reference should be made to Regulation 594/91 on substances that deplete the ozone layer.[100] For the release into free circulation in the Community of certain ozone depleting substances a license issued by the Commission is necessary. In addition, Article 13 of Directive 90/220 concerning genetically modified organisms can serve as an example. In this directive too, powers of decision are found in relation to the bringing onto the market of products. Finally, it should be noted that the Commission has powers in order to finance projects in the context of the structural funds.[101] These must comply as stated in Article 7(1) of the regulation, with Community environmental law and policy. Once more, the need for judicial protection against decisions taken by the Commission which have insufficiently taken European environmental law into account can therefore arise.

Those to whom decisions of the Commission with an environmental impact are addressed can appeal on the basis of Article 173. This appeal will presently have to be lodged with the Court of First Instance.

In the above mentioned examples it is often the Member State which is addressed by the decision. It is the Member State which is allowed to grant environmental state aid or not and it is the Member State which can be considered the beneficiary from structural fund projects. In the case of the Ozone Regulation however, it is the importer who should be considered the applicant and the addressee. In the case of decisions on the basis of the competition provisions of Articles 85 and 86 the undertakings concerned should be regarded the addressees.

Apart from the addressees of a Commission decision with environmental implications, affected third parties can pursue their interests through the Article 173 procedure if they have been directly and individually affected by the decision. Broadly speaking two types of affected third parties can be distinguished. In the first place there are those who are in competition with

---

[98] OJ 1994 No. C 72.
[99] See for example the *VOTOB* case, XXIInd Competition Report [1992] points 177–86
[100]   OJ 1991 No. L 67 and OJ 1992 No. L 405.
[101] Regulation 2052/88, OJ 1888 No. L 185.

undertakings which have benefited from the Commission's decision. In respect of the Commission's decision to approve Dutch State aid measures to establish manure processing installations, the artificial fertiliser industry should be considered a disadvantaged third party and, in my opinion, be eligible in a procedure for annulment. Also, in the case of exemptions on the basis of Article 85(3), for example in the context of an environmental covenant, competitors who consider themselves disadvantaged should be admissible and the judgment of the European Court in case C–295/92 indeed points in this direction.[102] The case concerned the plans of the Dutch legislator to adapt taxes on fossil fuels in such a way that they would be for fifty percent related to the energy content of the fuel and for the other fifty percent to their carbon content. The measure contained a number of exemptions, amongst others for industrial large-scale users. The measure had been reported to the Commission as a State aid. The Commission considered the measure compatible with the common market but the Dutch Agricultural Association (*Landbouwschap*) considered the exemption for industrial large-scale users illegal and lodged an appeal. The case has to be appreciated against the background of many years of discussion conducted by the Agricultural Association regarding the price of gas for the glasshouse sector. The European Court ruled the Agricultural Association inadmissible, because the State aid in question would only benefit a group of big industrial undertakings, which were not in competition with either the Agricultural Association itself, or the glasshouse farmers represented by it. According to the Court, the interests of the Agricultural Association would not be affected in any way by upholding or annulling the Commission decision. *A contrario,* however, it can be inferred from this that when an affected third party is in direct competition and the interests of the third party have been affected by the decision, the appeal is admissible.

In the light of existing case law the legal protection of the first group of affected parties would in my opinion cause few problems. The most important condition is that there must be a competitive relationship between the party ultimately benefiting from the decision and the party lodging the appeal.

Much more complicated is the admissibility of affected third parties who have objections against a decision of the Commission on environmental grounds. One could think of those living in the vicinity or environmental interest groups and the question arises when they would be directly and individually affected? The following two cases must be mentioned. First, the Irish environmental protection organization An Taisce has invoked

---

[102] *Landbouwschap v Commission,* not yet reported.

Article 173 against a decision by the Commission to make funds from the Structural funds available to the Irish government to establish a visitors centre in a nature reserve in Mullaghmore.[103] However, the Court of First Instance came to the conclusion that the Commission did not take any decision not to suspend or reduce Community financing. The Commission did however decide not to initiate a Treaty infringement procedure. (Article 169) Consequently the applicants were declared inadmissible.

Another case currently pending is T–585/93 *Stichting Greenpeace Council v EC Commission.*[104] In this case the dispute centres on a decision by the Commission to finance a number of infrastructure projects out of the ERDF, in particular two electricity plants. In this case the environmental protection organization Greenpeace has brought an action for annulment.

It remains to be seen whether the European Court will take a similarly broad interpretation of admissibility in environmental disputes as is customary in Dutch environmental law. This is far from certain, as it has to be borne in mind that in some other Member States, such as Germany and the United Kingdom, much more restrictive criteria for *locus standi* apply than in the Netherlands.

---

[103] Case T–461/93, order of 23.9.94 not yet reported.
[104] Case T–585/93, order of 9.8.95 not yet reported.

6. Direct Effect of EC Environmental Law

Ludwig Krämer

I INTRODUCTION

The doctrine of direct effect was developed by the Court of Justice of the European Community. It was recently formulated in a case where an environmental directive was at issue[1] in the following way:

> The Court has consistently held that wherever the provisions of a directive appear, as far as their subject-matter is concerned, to be unconditional and sufficiently precise, those provisions may be relied upon by an individual against the State where the State fails to implement the directive in national law by the period prescribed or where it fails to implement the directive correctly.

The doctrine of direct effect has produced an abundant amount of legal discussion. The core of the doctrine seems to be widely recognized. However, many questions remain and although in cases of doubt as to the direct effect of a provision of Community law, under Article 177 EC, a preliminary reference needs to be requested from the Court of Justice, national courts have shown some reluctance to do so. This being so, it becomes even more important that the doctrine itself be clear, precise and unambiguous. It is doubtful whether this is presently the case.

This chapter will, therefore, attempt to examine some of the issues relating to the direct effect of EC environmental law and will concentrate on the judgments of the Court of Justice itself, rather than discuss the numerous concepts which have been developed or construe new theories. I will first discuss the general aspects of the direct effect doctrine (II); and then examine the Treaty provisions on the environment (III); next, the extent to which environmental regulations and directives produce direct effects will be examined (IV); and section (V) will address the question whether the direct effect doctrine is applicable in relations between private persons.

---

[1] Court of Justice, case C–236/92 *Difesa della Cava*, [1994] ECR I–485.

Section (VI) will examine the effect of provisions of EC law generally. Some general observations will serve to conclude the discussion (VII).

II GENERAL ASPECTS OF THE DIRECT EFFECT DOCTRINE

For the purpose discussing the 'direct effect' of provisions of EC law, a distinction needs to be drawn between provisions of the EC Treaty and provisions of secondary Community law, i.e. regulations and directives. Historically, the Court of Justice developed the doctrine of direct effect for the first time in a decision of early 1963, in case 26/62 (*van Gend en Loos*).[2] In this case, the Court had to decide whether an individual was entitled to invoke the Article 12 EC in order to claim the illegality of a specific national measure.

The Court of Justice argued that the European Economic Community (EEC) – now the European Community (EC) – constituted a new legal order, the subjects of which were not only Member States but also their citizens. EC law therefore intends to grant rights to individuals which become part of their legal heritage. These rights arise not only where they are expressly granted by the Treaty, but also by way of obligations which the Treaty places in a clearly defined way on Member States or EC institutions. After the entry into force of the Treaty, Article 12 protected individuals against increases of custom duties and such an increase was therefore illegal.

This landmark decision contains a number of elements which are important for the relationship between EC law and national law:
   a) EC law constitutes a new legal order where the classical rules of public international law do not automatically apply;
   b) EC law is superior to national law and therefore EC (Treaty) law cannot legally be amended by subsequent national law. In other words, the rule '*lex posterior derogat legem anteriorem*' does not apply to the relationship between EC law and national law; and
   c) individuals may invoke rules of EC law which are in their favour.

In its later case law the Court examined, for each individual provision in the Treaty, whether it conferred rights upon individuals which they can invoke against Member States. Thus, the Court of Justice decided that Articles 13

---

[2]   Court of Justice, case 26/62, *van Gend en Loos*, [1963] ECR 1.

and 16,[3] Article 30,[4] Articles 48, 52 and 59,[5] Article 95[6] and Article 119[7] of the EC Treaty produced direct effect.

As regards secondary legislation, the Court proceeded in similar fashion. It did not examine a directive as such but assessed, for each individual provision, whether it conferred rights upon individuals. However, unlike regulations which according to Article 189 are directly applicable, directives are addressed to Member States but not to individuals.[8]

The Court overcame that problem by arguing that directives, too, could under certain conditions be directly effective and that 'to assume otherwise would be incompatible with the binding effect of directives.'[9] Thus, the denial of the direct effect of directives would have meant that Member States could avoid the effect of a directive simply by not transposing it into national law. Furthermore, the effectiveness of directives would be impaired if individuals could not rely upon them before national courts. Thus, directives aim at achieving a legal result, not merely an obligation for Member States.[10]

It can be deduced from the Court's case law that the following conditions must all be satisfied for a provision of a directive to be directly effective:

1. the period for transposing the directive into national law must have expired;

---

3 Court of Justice, case 33/70, *SACE*, [1970] ECR 1213; case 18/71, *di Porro*, [1971] ECR 811.

4 Court of Justice, case 74/76, *Volpi*, [1977] ECR 557; case 83/78, *Pigs Marketing Board*, [1978] ECR 2347.

5 Court of Justice, case 2/74, *Reyners*, [1974] ECR 631; case 33/74, *van Binsbergen*, [1974] ECR 1299; case 41/74, *van Duyn*, [1974] ECR 1337; case 13/76, *Dona*, [1976] ECR 1333.

6 Court of Justice, case 57/65, *Lütticke*, [1966] ECR 258.

7 Court of Justice, case 43/75, *Defrenne*, [1976] ECR 455.

8 Article 189 EC Treaty provides:
In order to carry out their task and in accordance with the provisions of this Treaty, the European Parliament acting jointly with the Council, the Council and the Commission shall make regulations and issue directives, take decisions, make recommendations or deliver opinions.
A regulation shall have general application. It shall be binding in its entirety and directly applicable in all member-States.
A directive shall be binding, as to the result to be achieved, upon each member-State to which it is addressed, but shall leave to the national authorities the choice of form and methods ...

9 Court of Justice, case 8/81, *Becker*, [1982] ECR 53; case 148/78, *Ratti*, [1979] ECR 1629.

10 See for instance Court of Justice, case 41/74, *van Duyn*, see note 5 above; case 51/76, *Nederlandse Ondernemingen*, [1977] ECR 113; case 148/78, *Ratti*, see note 9 above; case 8/81, *Becker*, see note 9 above; case 190/87, *Moormann*, [1988] ECR 4714.

2. the Member State has not or incorrectly transposed the provision of the directive into national law;
3. The provision must be unconditional;
4. The provision must be sufficiently precise; and
5. The provision must explicitly or implicitly confer rights upon individuals as against Member States.

These different conditions will now be discussed one by one.

1. The Expiry of the Directive's Deadline for Implementation

All[11] EC directives contain a provision indicating the period within which Member States have to transpose its provisions into national law.[12] The provisions of a directive take effect from that date onwards within the whole of the EC and thus also within individual Member States. Before the transposition date has expired, Member States are not obliged to transpose and to apply the EC provisions. In case 148/78 (*Ratti*), the Court of Justice rightly decided that prior to the deadline for implementation a provision of a directive could not be directly relied upon and that national law is therefore applicable.[13]

However, Member States may choose to transpose a directive before the period for transition has expired. Where a Member State chooses to do so EC law, as transposed by the national provisions, applies from that earlier date. The Member State in such cases is obliged to respect the provisions of the directive from the date which itself has fixed. Hence, the dates for transposition contained in directives are final dates which allow earlier compliance.

2. Absence of Transposition or Incorrect Transposition

Where a Member State fully and correctly transposes the provisions of a directive into national law, the rights and obligations of individuals flow from the implementing legislative measure and not from the directive itself. In those (normal) cases the directive deploys its full effect through the national implementation measure. The doctrine of direct effect only comes into

---

[11] It seems that Directive 76/464 on pollution caused by certain dangerous substances discharged into the aquatic environment of the Community, OJ 1976 No. L 129, p. 23 is the only exception. For the general rules of entering into force of directives see Article 191 EC Treaty.

[12] Example taken from Directive 80/68 on the protection of groundwater against pollution caused by certain dangerous substances, Article 21, OJ 1980 No. L 20, p. 43.

[13] Court of Justice, case 148/78, *Ratti*, see note 9 above.

operation where a Member State commits a failure because it 'fails to transpose a directive' (a) or 'it fails to implement the directive correctly' (b).

a Absence of a national legislative measures

The cases where Member States fail to transpose the provisions of a directive into national law are the most common. The Court of Justice has ruled on a number of these cases although not as yet in respect of environmental matters.

An example is case 8/81 (*Becker*) which concerned Directive 77/388 on VAT.[14] Article 13 of that Directive provided that Member States had to take measures in order to provide for a zero turnover tax rate for granting and negotiating credit. Germany had failed to transpose the directive into national law within the prescribed period. The German finance authorities continued to charge Ms. Becker, a self-employed credit-negotiator, turnover tax. The Court of Justice decided that Ms. Becker could rely on Article 13 and refuse to pay the tax. For the Court, it was decisive that Germany had not taken the necessary legislative measures. Had it done so, Ms. Becker would have been exempted from the turnover tax. German authorities could not hold Germany's failure to take the necessary steps against Ms. Becker.

The Court of Justice has clarified, in a number of decisions, that the fact that provisions of a directive are directly effective does not mean it is superfluous to transpose the directive into national law.[15] Whilst it is rare for all provisions of a directive to be directly effective, there is also an element of legal certainty which is ensured by a legislative or regulatory measure. It would be difficult for citizens, foreign investors or other Member States to ascertain their rights and obligations if there were no legislative provision within their national system of law informing them. In any event, it should be noted that the different directives oblige Member States to adopt transposition measures and to inform the Commission thereof. Although these provisions are not directly effective (since they do not confer rights on individuals) they do contain clear obligations under EC law, the breach of which may be pursued by the Commission under Article 169 EC.

b Failure to implement a directive correctly.

According to the last formulation of the Court quoted above,[16] the doctrine of direct effect also applies where a Member States transposes a directive

---

[14] Court of Justice, case 8/81, *Becker*, see note 9 above.

[15] Court of Justice, case 102/79, *Commission v Belgium*, [1980] ECR 1473; case 322/86, *Commission v Italy*, [1988] ECR 4004.

[16] Court of Justice, case C–236/92, *Difesa della Cava*, see text to note 1 above.

incompletely or incorrectly. Indeed, from the perspective of the individual there arguably is no difference with the situation where there are no implementation measures at all: in the absence of the direct doctrine of direct effect the protection granted by the directive's provision would remain illusory.

In addition, the language of the Court – 'where (a Member State) fails to implement the directive correctly' – shows that it is not just the legislative national act which is at issue. It is quite possible that national legislation complies word for word with the requirements of a directive but that administrative practice is not in accordance with the directive's requirements. By way of example, whereas national legislation transposing Article 1(5) of Directive 85/377[17] could correctly provide that no environmental impact assessment is necessary for 'projects the details of which are adopted by a specific act of national legislation' in a given case this provision could be erroneously applied to a project which was merely approved by governmental decree. Although the national legislation correctly and completely transposes the provision of the directive, in the concrete case it is incorrectly applied. Another example would be a national provision implementing Directive 90/313[18] granting individuals a right to access to information relating to the environment, but where in a concrete case the administration refuses to give access to a specific study on the environment, arguing that it is of poor quality.

The Court's statement quoted above therefore would seem to cover both incorrect transposition into national law as well as incorrect application in a concrete case. Doubts remain, however, in this respect. In the first place, the last words of the statement – 'or where it fails to implement the directive correctly' – do not appear in earlier manifestations of the doctrine, where instead only the absence of implementing measures is referred to. In addition, the distinction between 'direct effect' and 'effect' seems to have been confused in as far as incorrect implementation is concerned. 'Direct effect' can only mean that an EC provision applies without having been transposed into the national legal order. This follows from the wording of Article 189 EC itself which refers to 'direct application' of regulations. It also corresponds with the direct effect of the Treaty provisions which are not transposed into national law either. Where a provision has been incorrectly transposed or where it has been correctly transposed but is incorrectly applied, on the other hand, it is artificial to talk of the EC

---

[17] Directive 85/337 on the assessment of the effects of certain public and private projects on the environment, OJ 1985 No. L 175, p. 40.

[18] Directive 90/313 on the freedom of access to information on the environment, OJ 1990 No. L 158, p. 56.

provision as being 'directly applicable' or 'directly effective'. Rather, there exists a conflict between the EC provision and the national implementing provision which needs to be resolved according to general principles of conflict between EC provisions and national provisions. This is a different issue which has nothing to do with questions of direct effect. This argument is supported by the fact that the same problem occurs where an EC provision is not unconditional and sufficiently precise: in such a case the Court's doctrine of direct effect does not apply. Yet, a person may invoke the provisions of EC law in legal procedures and the national court would have to resolve the conflict between national and EC law.

In addition, it is difficult to find any decision of the Court of Justice where it applies the doctrine of direct effect to a case where there is a national provision transposing the EC provision but where this national provision does not correspond with the EC provision or, where it does correspond, is not correctly applied. The most recent example is case C–396/92 (*Bund Naturschutz*)[19] where the validity of a German provision was at issue. Germany had transposed Directive 85/337 on environmental impact assessment with some delay into national law. Furthermore, it had provided that projects where planning permission had been requested prior to the entering into effect of the German transposing law did not need to undergo an environment impact assessment. The Court of Justice decided that Directive 85/337 had entered into effect three years after its notification to Member States, thus on 3 July 1988. A Member State could not validly change this date, be it in respect of some projects or for some time only. The Court of Justice did not even mention the doctrine of direct effect and instead only generally referred to the effect of EC law.

It seems thus to be more appropriate to reserve the doctrine of direct effect for those cases where a provision of EC law and in particular of a directive has not been transposed into national law at all. The other cases, which will be discussed below in section VI, do not really belong to this category.

3. Unconditional Character of a Provision

The Community law provision to be directly relied upon must be unconditional. The Court has stated in this regard:[20]

A Community provision is unconditional where it is not subject, in its implementation or effects, to the taking of any measure either by the institutions of the Community or by the Member States.

---

[19] Court of Justice, case C–396/92, *Bund Naturschutz*, [1994] ECR I–3717.
[20] Court of Justice, case C–236/92, *Difesa della Cava*, see note 1 above.

Hence, a provision is unconditional where, in substance, it independently guarantees the protection of individuals and does not require national (or Community) law to substantiate the protection. In order to determine whether a specific provision of EC law is unconditional it needs to be read very carefully. For instance, in case 8/81[21] the relevant provision of Article 13 of Directive 77/388 stated:[22]

> Member State shall exempt (specific transactions from value added tax) under conditions which they shall lay down for the purpose of ensuring the correct and straightforward application of the exemptions and of preventing any possible evasion, avoidance or abuse.

At first sight the provision is conditional upon the Member States taking measures. However, these measures are merely intended to ensure correct application, avoid abuse and to prevent fraud and they do not make the granting of the exemption of the VAT for certain professions conditional upon these national measures. Thus, the Court of Justice rightly held that in the absence of any transposing measure Article 13 could be directly relied upon. Germany could not rely on the fact that fraud might still be possible because the necessary provisions to prevent fraud had not yet been taken. Rather, had Germany transposed Directive 77/388 in time, Ms. Becker would not have had to pay tax, which was the question at issue. The risk of fraud is due to Germany's failure and cannot, therefore, be invoked against the plaintiff and work in favour of the German fiscal authorities.

Another example is provided by case C–91/92 (*Dori*)[23] where the question arose whether the provision on the cooling-off period in Directive 85/577 was unconditional.[24] Article 4 of that Directive provides that the consumer of a contract concluded away from business premises must be informed in writing of his right to cancel the contract. Member States must provide for appropriate sanctions in cases where this information is not provided. Article 5 stipulates that the consumer has the right to withdraw from the contract within at least seven days after having received the information on his right to cancel the contract. National legislation must arrange the details relating to the exercise of this right in practice.

The Court of Justice found that Member States had a certain amount of discretion as to how to organize the sanctions and how to fix the conditions under which the consumer could exercise his rights. However, the core of

---

[21] Court of Justice, case 8/81, *Becker*, see note 9 above.

[22] Directive 77/388 relating to turnover taxes – common system of value added tax: uniform basis of assessment, OJ 1977 No. L 145, p. 1, Article 13.

[23] Court of Justice, case C–91/92, *Dori*, [1994] ECR I–3325.

[24] Directive 85/577 to protect the consumer in respect of contracts negotiated away from business premises, OJ 1985 No. L 372, p. 31.

the protection was the consumer's right to cancel the contract within at least seven days after having received the information on his right to cool off, which was not conditional upon any act of the national legislator. For this reason, the Court of Justice correctly observed that the right to cool off within seven days was an unconditional provision of EC law.

4. Sufficiently Precise Provisions

As regards the required precision of provisions of Community law, the Court of Justice ruled:[25]

A provision is sufficiently precise to be relied on by an individual and applied by the court where the obligation which it imposes is set out in unequivocal terms.

Certain commentators often add that administrations must be left with no discretion as to the measure to take.

The Court had to deal with the precision of a provision in case 14/83 (*von Colson and Kamann*).[26] This case concerned Directive 76/206[27] which laid down the principle of equal treatment of men and women as regards access to employment. Article 3(2) of the directive provided that Member States had to take the measures necessary to ensure that any laws, regulations and administrative provisions contrary to the principle of equal treatment were abolished. Article 6 required Member States to introduce into their national legal systems such measures as are necessary to enable all persons who considered themselves wronged by discrimination to pursue their claims by judicial process. The Court of Justice rightly decided that the choice of sanctions was left to national law. The question whether the employer had to offer another post to the discriminated candidate, whether he lost his licence or had to pay a financial compensation, was to be decided by Member States. The Court of Justice concluded that the sanction had to be deterrent and offer real and effective protection to discriminated persons. Thus, it decided that the sanction of German law to pay, by way of compensation, the cost actually incurred for presenting oneself at the employer – for example, a ticket for the metro – did not satisfy these conditions.

However, the Court did not attempt to indicate the kind of sanctions which would be appropriate. Indeed, the directive did not offer any guidance to do so as it was simply not sufficiently precise and he Court therefore had to

---

[25] Court of Justice, case C–236/92, *Difesa della Cava*, see note 1 above.

[26] Court of Justice, case 14/83, *von Colson*, [1984] ECR 1891.

[27] Directive 76/207 on the implementation of the principle of equal treatment for men and women as regards access to employment, vocational training and promotion, and working conditions, OJ 1976 No. L 39, p. 40.

leave the matter to the national authorities. The latter enjoy a degree of discretion to determine the kind of sanction and the Court of Justice will – as indeed it did – merely check whether this discretion has not been exceeded. 'Sufficiently precise' thus means that the legal rule can itself be filtered out of the EC provision and that there is no discretion left to national authorities. By way of a test, one could construe the provision in question as if it were contained in a regulation rather than a directive, and then consider whether it could be directly applied or whether instead national provisions would be necessary further to clarify its meaning. Had Articles 3 and 6 of Directive 76/207 been incorporated in a regulation, the plaintiff would nevertheless not have been able to obtain a specific sanction since the provision merely provided: 'Member States shall fix effective and deterrent sanctions against discrimination.' In contrast, enshrined in a regulation the disputed provision in the *Becker*-case[28] would be: 'Credit negotiators shall not pay turnover VAT.' The provision in the *Dori*-case[29] would become: 'Consumers shall be entitled to withdraw from the contract within at least seven days after having been informed in writing of this right.'

5. Conferring Rights on Individuals

a The reasoning of the Court of Justice
This last requirement was not mentioned in the Court's definition of the doctrine.[30] However, previous judgments clearly indicate that this fifth condition must be satisfied too. Indeed, there are many provisions in EC directives which are unconditional and sufficiently precise and yet do not provide, after the date for transposition has expired and the Member State has failed to transpose the Directive, the possibility for an individual to rely on them. For instance, most directives contain a provision identical or similar to the following:[31]

> The Member States shall bring into force the laws, regulations and administrative provisions necessary to comply with this Directive within two years of its notification. They shall immediately inform the Commission thereof.

Clearly, at least as regards the requirement to inform the Commission, this provision is unconditional and sufficiently precise. However, applying the doctrine of direct effect is out of the question since the provision does not

---

[28] Court of Justice, case 8/81, *Becker*, see note 9 above.
[29] Court of Justice, case C–91/92, *Dori*, see note 23 above.
[30] See above p. 99.
[31] Directive 80/68, see note 12 above.

confer any rights on individual persons but concerns the relationship between the Commission and Member States.

In case 380/87 (*Cinisello Balsamo*) the Court of Justice had to deal with a similar question.[32] The mayor of Cinisello Balsamo, a village in Italy, had prohibited the supply to customers of non-biodegradable plastic bags. The measure had not been notified to the Commission in draft form even though Article 3(2) of Directive 75/442 states that:[33]

> They (Member States) shall inform the Commission in good time of any draft rules to such effect and, in particular of any draft rule concerning ... the use of products which might be a source of technical difficulties as regards disposal or lead to excessive disposal costs ...

The question was put to the Court of Justice, whether this provision gave individuals a right which they could enforce before national courts in order to obtain the annulment or suspension of national rules to which Article 3(2) applied on the ground that those rules were adopted without having previously been notified to the Commission. The Court found that the purpose of that provision was to ensure that the Commission was informed of any plans for national measures regarding waste disposal so that it could consider whether Community harmonizing legislation was called for and whether the draft rules were compatible with Community law and take appropriate measures if necessary. The Court concluded:[34]

> It follows from the foregoing that the above mentioned provision concerns relations between the Member States and the Commission and does not give rise to any right for individuals which might be infringed by a Member State's breach of its obligation to inform the Commission in advance of draft rules.

Another well-known example is Article 169 EC, which provides that if:

> the Commission considers that a Member-State has failed to fulfil an obligation under this Treaty, it shall deliver a reasoned opinion on the matter after giving the State concerned the opportunity to submit its observation.

This provision is unconditional and precise. However, it again concerns the relation between the Commission and the Member States and not the rights of individuals. Therefore, it is not possible to challenge the Commission in court for failure to have initiated procedures under Article 169 against a Member State.[35]

In all these cases, the fiction that the provision is enshrined in an EC regulation is a useful aid to find answers whether or not rights are granted to individuals. In the first case the provision would read: 'Member States shall

---

[32] Court of Justice, case 380/87, *Cinisello Balsamo*, [1989] ECR 2491.

[33] Directive 75/442 on waste, OJ 1975 No. L 194, p. 39.

[34] Court of Justice, case 380/87, *Cinisello Balsamo*, see note 32 above, paragraph 23.

[35] Court of Justice, case 247/87, *Star Fruit*, [1989] ECR 291.

inform the Commission of draft rules;' in the second case, the provision would read: 'If the Commission finds a breach of the Treaty, it shall start legal proceedings.' Clearly, these provisions do not create any individual rights.

b The notion of 'rights'

It is obvious from the case law that has been quoted that the notion of 'right' used by the Court of Justice is not limited to subjective rights, but covers any favourable position or legal interest, which a legal provision intends to protect or effectively protects. This is suitably illustrated by the van Gend en Loos case.[36] Article 12 EC does not grant a subjective right to importers for customs duties to be frozen. The prohibition contained in Article 12 rather reflects back on importers, putting them in a favourable position allowing them to invoke that provision against the State. In the same way, Article 13 of Directive 77/388[37] (*Becker*) does not give credit negotiators a subjective right, but it addresses Member States and obliges them to take steps in order to improve their legal position. It is this more favourable position which the Court obviously has in mind when it refers to 'rights'. It might thus be more appropriate to use the notion of 'interests' instead of 'rights'.

This is well illustrated by the situation which arose in case 148/78 (*Ratti*).[38] In that case, Italy had failed to transpose Directive 73/173 which contained rules on the labelling of solvents.[39] Italian legislation differed from the provisions of Directive 73/173 whilst non-compliance with the Italian labelling rules was made a criminal offence. Mr. Ratti complied with the labelling provisions of Directive 73/173 but, as a consequence, breached Italian law. The Court of Justice was asked whether Italy could impose criminal sanctions against Mr. Ratti on the ground that he had not complied with the Italian labelling provisions. It answered in the negative: Mr. Ratti's 'right' in this case consisted of the non-application of the Italian criminal sanctions against him. Obviously, this is not a (subjective) right which Directive 73/173 conferred on him since that directive merely fixes labelling rules. Rather, Mr. Ratti had an interest in seeing the provisions of Directive 73/173 applied. Italy could not prosecute him because it could not have prosecuted him had it correctly transposed Directive 73/173. Hence, Italy is barred from taking advantage of its own failure by denying Mr. Ratti

---

[36] Court of Justice, case 26/62, *van Gend*, see note 2 above.

[37] Directive 77/388, note 22 above.

[38] Court of Justice, case 148/78, *Ratti*, see note 9 above.

[39] Directive 73/173 relating to the classification, packaging and labelling of dangerous preparations (solvents), OJ 1973 No. L 189, p. 7.

the more favourable position to which the provisions of Directive 73/173 entitle him.

Once again, in all these cases the 'regulation-test' outlined above could be applied. Article 13 (of Directive 77/388) would then probably read: 'Credit negotiators shall not pay turnover VAT.' The legislator's intention to create a situation which is favourable to credit negotiators becomes obvious. The favourable position which is legally protected is equivalent to the 'right' mentioned by the Court of Justice. The labelling provisions (of Directive 73/173) in the *Ratti*-case would probably read: 'Products covered by this regulation shall be labelled in the following way...' It is clear that such a provision, which pursuant to Article 189 EC would be directly applicable, contrasts with the Italian national provisions, which requires different standards. Such a conflict has to be resolved according to the supremacy rules. In case 6/64 (*Costa v Enel*)[40] the Court of Justice ruled – and almost all national courts adhere to this – that in the case of conflicts between EC law and national law EC law prevails, and as a result national law does not apply.[41]

The issue of direct effect only arises in cases where an individual's position (or 'right') is affected favourably and does not extend to situations where his position is worsened. In case 80/86 (*Kolpinghuis*),[42] the Court of Justice had to address such a case. Directive 80/777 provides that only water from recognized sources may be marketed as mineral water.[43] Even though the Netherlands had not transposed the requirements of that directive, Dutch authorities charged an individual who had sold tap water as mineral water by relying directly on Directive 80/777. The Court held that direct reliance on the provisions of Directive 80/777, as regards the prohibition to sell tap water as mineral water, would have the effect of creating obligations rather than rights for the individual in question. The provision could therefore not be directly effective.

The rights which EC directives grant to individuals may be invoked only against the State – including all institutions, bodies agencies and authorities which represent the 'State' – but not against other individuals or private bodies.[44] The reasons for this limitation provided by Court of Justice are

---

[40] Court of Justice, case 6/64, *Costa v ENEL*, [1964] ECR 585.

[41] Court of Justice, case 14/68, *Wilhelm*, [1969] ECR 1; case 11/70, *Internationale Handelsgesellschaft*, [1970] ECR 1125; case 48/71, [1972] ECR 529; case 106/77 *Simmenthal*, [1978] ECR 629; case C–213/89, *Factortame*, [1990] ECR I–2466.

[42] Court of Justice, case 80/86, *Kolpinghuis*, [1987] ECR 3982.

[43] Directive 80/777 relating to the exploitation and marketing of natural mineral waters, OJ 1980 No. L 229, p. 1.

[44] Court of Justice, case 152/84, *Marshall*, [1986] ECR 737; see also case C–91/92, *Dori*, note 23 above.

twofold. In the first place a directive is addressed at Member States and not at individuals and hence cannot bind individuals. Secondly, the opposite conclusion would imply that directives would produce effects identical to those of regulations. Although this reasoning is generally used it cannot, as such, be sufficient. Indeed, the essence of the doctrine of direct effect is to assimilate directives to regulations, albeit only under certain conditions. It is therefore, not entirely clear why the assimilation of directives to regulations cannot be extended to the extent that, exceptionally, a directive also directly applies to relations between individuals. This issue will be discussed below in section V.

The true reason for limiting the direct effect to actions against the State, if one follows the additional reasoning of the Court of Justice, lies in the failure of the State. The Member State is in breach of its obligation to incorporate the directive's provisions into national law. Consequently, the State must be treated as if the transposition had taken place. This reasoning does not apply to individuals which have not committed a failure. The Court's reasoning is convincing as regards the direct effect of directives. However, it raises problems as regards the horizontal direct effect of the provisions of the EC Treaty itself, which the Court of Justice has continuously recognized. Indeed, Treaty provisions need not be transposed into national law. There can thus not be question of the Member State's failure, the '*venire contra factum proprium*' which is at the heart of the doctrine of direct effect.

Besides those already mentioned, the only other reason for justifying the direct effect of a provision of a directive which could be advanced is the need to give full effect to EC law, combined with the related issue of the supremacy of EC law. The efficiency of EC Treaty law – such as for instance the prohibition of measures having equivalent effects to quantitative restrictions (Article 30), the prohibition of mergers (Article 85) or the equality of rights of men and women (Article 119) – would be seriously impaired if it would not be directly effective but had to be implemented by provisions of secondary law. These questions of 'full effect' and 'supremacy' will not be discussed further here. Instead, the next section will examine the question whether environmental provisions in the Treaty are directly effective.

III DIRECT EFFECT OF ENVIRONMENTAL PROVISIONS IN THE EC TREATY

Of the five conditions developed in section I for the application of the doctrine of direct effect the last three – unconditional and sufficiently precise provision, granting a right to individuals – are without further discussion capable of being applied to provisions of the EC Treaty. The second – absence of transposition into national law – clearly cannot apply, since the Treaty is not to be transposed into national law. The first requirement – the date for transposition must have expired – could perhaps, with some strain, be applied, in the sense that the Treaty must have come into effect. This being as it may: in essence 'direct effect' of EC Treaty provisions is dependent on the question whether these provisions are unconditional and sufficiently precise.

Article 130r(1) describes the objectives of EC environmental policy, to the pursuit of which the policy shall contribute. The general statement – 'shall contribute' – and the use of the word 'policy' demonstrate that a general declaration is made, which needs to be implemented by specific measures. The paragraph is therefore neither unconditional nor sufficiently precise to be directly effective.

Article 130r(2) phrase one, again uses the word 'policy' and stipulates that it shall 'aim at' a high level of protection. Since this instruction refers to the whole of the policy, it is not sufficiently precise to be applied to individual situations. Indeed, implementing measures are necessary in order to flesh out the notion of 'policy'. The phrase thus has no direct effect.

Article 130r(2), phrase two, declares that the policy shall be based on certain principles. The wording could be compared, for instance, with Article 30 ('measures having equivalent effect shall be prohibited') or with Article 85 ('The following shall be prohibited ...: all agreements between undertakings...') which, rather than referring to the principle of free circulation of goods or the principle of free competition, are direct, precise and unconditional in their core statement. In contrast, the wording of Article 130r(2) refers to principles of the policy, not to individual measures, and even uses the word 'should' instead of 'shall'. Whereas a statement such as 'persons polluting the environment shall pay for the damage' would be unconditional and precise; a provision that 'policy shall be based on the principle that the polluter should pay' is neither unconditional – since individual measures are necessary – nor precise, because a principle always is subject to exceptions. In addition, it remains unclear under which conditions the term 'should' turns into 'shall'; one cannot really speak of an obligation being set out in unequivocal terms. In case C–2/90 (*Wallonian*

Waste), the Court used the principle of Article 130r(2) that environmental damage should be rectified at source to justify, amongst others, that Belgian regions were entitled to prohibit the import of waste from other Member States.[45] This judgment does not contradict the present conclusion. Indeed, the Court had to balance the principle of free circulation of goods (including wastes) under Article 30 EC Treaty with the principle which the Court had developed itself to the effect that Member States are entitled to restrict the free circulation of goods for important reasons of general interest.[46] In weighing these interests the Court used the principle of Article 130r(2). But there is not the slightest indication, in the Court's judgment, that that provision is to be regarded as being directly effective.

Phrase three of paragraph 2 addresses the EC institutions which are under the general obligation to define and implement the different Community policies that are enumerated in Article 3 EC. There is no further measure necessary for the implementation of the principle which therefore can be considered unconditional. It remains doubtful, however, whether it is precise. The word 'integrated' in itself is all but unequivocal; it means 'entering into a whole', becoming part of something. Would this mean that other policies have to take account of environmental protection requirements or would they have to completely respect these requirements? Would each individual measure – directive, regulation, decision – have to respect the requirements, or rather the policy as a whole? And what are the requirements, the objectives of Article 130r(1) or (also) those of paragraph 2; all of them or only some? In which order of priority? The questions themselves show that there exist many possible interpretations of the phrase. Furthermore, EC institutions have a large degree of discretion as to how and with which speed to integrate these requirements into the other policies. It is therefore to be concluded that the provision is not sufficiently unequivocal to be directly applicable.[47]

Article 130r(3) instructs the EC to 'take account of' certain guide-lines when preparing its policy but there is no obligation to take these aspects into account for each individual measure. Nothing is said about the extent to which these aspects have to be taken into consideration. In any event, it is not apparent how individuals could obtain a favourable position by the

---

[45] Court of Justice, case C–2/90, *Wallonian Waste*, [1992] ECR I–4431.
[46] See in particular Court of Justice, case 120/78, *Cassis de Dijon*, [1979] ECR 649 where the general principle was developed; case 302/86, *Danish bottles*, [1988] ECR 4607, where the general principle first was applied to environmental measures.
[47] See also the old version of this phrasing, which was in force between 1987 and 1993: 'Environmental protection requirements shall be a component of the Community's other policies'. It may well be argued that this provision did have direct effect.'

correct and complete application of this paragraph. Thus, this provision is not directly effective.

Article 130r(4) distributes competencies between the EC and Member States. Article 130s deals with the decision-making procedure and Article 130t allows Member States to introduce or maintain more stringent protective measures. These provisions do not confer 'rights' or 'obligations'. In conclusion it appears that there is no provision in Title XVI of the EC Treaty which is directly applicable.

IV DIRECT EFFECT OF SECONDARY ENVIRON-MENTAL LAW

When examining secondary legislation, one should be aware of the rather limited field of application of the doctrine of direct effect which, in the reasoning adopted here, only applies where all of the above-mentioned conditions are fulfilled. I will examine in this section, different categories of provisions of EC environmental legislation; the decisions of the Court of Justice on direct effect of environmental provisions examined; and the situation where a Member State has incorrectly implemented a provision of a directive explored.

1. Directly Effective Environmental Provisions

A first group of environmental provisions in EC law which have direct effect are those provisions which fix numeric maximum values, maximum concentrations, limit values, etc. The provisions with numeric values are unconditional and precise – on this there can hardly be a dispute. Where they concern water and air pollution, the respective directives often provide that they aim to contribute to the protection of human health.[48] This objective already follows from Article 130r(1), which expressly provides

---

[48] See for instance Directive 76/160 concerning the quality of bathing water, OJ 1976 No. L 31, p. 1, first recital: 'Whereas, in order to protect the environment and public health, it is necessary to reduce the pollution of bathing water ...'; Directive 80/778 relating to the quality of water intended for human consumption, OJ 1980 No. L 229, p. 11, first recital: 'Whereas, in view of the importance for public health of water for human consumption...'; Directive 80/779 on air quality limit values and guide values for sulphur dioxide and suspended particulates, OJ 1980 No. L 229, p. 30, Article 1: 'The purpose of this Directive is to fix limit values ... and guide values ... for sulphur dioxide and suspended particulates in the atmosphere and the conditions for their application in order to improve: – the protection of human health, – the protection of the environment.'

that environmental policy shall contribute to the protection of human health. This reference to the interests of persons in the protection of their health implies that the fifth condition is satisfied, i.e. the granting of a favourable position to individuals by the EC provision.

To this category of rules belong provisions fixing emission standards and quality objectives on discharges of mercury, cadmium, HCH and other substances into water.[49] Not only the emission values, but also the quality objectives are sufficiently precise and unconditional. By way of example, the following quality objectives might be quoted:

> The concentration of dissolved cadmium in estuary waters ... must not exceed 5 ug/l;[50]
> The total concentration of mercury in inland surface waters affected by discharges must not exceed 1ug/l as the arithmetic mean of the results obtained over a year.[51]

The maximum concentrations of undesirable substances in drinking water also belong to this group of provisions.[52] In the same way, the limit values for air pollution, concerning the concentrations of sulphur dioxides and suspended particulates,[53] lead[54] and nitrogen dioxide[55] are directly effective. The various directives in question explicitly specify that the limit values have been fixed in order to protect human health and that they must not be exceeded throughout the territory of Member States.

A second group of provisions in environmental directives are those containing prohibitions such as prohibitions to use certain substances, to use instruments to catch animals, to discharge substances into the water or the soil, etc. These prohibitions are practically all unconditional and sufficiently precise and in as far as they protect, explicitly or implicitly, interests of individuals they are directly effective. Examples are the ban of chemicals

---

[49] Directive 82/176 on limit values and quality objectives for mercury discharges by the chlor-alkali electrolysis industry, OJ 1982 No. L 81, p. 29; Directive 83/513 on limit values and quality objectives for cadmium discharges, OJ 1983 No. L 291, p. 1; Directive 84/156 on limit values and quality objectives for mercury discharges by sectors other than the chöoralkali electrolysis industry, OJ 1984 No. L 74, p. 49; Directive 84/491 on limit values and quality objectives for discharges of hexachlorocyclohexane, OJ 1984 No. L 274, p. 11; Directive 86/280 on limit values and quality objectives for discharges of certain dangerous substances included in list I of the Annex to Directive 76/464, OJ 1986 No. L 181, p. 16.

[50] Directive 83/513, note 49 above, Annex II No. 1.2.

[51] Directive 82/176, note 49 above, Annex II No. 1.3.

[52] Directive 80/778, note 48 above.

[53] Directive 80/779, note 49 above.

[54] Directive 82/884 on a limit value for lead in the air, OJ 1982 No. L 378, p. 15.

[55] Directive 85/203 on air quality standards for nitrogen dioxide, OJ 1985 No. L 87, p. 1.

under Directive 76/769,[56] the prohibition to market petrol with a higher lead content than 0,15 g/l under Directive 85/210,[57] the ban of direct discharges of certain dangerous chemicals into the groundwater under Directive 80/68[58] or the deliberate killing of birds, the destruction of nests and eggs and the taking of eggs of birds under Directive 79/409.[59] The precise and unconditional character of such prohibitions is not undermined by the fact that under certain circumstances derogations are allowed. The mere possibility to derogate does not affect the clear instruction of the legal rule.

A third category consists of obligations for the administration to act. For instance, Directive 85/337 requests Member States to carry out an environmental impact assessment (EIA) before authorising certain public or private projects, mainly infrastructure projects.[60] This EIA procedure is compulsory for particularly important projects listed in Annex I such as the construction of motorways, big airports or ports or incineration installations for dangerous waste. For other projects, listed in Annex II, an EIA is required where significant effects of the project on the environment are likely to occur.[61] Where an EIA is carried out, the public concerned must be consulted. The provision requiring an EIA for Annex I projects is precise and unconditional. The interest of the individual – to the extent to which such a person belongs to the 'public concerned' – follows from his right to be consulted and to argue against, for instance, planned infrastructures, noise protection measures etc. Therefore, even in the absence of national legislation, an individual which belongs to the 'public concerned' can invoke the obligation that the administration is obliged, since the coming into effect of Directive 85/337, to undertake an environment impact assessment for Annex I projects.

In contrast, national administrations are left a margin of discretion as regards Annex II projects. The 'regulation-test', outlined above would result in the following wording: 'For annex II-projects, the administration shall examine whether they are likely to have significant effects on the environment; where this is the case an environment impact assessment shall be carried out.' Thus, there is an obligation to examine, not to act. The question arises whether this precise and unconditional obligation to examine

---

56 Directive 76/769 relating to restrictions on the marketing and use of certain dangerous substances and preparations, OJ 1976 No. L 262, p. 12; this Directive has been amended twelve times.

57 Directive 85/210 on the lead content of petrol, OJ 1985 No. L 96, p. 25.

58 Directive 80/68, note 12 above.

59 Directive 79/409 on the conservation of wild birds, OJ 1979 No. L 103, p. 1.

60 Directive 85/337, note 17 above.

61 Directive 85/337, note 17 above, Article 2.

gives rise to some sort of a protected position for members of the 'public concerned', whether the provision is directly effective.

It is argued that this is not the case.[62] National administrations are under a certain obligation to examine. However, at that stage, the issue of public participation does not (yet) arise. It is, therefore, an obligation which is placed upon administrations in the general interest, but which does not create a right for individuals to insist that this examination is taking place. Therefore, where an administration fails to make this examination, there is no right under EC law to raise this matter before a national court. Nevertheless, there would be a breach of provisions of EC law which national courts, under national procedural and substantive rules, should consider and which the Commission, too, could pursue under a procedure of Article 169 EC.

Occasionally, it has been argued that even the provisions relating to Annex I projects are not directly effective on the ground that an environmental impact assessment obliges the administration to require from developers the documentation mentioned in Article 5(2) of Directive 85/377. Because this constitutes an obligation for individuals (the developer), a legislative measure would be necessary. However, this opinion would only be correct if developers had a right, under national law, to realize a project. Alternatively, the administration would be able not to decide on the project until it had received all the documents under Article 5(2). Such a 'right' to realize a project seems to exist in only a minority of Member States[63] and even in those cases it should be noted that the obligation to make an EIA rests upon the administration. The mere fact that a government has failed to ensure the transposition of the directive in time does not rid the administration of this obligation. Where the administration is genuinely unable to obtain from the developer all the documents and information required by Article 5(2) it must attempt to find the necessary information elsewhere, for instance by making the necessary studies itself. In any event, it has to consult the administrations dealing with environmental questions (Article 6(1)) and allow the public concerned to express its opinion on the project (Article 6(2)). It might even be under an obligation to draft the summary of Article 5(2) and which must be submitted to the public concerned itself. It must not be forgotten that it is due to the Member State's

---

[62] It appears that only in Germany there exists a subjective right of a developer to obtain planning permission as soon as all requirements fixed by legislation are complied with.

[63] Directive 84/360 on the combating of air pollution from industrial plants, OJ 1984 No. L 188, p. 20.

own failure to transpose Directive 85/337 in time that all these difficulties have arisen.

A similar obligation stems from Article 9 of Directive 84/360 on air pollution from industrial plants.[64] This provision requires that:

> applications for authorization and the decisions of the competent authorities (to emit pollutants into the air) are made available to the public concerned.

Even where this provision has not been transposed into national law, the individual may compel the administration to comply with this provision, since the five conditions for direct effect are satisfied.

Article 8 of Directive 82/501 provides that the population living in the vicinity of an industrial plant covered by the directive shall be informed of the risk emanating from the plant and of the measures to take in the case of an accident.[65] Article 8 does not specify whether this information must be provided by public authorities or by the plant owner. Since, however, the directive is addressed at Member States, an administration could not refuse to give that information where the directive has not been transposed as this would mean that the right of the adjacent population to be informed would be jeopardized in such a case.

Directive 90/313 requires that the administration makes available to individuals, upon request from, information on the environment which is in the hands of the administration.[66] The directive enumerates a number of situations, in which a Member State may provide that the information is not granted such as cases of secrecy of governmental deliberation, defence aspects, commercial and professional secrecy, etc. The provision to supply information is unconditional and precise and is directly effective. A Member State which has not transposed the provision of the directive cannot invoke the exceptions since the directive expressly stipulates that a Member State 'may' refuse information in such cases. Since there exists a discretion to refuse, the exception cannot itself be directly effective. An exception arises in cases where the supply of information would itself violate human rights of a person, for instance where information on the privacy of persons is to be supplied.

The above-mentioned provisions reflect examples of directly effective provisions of secondary environmental law. Normally, however, provisions which create an obligation to act for the administration are not directly effective in that they fail to satisfy the fifth condition, i.e. that of granting a 'right', a favourable position to individuals. Thus, where an administration

---

[64] Directive 82/501 on the major accident hazards of certain industrial activities, OJ 1982 No. L 230, p. 1.

[65] Directive 90/313, note 18 above.

[66] Court of Justice, case 372 to 374/85, *Traen*, [1987] ECR 2141.

is obliged under an EC directive to draw up a clean-up programme for water, air or soil, or a monitoring programme for waste, such an obligation is not in itself improving the individual's position vis-à-vis the administration. The same applies where the administration has to grant authorizations to companies, install measuring stations, measure and assess the pollution of water or air, create habitats, publish data or reports, etc. The majority of these provisions are unconditional and sufficiently precise; yet they generally concern the normal administrative activity which does not impact on rights of individuals. To this category also belongs the case where an individual in the context of an Annex I project invokes the obligation to act but does not belong to the 'public concerned'. In such a situation, Directive 85/377 does not confer a right on that individual because the provision of Directive 85/377 produces direct effects for individuals who belong to the 'public concerned', but not for other persons. This difference between (unconditional and precise) provisions with direct effect and (unconditional and precise) provisions without such effect will be further illustrated by the jurisprudence of the Court of Justice in environmental cases.

2. The Court of Justice and Direct Effect of Environmental Provisions.

As noted above, there are very few decisions where the Court of Justice ruled on the direct effect of an environmental provision.

In cases 372 to 374/85 (*Traen*),[67] the Court was asked in a procedure under Article 177 EC whether Articles 8 and 12 of Directive 75/442[68] applied directly to economic operators or whether Member States had to take specific measures in order to implement them. The Court found that the provisions in question imposed obligations on operators, but did not grant them rights and concluded therefore that the provisions in question were not directly effective.

In case 14/86 (*Pretore di Salò*)[69] the Court in a procedure under Article 177 EC dealt with the question concerning whether the provisions of

---

[67] Directive 75/442, note 33 above, Article 8: 'Member States shall take the necessary measures to ensure that any holder of waste: – has it handled by a private or public waste collector or by an undertaking which carries out the operations listed in Annex IIA or B, or – recovers or disposes of it himself in accordance with the provisions of this Directive'; Article 12: 'Establishments or undertakings which collect or transport waste on a professional basis ... where not subject to authorisation, shall be registered with the competent authorities'.

[68] Court of Justice, case 14/86, *Pretore di Salò*, [1987] ECR 2545.

[69] Directive 78/659 on the quality of fresh waters needing protection or improvement in order to support fish life, OJ 1978 No. L 222, p. 1.

Directive 78/659 on the quality of fresh water to protect fishlife[70] were sufficiently precise and unconditional to be used in criminal proceedings against a person. The Advocate General advised against direct effect of the Directive because Member States enjoy discretion in designating the waters falling with the application of the Directive.[71] The Court did not examine the provisions of Directive 78/659 as to their direct effect, but argued that their use against a person in criminal proceedings would impose 'obligations' rather than create rights which was ruled out.

In case 380/87 (*Cinisello Balsamo*),[72] the Court of Justice was asked a number of questions by an Italian court relating to the direct effect of Directive 75/442(73). Specifically the court was asked:

1. whether the directive's provisions gave individuals the right to sell plastic bags or containers.

In *Cinisello Balsamo*, the Court stated that the directive did not create, directly or indirectly, any such right. Rather, Article 3 provided, *inter alia*, that national measures should be taken in order to prevent the generation of waste. The prohibition to use certain substances in products – the Italian measure prohibited the use of non-biodegradable plastics – was an appropriate measure to contribute to the prevention of generation of waste. The Court was also asked to address:

2. whether Article 3(2) of the Directive gives individuals a right which they may enforce before a national court in order to obtain the annulment or suspension of rules which had been adopted at national level without having been previously been communicated to the Commission.

The Court answered that Member States were under an obligation to inform the Commission of all measures which they intended to adopt by virtue of Article 3(2). It stated that:

> Neither the wording nor the purpose of the provision in question provides any support for the view that failure by the member States to observe their obligations to give prior notice in itself renders unlawful the rules thus adopted. It follows from the foregoing that the above mentioned provision concerns relations between the Member States and the Commission and does not give rise to any right for individuals.

Thus, although the obligation of prior notice was unconditional and precise, it did not create rights for individuals.

---

[70] Court of Justice, case 14/86, note 69 above, opinion of the Advocate General, paragraphs 9 and 10.

[71] Court of Justice, case 380/87, *Cinisello Balsamo*, note 32 above.

[72] Court of Justice, case C–236/92, *Difesa della Cava*, note 1 above.

The same Italian court submitted various questions to the European Court in case C–236/92 (*Difesa della Cava*).[73] In 1989 and 1990 the Lombardy Region adopted a plan for a tip for solid urban waste to be established in a municipality within the regions. A number of individuals instituted proceedings against those decisions, claiming that their rights were affected. They argued that Italy had transposed Directive 75/442 by provisions which provided for the disposal of waste almost exclusively by means of tipping. No measures intended to encourage the recycling of waste had been adopted, so that it would be necessary to use tips for waste disposal. If Italy had taken the measures necessary to encourage waste recycling as soon as the directive had come into force, there would not have been any need to establish further tips.

The Italian court asked the following question:

> Does Community environmental law, in particular Article 4 of Council Directive 75/442/EEC of 15 July 1975 on waste, grant to individuals 'subjective rights' ('diritti soggettivi') which the national court is required to protect?

The Court of Justice replied that Article 4:

> essentially repeats the terms of the third recital in the preamble [and] indicates a programme to be followed and sets out the objectives which the Member States must observe in their performance of the more specific obligations imposed on them by Articles 5 to 11 of the directive. Thus, the provision at issue must be regarded as defining the framework for the action to be taken by the Member States regarding the treatment of waste and not as requiring, in itself, the adoption of specific measures or a particular method of waste disposal. It is therefore neither unconditional nor sufficiently precise and thus is not capable of conferring rights on which individuals may rely as against the State.

The Court produced the correct result. Indeed, it is not possible to deduct from Article 4 the obligation for a Member State to promote recycling rather than provide for the tipping of waste. The 'regulation test' applied to this provision would probably read: 'Waste must be disposed of without harm to man or the environment.' There is no support in Article 4 for a right for individuals to have waste recycled rather than tipped. Therefore, to the extent that the Italian individuals opposed the waste disposal tip as such, their claim had no foundation in Directive 75/442.

However, the answer by the Court of Justice seems to go beyond the specific case and seems too general. It reads:

> Article 4 of Council Directive 75/442/EEC of 15 July 1975 on waste does not confer on individuals rights which the national courts must safeguard.

There are four arguments used by the Court to reach this conclusion:

---

[73] See Court of Justice, case C–236/92, *Difesa della Cava*, note 1 above, Advocate General's opinion, paragraph 24.

1) Article 4 essentially repeats the third recital;
2) it sets out the objectives, which Member States must observe, when taking measures under Articles 5 to 11;
3) the Court has already held so in cases 372 to 372/85 (*Traen*); and
4) thus, Article 4 sets the framework for action.

These arguments will now be examined seriatim.

Concerning the first argument, this proposition was advanced by the United Kingdom government during the proceedings.[74] However, a simple comparison of the third recital with Article 4 shows a significant difference.[75] Article 4 is not simply repeating that each national provision shall protect man and the environment. Rather, it lays down very specific requirements for these measures. To be sure it is one thing to require planning, supervision and monitoring measures – which are the subject-matter of Articles 5 to 11 – aimed at preventing harm to man or the environment (third recital). However, it is most extraordinary that in a 'framework for action' it should be specified that there should be no odours, or that fauna and flora should not be affected. Paragraph 2 of Article 4 goes even so far as prohibiting uncontrolled disposal of waste which is a ban on specific actions and which could hardly be expressed in a more unconditional and precise fashion. It is not clear, however, whether the Court discussed Directive 75/442 in its original form or in the form after amendment by Directive 91/156[76] which inserted paragraph 2 and slightly amended paragraph 1. The text used by the Court suggests that the old version of Article 4 was used, although the new version was in force at the time of the judgment.[77] In short, Article 4 does not repeat 'essentially' the terms of the third recital, but goes considerably beyond it.

In respect of the second argument, the fact that Article 4 sets out objectives does not prevent it from being applied to a concrete case. If one

---

[74] See Directive 75/442, note 33 above, 3rd recital: 'Whereas the essential objective of all provisions relating to waste disposal must be the protection of human health and the environment against harmful effects caused by the collection, transport, treatment, storage and tipping of waste;'

[75] Article 4: 'Member States shall take the necessary measures to ensure that waste is recovered or disposed of without endangering human health and without using processes or methods which could harm the environment, and in particular:
 – without risk to water, air, soil and plants and animals;
 – without causing a nuisance through noise or odours;
 – without adversely affecting the countryside or places of special interest.
 Member States shall also take the necessary measures to prohibit the abandonment, dumping or uncontrolled disposal of waste.'

[76] Directive 91/156, OJ 1991 No. L 42, p. 43.

[77] According to its Article 2, Directive 91/156, note 76 above, entered into force on 1 April 1993.

considers the interpretation of Articles 12, 59, 85 or 119 EC Treaty, it is obvious that these provisions all (also) include objectives to be reached. However, according to the Court, this does not prevent them from being capable of being applied in the relationship between individuals and the State. Article 4 refers to 'measures', while the third recital uses the notion of 'regulations', a difference which should at least have suggested that Article 4 also refers to concrete measures.

As for cases 372 to 374/85,[78] the Court in these cases did not examine Article 4 but Article 10 of Directive 75/442.[79] It had concluded that Article 10 afforded a wide margin of discretion to Member States and did not require a specific way of organizing the supervision of waste activities. However, Member States had to take account of the objectives of the third recital and Article 4.

Finally, as noted earlier, there is nothing in Article 4 entitles an individual to claim the illegality of specific measures on the basis that the national legislation has failed to provide for recycling measures and had relied on disposal by tipping instead. Nevertheless, the Court's reasoning fails to explain why a specific waste tip could not be challenged by an individual on the ground that it adversely affected, for instance, bird habitats or that it caused nuisance through excessive noise or odours etc. In the same way, an individual could turn against an unauthorized waste tip and request a statement by the national court that that tip contradicted the amended version of Article 4(2) of Directive 75/442.

The Advocate General seems to have considered this eventuality. Indeed, paragraph 37 of his conclusion reads:

> On the other hand, as far as the location of tips is concerned, Article 6 requires the competent authorities to draw up plans for 'suitable disposal sites'. After the sites are decided upon, the authorities must make certain that waste is disposed of without endangering human health and without harming the environment, for which purposes the objectives laid down in Article 4 must be observed.

This opinion reflects the current writer's position: The individual disposal of waste must respect the requirements of Article 4. Since these requirements are expressly considered to prevent the endangering of human health, the individuals should be allowed to rely on them. In conclusion, I contend that Article 4 of Directive 75/442 is unconditional and sufficiently precise to be directly effective as far as individual measures are concerned.

---

[78] Court of Justice, case 372 to 374/85, note 67 above.

[79] Directive 74/442, note 33 above, Article 10: 'For the purposes of implementing Article 4, any establishment or undertaking which carries out the operations referred to in Annex II B must obtain a permit.'

As regards regulatory measures to be taken by Member States, it does not give individuals the right to insist on regulations with a specific content.

V DIRECT EFFECT OF DIRECTIVES BETWEEN PRIVATE PARTIES

The Court of Justice has always held that provisions of EC secondary legislation can only have direct effect as regards the relation between individuals and the State. It is not possible to extend the doctrine of direct effect to relations between private parties. The leading case in this respect is case 152/84 (*Marshall*).[80] In that case Ms. Marshall considered her dismissal to be unlawful as she had been discriminated on the basis of her sex. Her employer was a private law body and hence not an emanation of the State. The Court of Justice was of the opinion that Ms. Marshall's dismissal was in breach with Directive 76/207[81] but that this provision could not be relied upon against private individuals. It stated that directives were, under Article 189 EC, addressed at Member States and could therefore not impose obligations on individuals. Even in cases where Directive 76/207 had not been transposed into national law, the applicant could thus not rely on its provisions where discrimination by a private employer was at issue.

This decision has given rise to a significant amount of criticism. In particular, it has been argued that the distinction between public and private bodies, for the purposes of direct effect, was not an appropriate one. After all, the Court had recognized that provisions of the EC Treaty, in particular Article 119, could be invoked between individuals.[82] This criticism led the Court, in case C–91/92 (*Dori*),[83] to reconsider its doctrine as regards horizontal direct effects of directives. In that case, Ms. Dori had concluded, at Milan station, a contract with an Italian company on English by correspondence. Milan station was not the regular business premises of that company. Some days later, Ms. Dori withdrew from the contract. The company did not accept the withdrawal and the matter was referred to an Italian court. Directive 85/577 provides that contracts which are concluded away from the business premises of the trader may be withdrawn within one

---

[80] Court of Justice, case 152/84, *Marshall*, note 44 above.
[81] Directive 76/207, note 27 above.
[82] Court of Justice, case 43/75, *Defrenne*, [1976] ECR 455.
[83] Court of Justice, case C–91/92, *Dori*, note 23 above.

week after the consumer having been informed of his right of withdrawal.[84] Italy had not transposed that directive into national law.

The Court of Justice ruled that the provisions of Directive 85/577 were unconditional and sufficiently precise for them to be directly effective. They also aimed to protect the consumer and, in principle, all five conditions for applying the doctrine of direct effect were fulfilled. The Court nevertheless refused to apply it in the *Dori*-case, stating that Article 189 EC only provided that regulations were directly applicable. Directives were addressed at Member States, not at individuals. It was justified not to allow a Member State to invoke its own failure to transpose a directive and thereby deprive an individual of the rights which the directive in question intended to grant. But the same reasoning could not apply to individuals, which had not committed any failure. Deciding otherwise would mean to allow directives to have the same effect as regulations, whereas the EC Treaty expressly allowed the EC to adopt regulations in certain circumstances only.

The Court of Justice continued by stating that, even where a provision in a directive did not have direct effect, all national authorities of a Member State were obliged to take the general or specific measures necessary in order to ensure the implementation of an obligation laid down in an EC provision. Courts had thus to examine whether they were capable of interpreting national law in the light of the wording and the purpose of the directive, in a way which allowed the objectives of the EC provision to be achieved. The Court of Justice did not go as far as to require that the Italian court should interpret the cooling-off period of Directive 85/577 into existing Italian law. It concluded by stating that, where an interpretation of national law was not possible in a way so as to satisfy the rights of the individual, the Member State in question might be obliged to pay compensation in cases where a person had suffered damages caused by the fact that Directive 85/577 had not been transposed into Italian law.[85]

It appears from this decision, that there is no 'horizontal' direct effect of directives. Rather, the doctrine is limited to relations between individuals and State bodies. This confirms at the same time that the *ratio* of the Court's direct effect reasoning is the fact that the State should not be allowed to take advantage of its own failure (*venire contra factum proprium*). We now turn to address the general effect of an (environmental) directive in EC law.

---

[84] Directive 85/577, note 24 above.
[85] Court of Justice, case C–6/90 and C–9/90, *Francovich*, [1991] ECR I–5357; see also case C–91/92, *Dori*, note 23 above.

VI THE EFFECT OF EC ENVIRONMENTAL LAW

Irrespective whether an EC provision is directly effective, its effect in national law deserves consideration. In the following section, the general relationship between Community law and national law will be discussed. This will be followed by some observations on provisions which fall within the scope of the doctrine of direct effect and those which do not.

1. The Effect of EC Provisions in National Law

As early as 1964, the Court of Justice ruled on the relationship between national law and EC law. In case 6/64 (*Costa v ENEL*)[86] the Court decided that in cases of conflict, EC law prevailed over national law. No national legal provision could derogate from EC law and rules which existed prior to the EC rule were no longer applicable to the extent that they contradicted the EC provision. The Court justified its reasoning by virtue of the new legal order set up by the EEC Treaty, which had created a body of law which binds both individuals and Member States. National courts are bound to abide by this new legal order. Were Member States to be able unilaterally to derogate from it, EC law would lose its significance as an independent source of law.

In case 6/64 this principle of the supremacy of EC law over national law was developed with regard to Treaty provisions. At later stages, the Court extended this principle also to secondary legislation. Its main argument was derived from Article 189 EC, which states that regulations are directly applicable in all Member States. It would be impossible, according to the Court, to honour this requirement if subsequent national law were capable of prevailing over EC regulations since in that case the regulation would simply no longer be applicable. The principle of supremacy of EC law over national law is by now well recognized all over the EC and accepted and applied by national courts. It applies to Treaty provisions as well as regulations, directives and decisions.

2. Effect of Provisions Falling Within the Scope of the Doctrine of Direct Effect

Provisions of directives which are directly effective – and hence fulfil all five conditions mentioned above[87] – have the same effect as a regulation

---

[86] Court of Justice, case 6/64, *Costa v ENEL*, note 40 above.

[87] See above pages 101–2.

within the national legal order. The courts as well as administrations are obliged to apply them and national legislation which is in contradiction with directly effective provisions must be set aside by courts and administrations and may not be applied. The national provision does not become void: it continues to exist and is to be used within the national legal system, except in those cases where it enters into conflict with the superior rule of EC law. The 'regulation-test' implies that one should assume the directly effective provision to be a regulation. Such a regulation would need to be applied by all courts and administrations.

3. Effect of Provisions Which Are Not Directly Effective

According to Article 189 EC, a directive shall be binding upon each Member State to which it is addressed. Article 5 EC provides that Member States shall take all appropriate measures to ensure fulfilment of the obligations resulting from action taken by the institutions of the Community. The notion 'Member State' includes all emanations of the State and hence includes courts and administrations. In its landmark decision 6/64 (*Costa v ENEL*) and in a number of subsequent decisions, the Court of Justice has stated that, under Article 5 EC, Member States must do everything to ensure that EC law is fully and effectively applied. This obligation also rests on national courts, which have to interpret EC rules and national rules in a way which ensures that the letter and the spirit of EC law is fully respected. This obligation is not limited to EC provisions which are directly effective but applies to all EC provisions.

In case C–106/89 (*Marleasing*),[88] the Court of Justice was asked to interpret Article 11 of Directive 68/151 on company law.[89] This provision lists exhaustively the cases in which the nullity of a company may be ordered. Spain had not transposed that directive when in a civil case before a Spanish court the question was raised whether a company could be declared null by virtue of a ground other than those listed in Article 11 of Directive 68/151. The Court decided that Directive 68/151 did not produce direct effect, since this would have meant that obligations were placed on individuals, which is impossible in the absence of a national implementing provision. The Court then proceeded to hold that the national judge, by

---

[88] Court of Justice, case C–106/89, *Marleasing*, [1990] ECR I–4156.

[89] Directive 68/151 on coordination of safeguards which, for the protection of the interests of members and others, are required by Member States of companies within the meaning of the second paragraph of Article 58 of the Treaty, with a view to making such safeguards equivalent throughout the Community, OJ 1969 No. L 65, p. 8.

virtue of Article 5 EC, had a duty to interpret national Spanish law in the light of existing EC law, i.e. Directive 68/151 and that it was irrelevant that Spanish company law pre-dated the Directive. As a result, it was illegal for Spanish company law to provide for the nullity of a company on other grounds than those listed in Article 11 of Directive 68/151. This reasoning leads to the result that by interpreting national law in the light of EC law, a provision of national law becomes inapplicable in a concrete case where it contradicts the EC provision.

The Court chose almost exactly the same wording in the aforementioned case C–91/92.[90] The only difference is that the Court on this occasion did not go so far as to rule that any interpretation of national law, which did not grant a cooling-off period of at least seven days to the consumer, was in contradiction with the correct understanding of EC law and left this point open. Yet, the Court did add that the consumer could claim compensation against the defaulting Member State if national law was interpreted in a way so as not to provide the protection which EC law had intended to grant. In other words, the final result would be that either Ms. Dori should not be obliged to pay the contract price because the Italian court interpreted Italian law in a way that gave her a right to withdraw from the contract; or she could ask the Italian State for compensation of the damage which she had suffered as a result of her having to pay the contract price (and court litigation costs).

A separate instance concerns Directive 80/779 fixes limit values for sulphur dioxide concentrations in the air which may not be exceeded throughout the territory of Member States.[91] Since this directive aims at contributing to the protection of human health, it grants 'rights' to individuals. Nevertheless, individuals cannot turn against a neighbouring plant and claim a reduction in SO2-emissions where the Member State in question has not transposed Directive 80/779 into national law, since the directive needs to be transposed into national law in order to create obligations for that plant. However, in case of litigation, a national court might interpret a national rule of neighbour law which provides that unreasonable disturbance has to be avoided, in the light of the provisions of Directive 80/779 and consider that emissions which exceed of the limit values of Directive 80/779 are unreasonable.[92]

The next example only partly stems from a case actually decided by the Court of Justice. As mentioned above, the Court decided in case 380/87 that the obligation of Directive 74/442 to inform the Commission of draft

[90] Court of Justice, case C–91/92, *Dori*, note 23 above.
[91] Directive 80/779, note 48 above.
[92] Example taken from Zuleeg (1994) p. 168.

legislation for waste prevention or waste recycling was not directly effective since it only concerned the relations between Member States and the Commission.[93] If one imagines a case where within a Member State one specific official is charged to inform the Commission of such national draft legislation, that this official does not fulfil his duty and that therefore the administration tries to dismiss him from the national civil service, would the national court have to examine the provision of Directive 75/442 in order to see whether indeed it imposed obligations on Member States? The answer can should clearly be in the affirmative. Indeed, there is an obligation to be fulfilled under Directive 75/442 and this provision has effects in national law. It is clear that national courts cannot simply ignore the existence of EC provisions, even where these are not directly effective.

In France, an administrative act can be challenged in court on the ground that it is objectively contrary to legal provisions. Where a national court has to examine the existence and meaning of such legal provisions it also has to take EC provisions into consideration. This follows from Article 5 EC. It was in view of this doctrine that the administrative court of Pau examined, in 1993, the legality of an administrative decision to grant planning permission for the construction of the Somport tunnel in the Pyrenees.[94] The court found that Directive 85/337 required, in the course of an environmental impact assessment of a project, an examination of the direct and indirect effects of a project on the environment.[95] French law only required the direct effects to be examined. The court of Pau decided that, in the light of the EC provision, the French administrative act was illegal since it had not examined the indirect effect – the increase of traffic at the access routes to the tunnel – of the project.

Hence, there is a consistent line of decisions from the Court of Justice from which it can be concluded that the obligation of the national court to interpret national law in the light of existing EC provisions is neither restricted to directly effective EC provisions nor to those provisions which are unconditional and sufficiently precise. Indeed, in cases which were submitted to the Court of Justice, under Article 177 EC Treaty, it has sometimes been argued that only directly effective EC provisions can be the subject of a submission to the Court under Article 177. The Court of Justice has always rejected this restrictive interpretation, arguing that national law

---

[93] Court of Justice, case 380/87, *Cinisello Balsamo*, note 32 above.

[94] Tribunal administratif de Pau, case 91/855 and others, judgment of 2 December 1992.

[95] See Article 3 of Directive 85/377, note 17 above: 'The environmental impact assessment will identify, describe and assess ... the direct and indirect effects of a project ...'

had to be interpreted in conformity with all EC provisions.[96] Hence, it follows that national courts are under an obligation, by virtue of Article 5 EC, to interpret national rules in the light of existing EC provisions, irrespective of the question whether these provisions are directly applicable or not. In particular, it must be noted that this obligation is not restricted to:

a) unconditional and precise provisions of EC law;
b) to rules which have a direct effect; and
c) to cases, where the position of the individual with regard to the State is in question.

These points clarify the difference between the doctrine of direct effect and the obligation to interpret national law in the light of EC rules of law. While the first doctrine is based on a failure of the Member State in question, the second is based on the principle of the supremacy of EC law. Therefore, the first doctrine is limited to cases where a failure by a Member State exists, jeopardizing the protection that EC law offers to individuals The second theory is broader, in that it generally applies and is not conditional upon a favourable position of individuals.

So far, all cases have dealt with the question of the interpretation and application of EC rules by courts. It is doubtful, however, whether the same principles also apply to the administration. The Court of Justice has not yet clearly pronounced itself on that matter. In case 103/88 (*Fratelli Costanzo*)[97] the Court of Justice was confronted with a question of the direct effect of a provision of Directive 71/305,[98] as regards a local authority. In that case, all five above-mentioned conditions were fulfilled. The Court of Justice decided:

> An authority, including a local authority, has the same duty as a national court to apply Article 29(5) of Council Directive 71/305 and not to apply those provisions of national law that are incompatible with it.

The doctrine of direct effect also applies to the administration. This judgment has been criticized on the basis that the doctrine of direct effect ought to be limited to court decisions and should not be extended to administrative decisions. The most relevant legal argument is that a court may, under Article 177 EC Treaty, refer a preliminary question to the Court of Justice and whether a provision is directly effective. An administration does not have any such opportunity.

---

[96] Court of Justice, case 111/75, ECR 1976, p. 657; case 32/74, *Haaga*, [1974] ECR 1201.

[97] Court of Justice, case 103/88, *Fratelli Costanzo*, [1988] ECR 339.

[98] Directive 71/305 on award procedures for public construction projects, OJ 1971 No. L 185, p. 5.

While this interpretation is correct, it should be understood that the administration is also representing the State, and therefore all the justifications for the doctrine of direct effect also apply to the administration. Thus, a Member State would benefit from its own failure and remove from individuals the favourable position which EC law has granted them. It is interesting to note that Germany followed this interpretation. When Germany had not transposed Directive 90/313 on access to environmental information[99] into national law when the directive came into force it sent a circular to the administration, informing that it had to apply the provisions of Directive 90/313, despite the absence of national legislation since the provisions of that Directive were directly effective.[100]

Similar considerations apply to the question whether the administration is under an obligation to give effect to EC rules which are not directly effective. The general obligation flows from Article 5 EC and therefore again is not restricted to courts. It is obvious that the administration of a Member State has a greater discretion as to the meaning and relevance of the EC provision. However, this does not affect the general obligation to give effect to EC provisions. For instance, in the *French Somport*-case mentioned above,[101] the construction of the Somport tunnel was a project which came under Annex II of Directive 85/337.[102] Therefore, the French administration in principle enjoyed a degree of discretion as to whether to require an environmental impact assessment or not. However, in the concrete case the tunnel and the access road were in the centre of the last habitat for the brown bear in France. Thus, the discretion of the French authorities was effectively eliminated and any other decision than requiring an environmental impact assessment would have constituted improper use of this discretionary power. French authorities assessed the problem in the same way and did therefore undertake the assessment.

More generally, the Commission is taking action under Article 169 EC against Member States if Annex II projects are not subject to an environment impact assessment even though there is, in view of the particular circumstances, no margin of discretion for the administration.

---

99   Directive 90/313, note 18 above.
100   Circular of the Environmental Minister of the Federal Government of Germany to the environmental departments of the Länder, of 23 December 1992. In July 1994, Germany transposed the Directive into national law.
101   See reference in note 94 above.
102   A road tunnel project comes under Annex II of Directive 85/337, note 17 above, for which Member States enjoy discretion to decide whether an environmental impact assessment is to be made. The relevant provision in the *Somport*-case was Article 3 of Directive 85/337, which provides that 'the direct and indirect effects of a project' should be identified, described and assessed.

Such cases concerned in the past, for instance, the construction of a dam which would inundate a protected habitat, the planning permission to extract lignite which requires some 15,000 persons to leave their homes, or the construction of a tourist village for several thousand persons within a protected habitat.

This practice shows that the national administration is under an obligation to consider how it can give full effect to all the provisions of EC law and not just those which are directly effective. While its discretion may be considerable, it is by no means unlimited.

VII CONCLUSION

The doctrine of direct effect of EC provisions was originally developed in cases involving provisions of the EC Treaty and later extended to provisions of directives. The justification for directly applying provisions of the EC Treaty and directives are different: whilst the reasons for directly applying Treaty provisions resides in the nature and the wording of those provisions, the justification for directly applying provisions of a directive essentially lies in the failure of a Member State to transpose the provision into national law.

There are five conditions, which all must be fulfilled in order for a provision of a directive to be directly effective: the deadline for transposition must have expired; transposition must not have taken place; the provision must be unconditional; the provision must be sufficiently precise and it must grant individuals certain 'rights' or a favourable position with regard to public authorities.

None of the provisions in Articles 130r to 130t EC Treaty appear to be unconditional and sufficiently precise to be directly effective.

As regards environmental directives, provisions which contain emission standards, or concentrations of pollutants, expressed in a numeric value are directly effective as are provisions containing a ban or prohibition. Generally, provisions which oblige the administration to take action are not directly effective, since there is normally no corresponding right granted to individuals. Articles 2 and 4(1) of Directive 85/337 are directly effective and can be invoked by the persons concerned to the extent that they require a project which is covered by Annex I of that directive to undergo an environmental impact assessment prior to its approval. In respect of Annex II projects, these are not directly effective. Article 4 of Directive 75/442 is directly effective in so far as it allows an individual to challenge the nuisance caused by a specific waste elimination installation.

Provisions in directives which are unconditional and precise, but which create obligations for individuals are not directly effective. Provisions in directives which are unconditional and precise and which create rights for individuals nevertheless cannot be invoked against other individuals or private bodies. This is because whereas the doctrine of direct effect has as its basis in the failure of the State to transpose a directive into national law, individuals have not committed this kind of failure. For this reason, directives cannot create obligations for individuals without prior transposal of those provisions into national law. Provisions in directives which are unconditional and precise, but which only refer to the relationship between Member States and the Commission, without granting 'rights' to individuals are not directly effective.

It follows from Articles 5 and 189 EC that provisions of Community law prevail over national provisions, irrespective of the question whether these national provisions were adopted before or after the provisions of Community law. Therefore, where there is a conflict of rules, national courts have to give priority to the EC provision. This obligation does not only apply to provisions which are unconditional and precise, or which create 'rights' for individuals, but to all provisions of EC law.

National courts are therefore under the obligation to interpret national (environmental) law in a way which best ensures the full effectiveness of the EC provision. Where an EC provision is directly effective, national courts have to set aside the national rule which is at variance with that provision and apply EC law. Where an EC provision is not directly effective, national courts have to interpret national provisions as far as possible in the light of the EC provision thus ensuring the full effectiveness of the latter. In case of doubt national courts may, under Article 177 EC, request a preliminary ruling from the Court of Justice whereas they are obliged to do so if their decision, according to national procedural law, is not open to appeal. National, regional or local administrations have to apply directly effective EC provisions and set aside national conflicting provisions in the same way as courts. In respect of other provisions of EC law, they must interpret national provisions in the light of EC provisions and try to give full effect to these EC provisions in the same way as national courts.

7. *Francovich* and its Application to EC Environmental Law

Han Somsen

There is a hierarchy of values:
necessity in the first place,
politics in the second, and the law
only in so far as one is able to respect it.[1]

I THE ENFORCEMENT OF EC ENVIRONMENTAL LAW AS THE WEAKEST LINK OF THE REGULATORY CHAIN

Environmental policy is often compared with a regulatory chain.[2] The metaphor is illustrative because it implies that such a policy necessarily is only as strong as its weakest link. Applied to the European Community's environmental policy, the first link of the chain would consist of the formal competences enshrined in the Treaties to pursue an environmental policy. Indeed, academic debate in the 1970s focused on the question to what extent environmental goals belonged to the tasks of the Community, and whether the Treaties, as later amended by the Single European Act, provided the institutions with the powers to carry out those tasks.[3] The entry into force of the Treaty on European Union which extended the

---

[1] General De Gaulle as quoted in Mackenzie Stuart, *Hamlyn Lectures* (1977).

[2] Most recently in the Dutch Advisory Committee, 'Product and Environment' in *Zo sterk als de Zwakste Schakel* (*As Strong as the Weakest Link*), 18.2.1993. See Temmink 1993.

[3] For some analyses see Freestone 1991a pp. 135–54; Krämer 1990a; Sagio 1990 pp. 39–50; Scheuning 1989 pp. 153–92; Vorwerk 1990.

Community's environmental powers whilst paradoxically at the same time making their exercise conditional upon compliance with the principle of subsidiarity, has revitalized this debate.[4]

The second link of the chain consists of the body of secondary legislation and other instruments adopted by the institutions of the Community in furtherance of the Union's environmental goals. After a period of rapid expansion, concerns have been increasingly expressed about the *quality* of environmental directives, including the question of proportionality, and the appropriateness of legal instruments as such to bring about behavioural change.[5] Meanwhile, the application of the principle of subsidiarity to the existing body of secondary environmental law should give rise to a welcome process of consolidation and clarification, rather than a wholesale retreat of the Community in this field.[6]

The next two links bridge the gap between the Union and the Member States. One consists of the incorporation of EC environmental legislation in the national legal orders, popularly termed 'formal implementation'. Under Article 189(c) EC, in conjunction with Article 5 EC, Member States are under a duty to take all the necessary legal and administrative steps to ensure the fulfilment of the obligations arising out of environmental directives. This necessarily implies that they must not only transpose the provisions of the directive into their national legal orders by way of the adoption of legal or administrative provisions, but that they must also take the necessary *practical* steps such as the identification of bathing waters under Directive 76/160[7] or the classification of special protection areas for the purpose of Article 4(1) of Directive 79/409 on the conservation of wild birds.[8] This link of the chain is usually termed 'practical implementation'. Incomplete implementation of EC environmental law by Member States has long been regarded the achilles heel of the Union's environmental policy and from the mid-80s onwards political scientists and lawyers have predominantly focused their attention on questions of implementation. The institutions of the Community, too, have acknowledged the need for improvements in this field, and Member States have attached a separate declaration to the TEU to this effect.[9]

---

4   Epiney and Furrer 1992 pp. 369–409; Thieffry 1992 pp. 669–85.
5   See Jans 1990 p. 503 and more generally Haigh 1993. Also, Fifth Environmental Action Programme, *Towards Sustainability*, COM(92) 23 final.
6   See Commission report to the European Council on the adaptation of existing legislation to the subsidiarity principle COM(1993) 545 final. Also, Brinkhorst 1991.
7   OJ 1976 No. L 31.
8   OJ 1979 No. L 103.
9   See Haigh 1993; Jans 1989; Siedentopf and Ziller 1989.

Whereas such political commitment is to be applauded, without the appropriate enforcement mechanisms uniform and faithful compliance with Community environmental law will almost certainly remain illusory. The final link closing the chain hence consists of the enforcement mechanisms at the disposal of the institutions of the Community and private parties enabling them to secure compliance with EC environmental laws. As will be seen, it can be argued that the Community legislator should harmonize some of the procedural laws governing the availability of remedies for breaches of environmental laws. This raises questions about the Community's formal powers to adopt such provisions, at which point we have returned to our point of departure.

There are a number of factors suggesting that the enforcement of EC environmental law represents the weakest link of the Community's environmental policy. On the one hand, there are various characteristics peculiar to environmental directives which arguably make their effective enforcement more crucial than any other body of Community law; at the same time, enforcing EC environmental law has proved more complex than other spheres of Community law. Thus, once environmental damage has occurred it often is no longer possible to remedy the situation. Indeed, in case C–236/85[10] the Court stressed that the faithful transposition of Community obligations becomes *especially* important in respect of environmental directives 'as the management of the common heritage is entrusted to Member States as regards their respective territories'. However, as the Commission has rightly observed, the business community has less direct interest than in other spheres in seeing these standards effectively applied. This, evidently, implies that because the vigilance of private individuals to protect their rights is to a large extent absent in the case of EC environmental directives, more of the Commission's already scarce resources should be allocated to monitoring the implementation of environmental directives than to other areas of Community law. There are indications, however, suggesting that the Commission has instead used its resources mainly to secure the successful completion of the internal market programme.[11] The reactive nature of the infringement procedure under

---

[10] Case 236/85, *Commission v Netherlands*, [1987] ECR 3989 (in respect of Directive 79/409 on the conservation of wild birds).

[11] In its fifth supervision report, for example, the Commission states: 'In this respect, Article 169 of the EEC Treaty is now an instrument for the achievement of a policy, and not solely an essential legal instrument. The objective of Article 8a of the Treaty, namely to achieve by 1992 an area without frontiers, is now the Commission's priority objective and requires a strict application of existing Community law.' (Fifth Annual Report to the European Parliament on Commission

Article 169 EC, too, is incompatible with the need to prevent environmental harm, especially since very scarce use has been made of the powers under Article 186 'to prescribe any interim measures'. In any event, the Commission's investigative powers do not appear sufficient for it to effectively monitor practical compliance.

The possible direct effect of environmental directives although harbouring great potential, has so far failed to offset the shortcomings of the infringement procedure in the sphere of the environment. As recently illustrated in case C–236/92, even though the Court has significantly lowered the threshold for direct effect, the programmatic nature of much of EC environmental law will still often prove an insurmountable obstacle for individuals seeking to rely on those provisions before their national courts.[12] Even where environmental directives are directly effective, there remain doubts about the extent to which Community law prescribes the national procedures and remedies for the enforcement of those rights.[13] An 'enforcement gap'[14] can therefore be said to exist in the sphere of EC environmental law, which could seriously undermine its effectiveness.

One of the most important motivations leading the Court to embrace the doctrine of direct effect of Community law in 1962 was the introduction of an element of private enforcement of Community law[15] and the success of this policy almost seems to have caught the Court by surprise.[16] More than 20 years later, the same concern inspired the Court to endorse the principle that Member States can be liable for damages suffered by private individuals as a result of breaches of Community law.

---

monitoring of the application of Community Law – 1987 – COM(1988) 425 final.) See in similar vein the most recent 11th report OJ 1994 No. C 154 at p. 8.

[12] Case C–236/92, *Comitato di Coordinamento per la Difesa della Cava and Others and Regione Lombardia and Others*, [1994] ECR I–485. The case revolved around the question whether Article 4 of Directive 75/442 could produce direct effect. Krämer had earlier argued that such would be the case (Krämer 1992 p. 163). The Court, however, now seems to have rejected this interpretation. See also Chapter 6 of this volume.

[13] On this question see Jakobs 1993 pp. 969–83 and section II below.

[14] The term 'enforcement gap' is used to paraphrase the notion of an 'implementation gap' used by Rehbinder and Stewart 1985.

[15] Case 26/62, [1991] ECR I–5357: 'The vigilance of private individuals to protect their rights amounts to an effective supervision in addition to the supervision entrusted by Articles 169 and 170 to the diligence of the Commission and the Member States.'

[16] Thus, in its judgment in cases C–267 and C–268/91, *Bernard Keck and Daniel Mithouard*, [1993] ECR I–6097, the Court remarked:
'In view of the increasing tendency of traders to invoke Article 30 of the Treaty as a means of challenging rules whose effect is to limit their commercial freedom even where such rules are not aimed at products from other Member States, the Court considers it necessary to re-examine and clarify its case-law on this matter' (para. 14).

In the remainder of this paper an attempt will be undertaken to examine to what extent this principle of non-contractual State liability can be expected to narrow the enforcement gap described above.

II STATE LIABILITY FOR BREACHES OF EC ENVIRONMENTAL LAW AFTER *FRANCOVICH*: GENERAL BACKGROUND

Before examining in some detail the extent to which the conditions for State liability for breaches of Community law can be satisfied in principle for the various types of environmental provisions, it appears useful to place *Francovich* in the wider context of the Court's case law on national procedures and remedies. The facts of joined cases C–6/90 and C–9/90, *Francovich and others v Italian Republic*[17] are by now well known and need therefore only be briefly summarized.

The case arose when, after bankruptcy of two Italian firms, a number of employees risked losing substantial sums in unpaid salaries. The applicants then brought proceedings seeking payment of the compensation under Directive 80/987,[18] or in the alternative damages. According to Article 11 of the directive, the deadline for implementation had expired in October 1983. In an action under Article 169 EC, the Court had earlier already established that Italy had failed to implement the directive.[19] Two Italian courts of first instance (*Pretore*) referred the following questions pursuant to Article 177 EC:

a) whether the provisions of the directive in relation to payment of the guarantee debts were directly effective;

b) whether there was State liability in damages arising from its failure to implement the directive.

The Court found that the directive was not directly effective. However, in respect of the second question it ruled that it was a general principle, 'inherent in the scheme of the Treaty', that 'a Member State is liable to make good damage to individuals caused by a breach of Community law for which it is responsible.'

---

[17] [1991] ECR I–5357.

[18] OJ 1980 No. L 283/23.

[19] Case 22/89, *Commission v Italy*, [1989] ECR 143.

Three characteristics of the Treaty in particular were advanced to justify this conclusion; the autonomous character of the Community legal order,[20] the principle of effectiveness and protection of the rights of individuals and the principle of solidarity as expressed in Article 5 EC.[21]

An indispensable prerequisite for liability of a Member States was the nature of the infringement of Community law; only breach of a fundamental Community obligation could give rise to such liability.[22] As for the required seriousness of the breach, in *Brasserie du Pêcheur* and drawing upon its case law pursuant to Article 215 EC, the Court indicated that the decisive test for finding that a breach of Community law is sufficiently serious is whether the Member State manifestly and gravely disregarded the limits of its discretion.[23] The Court left little doubt that a breach of Community law will always be sufficiently serious if it has persisted despite a judgment finding the infringement in question to be established or a preliminary ruling or settled case law of the Court on the matter from which it is clear that the conduct in question constituted an infringement. Such a breach of a fundamental Community obligation in itself does not suffice for a Member State to become liable, however. In addition, liability for Member States depended on three conditions:

1) the result required by the directive includes the conferring of rights for the benefit of individuals,
2) the content of those rights is identifiable by reference to the directive,
3) there exists a causal link between the breach of the State's obligations and the damage suffered by the persons affected.

Importantly, the Court noted that these three conditions are 'sufficient'.[24] Fault or negligence on the part of the Member State is therefore not required.

Few cases decided by the European Court of Justice have given rise to more debate and controversy. On the one hand this seems understandable since, unlike the liability of the Community,[25] no reference to State liability is found in the Treaty.

---

[20] The Court in particular invoked case 2/62, *Van Gend & Loos*, [1963] ECR 1 and case 6/64, *Costa*, [1964] ECR 585.

[21] For the constitutional importance of this provision see Temple-Lang 1990 pp. 645–82.

[22] See Bebr 1992 at p. 570.

[23] Joined cases C-46/93 and C-58/93, *Brasserie du Pêcheur SA* and *Federal Republic of Germany* and between *The Queen* and *Secretary of State for Transport ex parte: Factortame Ltd and Others*, 5 March 1996 (not yet reported) para. 55.

[24] *Op. cit.* note 17, para. 41.

[25] Article 215 EC.

On the other hand, however, the *principle* of State liability for breaches of Community law was explicitly accepted more than 20 years ago, albeit subject to conditions governed exclusively by national law.[26]

More generally, the Court has been consistently emphasizing the importance of effective national remedies for breaches of EC law and has incrementally restricted the extent to which national procedural laws can fetter the enforcement of rights conferred by Community law. Initially it was merely held that, in the absence of Community rules, it is for the national legal order of each Member State to lay down the procedural rules for proceedings designed to ensure the protection of rights which individuals acquire through the direct effect of Community law provided that such rules are not less favourable than those governing the same right of action on an internal matter and those rules do not make it impossible in practice to exercise those rights.[27] In other words, national courts were not under any obligation to create new remedies. In *Simmenthal* the Court went significantly further by ruling that, if necessary, national courts must refuse to apply any conflicting provisions of national law, even if adopted subsequently.[28] Finally, a positive obligation to grant interim relief even where national law did not endow the court with the power to suspend the application of Acts of Parliament was construed in *Factortame*.[29] Earlier, in *von Colson and Kamann v Land Nordrhein-Westfalen*[30] and *Harz v Deutsche Tradax*, the Court ruled that Member States must adopt measures which ensured that the objective of the directive was achieved. If, as in the present case, a system of compensation was chosen then that compensation had to be adequate in relation to the damage sustained.

---

[26] Case 39/72, *Commission v Italy* [1973] ECR 101:
'... in the face of both a delay in the performance of an obligation and a definite refusal, a judgment of the Court under Articles 169 and 171 of the Treaty may be of substantive interest as establishing the basis of responsibility that a Member State may incur as a result of its default as regards other Member States, the Community or private parties.' (para. 11) Note also that the Court elaborated proposals regarding State liability in 1975 (EC Bulletin, supplement No. 9/75, p. 18).

[27] Case 33/76, *Comet*, [1976] ECR 1989.

[28] Case 106/77, *Simmenthal*, ECR 629.

[29] Case C–213/89 [1990] ECR I–2433. This rule could arguably already be distilled from case 13/68, *Salgoil*, [1968] ECR 661 and case 179/84, *Bozzetti*, [1985] ECR 2301 where the court stated:
'it is for the legal system of each Member State to decide which court has jurisdiction to hear disputes involving individual rights derived from Community law, *but at the same time the Member States are responsible for ensuring that those rights are effectively protected.*' (emphasis added)
See generally Schockweiler 1993 at p. 111.

[30] Case 14/83 [1984] ECR 1891.

Francovich, is therefore, remarkable not so much because it establishes the principle that Member States can be held liable for damages suffered by individuals caused by violations of Community law, but because it clarifies the legal basis for such liability. Hence, State liability for breaches of EC law is inherent in the Community legal order and the conditions for its applicability therefore governed by Community law and, although for the enforcement of this liability national procedural rules will still apply, even these procedural rules must comply with the general principles outlined above.

It is against this background, in conjunction with the Court's concern that EC law should be effectively and uniformly enforced, that the importance of the case for securing Member State compliance with EC environmental law should be appreciated.

1. State Liability for Breaches of EC Environmental Law: the Conditions

As already noted, the most significant aspect of the Court's judgment in *Francovich* is its inference from the autonomous character of the Community legal order that the conditions for State liability are governed by Community law. Simply put, this means that national legal systems which previously did not provide for a system of public authority liability or which made such liability subject to more restrictive conditions will now have to apply the system of liability introduced by the Court. Only the enforcement of the liability will be governed by national procedural laws and even those will have to comply with the general principles established by the Court.[31]

Under Article 215(2) EC the Court has developed the conditions for the non-contractual liability caused the institutions of the Community or by its servants in the performance of their duties. In *Brasserie du Pêcheur* the Court observed that the conditions under which the State may incur liability for damage caused to individuals by a breach of Community law cannot, in the absence of a particular justification, differ from those governing the liabiliy of the Community in like circumstances.[32] In essence, this means that the same strict approach towards the liability of the Community in the exercise of its legislative activities will in principle also apply to State

---

[31] See Ross 1993, who warns of the possible consequences if English courts are to choose to incorporate the judgment into the existing English system.

[32] Joined cases C-46/93 and C-58/93, *Brasserie du Pêcheur SA* and *Federal Republic of Germany* and between *The Queen* and *Secretary of State for Transport ex parte: Factortame Ltd and Others*, 5 March 1996 (not yet reported).

liability for legislative acts. This was underlined in *British Telecommuniations* where the Court, in respect of State liability for defective implementing acts, ruled:

> A restrictive approach to State liability is justified in such a situation, for the reasons already given by the Court to justify the strict approach to non-contractual liability of Community institutions or Member States where exercising legislative functions in areas covered by Community law where the institution or State has a wide discretion - in particular, the concern to ensure that the exercise of legislative functions is not hindered by the prospect of actions for damages whenever the general interest requires the institutions or Member States to adopt measures which may adversely affect individual interests.[33]

However, as the Court rightly observes, the national legislature does not systematically have a wide discretion when it acts in fields governed by Community law. In cases where the national legislature merely acts as an agent for the Community legislature in the framework of Article 189 EC the strict conditions applicable to liability of the Community will obviously not apply.

Following the Court's judgment in *Brasserie*[34] it is now clear that the same 3 conditions which govern State liability for breaches of directives also apply to State liability for breaches of provisions of primary Community law, *i.e.* the breach must be sufficiently serious, the rule of law infringed must be intended to confer rights on individuals, (breach of a fundamental Community obligation) and there must be a direct causal link between the breach of the obligation resting on the State and the damage sustained by the injured parties.

A final point that should be raised before turning to an examination of the three conditions formulated by the Court in the light of the numerous provisions of EC environmental law relates to the way in which the breach should be established. In *Francovich*, Italy's failure to transpose the directive was beyond doubt given the Court's earlier judgment to that effect in case 22/89.[35] The question arises whether the availability of the *Francovich* remedy is conditional upon such a prior judgment pursuant to Article 169 EC, however. In *Brasserie* the Bundesgerichtshof had asked whether the damage for which reparation may be awarded extends to harm sustained before a judgment is delivered by the Court finding that an infringement has been committed. The Court observed in this regard that, were the obligation of the Member State concerned to make reparation to be confined to loss or damage sustained after delivery of a judgment of the

---

[33] Case C-392/93, *Tje Queen* and *HM Treasury ex parte: British Telecommunications plc*, 26 March 1996 (not yet reported) para. 40

[34] *Op. cit.* para. 51.

[35] Note 19 supra.

Court finding the infringement in question, that would amount to calling into question the right of reparation conferred by the Community legal order.[36] The answer, therefore, is in the negative. A national court may, preferably after having referred a question as to the interpretation of a provision of an environmental directive, rule on the compatibility of national laws with that directive.[37] Evidently, a prior judgment under Article 169 EC is of great assistance to individuals seeking to enforce their rights and the Commission ought to bear this in mind in the use of their discretion. Advocates General and the Commission in a number of recent environmental cases have acknowledged this interaction between the infringement procedure and the *Francovich* remedy.[38]

a. Conditions 1 and 2: the result prescribed by the directive entails the grant of rights to individuals, the extent of which follows from the wording of the directive

Since the principle of State liability for breaches of Community law was justified by virtue of the fact that EC law is intended to create rights for individuals,[39] it seems logical that such liability can arise only if the provision of Community law breached entails the grant of rights to individuals. The first requirement hence bears some resemblance with what is sometimes referred to as the *Schutznorm* in the civil law tradition; for liability to arise it must be shown that the protection of those rights belongs to the objectives of the norm breached.

Although, this condition may prove a serious obstacle for individuals seeking reparation for harm suffered as a result of Member States' failure to adhere to environmental directives, in many ways it is still less restrictive

---

[36] *Op. cit.* para. 94.

[37] National courts were required to do this, for example in case 172/82, *Inter Huiles*, [1983] ECR 575, case 295/82, *Rhône Alpe Huiles*, [1984] ECR 575, case 240/83, *ABDHU*, [1985] ECR 531 (all waste oils) and case 169/89, *Gourmetterie van den Burg* (wild birds). See also Schockweiler 1993 at p. 116.

[38] Thus, in case C–237/90, *Commission v Federal Republic of Germany* [1992] ECR I–5973, when the Court enquired whether the Commission wished to maintain its complaint in respect of an infringement which had been rectified in the course of the proceedings the Commission responded:
'The Commission considers that (...) in view of a possible claim for damages, it would be useful if the Court of Justice would establish as a point of law that the *Trinkwasserverordnung* was not compatible with the directive, at least in its version prior to 1.1.1991 (...)'
Advocate General Lenz in Case C–337/89, *Commission v United Kingdom of Great Britain and Northern Ireland*, [1992] ECR I–6103, suggested that the ruling to the effect that the United Kingdom had failed to fulfil the obligations arising out of the drinking water directive could provide a basis for actions for damages.

[39] Para. 28 of the judgment.

than the conditions elaborated for the direct effect of environmental directives which after all must be shown to be precise and unconditional.[40] Hence in *Francovich* the applicants failed to negotiate the obstacle posed by the conditions for direct effect, but were successful in their bid to hold the State liable for the damage suffered. Indeed, it is widely argued that the most important rationale's behind the Court's acceptance of State liability for breaches of EC law was to compensate for some of the problems caused by the fact that it is often impossible for individuals to invoke directives, if only because the Court has denied their horizontal effect.[41] If this is so, it may be expected that the Court will interpret this condition in this light.

The crucial question, for the purpose of the usefulness of the *Francovich* remedy in the sphere of the environment, appears to be how 'environmental rights' should legally manifest themselves. Schockweiler argues that:

> The requirement that [the provision breached] should confer rights means that the Court excludes State liability or at least does not require such liability for breaches of mere *interests* protected by directives as for example is the case with numerous environmental directives.[42]

Against this interpretation one might invoke cases C–131/88[43] and C–361/88,[44] where the Court in unambiguous terms accepted that Directive 80/68[45] (on dangerous substances in groundwater!) and Directive 80/779 on sulphur dioxide and suspended particles in air[46] create rights for individuals.[47] Similarly the directive on the quality of drinking water has been regarded, at least by AG Lenz, as conferring rights upon individuals which they may enforce by way of an action for damages against the State.[48]

Schockweiler's restrictive interpretation of the first condition is probably a reflection of the common and legitimate concern that 'if every *prima facie* breach of Community law by a Member State which occasioned harm to an individual were to lead directly to a finding in damages, the amount of damages paid out would be astronomical, with serious consequences for the

---

[40] This is the simplified test the Court applied in case C–236/92, *op. cit.* note 12.

[41] Schockweiler 1993 p. 113 *et seq*; Steiner 1992 pp. 3–22.

[42] Schockweiler 1993 p. 119 (my translation and my emphasis).

[43] Case C–131/88, *Commission v Germany*, [1991] I ECR 825.

[44] Case C–361/88, *Commision v Germany*, [1991] I ECR 2567.

[45] OJ 1980 No. L 20.

[46] OJ 1980 No. L 229.

[47] Schockweiler counters this argument by remarking *op. cit.* p. 115:
'In this regard it must be observed that the Francovich case merely lays down minimum standards and does not rule out national provisions embracing more stringent liability regimes.'

[48] Note 37 supra.

ability of governments to intervene in the running of society.'[49] It is difficult to see how the extension of public authority liability to breaches of EC law could have this effect. As to the extent of reparation, in *Brasserie* the Court repeated its settled case law to the effect that in the absence of relevant Community provisions, it is for the domestic legal systems of each Member State to set criteria for determining the extent of reparation subject to the conditions that those criteria must not be less favourable than those applying to similar claims based on domestic law and must not be such as in practice to make it impossible or excessively difficult to obtain reparation.[50] In particular, the injured party will normally have to show reasonable diligence in limiting the extent of the loss or damage, or risk having to bear the damage himself.[51] If, however, this restrictive interpretation were to prevail, what kind of environmental rights could be protected by means of the *Francovich* remedy?

A first example, in the present writer's opinion, would be Article 4(1) of Directive 85/337 on environmental impact assessment providing that projects of the classes listed in Annex I shall be made subject to an environmental impact assessment.[52] The right of individuals to participate in the formulations of direct concern to their environment is has been clearly recognized outside as well as within the Community.[53] Similar observations apply to Directive 90/313 on freedom of access to information.[54] Article 4 already establishes that persons who consider that their request for information has been unreasonably refused or ignored, or has been inadequately answered by a public authority, may seek judicial or administrative review. Both these directives are intended to endow individuals with a right to participate in the formulation of decisions of

---

[49] Coppel 1993 at p. 27.

[50] *Op. cit.* para. 83.

[51] Joined cases C-104/89 and C-3/90, *Mulder and Others v Council and Commission,* [1992] ECR I-3061, para. 33.

[52] OJ 1985 No. L 175.

[53] Principle 23 of the World Charter for Nature, for example provides: 'All persons in accordance with their national legislation, shall have the opportunity to participate, individual or with others, in the formulation of decisions of direct concern to their environment, and shall have access to means of redress when their environment has suffered damage or degradation.' (*Op. cit.* note 5)
See also Rio Declaration Principle 10 and the Fifth Environmental Action Programme proclaiming: 'Individuals and public interest groups should have practicable access to the Courts in order to ensure that their legitimate interests are protected and that prescribed environmental measures are effectively enforced and illegal practices stopped.'
See generally Kiss and Shelton p. 21 *et seq.*

[54] OJ 1990 No. L 158.

direct concern to their environment whilst the extent of the right directly follows from the directives in question.

A second category of directives clearly creating rights rather than interests for individuals consists of those which are primarily concerned with the protection of human health. An example can be found in Directive 87/217.[55] Article 1 of this directive provides:

> The objective of this directive is to lay down measures and to supplement provisions already in force, with a view to preventing and reducing pollution by asbestos in the interests of the protection of human health and the environment.

Other examples in this category are Directive 80/779 on air quality limit values and guide values for sulphur dioxide and suspended particulates,[56] Directive 75/440 on the quality of surface water intended for the abstraction of drinking water[57] Directive 90/219 on the contained use of genetically modified micro-organisms[58] and Directive 90/220 on the deliberate release of genetically modified organisms.[59] In all these cases, the directives have established rights for individuals for their health to be protected against the adverse effects of certain types of pollution by creating a corresponding obligation for the State to take certain circumscribed steps.

Another class of environmental directives creating rights for individuals are those laying down requirements which, if satisfied, are intended to guarantee the free movement of those products throughout the internal market. An example would be Directive 70/220 on emissions from motor vehicles[60] and Directive 67/548 on the classification, packaging and labelling of dangerous substances.[61] If a private party were to suffer

---

[55] OJ 1987 No. L 85.

[56] Under Article 3 of this directive Member States are obliged to take appropriate measures to ensure that as from 1 April 1993 the concentrations of sulphur dioxide and suspended particulates in the atmosphere are not greater than the limit values given in Annex I. Limit values are set, in particular, to protect human health (Article 2).

[57] OJ 1975 No. L 194. The primary objective of this directive is clearly the protection of human health. Article 8(d), for example provides:
'In no case may the exceptions provided for in the first subparagraph disregard the requirements of public health.'

[58] OJ 1990 No. L 117.

[59] *Ibid.*

[60] OJ 1970 No. L 76. Article 2 of this directive provides:
'No Member States may refuse to grant EEC type-approval or national type-approval of a vehicle on grounds relating to air pollution by gases from positive ignition engines of motor vehicles (...) where that vehicle satisfies the requirements contained in Annexes ...'

[61] See case 278/85, *Commission v Denmark*, [1987] ECR 4609, where the Court ruled that the directive pursued total harmonization and that Member States were barred from introducing more stringent requirements.

damage or loss as a result of a Member State's non implementation of such product standards it could therefore invoke the principle of State liability.

From this brief sketch it appears that, even if the Court were to adopt a more restrictive interpretation of the concept 'environmental right' than suggested in its previous case law under Article 169, there are still many environmental directives where the principle could be invoked.

The extent to which this conclusion is correct, however, depends also on the relationship between the doctrine of direct effect, and the possibility to hold the State liable for their breach. Put differently, the question must be asked whether individuals can invoke the liability of the State also when a provision is directly effective, or whether the *Francovich* remedy should only be attributed a subsidiary role. There is support for the view that the remedy is intended to function as an additional safety net, only applicable in cases where individuals cannot rely on the direct effect of the provisions.[62] In this view, the following hierarchy of remedies emerges. Individuals can rely on the direct effect of provisions of EC environmental law only if these are not faithfully or timely transposed into the national legal order. If a provision lacks direct effect, national courts are under a duty to interpret their provisions in the light of the wording and the purpose of the directive in order to achieve the result pursued by the latter and thereby comply with the third paragraph of Article 189 of the Treaty.[63] Only if a directive does not produce direct effect may individuals rely on the *Francovich* formula to enforce their rights.

Although this pyramid has its conceptual charms and moreover the advantage of acting as a safety-valve against over-use of the *Francovich* formula, its drawbacks cannot be ignored. If, for example, an individual suffers loss or injury attributable to a breach of a water directive creating rights for individuals, that individual cannot effectively enforce his rights by relying directly on the limit values or quality objectives breached. It is even conceivable that individuals suffer loss precisely because they have adhered to directly effective directives, rather than national laws incompatible with those provisions.[64] Indeed, in *Brasserie* the Court categorically rejected the

---

[62] See Schockweiler 1993 at p. 119, similarly Coppel 1993 at p. 28. Seemingly contra Bebr 1992 at p. 576 who argues that rights for individuals:

' ... are either explicitly formally granted, as in the given instance, or deduced from a provision having direct effect. In both instances, their breach may justify an action in damages.'

[63] Case C–106/89, *Marleasing v Comercial Internacional de Alimentación*, [1990] ECR I–4135.

[64] This could occur under circumstances similar to those in case 148/78, *Pubblico Ministero v Ratti*, [1979] ECR 1629, for example because by so doing an undertaking

argument put forward by the German, Irish and Netherlands Governments that Member States are required to make good to loss or damage caused to individuals only where the provisions breached are not directly effective. It emphasized that it had consistently held that the right of individuals to rely on the directly effective provisions of the Treaty before national courts is only a minimum guarantee and is not sufficient in itself to ensure the full and complete implementation of the Treaty. Direct effect, it added, could not in every case secure for individuals the benefit of the rights conferred on them by Community law and, in particular, avoid their sustaining damage as a result of a breach of Community law attributable to a Member State.[65] In conclusion, therefore, the *Francovich* remedy is also available in cases where individuals cannot effectively enforce their rights by relying on directly effective provisions of Community law.

b. Condition 3: a causal link between the breach of the State's obligations and the damage suffered by the persons affected.

As far as causality is concerned, this requirement is hardly controversial. Some observations are important in this context, however.

In the first place, it is useful to bear in mind the Court's case law under Article 169 and the way in which it has dealt with Member States' justifications for their failure to implement environmental directives. Thus, the argument that the deadline for implementation agreed upon in the Council were unrealistic has been consistently rejected,[66] as has been the claim that the exact scope of an environmental directive was unclear.[67] Unforeseen circumstances such as governmental crises,[68] or unexpected environmental problems requiring priority treatment at the expense of the implementation of EC environmental directives[69] have all been raised to no avail. It can therefore be expected that the Court will deal with such defences in the context of actions for damages against the Member States. As has already been noted, Member States are liable if the three conditions formulated by the Court have been fulfilled and fault or negligence need not be shown.

A second observation relates to the meaning of the notion 'State'. As pointed out by Bebr, from an examination of the Court's jurisprudence it

---

suffers a competitive disadvantage as compared to other undertakings adhering to the provisions of national law.

[65] *Op. cit.* note 32, para. 20.

[66] See for example case 301/81, *Commission v Belgium*, [1983] ECR 467 (directive 77/80).

[67] Case 301/81, *ibid.*

[68] Case 52/75, *Commission v Italy*, [1976] ECR 277.

[69] Case 291/84, *Commission v Netherlands*, [1987] ECR 3483 (directive 80/68).

appears that this concept encompasses municipalities, local authorities and professional societies entrusted with public functions.[70] One might even argue that the proper analogy is with case 248/81 (*Buy Irish*) which would suggest liability of private bodies whose activities are subject to direct or indirect governmental control.[71] If the Court were to adopt this interpretation this would mean, for example, that the privatized water companies could be held liable for breaches of the drinking water directive.

III CONCLUSION

Despite the many uncertainties surrounding the interpretation of the *Francovich* judgment, it is not unrealistic to predict that Member States may soon find themselves liable for damages caused by non-implementation of EC environmental directives. The mere possibility of individuals bringing such cases before their national courts may in itself work as a stimulus for Member States to faithfully respect environmental obligations.

Since Member States now *must* create a system of public authority liability for breaches of EC environmental directives whereas no such obligation exists for breaches of laws which are purely internal to the Member States concerned, the curious situation is now created that it may be easier to enforce EC environmental laws than national environmental laws. As the environment should be regarded as indivisible, the time may now have arrived to consider the adoption of harmonizing legislation to address this problem. Harmonization at the same time would ensure that the impact of *Francovich*, at least in so far as the enforcement of EC environmental law is concerned, would be more uniform in all Member States.

---

[70] Bebr 1992 at p. 578.

[71] Case 249/81, *Commission v Ireland*, [1982] ECR 4005, as argued by Coppel 1993 p. 25.

8. *Locus standi*, Community Law and the Case for Harmonization

Eckard Rehbinder

I INTRODUCTION: A SURVEY OF THE DEVELOP-
MENT OF THE LAW OF ENVIRONMENTAL STANDING
IN THE MEMBER STATES

In the last two decades throughout the European Community advocates of
environmental concerns have to an ever increasing extent been granted
access to courts or administrative tribunals in order to control the proper
implementation, application and enforcement of environmental laws.[1] The
broadening of locus standi, or – in the American terminology – standing,
particularly relates to formally organized environmental associations; to a
lesser degree, informal, ad hoc environmental groups as well as individuals
have been accorded standing.

The similarity of this development is amazing because the national
systems of judicial review of administrative action are quite diverse.[2] In
some Member States such as France and Belgium, judicial review of
administrative action is primarily perceived as a means of controlling the
proper functioning of the administration in the public interest (objective
review). Judicial review of administrative action is a constituent part of the
rule of law whereby all state organs must observe the legal order. The
function of standing is then to select suitable plaintiffs and thereby ration
scarce judicial resources. Consequently, the administrative tribunals have no
reason to establish insurmountable barriers to access of environmental
advocates to judicial review. The standing criteria tend to be liberal,

---

[1] For a survey of this development see Winkelmann 1992; Führ et al., 1992 pp. 13–29;
Bizer et al., 1990 pp. 40–50.

[2] See Auby & Fromont 1971 pp. 455–6.

enabling environmental associations as well as individuals affected by administrative action or inaction in a diffuse fashion to challenge the legality of this action or inaction.

In other Member States, judicial review of administrative action primarily serves to protect subjective rights or legally protected interests of individuals (subjective review). These jurisdictions tend to limit standing to individuals who have suffered some individualized harm as a consequence of administrative action or inaction. Association suits in a representative function – the association representing members who would have standing as individuals – may be allowed or conversely, following a radically individualistic concept of right or interest, be disallowed. Examples of fairly divergent approaches to association standing in this group of countries are the Netherlands, Denmark and Italy on the one hand, Germany and Spain on the other.

Finally, there are Member States such as England that possess a mixed system of judicial review of administrative action – both objective and subjective depending on the kind of remedy; standing criteria may vary accordingly.

In the latter two groups of Member States, the modern judicial or legislative development has led to a considerable broadening of standing for environmental advocates, especially environmental associations.

One rationale underlying this development is the paradigm of diffuse interests which posits that all citizens or at least all citizens in a region are individually affected by administrative action or inaction relating to the environment, although in a diffuse, non-particularized fashion.[3] This concept negates the traditional distinction between private and public interest, maintaining that the public interest in environmental protection is no more than the sum of the individual interests of all citizens. This enables the judiciary or legislature to accord environmental standing to everybody, such as in the Netherlands or Ireland, or to recognize association standing in a representative capacity, such as in Italy.

Another rationale, which cannot always be clearly separated from the former, is the paradigm of 'private attorney general'.[4] While maintaining the paramountcy of subjective judicial review of administrative action, one recognizes that there is a specific need for environmental watchdogs which, by bringing court actions, control the proper functioning of the administration in the field of environmental protection and thereby ensure the proper implementation, application and enforcement of environmental law. This is particularly the case in Germany where 11 out of 16 Länder,

---

[3] See Cappelletti 1989 pp. 25–8, 272–8.

[4] *Ibid.* pp. 272–4, 283–99.

relying on this idea, have introduced a right of action for associations in the field of protection of nature and landscape. Under federal law, the jurisprudence of the Federal Administrative Court recognizes association standing for the annulment of administrative decisions rendered in violation of participation rights of these associations.[5] Denmark and – subject to some qualification – also England, in the light of some recent High Court decisions,[6] present other examples of public interest standing.

Finally – and overlapping with the two former rationales – the modern trend towards granting more or less extensive rights of action to environmental advocates can be explained by the erosion of the traditional liberal concept of separation of state and society and of the state-oriented understanding of democracy. There is a growing acceptance of a concept of a civil society in which environmental advocates are no longer considered as undesirable intermeddlers but as citizens who exercise their democratic rights.[7]

However the existence of a definite tendency towards broadening environmental standing does not mean that there is a true convergence throughout the European Community or that, looking at the Community as a whole, a satisfactory level of judicial protection of environmental interests has already been achieved. Therefore it is worthwhile reflecting on the possible Community role in this field. The question is whether there is a need for harmonization of the law of the Member States relating to environmental standing, and, if this question is answered in the affirmative, what should be the scope and extent of such harmonization.

Community involvement could pursue two quite different objectives:
- Harmonization could be a procedural means of ensuring the proper implementation, application and enforcement of substantive provisions of Community environmental directives (ancillary to Community law),
- beyond that, it could set a procedural framework for preventive action for the protection of the environment in the Member States by strengthening implementation, application and enforcement of the Member States' environmental law in non-harmonized areas (independent harmonization).[8]

---

5 BVerwGE 87, 63.
6 *Rex v Swale Borough Council and Medway Port Authority ex parte The Royal Society for the Protection of Birds*, [1991] JEL 135 (Q.B. 1990); *R v Poole Borough Council ex parte Beebee*, [1991] JEL 293 (Q.B. 1990); especially *R v HMIP and MAFP ex parte Greenpeace*, The Independent 30/9/93 (Q.B. 1993); cf. Schiemann 1990 pp. 342–53.
7 See Feldmann 1992 pp. 44–72; Rehbinder, Burgbacher & Knieper 1972 pp. 134–40.
8 This distinction is not made by Führ et al., 1994.

II ENVIRONMENTAL STANDING AS A MEANS OF ENSURING THE IMPLEMENTATION, APPLICATION AND ENFORCEMENT OF COMMUNITY ENVIRONMENTAL LAW IN THE MEMBER STATES

1. Implementation Problems of Community Environmental Law

The Community legal system is based on the premise that, while the Community organs primarily have a legislative function and are empowered to adopt regulations and directives, it is the task of the Commission to supervize compliance by the Member States with Community law. The Member States are in principle exclusively competent for implementing, applying and enforcing Community law. This is especially true of directives which play a central role in the field of environmental protection. The Member States are obliged to promptly and fully incorporate Community directives into the national legal system, adopt the necessary implementing regulations and administrative rules, organize the relevant administrative agencies, apply the harmonized provisions on the ground and enforce them in case of non-compliance. It is well established that in all Member States there is a considerable implementation and enforcement deficit with respect to environmental directives, although its extent varies from Member State to Member State and from directive to directive.[9] The annual reports of the Commission about the control of the application of Community law in the Member States,[10] which among others list the number of infringement proceedings instituted against Member States, give a first impression of this endemic feature of Community environmental law. However, they only indicate the tip of an iceberg. The Commission, in fulfilling its task set forth under Articles 155 and 169 of the Treaty to monitor and enforce compliance by the Member States with Community environmental directives, has for obvious reasons concentrated on formal implementation, i.e. transposition of directives into national law and compliance with formal reporting and other procedural obligations, while infringement proceedings tackling practical implementation in the broad sense have been extremely rare.

---

[9] See, e.g., House of Lords Select Committee on the European Communities, Implementation and Enforcement of Environmental Legislation; European Parliament, Commission on Environment, Public Health and Consumer Protection on Implementation of the Environmental Law of the European Community, PE 152.144 final (6 January 1992); Meier Reitzes 1992; Smith & Hunter 1992 pp. 10112–14.

[10] See the Eleventh Annual Report of the Commission on the Implementation of Community Law, OJ 1994 No. C 54 p. 1.

Although the number of complaints relating to practical implementation is high and tends to increase year-by-year, there are very few cases where the Commission has instituted formal infringement proceedings against misapplication of Community environmental directives on the ground. An example is the *Leybucht Dykes* case[11] where the issue was whether Germany, in authorizing the construction of a dyke that encroached upon wetlands protected under the bird directive, had violated that directive. Other examples concern the quality of drinking water. To my knowledge, the Commission has never tackled cases of lack of, or insufficient, organization of environmental agencies or lack of enforcement of Community environmental law against polluters.

2. Community Remedies

Under the EC Treaty, there are Community remedies that are specifically designed to tackle violations by Member States of the obligation to implement and enforce Community directives, including environmental directives. In the first place, this is the infringement procedure laid down in Article 169 EC. In the second place, the reference procedure laid down in Article 177 EC has, at least objectively, the function of remedying violations of Community environmental law. Although it does not fully reach administrative implementation and enforcement because the application of harmonized environmental law to the facts of a particular case is normally beyond the scope of Community jurisdiction, in practice, the uncertain delimitation between interpretation of Community law and its application allows the European Court of Justice to exercise a considerable influence on application of Community law on the ground.

Since 1978, the Commission has, subject to some exceptions, routinely instituted infringement proceedings wherever it had sufficient information about deficient formal implementation of an environmental directive, while in the field of practical implementation political judgment still seems to play some role. Moreover, the establishment of an informal complaint procedure enables all Community citizens, including environmental organizations, to bring alleged infringements to the attention of the Commission.[12] However, the growing number of infringement proceedings in environmental matters and the limited capacity of the Commission Directorate General XI for policing complaints and gathering information about infringements on the ground, which have resulted in an average

---

[11] Case C–57/89, *Commission v Federal Republic of Germany*, [1991] ECR I–883.

[12] Communication of the Commission, OJ 1989 No. C 26 p. 6; House of Lords, *op. cit.* note 9, pp. 30–1.

duration of infringement proceedings of more than four years, demonstrate the inherent limitations of the infringement procedure. In addition, due to the quasi-political character of the procedure that exposes the Member States to a sort of public censure by the European Court of Justice, there also is a certain acceptance problem. Without a substantial degree of decentralization of institutions that are designed to, or function as, guardians of the Community interest in compliance, the implementation and enforcement deficit in Community environmental law is bound to remain endemic.

3. The Need for Decentralization of Supervisory Powers

This focuses attention on strengthening national institutions that could handle infringements themselves and, only where necessary, trigger the reference procedure under Article 177 EC Treaty. The limitations of the procedure of incidental control of interpretation of Community law are that access to the procedure is conditional on access to the national courts and, as stated, the procedure does not fully reach administrative implementation and enforcement. Harmonization of standing rules would contribute to overcoming the first of these limitations and beyond, concentrate litigation for non-compliance on the national judicial systems. In order to avoid overloading the national court system and take advantage of administrative routine, one could create independent complaint boards which must be addressed before instituting court proceedings. Environmental advocates, especially environmental associations, who have broad access to national complaint boards and tribunals could vindicate the Community interest in adequate implementation, application and enforcement of Community environmental law there and ultimately, where necessary and to the extent possible, before the European Court of Justice in the reference procedure.[13] Such standing rights have the desirable result that they would to a certain degree depoliticize infringements of Community environmental law; as long as national complaint boards and tribunals are exclusively involved there is no direct confrontation between a Community organ and the relevant Member State. Where deemed necessary or expedient, the Commission could still institute infringement proceedings which are not even precluded

---

[13] Stein & Vining 1976 p. 241; Rehbinder & Stewart 1985 pp. 337–41; Führ et al., 1992; Führ et al., 1994; Koppen & Ladeur 1991 p. 45; Stewart 1992 pp. 30–6; Select Committee, *op. cit.* note 9, No. 159

where the case has already been referred to the European Court under Article 177 EC.[14]

Rights of action of environmental advocates, in particular environmental associations, would remove or at least mitigate the usual disequilibrium in the political and administrative process between societal forces that militate against environmental protection and hence against application of Community environmental law and those that defend these interests.[15] The establishment of procedural parity of environmental with economic, development- and employment-oriented interests would also – and above all – have a preventive effect in that it would strengthen the position of environmental advocates in administrative proceedings and thereby indirectly improve participation. This will in turn lead to better compliance with Community environmental law by public authorities. Due to their familiarity with local and regional conditions and the information input from members of the public and membership organizations, environmental advocates would focus on deficient application and enforcement of Community environmental law on the ground where the implementation deficit arguably is greatest thereby ensuring a higher degree of overall compliance with Community law.

On the other hand, one should also acknowledge the inherent limitations of a primarily court-based model of remedying the implementation and enforcement deficit in Community environmental law. Social science research on implementation teaches us that the reasons for implementation deficits are quite varied.[16] Deficiencies of the normative program, the interest structure of a given society, the procedural position of actors, the organization and budgeting of environmental agencies, the attitudes of administrators and the general political-administrative culture of a given country play a role. It is clear that not all of these factors can be influenced by judicial review of administrative action or inaction and that judicial review may to some extent merely have a symbolic function.[17] Nevertheless access to courts and administrative tribunals constitutes an important contribution to reducing the implementation and enforcement deficit, the more so since environmental litigation, beyond the legal force of court judgments, also has a mobilizing effect, strengthens the environmental movement and increases public awareness of environmental problems.

---

[14] European Court of Justice, case 26/62, *Van Gend*, [1963] ECR 1; case 31/61, *Export rebates case*, [1970] ECR 25, at pp. 33–4
[15] Rehbinder, Burgbacher & Knieper 1972 pp. 134–40; Führ et al., 1994 p. 4.
[16] Mayntz 1983a; Mayntz 1983b; Mayntz 1988.
[17] Snyder 1993 pp. 52–3.

4. Precedents in Community Law

I think that the more recent legal development in the Community provides strong arguments in favour of harmonization of the law of standing for the sake of enforcing envir onmental directives. First of all, the expanding doctrine of direct effect of directives is based on the premise that Member States' citizens should act as guardians of Community law.[18] It is true that direct effect requires the finding of a subjective element, namely that the provision of the directive in question, by its very nature, is amenable to conferring rights on individuals. However, the understanding of the notion of right is broad. Recent European Court decisions in related areas support this view. In the infringement cases concerning national incorporation of Community environmental standards by administrative rules,[19] the Court seems to recognize an implicit Community right of action for the enforcement of directives already transposed. The *Francovich*[20] case practically further extends the direct effect doctrine by establishing state compensation obligations for non-compliance even in the absence of a direct effect in the strict sense (e.g. 'horizontal' directives or lack of precise and unconditional provisions that are designed to create rights for Community citizens). The rationale underlying these clearly interrelated, although still evolving doctrines is not the protection of subjective rights but, rather, to ensure the proper implementation of Community law by the Member States; consequently, the concept of right arguably is close to that of sufficient interest as used in national jurisdictions that recognize objective judicial review of administrative action.

Secondly, while it is true that the enforcement of Community environmental law is in principle entrusted to the Member States subject to the domestic administrative and civil procedure law, there are some minimum standards set forth by Community law. These minimum requirements have been stiffened in the recent jurisprudence of the European Court of Justice. The *Rewe* case[21] still showed great respect for national procedural law holding that the Member States are in principle free to apply their domestic administrative and civil procedural law, provided it does not discriminate against foreigners, is not unreasonable and does not entirely preclude judicial review. However, the more recent decisions of the

---

[18] Timmermans 1979 pp. 533–55; Mathijsen 1990 pp. 113–14, 307–10.

[19] Case 131/88, *Commission v Federal Republic of Germany*, [1991] ECR I–825; case C–59/89, *Commission v Federal Republic of Germany*, [1991] ECR I–2607; case 361/88, *Commission v Federal Republic of Germany*, [1991] ECR I–2567; cases C–13, 14 and 64/90, *Commission v French Republic*, [1991] ECR I–4339.

[20] Cases C–6 and 9/90, *Francovich*, [1991] ECR I–5357.

[21] Case 158/80, *Rewe v Hauptzollamt Kiel*, [1981] ECR 1805.

European Court, especially in the cases *Johnston*[22] and *Factortame*,[23] suggest that there is a Community minimum standard of providing effective judicial review including interim injunctive relief against alleged misapplication of Community law, at least where it has direct effect.

I do not conclude from these judgments that primary Community law already mandates the introduction of rights of action for environmental advocates, especially environmental associations, but it provides a strong political argument in favour of harmonization of national rules relating to standing in order to ensure the proper implementation, application and enforcement of Community environmental directives.

The Commission proposal on liability for waste,[24] taken together with the substantive waste disposal directives, is based on the same premise in calling for association standing for the compensation of environmental damage. I will show below that this proposal has its deficiencies because it does not sufficiently consider the role of public authorities in the restoration of environmental damage. However, its general approach, namely that environmental associations are needed as watchdogs for compliance with Community law, is unaffected by this deficiency and generally reasonable. The serious nature of the implementation deficit of Community environmental law even justifies considerable encroachments on national procedural law in order to ensure a minimum of equal implementation, application and enforcement of the environmental directives throughout the Community. Since harmonization is ancillary to substantive harmonization, its function being to effectuate existing directives, counter arguments based on the principle of subsidiarity are less pertinent. The Fifth Environmental Action Programme[25] expressly calls for a greater role of the public in order to overcome the implementation deficit. Given the modern tendency in most Member States towards recognizing association standing, it would make sense to impose a minimum standard of effective judicial review for the sake of enforcing Community environmental law.

5. Minimum Harmonization

The subsidiarity principle is more relevant as regards the concretization of this minimum standard. Thus, the Member States could be empowered to

---

[22] Case 222/84, *Johnston*, [1986] ECR 1651.

[23] Case C–213/89, *R v Secretary of State for Transport, ex parte Factortame Ltd. and others*, [1990] ECR I–2433; see also cases 143/88 and 92/89, *Zuckerfabrik Süddithmarschen v Hauptzollamt Kiel*, [1991] ECR I–415.

[24] Amended Proposal for a Directive on civil liability for damage caused by waste, OJ 1991 No. C 192.

[25] COM (92) 23 Final, sections 3.2, 3.3 and 9.

determine the general prerequisites for conferring standing on environmental associations. In some Member States, the aversion against self-
appointed guardians of the public interest or, more generally, concern about
the legitimation of environmental associations for acting as advocates of the
public interest has led to the introduction of formalized authorization
(recognition) procedures for environmental associations to be granted standing. For a somewhat restrictive example, Germany requires that
environmental associations at least be regional, have no economic interest
in protecting nature, ensure a proper fulfilment of their public interest
functions, considering the kind and extent of their past activities, the kind
and number of members and their financial resources, be declared tax-
exempt for pursuing the public interest, and allow access to everybody who
supports the objectives of the association.[26] In other States, the judge
reserves upon himself the right to reject an association that, in a particular
case, is not deemed to be an appropriate plaintiff. Moreover, in many
countries the association must to the extent possible have participated in the
previous administrative proceedings and/or exhausted administrative
remedies. These national procedural prerequisites for granting standing
could be retained, provided they are not excessively restrictive. Conversely,
Member States should be left the freedom to go beyond the Community
minimum and also confer public interest standing on individuals.

III INDEPENDENT HARMONIZATION OF THE NATIONAL LAW RELATING TO STANDING AS A PREVENTIVE MEANS OF STRENGTHENING THE IMPLEMENTATION AND ENFORCEMENT OF NATIONAL ENVIRONMENTAL LAW

1. Need for Independent Harmonization?

Harmonization of national laws relating to environmental standing does not
need to be limited to the enforcement of Community environmental
directives. It could also aim at generally strengthening the implementation
and enforcement of the autonomous body of domestic environmental law.
Such harmonization, which one could denote as 'independent' – as opposed
to 'ancillary' – harmonization, raises more touchy political as well as legal
issues. By requiring Member States to broaden access to domestic courts

---

[26] S. 29(2) Federal Act on Protection of Nature and Landscape (Bundesnaturschutz-
gesetz), (1987) Bundesgesetzblatt I p. 889.

and administrative tribunals, Community law could make a quite important contribution to reducing the implementation and enforcement deficit that exists to a larger or lesser degree in all Member States and thereby improve the level of environmental protection in the Member States. In this sense, harmonization of the rules relating to standing is a procedural expression of the precautionary principle set forth in Article 130r EC Treaty. The basic assumptions underlying the modern tendency in the Member States to extend standing to environmental advocates, especially environmental associations, have already been stated. They are also valid for harmonization by the Community.

However, compared with the wide range of rationales that can be sustained for broadening access of environmental advocates to judicial review of administrative action or inaction in the national context, the case for harmonization rests on a relatively small basis. In particular, the concept of diffuse interests, the democratic argument for environmental standing as well as the rule-of-law rationale are outside the reach of the Community. It is not the task of the Community to protect diffuse interests of the citizens of the Member States in non-harmonized areas of environmental regulation; the Community is not called upon to improve the democratic process in the Member States nor has it any say in the definition of the democratic principle as regards domestic matters; finally, the integrity of the legal order in the Member States as such is in principle their own responsibility. Rather, the Community would have to rely exclusively on means-ends-rationality. It would have to conceive harmonization of the national standing rules as a procedural instrument of strengthening, directly or indirectly, the implementation, application and enforcement of domestic environmental law in the Member States by ensuring parity of environmental groups with other interest groups in the political and administrative process and enabling them to initiate judicial review where necessary. Of course, this rationale exposes the instrument chosen compared to alternatives such as parliamentary controls, administrative review and oversight by ombudspersons.

Even if one recognizes the relative weakness of the case for independent harmonization of national rules relating to environmental standing, it is interesting to note that such harmonization is in line with the more recent tendency in Community environmental law to supplement traditional environmental regulation (command-and-control regulation) by soft instruments, involving all sectors of society, i.e. the potential polluters as well as environmental associations and the public at large, in order to improve the degree of protection and add precautionary elements. Directives or regulations so diverse as those concerning environmental impact assessment, public access to environmental information, eco-label, eco-audit and the proposal in the field of environmental liability[27] are an expression of this new paradigm of Community environmental law.

2. Subsidiarity and Independent Harmonization

One problem is that in the past, the Community was very reluctant to legislate in the field of administrative procedure, even in harmonized areas. Although the Community possesses legislative competence under Article 130r EC, the new principle of subsidiarity provides strong arguments against any Community activity in the field of administrative procedure. The subsidiarity principle mandates legislative restraint by the Community. It shall only act where the objectives of the measures envisaged cannot sufficiently be achieved at the level of the Member States and therefore, because of their extent and effects, can better be achieved at Community level. In applying this principle, beyond a mere result-oriented comparison of the relevant measures, a balancing of Community and Member State interests is necessary. Unreasonable encroachments on national legal and administrative systems must be avoided.[28] The rules relating to standing are deeply imbedded in the respective domestic system of judicial review, they are an expression of basic constitutional concepts and function in the framework of domestic political-administrative and social cultures. Any Community intervention, even if limited to setting minimum standards, would result in a considerable degree of distortion of the established pattern of judicial review of administrative action in the Member States.

On the other hand, there already are some precedents of Community harmonization of administrative procedure law in the field of environmental protection that demonstrate that cautious intervention which respects the national prerogative can easily be absorbed by the national legal and administrative systems. Indeed, the Environmental Impact Assessment Directive[29] compels Member States to modify considerably their administrative procedural law relating to public participation, cooperation of different agencies, and reasoning and publication of administrative

---

[27] Directive on the assessment of the effects of certain public and private projects on the environment (85/337), OJ 1985 No. L 175; Directive on the freedom of access to information on the environment (90/313), OJ 1990 No. L 158; Regulation on voluntary participation of enterprises in a Community system of environmental management and environmental audit (No. 1836/93), OJ 1993 No. L 168; Council Regulation on a Community Award Scheme for an Eco-Label (No. 880/92), OJ 1992 No. L 99; as for the waste liability proposal see *op. cit.* note 24.

[28] See Subsidiarity: The Challenge of Change 1991; Wilke & Wallace 1990.

[29] *Op. cit.* note 25.

decisions. The Directive on public access to environmental information[30] rejects the traditional principle of secrecy of administrative proceedings and opens agency files to public inspection or at least accords every citizen an unconditional right of access to information on environmental data.

The serious nature of the implementation and enforcement deficit in virtually all Member States would seem to justify further harmonization of national administrative procedure law with the aim of strengthening the role of environmental advocates as motors for improving the implementation, application and enforcement of national environmental law. The result would be a – relative – improvement of the level of environmental protection in all Member States, although harmonization of standing rules alone is of course not capable of raising the level of substantive protection provided by the respective national laws. One cannot rule out that environmentally more advanced Member States might oppose to such harmonization on the ground that it does not remove the competitive advantages enjoyed by less environmentally conscious Member States. From a Community perspective, even a relative improvement of environmental protection is important. Moreover, since the environmentally less conscious Member States normally also are those in which implementation and enforcement deficits are greatest, arguably one can expect the most important improvements in these countries.

IV SCOPE AND EXTENT OF HARMONIZATION

Independent of the general objective of harmonization of national standing rules – ancillary or independent harmonization – it is doubtful whether simple harmonization of national rules relating to formal access to judicial review would be sufficient to strengthen the role of environmental advocates in securing compliance with Community or domestic environmental law. The function of standing rules is to determine who can initiate judicial review, thereby rationing access to scarce judicial resources and determining the distribution of decision-making powers in the relationship between courts and administrative tribunals and agencies. However, the effectiveness of judicial review of administrative action also depends on the availability of, and access to, administrative review, the remedies of the parties and powers of the court, including the availability of interim relief, the kind of decisions that are subject to judicial review, the scope of judicial review as to procedure and the merits, and the distribution

---

[30] *Ibid.*

of the costs of litigation. There are great differences between the Member States in this respect.[31]

For example, in some Member States judicial review is merely cassatory; the administrative tribunal can only annul an illegal administrative decision and has no injunctive powers. To a certain extent, this may be compensated by the grant of rights of action for compensation of harm suffered as a consequence of breach of official duty or the availability of injunctive relief directly against polluters under private law. Furthermore, an action brought before an administrative tribunal seldom has an automatic suspensive effect. Where, as in most Member States, such an effect is denied, the degree to which the tribunals can – and do in practice – grant interim relief is quite varied. Likewise, the kind of administrative decisions that are subject to judicial review varies from country to country. In some Member States, only individual decisions are reviewable. In other Member States, generic decisions such as environmental standards, administrative rules, programs and/or plans can also be challenged before the court or administrative tribunal. Also, the scope of judicial review, especially the degree of de-ference to agency interpretation of broad statutory terms, appreciation of facts and exercise of discretion, is very different throughout the Community. And finally, in some Member States, costs of litigation are a real barrier to access to administrative justice.

In view of these differences, 'deep' harmonization of the whole body of the relevant national administrative procedure law would not seem to be feasible nor desirable as a matter of policy. The subsidiarity principle provides strong arguments against such extensive harmonization. On the other hand, generous formal access to judicial review can be frustrated by lack of real access to administrative justice. Therefore, a Community minimum standard relating to key elements that have a bearing on the effectiveness of judicial review of administrative action, especially relating to the remedies, court powers and kind of reviewable decisions as well as the distribution of the costs of litigation, would seem warranted.[32] Of course, this adds to the complexity of the harmonization task and does not facilitate reaching a consensus in the Community political process.

Another question pertaining to the extent of harmonization relates to the availability of rights of action for vindicating the public interest in compliance with environmental law directly against polluters. Only very few Member States such as the Netherlands and – limited to injunctory

---

[31] See Rehbinder & Stewart 1985 pp. 153–4, 157; Frowein 1993; Auby & Fromont 1971.

[32] In the same sense Bridge 1984 pp. 39–42; Snyder 1993 p. 51.

relief – Belgium recognize standing in such situations.[33] Therefore, harmonization could not be justified with the argument that Community law is only codifying an existing trend in the Member States.

The need for introducing rights of action directly against polluters very much depends on the availability of remedies at the disposal of environmental associations and citizens against the public authorities. Where a national legal system accords public interest plaintiffs injunctory relief against the authorities and the scope of judicial review of enforcement action or inaction is broad, the need for having direct recourse against polluters is slight. On the other side of the scale, there is a clear need for such rights of action where injunctory relief against the authorities is not available or the discretion the authorities normally enjoy in the field of enforcement is not reviewable. If one assumes harmonization of national law relating to standing will be accompanied by a reasonable degree of harmonization with respect to remedies and court powers, arguably the introduction of standing directly against polluters is not an urgent task. However, the example of the Netherlands shows that one can also decide to reinforce the legal position of public interest plaintiffs by according them access to both channels of judicial review – review of administrative action or inaction as well as recourse directly against polluters.

The introduction of rights of action directly against polluters by Community law can only be a constituent part of a systemic view of judicial review for protecting the environment. Such a concept is entirely missing in the Commission proposal on liability for waste,[34] which would grant environmental associations standing for requiring polluters to cease a waste disposal activity that threatens natural resources and/or restore a natural resource already damaged to its previous state without considering the possible role of the authorities. Therefore, in my opinion the proposal is ill-conceived. One would expect an explanation why such a direct action is needed, what is the relationship between this action and enforcement action by the competent authorities, in particular whether there must be a 'waiting period' during which the authority is exclusively competent to act against the polluter, who decides on the necessary restoration measures, etc. In any case one should not try to determine these policy questions by simply classifying the problem as one of private law of compensation.

All in all, although I have some personal sympathy for the Dutch model of a civil society in which public interest groups and individuals do not

---

[33] For the Netherlands Hoge Raad, *Nieuwe Meer* case, [1986] Milieu en Recht, p. 324; *Kuunders* case, [1993] Milieu en Recht p. 234; for Belgium Act of 12 January 1993 concerning a right of action in environmental matters.

[34] *Op. cit.* note 24.

necessarily need to take the 'detour' via the authorities in order to enforce the public interest in a better environment against illegal encroachments, I tend to think that in the present state of the development of the Community harmonization in this field is somewhat premature.

V CONCLUSION

To conclude, there are good arguments in favour of ancillary harmonization of standing rules that aims at enabling environmental advocates to vindicate the Community interest in adequate implementation, application and enforcement of Community directives in the field of the environment. The case for independent harmonization of national rules relating to standing of environmental advocates that would not be limited to the enforcement of Community law is weaker. However, such harmonization could be justified with the recent tendency in Community environmental policy to supplement traditional command and control regulation by soft instruments. In any case, harmonization cannot halt at formal access to courts and administrative tribunals, but must also include key elements of material access to administrative justice.

9. The Enforcement of EC Environmental Law and the Role of Local Government

Jamie Woolley

Local and Regional Authorities have a particularly important part to play in ensuring the sustainability of development through the exercise of their statutory functions as 'Competent authorities' for many of the existing directives and regulations and in the context of practical application of the principle of subsidiarity.[1]

I THE STRUCTURE OF LOCAL GOVERNMENT IN THE UNITED KINGDOM

No constitutional guarantees exist for local government in the United Kingdom and the UK Government has refused to sign the Council of Europe's European Convention on Local Government, known as the European Charter of Local Self-Government although it has been signed by 22 other European Countries and ratified by 18 of them. The Charter sets out the basic principles of a democratic local government system. Local Government is purely the creature of statute with separate legislation for England and Wales, Scotland and Northern Ireland. Only a small proportion of local government finance is permitted to be raised locally, the major part being funded by Central Government, undermining local autonomy and accountability. Local Government has no independent legislative powers worthy of the name and whilst there is a strong tradition allowing local government to speak on behalf of its community, this is inadequately supported in law.

---

[1] COM(92) 23 Final – Vol II, p. 26.

In England and Wales, except in the major conurbations (the 'Metropolitan Areas'), there are two tiers of local government: County and District. Separate exercises have addressed the abolition of these two tiers in both England and Wales and the creation of unitary authorities in their place in many areas of both countries. In the Metropolitan areas of Tyne and Wear, Merseyside, Greater Manchester, West and South Yorkshire, West Midlands and Greater London most functions are carried out by unitary authorities: the Metropolitan District authorities and the London Boroughs. (Some functions are carried out through joint arrangements of a statutory or non-statutory kind.)

In Scotland the equivalent two tiers are Regional and District Councils with Island Councils being essentially discharging the functions of both. Proposals also exist to abolish a number of the Regional Councils.

In Northern Ireland local government's functions have been restricted during the continuing troubles, so that although they retain a number of environmental responsibilities, planning responsibilities are discharged through a chain of local offices of the Department of the Environment.

II THE CONTEXT FOR LOCAL GOVERNMENT

These proposals for reorganization are part of the ongoing policy of the Conservative Government to erode the importance of local government. Other functions have been abolished, centralized, privatized, made subject to compulsory competitive tendering, been made impossible to finance or been made the subject of voluntary opt outs or transferred to quangos. As a result, local authorities have no longer, for the most part, any direct responsibility for running public transport, have had their roles in the provision and maintenance of housing and schools considerably reduced, have had their control of planning decisions reduced by the readiness of Central Government to overrule on appeal, been deprived of their direct responsibility for waste management, been required to put their function of waste collection out to tender and will see their waste regulation function transferred to the Government's Environment Agency in due course. The statutory mechanism also exists to transfer much of their air pollution control functions to Her Majesty's Inspectorate of Pollution. In Scotland air pollution functions are to be transferred to the Scottish Environment Protection Agency. Local Government is not in good shape to progress environmental matters with the resources, personnel and verve that it would like.

III LOCAL GOVERNMENT AWARENESS OF EC LAW AND CONSULTATION IN THE EC LEGISLATIVE PROCESS

Local Government is primarily aware of the EC dimension in respect of EC grants, public procurement, equality and employment issues, health and safety and Sunday trading. As multifunction agencies, democratically governed and geographically dispersed, the concentration of awareness of the EC dimension in environmental law found in HMIP or the NRA is not similarly exhibited by individual local authorities but is growing.

Article 198a of the Rome Treaty inserted by the Maastricht Treaty creates the Committee of the Regions (COR) and this represents the first occasion on which the EC Treaties have recognized the existence of local and regional government. The Committee must be consulted where the Treaty provides, and may be consulted where the Council or Commission consider it appropriate. The COR may offer opinions in addition at its discretion without prior request. Although the Treaty requires that it be consulted for public health matters it does not so require for environmental matters falling within Article 100a (internal market) or 130r (environment) which is at odds with the quotation from the 5th Action Programme set out at the beginning of this paper. Nonetheless it is envizaged that the Committee will wish to comment on aspects of draft environmental legislation. The UK has 24 members on the Committee, which has established a number of Commissions. Commission No 5 on Environment and Planning meets monthly and, for example, will be considering the draft amendments to the EIA directive at its next session.[2] A uniform local government perspective is unlikely since, just as with the Parliament, transnational political alliances will also be formed that will shape different perceptions.

The Council of European Municipalities and Regions (CEMR) provides a permanent local government presence in Brussels and accommodation for national representatives of individual Member State's local government organizations. British local government has some twenty offices in Brussels shared with other regional organizations and in the main with very small staffs. The CEMR has established an Environment Committee which is serviced by an officer advisory group. The Committee meets with Commission officials. In addition its President sits as one of four required local and regional government representatives on the European Commission's 32 member General Consultative Forum on the Environment established at the end of 1993 with the formal objective of assisting

---

2   COM(93) 575 OJ No. C 130.

progress towards the sustainability envisaged by the 5th Action Programme.[3] It meets three times a year.

Of course many other routes for informal dialogue exist through local MEPs, lobbies of officials, involvement of officers in some expert groups, and evidence to Parliamentary Select Committees.

Consultation procedures also exist within the UK for the implementation of directives but by then the die is to a considerable extent cast. There is no statutory requirement to consult before imposing EC derived environmental obligations on local government.

IV LOCAL GOVERNMENT POLICY FORA

There are currently more than five local government associations in the UK including the Confederation of Scottish Local Authorities, the Association of Local Authorities of Northern Ireland, the Association of County Councils, the Association of Metropolitan Authorities and the Association of District Councils. Amalgamation of the last three English and Welsh organizations is planned. All associations are represented on the Local Agenda 21 Steering Group, which provides an advisory role to local authorities on implementing Agenda 21 and is serviced by the Local Government Management Board.

V OVERVIEW OF THE ENVIRONMENTAL RESPONS-IBILITIES OF UK LOCAL GOVERNMENT

Local authorities as a whole have environmental protection responsibilities in the fields of planning (including construction, change of use and mineral extraction), transport, air pollution control, control of nuisances including noise, waste collection/management and disposal/regulation, litter control, emergency planning, food hygiene, health and safety but no major responsibilities relating to drinking water or river quality. Local authorities' jurisdiction does not in general extend beyond low water mark, although tidal estuaries, harbours and bays can prove exceptions to this principle, so, for example, dredging of marine aggregates in some parts of the Bristol channel is subject to local authority planning control.

---

3   See Commission Decision 93/701 of 7th December 1993 OJ No. L 328.

VI LOCAL GOVERNMENT IN EUROPEAN COMMUNITY LAW

In *Fratelli Costanzo SpA v Comune di Milano* the ECJ decided that administrative authorities of the State including municipal authorities are under the same obligation as a national court to apply the provision of a directive (or to refrain from applying national provisions of national law which conflict with a Community provision), where its subject matter is unconditional and sufficiently precise and the due date for implementation has passed without implementation occurring (i.e. it is directly effective).[4] This is so because the obligation to implement is binding on all authorities of the Member State. In so finding the Court pointed out that if a court was required to implement by its decision such a provision, then '... all organs of the administration, including decentralized authorities such as municipalities, are obliged to apply those provisions.' Underlying this rationale was Article 5 of the EC Treaty:

> Member States shall take all appropriate measures, whether general or particular, to ensure fulfilment of the obligations arising out of this treaty or resulting from action taken by the institutions of the Community. They shall facilitate the achievement of the Community's tasks. They shall abstain from any measure which could jeopardize the attainment of the objectives of this Treaty.

The result is that local authorities are given the responsibility of ensuring fulfilment of EC law by 'applying' it, although denied the legislative competence to ensure fulfilment. When in doubt about the direct effectiveness of a provision, there is no recourse available in the UK to a court for an advisory opinion or directly to the European Court of Justice. (Misunderstandings about access to the ECJ are very prevalent.) However there does seem to be scope to apply for a declaration regarding failure to implement EC law following the House of Lords decision in the recent *Equal Opportunities* case referred to below.

Uncertainty will therefore predominate. Note that an authority which wishes to comply with a clearly directly effective provision of a directive, faces further problems. Even if part of a directive meets the requirements of direct effect, it does not necessarily follow that the authority will be adequately clear about its obligations as a whole: in *Emmott v Minister for Social Welfare*,[5] the ECJ stated:

> So long as a directive has not been properly transposed into national law, individuals are unable to ascertain the full extent of their rights. That state of uncertainty for individuals subsists even after the Court has delivered a judgment finding that the

---

4 Case 103/88, [1989] CMLR 239 at p. 257.
5 [1991] IRLR 387 at p. 390.

Member State in question has not fulfilled its obligations under the directive and even
if the Court has held that a particular provision or provisions of the directive are
sufficiently precise and unconditional to be relied upon before a national court. Only
the proper transposition of the directive will bring that state of uncertainty to an end
and it is only upon that transposition that the legal certainty which must exist if
individuals are to be required to assert their right is created.

The converse of this is that local authorities will often be unable to ascertain
the full extent of their obligations in these circumstances so that the legal
certainty which ought to exist if local authorities are to carry out their
obligations accurately will not have been created. Note also that Councillors
charged with decisions can be anxious about striking out on an apparently
novel course against the background of the potential sanction of surcharge
for acting beyond their legal powers.

VII EC DERIVED ENVIRONMENTAL RESPONSIB-
ILITIES OF UK LOCAL GOVERNMENT

I list some of the more important requirements and some points of interest.

1. Environmental Information:

Directive 90/313 is implemented by the Environmental Information
Regulations 1992. Article 3 of the directive states that 'Member States shall
define the practical arrangements under which such information is
effectively made available'. The UK Government has simply passed this
obligation to the competent authorities requiring them to define the practical
arrangements. However to make the arrangements practical training, staff
time and the reorganization of resources is necessary. This costs money but
the Government as the Member State has not made additional money
available so practical arrangements in reality cannot be implemented. The
spirit of the directive has been studiously ignored.

2. Physical Planning

- The environmental assessment Directive 85/337. (This is considered in
  more detail elsewhere in this paper.)
- The birds Directive 79/409.
- *Kincardine and Deeside District Council v The Forestry Commission*:[6]
  Articles 2 and 4 respectively aimed at maintaining the population of

---

6 [1993] *Env. L.R.* 151.

species and providing special habitat conservation measures and protection areas were not sufficiently precise and unconditional and therefore not of direct effect, although Article 5, 6.1 and 8 'might be regarded as precise ...'

- The habitats Directive 92/43.[7]
- Proposed COMAH Directive[8] to replace the Seveso Directive. Although European Parliamentary consideration of this has been deferred until the autumn, draft article 9(g) requires the operator to produce a safety report for the purpose of providing sufficient information to the relevant authorities to enable decisions to be made in terms of the siting and land use for new establishments and developments around existing establishments.

3. Air Pollution

Directives 80/779, 82/884 and 85/203 setting health protection standards for smoke and sulphur dioxide, for lead and for nitrogen dioxide, respectively. (Article 11 of the last is directly effective.[9])

Directive 84/360 on the combating of air pollution from industrial plants within the UK has been implemented under Part I of the Environmental Protection Act 1990. It gives local authorities specific responsibilities for some categories of plants listed in Annex 1 to the directive, namely foundries, works for the industrial finishing of asbestos-based products, plants for the production of glass and for ceramics, hospital incinerators and some incinerators for solid and liquid waste. The proposal for a directive on integrated pollution prevention and control [10] would appear capable of requiring local authorities to introduce integrated pollution controls to some processes that they currently authorize solely for air pollution. Alternatively the authorities may simply lose some processes to Her Majesty's Inspectorate of Pollution – see for example installations for the production of glass with a capacity of 5000 tonnes output per year, currently a part B process but listed in the draft directive's Annex 1.

Under Directive 87/101 on the disposal of waste oils local authorities have specific responsibilities for combustion works burning waste oils with a gross thermal input of less than 3 MW.

---

[7] See now the Town and Country Planning (Habitats) Regulations 1994 and the Planning Policy Guidance on Nature Conservation anticipated to be issued at the time this paper was delivered later in 1994.

[8] COM(94) 4 Final.

[9] Case C–186/91, *Commission v Belgium*, [1993] ECR I–851.

[10] COM(93) 423 Final.

Reference also needs to be made to Directive 89/369 on the prevention of air pollution from new municipal waste incineration plants and 89/429 from existing municipal waste incineration plants (where these belong to the authority or are under the control, direct or indirect, of a local authority waste disposal company).

4. Waste Regulation

In this context Directive 75/442 on waste and 91/689 on hazardous waste and Directive 80/68 on the protection of groundwater against pollution by certain dangerous substances are relevant. The latter is finally legislated for in the context of waste management by Regulation 15 of the Waste Management Licensing Regulations 1994. DOE Circular 11/94 concedes at page 137:

> The Department now accept that the directive requires us to apply the approach in the directive by more formal legal means (than DOE Circulars 4/82 and 20/90).

Note in particular the need for prior examination of the hydrogeological conditions of the area concerned.[11] The draft Directive on the landfill of waste[12] also has implications for local government.

5. Emergency Planning for Industrial and Radiation Hazards

In this area, the following directives are particularly relevant:
- Directive 82/501 as amended (the 'Seveso' Directive) to be replaced by the proposed COMAH Directive.[13]
- Directive 89/618 on public information for radiological emergencies. The latter remains incompletely transposed because no competent authority has been given the task of actually informing the public in the event of a radiological emergency. The UK implementing regulations (Public Information for Radiation Emergencies Regulations 1992) merely require local authorities to draw up arrangements but they are specifically given no responsibility to implement them.[14]
- The revised draft basic safety standards Directive for the protection of workers and the public from ionising radiation[15] does not specify

---

[11] Regulation 15(2).
[12] OJ No. C 1909 of 22 July 1991 as amended on 5th August 1993 and presently before the Council.
[13] COM(94) 4 Final.
[14] See Regulation 4(1).
[15] COM(93) Final, 20.7.93, draft Article 47.

matters in anything approaching the detail of the proposed COMAH Directive.

VIII THE FAILURE OF LOCAL AUTHORITIES TO OBSERVE EC ENVIRONMENTAL DIRECTIVES

The relevant cases on the environmental impact assessment Directive 85/337 may be fairly familiar: they demonstrate a poor appreciation of EC-derived responsibilities matched by poor judicial analysis. It is difficult to avoid the thought that insular planners and judges may resent the continental intrusion, viewing environmental assessment as a nuisance rather than a tool to improve the quality of decision-making.

In *R v Swale Borough Council ex parte RSPB*:[16] the applicants challenged the grant of planning permission for land reclamation of mud-flats which were used as feeding grounds for wintering birds. Simon Brown J. held that whether any particular development is or is not within scheduled descriptions in the environmental assessment regulations is exclusively for the planning authority in question subject only to *Wednesbury* challenge. Questions of classification were essentially questions of fact and degree, not of law. This approach has been the subject of trenchant criticism essentially along the lines that the question of significance for the purpose of projects in Annex 2 of the directive is an objective rather than subjective test, and that the issue of classification is essentially one of law. He also noted that the regulations provided for assessment of '... the reclamation of land from the sea for the purpose of agriculture' where significant effects were likely but that the reference in the directive to '... land reclamation for the purpose of conversion to another type of land use' had been omitted entirely from the regulations. He did not address what obligation either the court itself or the council as part of the State had in remedying this omission merely finding that he could not construct the UK regulations so as to remedy this omission. Whether arguments about the *vires* of the regulations could have been raised to delete the restriction to agriculture or whether the duty of construction could have been applied to the primary legislation rather than the secondary legislation do not seem to have been explored. The case has given the green light to local authorities who would rather not consider the implications of projects too closely on environmental grounds, because of their concern to regenerate local economies.

---

[16] [1991] *JEL* 135.

In *R v Poole Borough Council ex parte Beebee*:[17] Poole BC had granted itself planning permission to build a housing estate on a part of Canford Heath, designated as an SSSI containing a number of protected species including sand lizards. The applicants applied for judicial review, *inter alia*, on the grounds that the council had failed to consider whether an environmental impact assessment should be carried out at all. (The two applicants represented the Worldwide Fund for Nature (WWF) and the British Herpetological Society (BHS)). Schiemann J. conceded standing to the first as it was mentioned in the terms of the planning permission, but would not have conceded standing to WWF alone, notwithstanding a long association with the heath and grant of aids to the BHS. Of particular interest in the discussion below was that he was impressed by the submission that he should be slow to find that others had sufficient interest where Parliament had created a body, the Nature Conservation Council, to protect the interest involved. The question of the capacity of one emanation of the State (NCC) to seek the enforcement of the directive against another, the Poole Borough Council was, semble, not addressed. Schiemann J. found that the significant factors (relating to environmental assessment) had been drawn as a matter of fact to the attention of the authority '..and so that authority had in their possession the substance of what they would have had if they had applied their minds to the 1988 regulations and had prepared an environmental statement. The substance of all the environmental information which was likely to emerge ... had already emerged ...' This also provides the green light for authorities not to take the rigorous assessment of environmental effects seriously.

IX THE DUTY NOT TO INTRODUCE LOCAL REQUIREMENTS INCOMPATIBLE WITH DIRECTLY EFFECTIVE EC LAW

Local authorities are vulnerable to arguments based on Community law that have been advanced by DIY stores, sex shops (both arguing on the basis of Article 30), the plastics industry and freight hauliers. Representatives of the last two sectors attacked local authorities' actions aimed at improving the environment by 'subsidiary' regulation.

In *Enichem Base v Comune di Cinisello Balsamo*,[18] the ECJ found that the introduction by the mayor of an Italian authority of a local ban on non-

---

[17] [1991] *JPEL* 543.
[18] Case 380/87, [1989] ECR 2491.

biodegradable plastic bags was not inconsistent with the policy objectives of the waste Directive 75/442, which created no right to sell such products. The Court did not consider the compatibility of the measure with Article 30 as the question had not been referred to it. However, the requirement in the directive to remit the draft of the ban to the Commission was a requirement that applied to a municipality as much as to a national government, although the requirement did not give rise to any directly effective right since the observance or non-observance of the requirement had no effect on the legal validity of the ban.

In *R v London Boroughs Transport Committee ex parte Freight Transport Association Ltd*,[19] the Court of Appeal found that the London Boroughs Transport Committee acting on behalf of 22 London boroughs and having regulatory powers was an emanation of the State and that therefore prohibitions in EEC Directives 71/320 and 70/157 for braking devices and exhaust systems were directly effective so that part of a permit imposed by the London Boroughs Transport Committee as a condition for the use of residential streets in Greater London by heavy goods vehicles was invalid as being in breach of the directives. On appeal the House of Lords disagreed as to the impact and relevance of the directives for traffic regulation as opposed to vehicle use but did not overturn the findings that they were of direct effect and that the LBTC was an emanation of the State.[20] What was most interesting in this case was Lord Templeton's specific reference to 'the Community objective of preserving, protecting and improving the quality of the environment' under article 130r of the EEC Treaty and the emphasis laid on the conditions as being 'consistent with article 130r and the Commission's Green Paper [on the Urban Environment] ...'. This seems an excellent example at the highest national level of the view that the European Court of Justice's approach to interpretation of European Law must be adopted by the national court when considering the meaning and application of an EC directive including therefore the consideration of the history of a directive and European environmental policy generally. It is noteworthy that whilst the House of Lords has felt it appropriate to consider and refer explicitly to EC environmental policy, lower courts, particularly in their decisions on environmental assessment mentioned above and further below, have not.

---

[19] [1990] 3 *CMLR* 495.
[20] [1991] 3 All ER 915.

X LOCAL AUTHORITY AWARENESS AND UNDER-STANDING OF THE EC DIMENSION: THE EXAMPLE OF THE WASTE FRAMEWORK DIRECTIVE 75/442

1. The Control of Pollution Act 1974

It is perhaps indicative of the timidity with which European points of law are advanced, the cool reception they receive from some of the UK judiciary or the ignorance that persists about the contents of directives that no reference was made to the waste framework directive in the judgment in Attorney General's Reference (no 2 of 1988).[21] In that case the Court of Appeal found that a Welsh District Council's waste licence condition which provided that 'the (waste disposal) facility shall at all times be managed and operated so as to avoid creating a nuisance to the neighbourhood' was void and that a prosecution for its breach therefore failed. The court pointed out that the sole grounds in UK law for refusing a licence where planning permission was in existence was where it was necessary for the purpose of preventing pollution of water or danger to public health, (section 5(3) Control of Pollution Act 1974) and that an authority was obliged to revoke a licence if pollution of water, danger to public health or serious detriment to the amenities of the locality would be caused. It was argued successfully that noise as a nuisance could not be controlled by the licence as a nuisance because other statutory controls existed and that the concept of nuisance was too wide for inclusion in a condition.

However Article 4 of the waste framework Directive specifically provided that:

> Member States shall take the necessary measures to ensure that waste is disposed of without endangering human health and without harming the environment, and in particular
> – without risk to water, air, soil, plants or animals;
> – without causing a nuisance through noise or odours;
> – without adversely affecting the countryside or places of special interest.

Further, the directive went on to provide for a permit system that had to take account of Article 4. This went considerably beyond the provisions of the Control of Pollution Act 1974 with its specific provision that waste was to be disposed of '... without causing a nuisance through noise or odour.' I do not know if any attempt was made to advance arguments based on the directive, but no reference to the directive appears in the judgment.

---

[21] [1990] *JEL* Vol. 2, No. 1 p. 80.

In 1991 Ludwig Krämer suggested that certain absolute prohibitions in a number of directives met the requirements of direct effect.[22] He instanced Article 5 of Directive 78/319 on toxic and dangerous waste which reads almost identically to Article 4 of the waste framework Directive 75/442 and argued that people living in the vicinity of waste disposal plants had the right to enforce these provisions through the courts.

In the UK the waste disposal licensing system was to be replaced under part II of the Environmental Protection Act 1990. This purported to bring matters in line with Article 4 by extending the basis for rejection of a licence application to cover pollution of the environment as a whole rather than just water.[23] However there were still question marks over whether this had fully transposed the then requirements of the framework directive. For example, reference to the countryside and places of special interest in the last part of Article 4 was not provided for. (See Bates 1992, para. 1.13.)

Directive 91/156 was then introduced amending the waste framework Directive with a transposition date of 1st April 1993.[24] The Department of the Environment aimed to introduce Part II of the EPA with new regulations to coincide with that date. The ramifications of the definition of waste, the full implications of the amended directive and the failure to provide adequately for Article 4 led the Department of the Environment to postpone the introduction of Part II to 1st June and eventually until April 1994. Effectively therefore Article 4 remained unimplemented in full in the UK from 1977 to 1994 and the amendments to the directive remained unimplemented for 12 months after their transposition date.

2. The Groundwater Directive

The additional failure to implement certain requirements of the EC Directive 80/68 on the protection of groundwater against pollution caused by certain dangerous substances for some 12 years in the context of waste management has already been alluded to above.

3. Local Authorities' Perceptions

Local authorities did finally become aware of discrepancies between national and Community waste law in 1993 but their understanding of the situation and the advice they received is a useful barometer of the extent to

---

[22] 'The implementation of Community Environmental Directives within Member States: Some implications of the Direct Effect Doctrine', *JEL*, Vol. 3 No. 1, 1991.

[23] See Section 36(3) EPA 90.

[24] OJ 1991 No. L 42.

which the role of the Commission is understood and the provisions of the directives fully appreciated. In the middle of 1993 County Councils with responsibility for waste licensing considered that they faced a double jeopardy because of the Department of the Environment's failure to introduce new waste licensing rules under Part II of the Environmental Protection Act 1990. The Association of County Council's environment committee was originally concerned on the one hand that the authorities as emanations of the State might themselves face legal action brought against them by the Commission, (a novel idea) but, semble, their fears were allayed regarding that, not by advice that it was the Member State's Government that would face any proceedings by the Commission, but by advice that the Commission would take such a long time before proceeding against any individual authority that the failure to transpose would have been rectified long before that. Their concern was that they might be breaking EC law if they continued to issue licences under the Control of Pollution Act 1974 as that Act did not incorporate all the requirements of the framework directive. Apparently it was not considered how they might issue licences in a manner that *would* conform with the directive's requirements which they would have been required or entitled to do in the light of *Costanzo*. Rather, they were concerned that they might face legal action for judicial review by contractors if they delayed issuing licences under the existing UK law which apparently was the only other option they considered.

4. The *Lombardia* Case

In the meantime the UK Government were able to intervene in Case C–236/92 *Comitato di Coordinamento per la Difesa della Cava and others v Regione Lombardia and Others*.[25] The Giunta Regionale of the Lombardy Region had approved by various decisions in 1989 and 1990 a plan for a tip for solid urban waste to be established in a municipality within the region. The national rules implementing Council Directive 75/442 provided for the disposal of waste almost exclusively by means of tipping, whereas the directive required Member States to adopt appropriate measures to encourage the prevention, recycling and processing of waste. The question arose whether Article 4 of the directive was of direct effect.

Advocate General Damon's view was that:

> Article 4 ... must be interpreted as meaning that it does not give individuals any right on which they may rely before national courts in order to obtain the annulment of a decision of a national authority falling within the scope of that provision *on the ground*

---

[25] Case C–236/92, [1994] ECR I–485.

that the national rules did not provide for the measures necessary to promote the method of treatment by recycling in order to dispose of waste. (my emphasis).

The Court itself found that it was neither unconditional nor sufficiently precise to confer rights on citizens upon which they may rely against the State, finding by implication that because Article 4 referred to the Member State having to take 'the necessary measures to ensure that waste is disposed of without endangering human health and without harming the environment ...', that there were measures which the Member State had to take and therefore the provision was not unconditional and secondly that the provision was not sufficiently precise because the obligation was not set out in unequivocal terms. The Court found that Article 4 indicated a programme or framework of action to be followed and set out the objectives which Member States must observe in their performance of the more specific obligations imposed on them by Article 5 to 11.[26]

5. Comments on the *Lombardia* Case

This is a disappointing finding but the case appears curious since the basis of the citizen's complaint appears to have been that the framework directive required the Member States to encourage the prevention, recycling and processing of waste and this suggested an order of priority. It may be that the finding that Article 4 of the directive was not of direct effect can be confined to the argument that it did not have the specific effect actually argued for which seems to be the basis of the Advocate General's view. However the Court seemed to go further. It still seems possible to argue that if damage was caused to an individuals health or property, Article 4 might form the basis for a claim on *Francovich* principles. However if Article 4 does not confer on individuals rights which the national courts must safeguard this looks difficult to advance as a proposition. The Court did not however state that the Member State was not bound by Article 4, merely that it did not provide citizens with enforceable rights. (As in *Enichem* this would equally bind local authorities.) Consequently paragraph 2(1) of Schedule 4 to the waste management Licensing Regulations which places a general duty on planning and waste regulation authorities to 'discharge their ... functions ... with the relevant objectives' and the Department's advice in DOE Circular 11/94 that competent authorities will have discretion in applying the objectives in Article 4 could be said to be at odds with the Court's view that Article 4 sets out objectives which *must* be observed.[27] I

---

[26] See Bulletin of ECJ's Information Service, No. 06–94; case now reported in [1994] ECR I–485.

[27] See paragraphs 1.48 and 1.49 of the Circular.

anticipate that challenges will be mounted to decisions which do not observe the Article 4 objectives with demonstrable care and share the view that 'Article 4 is therefore likely to shake up the framework within which waste management decisions are taken, quite possibly by a good deal more than the Government has suggested.'[28] Local authorities will not be able to deal with these challenges without a careful understanding of this EC background.

XI THE ENFORCEMENT OF EC ENVIRONMENTAL DIRECTIVES BY LOCAL AUTHORITIES AGAINST OTHER COMPONENTS OF THE STATE

This gives rise to two interconnected problems: *locus standi* under UK law and the status of an emanation of the State to take advantage of the direct effect doctrine.

1. Environmental Assessment

In *Twyford Parish Council v Secretary of State for the Environment*,[29] two parish councils and three individuals queried the validity of the proposal to extend the M3 across Twyford Down near Winchester on the basis that no environmental impact assessment (EIA) had been carried out in breach of the EIA Directive: McCullough J. decided that the directive did not apply to projects already in the pipeline; however if he was wrong on that (and the Court in case C–396/92, *Bund Naturschutz* deliberately left this issue untouched[30]) he went on to find that the '... applicants (*sic*) were amongst those whom the directive was intended to benefit and (the directive's) provisions were unconditional and sufficiently precise ...'. *Locus* was therefore conceded (but he would have afforded no remedy all the same because in his view it was necessary for the applicants to show they had suffered and in his view they had not: this part of the decision has been widely criticized). It was an Annex I project. There was no discussion of the status of the two Parish Councils as themselves being emanations of the State.

---

28 *ENDS* Bulletin No. 231, April 1994, p. 16.
29 [1992] *Env. L.R.* 28.
30 But see now the judgment in that case, [1994] ECR I–3717.

In *Kincardine and Deeside District Council v The Forestry Commission*,[31] an application for a woodland grant was made five days after the directive should have been transposed and seven days before the Environmental Assessment (Afforestation) Regulations 1988 came into effect. The District Council objected to the application and appeared at a hearing of the Forestry Commissioner's Regional Advisory Committee for North East Scotland where they made representations that were in part based on prior consultation with the RSPB. Lord Coulsfield found as to *locus* that the Council '... can ... properly be said to have a reasonable concern with a major project in their area which may affect the economy or amenity of the area generally. That is, in my view, a material or sufficient interest.'

Lord Coulsfield found that the Forestry Commission was an emanation of the State. The respondents submitted that the directive could only be enforced by an individual if it conferred rights on that individual and asserted that the directive did not purport to confer any rights on the Council. Lord Coulsfield rejected that argument (but did not refer to the fact that the Council itself was an emanation of the State) but he found that Annex II projects such as the one in question were subject to large a degree of State discretion and therefore were not subject to direct effect; by contrast there was a 'powerful argument that Annex I projects were subject to direct effect ...'.

In *Wychavon District Council v Secretary of State for the Environment and Velcourt Ltd*,[32] the facts were that the EIA Directive should have been transposed by 3rd July 1988. A planning application was made to the District Council for permission to erect poultry houses capable of raising 350,000 poultry per year on 11th July. The UK Regulations were made on 12th July and came into effect on 15th July. The District Council refused permission. In October 1990 it transpired that the true throughput would be 1.25 million birds. The Inspector on appeal granted permission on 21st August 1991. Leave to quash that decision was sought on 1st October 1991.

So the application was made after the implementation date of the EIA directive but before the introduction of the UK Regulations and no EIA had been sought by the district council. (One might question why not.) The council submitted at the planning appeal that the major increase in poultry throughput meant that the matter should be treated as a new application, in this case post-dating the introduction of the EIA regulations, which therefore applied to the application. Indicative criteria in Circular 15/88 on the interpretation of Paragraph 2 of Appendix A to Schedule 2 of the Regulations provided that poultry rearing installations housing more than

---

[31] [1993] *Env. L.R.* 151.
[32] *Times Law Report* January 7, 1994; now reported at [1994] *Env.L.R.* 239.

100,000 broilers '..may require environmental assessment.' The inspector allowed the appeal finding that an environmental assessment could not be required. The planning authority applied for judicial review of that decision on the basis that an environmental assessment should have been required before the appeal could be decided.

Mr Justice Turner posed two questions:

1) Can a local planning authority in its capacity as respondent to an appeal from the refusal of a planning application made to it, (a) seek to enforce a directive if otherwise it is directly enforceable or (b) enforce such a directive against a private individual as opposed to a party which is an emanation of the State?

2) Is the directive itself of such a character that, in accordance with community law, it is directly enforceable?

He found that:

1a) the directive could not be relied on by the Council as against the planning applicant, a private limited company because that would be to allow the directive to have horizontal effect;

1b) the Council itself, because it was an emanation of the State could not be an individual for the purpose of seeking to enforce the requirement of the directive;

1c) the duty of construction (*Van Colson/Marleasing*) was not applicable because the court could not by exercise of its discretion interpret the applicable date of the UK Regulations as any other date and the Regulations post-dated the application for planning permission;

2) Articles 1.1, 2.2, 3.3, 4.2, 5.1, 5.2, 6.1 and 6.3 were all neither unconditional nor certain, so that the directive as a whole was incapable of direct effect.

I would comment as follows:

1a) It is true that it is well settled that a directive cannot cast obligations on private individuals,[33] so this would seem to support the view that Article 5 of the EIA Directive cannot be enforced against a private individual (see Duffy 1994 p. 442).[34] It is not clear how it came about that the developer was a party to the action to review the Secretary of State's decision although it is evident that the developer would have wished to intervene had the judicial review proceedings been solely brought against the Secretary of State.

The court's approach fails to distinguish between the obligations imposed on the State and those imposed on the developer. *Costanzo*

---

[33] Case 152/84, *M.H. Marshall v Southampton and South West Hampshire Area Heath Authority*, [1986] ECR 723.

[34] Court of Justice, case C–91/92, *Dori*, [1994] ECR I–3325.

clearly provides that the State must apply the provisions of the directive which are of direct effect against it where there has been a failure to implement: these requirements are:

- to ensure the assessment before consent is given (Article 2.1);
- to ensure the developer supplies the environmental information (Article 5.1, pace Mr Justice Turner);
- to ensure that other relevant authorities have the opportunity to comment on the request for consent (Article 6.1 pace Mr Justice Turner);
- to ensure the request for development consent is made publicly available for the expression of public opinion (Article 6.2);
- to take the relevant information into account in development consent procedure (Article 8).

The only part of the directive which could be said to purport to impose obligations on a private individual, i.e. the developer, is that contained in Article 5 requiring the Member State to ensure the developer provides the environmental information. But if the planning authority i.e. the Secretary of State in the case in question is bound to demand the information, it must do so, leaving the developer if necessary to refuse to do so if he wishes to take the point that this amounts to horizontal application of the direct effect doctrine. (Since under national planning law, the authority is already empowered under Town and Country Planning legislation to request the totality of the information that is required under a formal assessment, if this approach was taken a developer would then have no option but to provide the information in any event.)

1b) Because it seems that the applicants sought an order as against the private company, it would have seemed unnecessary in the light of the judge's first finding to consider the status of the local authority. Nonetheless finding that the authority was an emanation of the State and pointing to ECJ references to an individual having the right to enforce directly effective provisions, he went on to find that the authority could not enforce a directly effective provision.

Whether this argument would have been correct against the Secretary of State seems less certain in the absence of a relevant ECJ decision on this point. Mr Justice McCullough did not seem to experience the same problem in *Twyford*. Furthermore the decision now appears to be at odds with the House of Lords decision in *R v Secretary of State for Employment ex parte Equal Opportunities Commission and another*.[35]

---

[35] [1994] 1 All ER 910; [1993] 1 CMLR 918.

The Equal Opportunities Commission (EOC) challenged the legitimacy of differing qualifying periods for redundancy and unfair dismissal payments as between part time and full time workers, arguing that the distinction in fact discriminated against women, challenging a decision of the Secretary of State for Employment declining to accept this argument and seeking a declaration that the United Kingdom was in breach of its EC obligations. Lord Keith found that the EOC had sufficient interest and therefore *locus standi* to obtain a declaration by way of judicial review that UK law was not in conformity with EC law. By implication therefore the fact that the EOC was an emanation of the State did not prevent it from initiating legal action regarding unfulfilled Community law against a Government Minister for the benefit of its constituency: those discriminated against on the basis of gender. Local Government's power to litigate for the benefit of its constituency, namely its inhabitants[36] seems to provide a suitable parallel and Richard Gordon Q.C. has written

> that the EOC's reasoning ... compels the wider conclusion that local authorities now have standing to monitor the implementation of European legislation in the United Kingdom.[37]

It is also not impossible to conceive of a situation where an authority must seek judicial review of UK legislation which it believes would otherwise compel it to act, in its view, in contravention of EC law. This would seem to follow the logic of the decision in *Costanzo* and provide the authority's best opportunity of clarifying the law and respecting its Community obligations.

1c) The obligation on the courts to interpret domestic law to conform to EC requirements as set out in *Van Colson*[38] and *Marleasing*.[39] has always been subject to interpreting the caveats of the ECJ in each case '... in so far as a national court has a discretion under national law' and 'as far as possible'. The court refused to interpret the Regulations' commencement date so as to backdate it to apply to the application. 'No amount of interpretation, properly so called, can overcome this obstacle.' The more appropriate argument might, however have been

---

[36] Section 222 Local Government Act 1972 for England and Wales or, for a 'section of its inhabitants' under s189 of the Local Government (Scotland) Act 1973 for Scotland.

[37] 'Servants or Masters? Local Authorities in the European Judicial Review Arena', *Local Authority Law*, Issue 4, April 27 1994, p. 7.

[38] Case 14/83, [1984] ECR 1891.

[39] Case 106/89, [1990] ECR I–4135.

to construe the Town and Country Planning Act 1990 itself as requiring to be interpreted subject to the directive on the basis that the TCPA requirements in section 70(2) (and section 54A) to base decisions on, *inter alia*, 'material considerations' are silent on what those considerations are and therefore those considerations could have been interpreted subject to the directive, absent any effective UK regulations to include the requirement that the environmental information required by the directive should have been considered as a relevant consideration. This is consistent with the application of the *Marleasing* doctrine in the *Greenpeace* case considered below.

2) The argument about whether the directive was sufficiently precise and unconditional to be of direct effect was apparently advanced on the surprising note that Article 12 which dealt with the transposition date was precise, which seems of no great relevance. This was met by the court's view that a number of the other Articles were not precise and unconditional and that therefore the directive was incapable of direct effect. This is odd because it has never been necessary to show that an entire directive was precise and unconditional, only a particular provision. On this point the court seems to have plainly erred.

Disappointingly the court also found that the inspector had all the information before him that would have been covered by an assessment, so that it would have made no difference in any event. This second 'pragmatic' finding on the sufficiency of the information, following the Canford Heath case, regardless of the rigour or process required by the directive suggest that the courts may feel competent to make factual judgments for which they are ill equipped.

2. Radiation Protection

In *R v Secretary of State for the Environment, HMIP and MAFF ex parte Greenpeace and Lancashire County Council*, Lancashire County Council and Greenpeace challenged the validity of emission authorizations granted under the Radioactive Substances Act 1993.[40] Mr Justice Potts found that Article 6(a) of Euratom Directive 80/836 requiring prior justification of exposures to ionizing radiation had not been transposed into UK law. The court applied *Marleasing* and followed *Webb v Emo Air Cargo Ltd*,[41] finding that the Radioactive Substances Act 1993 was not inconsistent with the requirement of the directive, but was merely silent on the point. It followed that the Act could therefore be interpreted as being subject to the

---

[40] *The Independent*, Law Reports, 8th March 1994.
[41] [1993] 1 WLR.

requirements of the directive without creating any inconsistency with the Act and that accordingly the Ministers had erred in arguing that Article 6(a) of the directive was inapplicable. Lancashire County Council were statutory consultees under the terms of the Radioactive Substances Act and no argument was raised that because they were an emanation of the State they were not entitled to raise the requirement to observe Community law against three other emanations of the State.

3. Broadcasting

Article 12 of the broadcasting Directive 89/552 provides that 'Television advertising shall not: ... (e) encourage behaviour prejudicial to the protection of the environment.' This can be compared with the ITC Code of Advertising made under the Broadcasting Act 1990 which provides that:

> No advertisement may encourage or condone behaviour prejudicial to the protection of the environment. This does not preclude advertisements for products and services which may have some adverse environmental impact in normal use, e.g. motor cars. All claims relating to environmental impact must comply with guidelines approved by the [I.T.] Commission from time to time for this purpose.

I mention this to point up the future possibilities of local authorities combining to litigate for a more thorough observance of Article 12 than is presently provided for in the UK. If authorities can pursue matters in the same way as the EOC, as suggested above, such an action cannot be ruled out.

XII LOCAL AUTHORITIES, DIRECT EFFECT AND THE *FRANCOVICH* REMEDY

In *R v Legal Aid Area No 8 (Northern) ex parte Florence Emily Sendall*,[42] the court of appeal endorsed the rejection of leave to challenge by way of judicial review the decision of the Legal Aid Board to refuse legal aid for representation at a public inquiry as this was outwith its statutory powers. Although Article 6 of the EIA directive required Member States to ensure that 'the public concerned is given the opportunity to express any opinion before the project is initiated', it also provided that the detailed arrangements relating to this consultation were for the Member State to put into place. Since there were a number of avenues by which the end result could be achieved, the court would not compel the Legal Aid Board to be

---

[42] [1993] *Env. L.R.* 167.

enlisted in a response which had not been chosen by the Member State and which presented only one of a number of methods of meeting the directive's requirements. The choice of the legal aid board as the emanation of the State in these circumstances is understandable, although it was the planning authority that was required to take into account Ms Sendall's views.

In *Francovich*, the beneficiaries of the guarantee contemplated by Directive 80/987 and the content of the guarantee were sufficiently precise, but the identity of the institution liable for the guarantee was not sufficiently precise to allow individuals to rely upon the provisions of the directive to assert rights against the State in proceedings before national courts. If this is right, then merely because a provision of an unimplemented directive would most *sensibly* be expected to become an obligation of that authority in due course because of current responsibilities to which the content of the directive would naturally relate, an individual would not it seems automatically be entitled to enforce such a provision of an unimplemented directive against a local authority. In the case of the EIA directive, the competent authorities (as opposed to the 'guarantee institutions') '... shall be that or those which the Member States designate as responsible for performing the duties arising from the directive.' (Article 1.3.) Following *Francovich* a local planning authority presented with a direct effect argument for an unimplemented aspect of environmental assessment might just argue that the identity of the competent authority was not sufficiently precise to allow an individual to rely on it. If the citizen then were to bring an action against the Minister the same argument could be used, so that in the absence of actual damages as required in *Francovich*, no remedy would seem possible.

It has been suggested that the introduction of this additional remedy may have been deliberately designed as part of a judicial strategy to de-emphasise the direct effect doctrine with its inability to provide horizontal effect and to refocus liability where it belongs – on the defaulting Member State's Government.

If this was the intention, it can be said already to have had some impact on the position of local authorities. In *Kirklees BC v Wickes Building Supplies Ltd*, Lord Goff refused to require that the local authority provide an undertaking in damages as a corollary of any injunction against the DIY chain store notwithstanding the duty on the court to give in principle effect to the direct effect of Article 30 pending the final ruling of the European Court of Justice. His second reason for so deciding was that it was the Member State that was liable in damages in the judgment in *Francovich* so that it would be wrong for a council, performing its statutory duty under national law, to '... find itself under a liability in damages as a result of performing that duty.'[43] If this is correct, and some commentators have criticized this element of the judgment, it might also be a significant factor in an environmental case if an order were sought quashing a planning permission or licence on the basis of EC law and an intervening developer claims that the implementation of rights flowing from the permission or licence should only be stayed if the applicant can give the equivalent of an undertaking in damages. In these circumstances presumably the applicant could argue that any claim for damages should be against the Government for non-implementation of the directive and accordingly the protection of an undertaking ought not to be necessary. It remains to be seen how the ECJ tackles the issue of damages in *Factortame* (3).[44] (See also *R v Inspectorate of Pollution and another ex parte Greenpeace Limited*,[45] where, although one limb of the argument turned on the application of EC law, the argument based on Lord Goff's judgment does not appear to have been advanced.)

In the context of environmental directives it has been observed that their focus on the protection of the environment rather than the protection of individual's rights may make it difficult to see how the prerequisite for the application of the *Francovich* principle, namely that damages have been suffered, could arise. Commentators have postulated however that if a failure to observe drinking water quality standards occurred leading to actual damage to health or to the incurring of expenses to avoid damage to health or to secure the quality standards, e.g. by the installation of private filtering equipment or the purchase of bottled water, then the prerequisite for recovery would exist (see Somsen Chapter 7). However an action against a local authority rather than central government seems inappropriate in the light of general principles and the comment of Lord Goff quoted above. It is always possible however that a failure on the part of an authority to disregard a national law which is contrary to a directly effective provision of EC law might lead to a claim for damages against the authority itself.

---

[43] [1992] 3 All ER 717 at 735.

[44] Case C–46/93 and C–58/93, *Brasserie du Pêcheur SA and Federal Republic of Germany and between The Queen and Secretary of State for Transport ex parte: Factortame Ltd and Others*, 5.3.96 (not yet reported).

[45] Court of Appeal, [1994] 1 WLR 570.

XIII LOCAL AUTHORITIES AND ADMINISTRATIVE CERTAINTY: THE EFFECT ON PUBLIC ADMINISTRATION OF SUSPENSION OF TIME LIMITS FOR CHALLENGE FOLLOWING *EMMOTT*.

In *Emmott* the Court concluded that:

> ... until such time as a directive has been properly transposed, a defaulting Member State may not rely on an individual's delay in initiating proceedings against it in order to protect rights conferred upon him by the provision of the directive and that a period laid down by national law within which proceedings must be initiated cannot begin to run before that time.[46]

On this ground if the facts in the decision in Swale to deny relief on the basis of delay were to be repeated the decision might now be queried.[47] (Ward 1993 p. 235) There the application was made just two days short of three months, with Simon Brown J. actually finding that 'the challenge ought already to have been brought (before October 12)' i.e. within just less than two months.[48] This did not meet the requirement that the application should be made promptly under Order 53 of the Rules of the Supreme Court. Following *Emmott* it would appear that the delay would be irrelevant when dealing with claims to enforce directly effective environmental requirements. 'The judge must conduct an investigation on the direct effect of the directive before the complaint can be defeated by a limitation period.' (Ward 1993 p. 235)

If this is right, the six week period for challenges to the Secretary of State and the three month period for challenges to the local authority respectively in planning matters may not apply where questions of unimplemented Community law arise. A local authority which grants planning permission, as the result of which a developer enters into contracts, may be in an invidious position if that permission is subsequently challenged but it is clear that the limited periods in which challenges are normally allowed, may not be applicable and administrative certainty therefore not assured for some time. (The recent decision in the *Steenhorst-Neerings* case[49] suggests that the ECJ will not implement the ramifications of the *Emmott* judgment with all the consistency that might have been expected but does not affect the general proposition.)

---

[46] Case C–208/90, *Emmott v Minister for Social Welfare*, judgment of 25 July 1991.
[47] *R v Swale Borough Council and another ex parte RSPB*, [1991] 1 PLR 6.
[48] See p. 24 of the judgment cited note above.
[49] Case C–338/91, *Steenhorst Neerings*, [1993] ECR I–5475.

XIV THE COMPLAINTS PROCEDURE

I have lodged complaints with the Commission on behalf of local
authorities relating to:
- State aids in the energy field,
- delays and inadequacies in the introduction and implementation of
  radiation protection and public information directives,
- inadequacies in the implementation of the freedom of access to
  environmental information directive, in particular relating to the Health
  and Safety Executive's view that environmental information cannot
  include information of importance to human safety; that certain State
  controlled bodies assert that the directive does not apply to them and
  other matters relating to the transposition of the directive,
- inadequacies in the implementation of the environmental assessment
  directive.

I would comment that it is clear that the complaints procedure is overloaded
so that the Commission is unable to react promptly. It appears that DG X1
values the insights into Member State's efforts to transpose directives which
complaints afford and is concerned that implementation should be accurate
and in accordance with the spirit of the relevant directive but at the same
time is unsympathetic to complaints regarding radiation protection matters
and less concerned with the accuracy of transposition of Euratom directives
or the coherence of its own published Communications relevant to such
directives. The Community is committed by the Euratom Treaty to develop
the nuclear industries and does not seem to take a neutral attitude in dealing
with conflicts between its own radiation protection laws and its
developmental mission.

Complaints can bear, or appear to bear fruit. A complaint to the
Commission that the environmental information regulations fail to provide
an effective form of appeal against a refusal of information was followed
some months after, whether as a result or not I cannot state, by a proposal in
the White Paper on Open Government to establish a specific appeal
tribunal.[50] A complaint about the timetable for the transposition of a
directive led to earlier, albeit still late, transposition.

It has never been suggested by the Commission that it would not
countenance complaints from local authorities because of their particular
status. Of course because the Commission retains absolute discretion as to
the appropriate course of action to follow on receipt of a complaint, the

---

[50] Cm 2290 1993, HMSO at para. 6.16.

process can at times be frustrating especially when the complainant is in general bereft of any recourse to the ECJ should the Commission fail to act.[51]

---

[51] See *Star Fruit Co SA v EC Commission*, [1990] 1 CMLR 733.

10. Common Interest Groups and the Enforcement of European Environmental Law

John Faulks and Laurence Rose

I INTRODUCTION

The Royal Society for the Protection of Birds is Europe's largest voluntary nature conservation organization with 860,000 members and 800 staff in 13 offices across the UK. We are the UK partner organization in BirdLife International, a global network of bird conservation organizations represented in 110 countries. In the European Union there are BirdLife partners in every Member State. BirdLife International has a Brussels office which coordinates the work with the European Institutions.

The EU legislation we are most concerned with is, primarily, the birds Directive[1] and habitats Directive.[2] However, supporting measures. and in particular the directive on environmental impact assessment (EIA) and integration measures such as the environmental elements of the structural fund regulations, are also important.

The Commission has observed that:

The [environmental] Directives which cause the greatest difficulties are those relating to waste, discharges to the aquatic environment, the protection of wild birds and environmental impact assessment.

In 1993 birds, nature conservation and EIA were identified as the main implementation and application problems for Greece, Spain, France, Italy

---

[1] Directive 79/409 on the conservation of wild birds, OJ 1979 No. L 103.
[2] OJ 1992 No. L 206, Directive 92/43 on the conservation of natural habitats and of wild fauna and flora.

and the Netherlands.[3] BirdLife International holds some of the best and most up to date data on birds and their habitats, enabling us to determine in detail the measures required of Members States and the Commission in meeting the standards set out in the directives. We therefore readily detect breaches of these standards and are able to collate high quality evidence in the pursuance of cases.

The right to take legal action definitely strengthens an NGOs negotiating position. For example we have campaigned to ensure that licences to kill protected species suspected of damaging agricultural and fisheries interests are only issued where there is sound evidence of significant damage but progress has been slow. Now, after 10 years campaigning, we are challenging the issue of certain licences in court. There has been a marked change in attitude towards our concerns.

Yet, any legal action we may take in defence of our interest is not in preference to consultation.

II THE ROLE OF NGOs IN ENFORCEMENT

Principle 10 of the Rio Declaration, which covers the participation of 'all concerned citizens' in environmental issues, calls on States to give:

> effective access to judicial and administrative proceedings, including redress and remedy

The 5th Action Programme anticipates that:

> Individuals and public interest groups should have practicable access to the courts in order to ensure that their legitimate interests are protected and that prescribed environmental measures are effectively enforced and illegal practices stopped.

Experience from other jurisdictions shows the effectiveness of granting rights of action to citizens as a tool to safeguard the environment (OKO Institut 1993). The Commission has been working on improving access to justice in environmental matters for some time but it has not appeared in the legislative programme for the last two years. Instead the Commission is emphasizing:

1. better consultation before putting a measure in place;
2. better drafting;
3. promoting the informal network of national enforcement agencies (known as the Chester network or ECONET).

---

3 Eleventh Annual Report to the European Parliament on monitoring the application of Community law – 1993, OJ 1994 No. C 154.

One fundamental problem is that of the direct effect of the provisions of environmental directives. As shown by the contributions by Freestone and Krämer elsewhere in this book, it is not self evident whether the measures of most concern to the RSPB and BirdLife International, the birds Directive and the habitats Directive, create rights on which citizens can rely before national courts. The doctrine of direct effect has to be stretched to apply to provisions which cover site designation and site protection as the Member States are granted an element of discretion which through the European Court's case law is only gradually being eroded.[4]

The doctrine of direct effect can be usefully advanced in respect of procedural obligations such as those contained in the EIA directive. However, it needs to be borne in mind that obtaining adequate redress for procedural rights will not necessarily lead to the final result we are seeking. It is perfectly possible for the outcome of a 'negative' environmental assessment to be disregarded and hence for a site to be damaged for 'overriding issues of public interest'.

III PRACTICAL EXPERIENCE

In this paper, we pay special attention to one of the most important measures relating to biodiversity conservation at EU level: Article 4 of Directive 79/409 on the conservation of wild birds. This provision obliges Member States to designate and strictly protect the most important areas for birds according to certain criteria as Special Protection Areas (SPAs).

In order to enforce Article 4, the RSPB has sought to:

1. challenge Member States' failure to designate sites or to effectively protect them;
2. prevent damage from occurring or;
3. ensure the Commission does not approve acts or policies which harm biodiversity.

1. Actions Against the State

a. Complaints to the Commission

The complaints procedure was introduced by the Commission to assist it in fulfilling its duty to ensure that Treaty is respected. As far as the complainant is concerned it is not subject to strict procedural requirements

---

[4] See case C–355/90, *Commission v Spain* (Santoña), ECR [1993] I–4221 and case C–89/89, *Commission v Germany* (Leybucht), ECR [1991] I–883.

although in practice a certain set pattern is adhered to. The complainant makes a submission to the Commission alleging a breach of the Treaty, the Commission takes steps to investigate the allegation and, if it substantiates the allegation and is unable to achieve a negotiated settlement, it issues a so-called Reasoned Opinion. If the action proposed in the Reasoned Opinion is not taken within the deadline stipulated (usually 2 months) the Commission 'may bring the matter before the Court of Justice'.[5] Notable current or recent complaints which we or our partners have lodged include:

United Kingdom

– Cardiff Bay. failure to designate Cardiff Bay as Special Protection Area (SPA) under Article 4 of the birds Directive as this would obstruct plans to construct a barrage across the bay. The plans entail flooding mud flats which are home to internationally significant numbers of certain Annex I species. The procedure is ongoing.

– Lappel Bank: failure to include Lappel bank in the Medway Estuary SPA as it would obstruct the extension of the port of Sheerness. The European Court's judgment of 11 July 1996 represents a major victory for th RSPB (see below).

Greece

– Acheloos: a scheme to divert 40% of the flow of the River Acheloos to irrigate the plain of Thessaly has not been subjected to a comprehensive environmental assessment and presents grave risks to the integrity of the Messolonghi wetlands SPA. The procedure is ongoing and subject to domestic action.

Spain

– Jandia: EU funded wind turbines are being built in an area which qualifies as an SPA in Fuerteventura. The procedure is ongoing

– Tarifa: EU funded wind turbines have been built inside a designated SPA in Andalucia, threatening a vital migration bottleneck. The procedure is ongoing.

– Santoña: Case C–355/90 *Commission v Spain* of 3 August 1993 arose from a complaint against the failure to fully designate a site and building and drainage works damaging its integrity.[6] The case represents one of only two cases under Article 4 of Directive 79/409 to have led to a judgment by the European Court of Justice which in this case went against the Member State.

---

5 Article 169 EC. For a more detailed analysis, see Macrory's contribution in Chapter 2.

6 See note 4.

Portugal
- Tagus Bridge: a river-crossing to serve Lisbon will seriously damage a designated estuarine SPA. The procedure is ongoing and subject to domestic action.

Denmark
- Oresund Bridge: the proposed road bridge linking Denmark and Sweden is disrupting the food source for the largest colony of eider duck in Europe. Significantly, the Commission dropped the case during the Danish Presidency and at the Corfu summit of 24 June 1994 the project was declared a priority for the EU.

For NGOs the advantages of the complaints procedure are that it is cheap, easy to invoke and that there are no preconditions such as having to prove all other options have been exhausted. As a result many NGOs greatly value the procedure as a route to a remedy.

However, the disadvantages which will be outlined below considerably compromise its effectiveness as a means of preventing harm or achieving a quick result. The complainant is a whistle blower rather than a litigant and hence removed from the process. The following shortcoming are particularly significant in the context of dealing with breaches of EC environmental directives.

(i) Lack of political weight granted to environmental complaints An interesting illustration of the low political weight carried by environmental complaints is provided by two complaints about the Acheloos diversion scheme referred to earlier. A complaint on environmental grounds was made by several NGOs in June 1992. A year later a consortium of Greek companies complained to the Commission that the tendering for the scheme infringed the public procurement directives. This led to an urgent meeting between the single market Commissioner and the Greek Government Representative in Brussels and a remarkably speedy decision that the contract would have to be re-let. Thus the decision on the commercially based complaint took only 4 months and took effect before the Greek Parliament approved the contract. The much earlier environmental complaint remained stuck in the system.

This and several other cases have served to demonstrate the extraordinary power wielded by certain DGs, notably DG XVI (Regional Development Funding), over environmental interests represented by DG XI. DG XVI's meddling in environmental complaints extends even to issues, such as Cardiff Bay, where Community funds are not involved.

(ii) Lack of investigative powers   The issue of site designation and the question whether damage to sites is significant depends largely on scientific evidence. The opportunities to verify the data on which decisions are based are few and site visits are the exception rather than the rule. The contrast between DG IVs powers and those of DG XIs has already been alluded to by Lord Clinton-Davis. In the competition field the Commission has considerable powers to investigate alleged wrongdoing. In the environmental sphere, on the other hand, it has to rely on writing diplomatic letters to the defendant government which not rarely are completely ignored. This puts an exceptional onus on the complainant to prove infraction; recent decisions by the chefs de cabinet suggest that this burden is to increase substantially.

(iii) Lack of transparency   Although the Commission expresses the intention of keeping complainants informed and does make some efforts to this effect, the process remains basically secretive. Complainants seldom discover the arguments put forward by the defendant government or the true grounds on which the Commission reaches its decisions.

(iv) Reactive nature of the infringement procedure   A case clearly illustrating the reactive nature of the complaints procedure is that of Glendye (Kincardine & Deeside). Moorland in Scotland was targeted for afforestation and the RSPB complained to the Commission. Although the Commission agreed with the grounds of complaint it took them three years to do so by which time the moorland was planted and the trees were well grown so the damage had been done.

Even where the Commission has started Article 169 proceedings there is considerable difficulty in making a successful case for the grant of interim relief.[7]

(v) The process is political rather than legal   Any formal action to follow up a complaint requires a formal decision of the Commission. These must in principle be taken by all Commissioners, a task delegated to the regular meetings of the Chefs de Cabinet. Even where there are strong legal arguments for commencing proceedings, action is often prevented for political reasons which may be totally unconnected with the facts at issue.

In the 11th Report 'Reunions Paquet' are identified as one of the ways of improving the implementation and application of environmental law. These are the meetings held between the Commission and the representatives of national governments to discuss outstanding issues such as implementing

---

[7]   See for example the application in the *Leybucht Dykes* case, case 57R/89 [1990] 3 CMLR 651.

legislation and complaints. Although this may be a commendable initiative, the negotiated settlements that are reached have a tenuous legal basis. They are not necessarily publicized by the defendant government or the Commission, complicating monitoring and policing the conditions.

By way of illustration, it appears that a deal has been struck over Cardiff Bay. The Commission initially held that the UK was in breach of the Birds Directive. However because the Habitats Directive comes into force shortly which changes the circumstances in which a site may be damaged, it has decided not to any take action. It appears that in exchange the UK is to speed up its designation of sites, implement a national action plan for Dunlin and Redshank and provide new habitats by way of compensation. With no information as to whether the UK has accepted this or how they intend to fulfil these conditions, it is difficult to judge whether or not the compromise reached is acceptable.

It is clear, therefore, that the complaints procedure harbours numerous serious shortcoming in terms of its effectiveness as a tool to enforce EC environmental law. Arguably, however, it is useful for raising the profile of an issue and the rare case to reach the ECJ has a considerable significance for the rest of our work.

b. Enforcing EC environmental law through the national courts

BirdLife partner organizations have been involved in national court actions relating to Acheloos, Oresund, Tagus and Lappel Bank. In the UK we have initiated two judicial review cases:

Lappel Bank

We have challenged the Secretary of State's decision to exclude Lappel Bank from the Medway Estuary SPA. Lappel is recognized as an integral part of an estuarine system with international importance. We argued that he did not have discretion to exclude it on economic grounds particularly in the light of the *Santoña* case.[8] An application for judicial review was refused by the Divisional Court on 8 July 1994. The appeal against this judgment was rejected by the Court of Appeal on 18 August 1994. On 9 February 1995 the appeal was heard by the House of Lords, which decided to refer a question to the European Court of Justice. Advocate General Fennelly issued his Opinion on 21 March 1996. On 11 July 1996 the Court held that Article 4(1) or (2) of Council Directive 79/409 is to be interpreted as meaning that a Member State is not authorized to take account of economic requirements mentioned in Article 2 thereof when designating an SPA and defining it bounderies. It also held that Article

---

[8]   1995 *JEL* p. 245.

4(1) or (2) of the directive is to be interpreted as meaning that a Member State may not, when designating an SPA and defining its bounderies, take account of economic requirements as constituting a general interest superior to that represented by the ecological objective of that directive. Finally and importantly, it was also held that Article 4(1) or (2) of the directive is to be interpreted as meaning that a Member State may not, when designating an SPA and defining its bounderies, take account of economic requirements which may constitute imperative reasons of overriding public interest of the kind referred to in Article 6(4) of Directive 92/43 on the conservation of natural habitats of wild fauna and flora.

The *Lappel Bank* case is an important test case for the RSPB, affecting the designation of many more future SPAs and the Court's judgment therefore represents a major victory.

MAFF Licensing Policy on the Wye

Article 9 of the birds Directive allows Member States to issue licences for the killing of protected species if there is evidence that these are causing significant damage to certain interests. Whilst we do not disagree with this principle, we are challenging the basis for the issue of licences to kill goosander and cormorant which are alleged to pose a threat to fisheries on 2the River Wye. Applicants do not appear to have provided any evidence of serious damage and MAFF do not appear to have taken steps to verify the need for the licences.

(i) Standing Cases taken by interest groups provide some guidance on when environmental groups have standing in judicial review applications. Sufficient interest in the matter to which the application relates must be proved to (a) get the opportunity to argue the case and (b) to justify the remedy sought. Ultimately, both leave to apply and the remedies on judicial review are in the discretion of the courts.

From the case law, the following general points can be deduced about the standing of environmental groups in the UK.

1. No one with an arguable point of law is likely to be refused leave (Grosz 1994).
2. A group is likely to have sufficient interest if it has:
   - had a direct and long term involvement with a site,[9]
   - participated in the consultation process leading to the decision being challenged,[10]

---

[9]   *R v Poole Borough Council ex parte Beebee & others*, [1991] 2 PLR 27; [1991] *JPL* 643.

The following factors may also be taken into account:
- an established track record in the area of policy to which the decision relates,[11]
- a recognized 'client group' which is affected by the decision but which may be unable to bring a claim (in our case birds or priority habitat),[12]
- whether the group represents local residents.[13]
3. It is established that a national Court will be obliged to find an appropriate remedy for infringement of a directly effective right – however an applicant will have to demonstrate that damage has been caused by the failure to implement.[14]

Significantly, the House of Lords recently held that the Equal Opportunities Commission (EOC) had standing to seek a declaration that a UK statute was incompatible with EU law on sex discrimination.[15] It had standing by virtue of its statutory duty and public law role to eliminate discrimination. Ensuring that the relevant EC law was upheld was seen as a part of that role. It remains to be seen whether this adds anything new to the test of standing for NGOs.

The court must be satisfied that no alternative remedy could be pursued. Thus, in the *Canford Heath* case, the court went so far as to suggest that the Nature Conservancy Council was the body which should have been dealing with the matter rather than the applicants. Ironically, in the recent Friends of the Earth drinking water case, it was suggested that the complaints procedure might represent an alternative remedy which could persuade the Court not to grant relief.[16] Although, eventually, the point was not decided since the illegality of the decision challenged was not established, the trend harbours a real danger that it could take NGOs back to square one.

Hopefully the Law Commission will recommend a workable solution to these problems. We have submitted recommendations in our joint response

---

[10] Lappel Bank: *R v Swale Borough Council ex parte RSPB*, [1991] 1 PLR 6; *R v HMIP & MAFF ex parte Greenpeace*, [1994] 4 All ER 325.

[11] *R v HMIP & MAFF ex parte Greenpeace*, [1994] 4 All ER 325; *R v Lord Chancellor ex parte The Law Society*, Times, 25 June, 1993.

[12] *R v Poole Borough Council ex parte Beebee & others*, [1991] 2 PLR 27; [1991] *JPL* 643; *R v Secretary of State for Social Services, ex parte Child Poverty Action Group*, [1990] 2 QB 540; *R v Secretary of State for Health ex parte Alcohol Recovery Project*, draft judgment (unreported).

[13] *R v HMIP & MAFF ex parte Greenpeace*, [1994] 4 All ER 325.

[14] *R v SoS for Transport ex parte Twyford Parish Council*, [1992] *JEL* 273.

[15] [1994] All ER 916.

[16] *R v SoS for the Environment ex parte FOE & another*, Times, 4 April 1994.

with other NGOs to Law Commission Paper No 126 'Administrative Law: Judicial Review and Statutory Appeals'.[17]

2. Challenging the Commission

National courts do not have jurisdiction over the activities of the European institutions whilst NGOs only have limited rights before the ECJ.

a. Article 173

Under Article 173 EC any natural or legal person may institute proceedings before the ECJ to review the legality of an act of one of the European institutions.[18] This only applies where the applicant has suffered damage as a result of (i) a decision which is addressed to him or (ii) a decision which, although addressed to someone else or in the form of a regulation, is of 'direct and individual concern' to the applicant.

As a route for citizens to review the legality of decisions seen as environmentally damaging taken by the Commission, Article 173 initially looks attractive. However, because of the tests of admissibility established by the ECJ, particularly the interpretation of 'direct and individual concern' thus far it has proved to be of limited value in the environmental field.

There have been no successful environmental actions based on Article 173 although the issue has most recently been brought before the Court in two instances. The first relates to plans to build a visitor centre in an environmentally sensitive area of a site of international botanical importance at Mullaghmore in the Burren, Ireland.[19] Irish NGO, An Taisce and the Worldwide Fund for Nature are seeking to challenge the Commission's decision to close a complaint file thus allowing EU funds to be released for the construction of the visitor centre. This case appears to be turning on whether or not the decision to close the complaint file is one which is subject to the jurisdiction of the Court rather than whether the decision is of direct and individual concern to the applicants. The second case concerns a Commission decision to fund the construction of two coal fired power stations in the Canary Islands.[20] Local residents and Greenpeace International are challenging it claiming that the Commission acted illegally because it knew or should have known that obligations arising out of the environmental impact assessment directive had not been

---

[17] See Law Commission Paper 126.

[18] For a detailed analysis, see Sands' contribution in Chapter 3.

[19] Case T–461/93, *An Taisce & WWF(UK) v Commission*, [1994] ECRII–733.

[20] See case T–585/93, *Stichting Greenpeace Council v EC Commission*, order of 9 August 1995 (not yet reported), OJ 1993 No. C 43.

complied with. Thus, construction started before the EIA was completed, the public was not fully consulted and the environmental information supplied by the developer was inadequate particularly as it did not include examination of alternatives.

The RSPB and our partners in the EU are following these cases with particular interest since we are seriously contemplating challenging certain funding decisions of the Commission. The *Tarifa* case and, should funding be granted, the *Acheloos* case particularly merit consideration in this regard.

An interesting case in the national courts of Greece deserves to be considered in this connection too. EU funds were granted to build a fish farm in a wetland near Messolonghi which is protected under the birds Directive, causing serious damage. The Greek court, hearing a complaint by national NGOs, declared the planning decision illegal on the basis of a national law which automatically transposes the directive. Hence, the national court has declared an EU funded project to be, in effect, contrary to EU law. EU funding allocations are subject, through regulation 2052/88, to compliance with European Union environmental law.[21]

b. Article 175
Article 175 allows natural or legal persons to complain to the ECJ that an institution has failed to address to that person any act other than a recommendation or an opinion. However the case law on private applications has been described as a history of failure (see Sharpston 1993) and again it is difficult to imagine a legally binding act in the environmental field that would be addressed to an individual except perhaps a funding decision.

c. Third party interventions
A person not party to a case before the ECJ can intervene to support the position of one of the parties if they can establish an interest in the result. No citizen intervention has ever taken place in an environmental case but the European consumers organization BEUC has been admitted as an intervenor in a case brought by the Ford Motor Company against the Commission.[22]

d. Article 177
Article 177 EC gives the ECJ jurisdiction to give a preliminary ruling on the interpretation of the Treaty or Community legislation. If a national court is

---

[21] Article 7(1) Regulation 2052/88, OJ 1988 No. L 185 (as amended by Regulation 2081/93.

[22] Case 229/82, *Ford v Commission*, [1984] ECR 309.

faced with a question of Community law which it considers should be clarified by a definitive ruling from the ECJ it can use the Article 177 reference procedure. Article 177 EC is a useful avenue allowing citizens to enforce EU environmental law. A preliminary reference from the administrative court in Nantes in France recently obtained a ruling that the hunting seasons in France were contrary to the birds Directive.[23] It should be borne in mind that, although applicants can request a national court to make a reference, ultimately that court enjoys considerable discretion in its decision whether or not to refer.[24] Moreover, a decision to refer tends to lead to delays which may take a year to 18 months.

IV USING THE OTHER EUROPEAN INSTITUTIONS

1. European Parliament

Before the Treaty on European Union came into force, the European Parliament's role was largely limited to giving political momentum to an issue. However, following the adoption of the Treaty on European Union, the formal enforcement powers of the European Parliament have been strengthened by the establishment of the Ombudsman and Temporary Committees of Inquiry.

a. Ombudsman[25]
Any person can submit a complaint to the Ombudsman asserting 'maladministration' by one of the European institutions. If the complaint is substantiated the matter is referred to the relevant institution and a report is made to European Parliament. It remains to be seen what the standards of proof will be that will be required of the applicant.

b. Right of petition[26]
Citizens have an express right to petition the Parliament. Petitions are received and scrutinized by the Petitions Committee. A petition about the environmental impacts of the Oresund bridge case did lead to some useful

---

[23] See case C435/92, *Association pour la protection des Animaux Sauvages & Others v Prefet de Maine et Loire & Prefet de la Loire Atlantique*, [1994] 3 CMLR 685.

[24] Lower courts enjoy complete discretion in this respect whereas '...' must refer a question. Even the latter, however will enjoy a discretion in deciding whether a question is 'necessary'.

[25] Cf. Article 138e EC.

[26] Cf. Article 138d EC.

cross examination of the Commission by the Parliament. Moreover, the opportunity now exists for the European Parliament to act on petitions by calling a Temporary Committee of Inquiry.

c. Temporary committees of inquiry[27]

At the request of one quarter of Parliament's members, it can set up a Temporary Committee of Inquiry to investigate alleged contraventions of Community law or instances of maladministration in the implementation of Community law. 15 members must complete the investigation into the issue within 9 months. The President of the Parliament is obliged to 'take all the necessary steps to ensure that the conclusions of the inquiry are acted on in practice'. Presumably that could include taking another European institution to the ECJ pursuant to, for example, Articles 173 and 175 EC.

2. Court of Auditors

The Court of Auditors' remit is to ensure that Community resources are used efficiently and effectively. Individuals do not have the right to petition the Court directly but there are ways of trying to ensure that the Court becomes seized of a matter. Again the result of an inquiry by the Court of Auditors is only likely to influence future practice but can have significance. The Court of Auditors recently published their findings on the environmental impact of spending under the Structural Funds.[28] Their investigation was undoubtedly prompted by the growing outcry at the lack control and safeguards which existed at the time. The Court's report added considerable weight to arguments advanced by NGOs that the administration of the Funds was inadequate to safeguard compliance with EU environmental law. Significant changes were made to the structural funds regulations when they were renewed.

---

[27] Cf. Article 138c EC.
[28] See Court of Auditors Report, OJ 1992 No. C 247.

V CONCLUSIONS

As experts in their field, as 'watchdogs', as representatives of a very large group of European citizens and as champions of all citizens' rights to a clean, diverse environment, NGOs have a key role in the enforcement of EU law. In practice, this role cannot be fully realized under the present legal and administrative set-up within the European Union. It is unlikely that any isolated action will change this; rather, we propose a mixed solution which is likely to encompass all of the following:

1. *Treaty reform*
The intergovernmental conference in 1996 constitutes an important opportunity to revise the Treaty in a way so as to acknowledge the existence of environmental rights which the European Court of Justice must protect. The Treaty should give appropriate recognition to a right to a clean environment rich in diversity of species and habitats.

2. *A 'horizontal' directive on access to the legal process*
The existing draft proposal for a directive elaborated by the OKO institute (OKO Institut 1993) should be promoted as it includes a workable definition of an environmental organization, anticipates interim remedies and eases the burden of proving harm.

3. *Streamlining and de-politicizing the complaints procedure: towards arbitration?*
Despite the clear shortcomings of the complaints procedure presented in this paper, the advantages of the procedure – ease of access and cheapness – have made it of the utmost importance to NGOs. However, NGOs would greatly prefer access to an effective, quick and hopefully preventive remedy of a non-judicial nature, something which would surely suit governments and the Commission alike. Provided a means can be found of filtering out spurious, mischievous or otherwise ill-founded claims, it should be possible for the Commission to broker technical solutions in the majority of cases. The role of the Environment Agency as a collator and keeper of information will be important in achieving such solutions and its work programme and resources should reflect this.

11. Applying EC Environmental Law on the Ground

Peter Bird

I INTRODUCTION

This paper examines the practical implications of applying European Community legislation for the normal operations of the National Rivers Authority (NRA). It assesses the mode of incorporation of EC water directives into the legislative framework of the United Kingdom and some of the practical difficulties encountered in the structuring of sampling and analysis programmes designed by the NRA to comply with the obligations.

The implementation of Directive 91/271/EEC on the treatment of urban waste waters and directive 76/160 on the quality of bathing water are used as typical examples to examine the process of the incorporation of an environmental directive into UK legislation. A brief overview of some of the most important other water directives is provided showing how these have been used as building blocks in the construction of the NRA sampling and analysis programme.

II THE TRANSPOSITION OF EC WATER DIRECTIVES IN THE UK: THE EXAMPLE OF THE URBAN WASTE WATER DIRECTIVE

EC directives are binding legislative instruments which, once agreed by the Council of Ministers, must be implemented by Member States using their own legislative processes in a way so as to ensure that all their requirements are properly translated. Each Member State has its own legislative processes and it may not be possible in all cases to incorporate literally the wording from the directive directly into national legislation. Thus, whereas some Member States translate the provisions of a particular directive in their entirety, others have to reword or add schedules to existing legislation. When the Commission is examining whether environmental directives have been properly implemented, the former countries obviously easily pass inspection whereas the latter countries may require deeper probing to ensure that all aspects of the directive are honoured.

The obligation for European Community legislation to be properly implemented has highlighted some of the complexities in the UK legislative system. which has to take account of three separate legal systems, those for England and Wales, Scotland and Northern Ireland. There are also three regulatory bodies – the NRA for England and Wales, the River Purification Boards for Scotland and the Department of the Environment for Northern Ireland and it is necessary for a directive to be implemented properly in all three systems. In case C–337/89, for example the United Kingdom was found to be in breach of Directive 80/778 relating to water intended for human consumption, *inter alia*, because no suitable implementing legislation was in force in Northern Ireland.[1]

In the UK the implementation process has traditionally been undertaken through additions to current legislation by means of schedules or Statutory Instruments. Therefore, it has been necessary for Government departments to subject the legislation to detailed scrutiny. Before the schedules or Statutory Instruments are written, it must be ensured that the directive is properly understood so that its intention and the purpose are clearly reflected by such implementing legislation.

Before domestic legislation is drawn up, it has been the practice of the sponsoring Government department to form a group or committee from interested parties to examine a particular directive and highlight any areas requiring specific clarification or interpretation within the enabling legislation. A recent case providing practical insights in the process by which directives are implemented and the kind of problems encountered by the competent authorities is provided by the urban waste water directive

1. The Transposition of the Urban Waste Water Treatment Directive and the Work of the Implementation Group

Directive 91/219 on urban waste water concerns the collection, treatment and discharge of urban waste water and the treatment and discharge of waste water from certain industrial sectors. The objective of the directive is

---

[1] Case C–377/89, *Commission v United Kingdom*, [1992] ECR I–6103.

to protect the environment from the adverse effects of the above mentioned waste water discharges. (Article 1)

For the purpose of its implementation an 'Implementation Group' was formed in 1991 whose terms of reference were to examine and clarify the wording of the directive and to ensure that all potential participants in its application had an opportunity to develop a clear understanding of their role in the implementation and enforcement of the directive. The Implementation Group was set up by the Department of the Environment as soon as the directive had been approved by the Council of Ministers.

The Group consisted of representatives from the Department of the Environment, National Rivers Authority, Ministry of Agriculture, Fisheries and Food, Water Services Association, Office of Water Regulation, the Scottish Office, River Purification Boards, DoE Northern Ireland and the Treasury. The remit of the group was to advise the Government on the detailed interpretation of the directive and to recommend actions to be included in the Regulations for its implementation.

An initial reading of the directive provided general indications as to its thrust and spirit but it soon became clear that the interpretation of a number of key phrases would have a significant impact on the application of the directive in the UK. The intention of the DoE was that these issues should be examined in detail by the group to ensure that the Regulations, timetabled by the directive to be laid in June 1993, took full account of them and a clear unambiguous consensus was obtained. The group met at regular intervals and considered a wide range of issues in some detail, some of which will be discussed below. However, many other items of less import were also resolved in drawing up the Regulations.

a. The definition of 'normal operating conditions' (Annex 1(D)(4))
In respect of the reference methods for monitoring and the evaluation of results, the directive specifies that the failing samples taken under 'normal operating conditions' should not deviate from the parametric values by more than 100 per cent.

All analytical details used in testing compliance with the directive are to be displayed on public registers. There clearly will be occasions where dischargers do not comply with the required conditions through no fault of their own, such as electricity failure or vandalism at the plant. Where these unforeseeable non-compliances are recorded it would be misleading to assume that the directive had been breached. A full list of conditions considered to be outside 'normal operating conditions' therefore needed to be agreed which, if they applied, would be recorded on the public register.

b. 'Unusual weather conditions' (Annex 1(D)(5))
The directive also allows a derogation for 'unusual weather conditions'. Whilst waste water treatment plants are usually designed to cope with a wide variation of weather types giving rise to increased flow and temperature variations, extreme variations cannot be accommodated. The directive merely referring to 'unusual situations such as those due to heavy rain', agreement needed to be reached on exactly what kind of conditions justified derogations from the directive's requirements.

c. Composite versus spot sampling programmes (Annex 1(D)(1)
The directive requires composite samples to calculate performance of treatment works, whereas the general requirement in the UK for compliance calculation is for spot samples. To ensure that plant performance had been properly translated, it was necessary to agree a research project to compare the results of composite samples with spot samples taken at the same time.

d. Monitoring programmes (Article 15, Annex(1)(D))
The directive specifies a minimum sampling programme which depends on the size of the treatment plant. This Community sampling programme had to be integrated into the programme which existing UK legislation usually required to be specified in the consent conditions of the treatment works.

e. Definition of estuaries (Article 2)
The directive defines an 'estuary' as the transitional area at the mouth of a river between fresh-water and coastal waters but requires each Member State to define the outer (seaward) limits for the purposes of classifying discharges. Whereas the inner boundaries of estuaries were already defined under The Water Resources Act 1991, the outer boundaries required an agreed definition.

f. Primary treatment standards (Article 2)
The directive provides that discharges receiving primary treatment should have a specified percentage removal of contaminants. Thus, 'primary treatment' is defined as:

treatment of urban waste water by a physical and/or chemical process involving settlement of suspended solids, or other processes in which the biochemical oxygen demand (BOD5) of the incoming waste water is reduced by at least 20 per cent before discharge and the total suspended solids of the incoming waste water is reduced by at least 50 per cent.'

This was a novel concept for UK control and agreements had to be reached on where measurements had to be made and which parts of the process should be included.

g. Collecting systems (Article 3, Annex 1(A))
The directive stipulates that collecting systems have to be designed, constructed and maintained in accordance with the 'best technical knowledge not entailing excessive cost', notably regarding:
–volume and characteristics of urban waste;
–prevention of leaks;
–limitation of pollution of receiving waters due to storm water overflows.

It had therefore become necessary to define the design standards required, especially with respect to the prevention of storm water overflows which are the cause of environmental pollution. The operators and regulators co-operated on proposed sewer designs to eliminate these intermittent discharges.

h. Agglomerations (Article 2)
The definition of agglomerations in the directive was not very helpful in deciding whether certain settlements should have collecting systems and then treatment plants. Hence, according to Article 2(4) 'agglomeration' means 'an area where the population and/or economic activities are sufficiently concentrated for urban waste water to be collected and conducted to an urban waste water treatment plant or to a final discharge point.' Several examples of agglomerations were examined, all with very different implications for how discharges were to be treated under the directive.

i. Appropriate treatment (Articles 2 and 7)
Article 7 of the directive provides that Member States shall ensure that by 31 December 2005, urban waste water entering collecting systems shall before discharge be subject to 'appropriate treatment', a concept defined in Article 2(7) as:

> treatment of urban waste water by any process and/or disposal system which after discharge allows the receiving waters to meet the relevant quality objectives and the relevant provisions of this and other Community directives.

The types of treatment allowable under 'appropriate treatment' had to be agreed in such a way so as to ensure that all sewage discharges were properly treated.

j. Trade effluent regulations (Articles 11 and 13)

Article 11 of the directive provides that Member States must ensure that the discharge of industrial waste water into collecting systems and urban waste water treatment plants is subject to prior regulations and/or specific authorizations by the competent authority or appropriate body. Such regulations and/or specific authorizations must satisfy the requirements set out in Annex 1,C. In addition, in respect of biodegradable industrial waste water from plants belonging to one of the industrial sectors listed in Annex 3 and 2 which does not enter urban waste water treatment plants before discharging to receiving waters, the directive requires respect with prior regulations and/or specific authorizations in respect of all discharges from plants representing 4 000 population equivalent or more. By 31 December 1993, the competent authority was obliged to set requirements appropriate for the nature of the industry concerned for the discharge of such water.

Trade effluent discharges were therefore examined with a view to ascertaining whether discharges from particular industries could all be given a similar consent condition. It soon became obvious that similar industries give rise to very dissimilar effluents and that discharges should be controlled by their impact on the environment and not by a single standard.

k. Sludge disposal (Article 14)

Eutrophication of marine waters in the Mediterranean, the Baltic and the North and Adriatic Seas and the associated problem of algae blooms led the Third International Conference on the protection of the North Sea to pledge phasing out disposal at sea of sewage sludge by the year 1998. This commitment was implemented by the Community by means of Article 14 of the directive. Sludge disposal to sea therefore had to be eliminated by 1998, and safe alternatives for future disposal needed to be found.

m. Definition of sensitive and less sensitive areas (Articles 5 and 6)

According to Article 5 of the directive, Member States had to identify 'sensitive areas' by 31 December 1993. Before discharge into these sensitive areas, urban waste water entering collecting systems has to be subject to more stringent treatment than that described in Article 4 (secondary treatment). Similarly, Article 6 obliges Member States to identify 'less sensitive areas' where discharges must be subjected to treatment which is less stringent than Article 4, provided that such discharges at least receive primary treatment and that comprehensive studies indicate that such discharges will not adversely affect the environment.

Clearly, much of the impact of the directive therefore rested on the definition of sensitive or less sensitive area. Although the directive provides guidance on these terms, it still leaves the competent authorities with considerable discretion.[2] A great deal of time and effort was put into the examination of data to ensure that the definition of eutrophication and the comprehensive studies required for less sensitive areas were accurate thus putting scarce resources to the best use.

---

[2] Annex II provides the criteria for identification of sensitive and less sensitive areas as follows:

A. Sensitive areas

A water body must be identified as a sensitive area if it falls into one of the following groups:

(a) natural freshwater lakes, other freshwater bodies, estuaries and coastal waters which are found to be eutrophic or which in the near future may become eutrophic if protective action is not taken.

The following elements might be taken into account when considering which nutrient should be reduced by further treatment:

(i) lakes and streams reaching lakes/reservoirs/closed bays which are found to have a poor water exchange, whereby accumulation may take place. In these areas, the removal of phosphorous should be included unless it can be demonstrated that the removal will have no effect on the level of eutrophication. Where discharges from large agglomorations are made, the removal of nitrogen may also be considered;

(ii) estuaries, bays and other coastal waters which are found to have a poor water exchange, or which receive large quantities of nutrients. Discharges from small agglomerations are usually of minor importance in those areas, but for large agglomerations, the removal of phosphorus and/or nitrogen should be included unless it can be demonstrated that the removal will have no effect on the level of eutrophication;

(b) surface freshwater intended for the abstraction of drinking water which could contain more than the concentration of nitrate laid down under the relevant provisions of Council Directive 75/440 of 16 June 1975 concerning the quality required of surface water intended for the abstraction of drinking water in the Member States if action is not taken;

(c) areas where further treatment than prescribed in Article 4 of this Directive is necessary to fulfil Council Directives.

B. Less sensitive areas

A marine water body or area can be identified as a less sensitive area if the discharge of waste water does not adversely affect the environment as a result of morphology, hydrology or specific hydraulic conditions in that area.

When identifying less sensitive areas, Member States shall take into account the risk that the discharged load may be transferred to adjacent areas where it can cause detrimental effects. Member States shall recognize the presence of sensitive areas outside their national jurisdiction.

The following elements shall be taken into consideration when identifying less sensitive areas:

open bays, estuaries and other coastal waters with a good water exchange and not subject to eutrophication of oxygen depletion or which are considered unlikely to become eutrophic or to develop oxygen depletion due to the discharge of urban waste water.

The definition of sensitive and less sensitive areas hence was a crucial issue which needed to be covered in the guidance and a small sub-group of regulators was formed from NRA, RPBs, DoE, MAFF, SO and DoE NI to ensure that actions taken across the UK were compatible. The sub-group produced two consultation papers in 1992 concerning;

1. Criteria and procedures for identifying sensitive and less sensitive areas and polluted waters (Nitrates Directive); and
2. Methodology for identifying sensitive areas and methodology for designating vulnerable zones (Nitrates Directive).

The intention was to ensure that clear guidance was given for the identification of these areas in line with the directive's timetables and to ensure that these issues were covered in the Regulations being prepared by the Government

n. Relation with EC Directives on Habitats, Birds and Agricultural Nitrates

The directive requires that the operation of other directives is not adversely affected by the implementation of the directive. Of particular importance in this respect are the directives on habitats, wild birds and agricultural nitrates. This was illustrated particularly graphically in case C–355/90, *Commission v Spain*, the Court implied that specific waste water treatment plants needed to be constructed in the Marismas de Santoña even though Directive 79/409 itself is silent on the matter.[3] Waters in Special Protection Areas may well require further treatment than would be strictly necessary for a sensitive area in view of the provision in Annex 2A(c).

2. Further Work Undertaken by the Regulators

In England and Wales the NRA had been designated the competent authority for recommending sensitive and less sensitive areas. However, the NRA consists of 8 regional bodies which are responsible for the environmental data in their own area and in the course of collecting data for the sensitive areas and it was recognized that some regional diversity in the interpretation of data was taking place. A small NRA group was formed to give more detailed advice on the quality of data which was acceptable for sensitive area identification. This advice was standardized against methods in use in Scotland and Northern Ireland to ensure that an equivalent approach was being undertaken across the UK.

---

[3]   Case C–355/90, *Commission v Spain*, [1993] ECR I–4221.

The final recommendations for sensitive areas were made to the DoE by the NRA in 1993 and the list of sensitive areas was published in May 1994. The remainder of the statutory requirements of the directive were tackled in a similar fashion so that all the issues could be sorted out in time to meet the directive's deadlines which commence in 1998.

III MONITORING AND PRACTICAL IMPLEMENT-ATION: THE EXAMPLE OF THE BATHING WATER DIRECTIVE (76/160)

There are a number of water directives which have already been implemented and for which the sampling and reporting requirements need to be carefully programmed to ensure that targets in the directives can be met. The practical problems of implementation have been addressed in each individual directive. As more experience is gained, these guidelines may have to be reviewed; instructions are issued to regions on the construction of sampling and analysis programmes and these are reviewed on a regular basis taking account of new interpretations. A short review of some of these directives and some of the issues encountered in their implementation may serve to illustrate the sometimes difficult position of the NRA.

A particularly illustrative example is offered by directive 76/160 on the quality of bathing water, which has been the subject of much controversy. The directive[4] was first proposed by the Commission in March 1975.[5] In summary, it aims at raising or maintaining the quality of fresh, running, stagnant and sea water in areas where bathing is authorized or not prohibited and traditionally practised by a large number of bathers. For the achievement of these objectives, the preamble of the directive refers to the fixing of quality objectives. These are defined as 'a set of requirements which must be fulfilled at a given time, now or in the future, by a given environment or particular part thereof'.[6] In order to attain these objectives, the directive lays down 19 parametric values. In the case of 13 of the latter, the directive fixes both mandatory (I) and guide (G) values. Minimum sampling frequencies are prescribed as well as where and how samples must be taken.

The physical, chemical and microbiological parameters indicated in the Annex form an integral part of the directive (Article 2). For these

---

[4] Directive 76/160, OJ 1976 No. L 31.
[5] OJ 1975 No. C 67.
[6] First Report on the State of the Environment, (Brussels-Luxembourg, 1977) p. 19.

parameters, Member States must set, for all bathing areas or for each bathing area individually, the values for the parameters given in the Annex (Article 3(1)). Member States must set values at least as stringent as the (I) values but may decide not to fix any values for the parameters for which no values are given in the Annex until such time as figures have been determined. The legal significance of the guide values remains unclear, as Member States are merely required to endeavour – subject to the non-degradation principle of Article 7 – to observe them as guide-lines (Article 3(3)).

As the major concern is the role played by bathing water polluted by sewage effluent in the transmission of infectious diseases, the microbiological standards are undoubtedly the most important. Hence, the directive requires the monitoring of pathogenic bacteria such as coliform, streptococcic, salmonella and enterovirus. However, the directive is not exclusively concerned with protecting public health. This is evidenced by the remaining 14 physico-chemical parameters, some of which aim at ensuring a minimum standard of amenity rather than protecting public health. Thus, among the substances to be monitored are those imparting an unpleasant taste to water such as phenols and hydrocarbon oils and detergents. Importantly, bathing water is deemed to conform to the relevant parameters if a proportion (varying between 80 and 95 percent) of the samples conforms with the parametric values (Article 5). It is suggested that this refers to all samples examined in one year (see Gameson 1979 p. 207).

Total coliforms and faecal coliforms should be sampled fortnightly, but when a sampling produced in previous years produced results which are appreciably better than required by the directive and no new factor likely to lower the quality of the water has appeared, the sampling may be reduced by a factor of 2. The remaining 3 microbiological standards only require sampling when inspection in the bathing area shows that the substance may be present or that the quality of the water has deteriorated. From the 14 physico-chemical parameters colour, mineral oils, surface active substances, phenols transparency, tarry residues and floating materials are to be monitored fortnightly.[7] However, in the case of exceptional geographical or meteorological conditions provision exists for exceeding the limits of colour and transparency. Except for the parameters ammonia and nitrogen Kjehldahl, all remaining physico-chemical parameters must be checked by the competent authorities when an inspection in the bathing area shows that

---

[7]   All the substances to be sampled fortnightly are subject to the provision that sampling may be halved if samples in previous years showed results appreciably better than required by the Directive and meanwhile no factor likely to lower the quality of the water has appeared.

the substance may be present or that the quality of the water has deteriorated, leaving considerable scope for interpretation.

The directive also determines where and how samples should be taken. Sampling must be carried out at points where the number of bathers is highest and should begin two weeks before the bathing season. They should be representative of the stretch of water monitored and therefore undue collection of either the surface film or the bed material should be avoided. Samples should be taken 30 cm below the surface of the water except for mineral oil samples. In practice this may prove difficult during bad weather. As a result of pressure from the British participants at the early Brussels meetings, Article 6(3) recognizes the importance of visual inspection. Additional sampling must take place should an inspection by a competent authority or sampling operations reveal that there is a discharge likely to lower the quality of bathing water, or when there are any other grounds for suspecting that there is a decrease in water quality (Article 6(4)). Sampling programmes need to be constructed for each bathing season (May – September) to ensure that different days of the week and states of the tide are covered. All 419 bathing waters in the UK need to be analyzed for at least 20 samples per bathing season to ensure proper statistical interpretation. The directive only requires a minimum of 13 samples but this leads to difficulties as the standard requires 95 per cent compliance. There are no general requirements for sample handling, therefore the NRA has developed instructions to ensure all samples are treated in a similar manner.

Article 13 which originally provided that Member States shall, four years following the notification of the directive and at regular intervals thereafter, submit a comprehensive report to the Commission on their bathing water and the most significant characteristics thereof has been amended by Article 3 of Directive 91/692 of 23 December 1991 on standardizing and rationalizing reports on the implementation of certain environmental directives.[8] The bathing water directive occupies a special position in that Member States must submit reports annually and in sufficient time to inform the public of the quality of bathing water of the most recent period. The first report on the quality of bathing water was to be transmitted to the Commission by 31 December 1993 on the basis of the questionnaire contained in Decision 92/446 of 27 July 1992.[9] The Commission has since long published consolidated reports providing a comparative analysis of

---

[8] OJ 1991 No. L 377.
[9] OJ 1992 No. L 247.

bathing water quality throughout the Community[10] but under the amended Article 13 the Commission must publish a Community report on the implementation of the directive within four months of receiving the reports from the Member States. All bathing waters in the EU are classified using the same standards. This ensures comparability across member states even though the bathing waters may have quite different physical characteristics

The directive has been subject to intense criticism, some of which has been acknowledged by the Commission, which has proposed changes to the directive.[11]

1. Implementation in the UK

The process of formal implementation needed to be completed two years after notification of the directive (Article 12(1)). The original draft of the directive provided for a period of eight years to allow Member States to comply with the limit values of the directive. However, Article 4(1) now provides that Member States must take all the measures to ensure that within 10 years following notification of the directive, the quality of bathing water conforms to the limit values set in accordance with Article 3. For the majority of Member States, this period expired in December 1985. A distinction is drawn between existing and new bathing waters. Bathing waters created after December 1975 had to comply with 'I values' from the moment bathing was first permitted with the caveat that those bathing areas created during the two years following notification the values needed not to be observed until the end of that period i.e. December 1977 (Article 4(2)).

Crucially, the Court has ruled that the time limits laid down in Article 4(1) and 4(3) begin to run from the date of notification of the directive and not from the moment when waters are identified as bathing waters.[12] In other words, the scope of application of the directive and hence the deadlines for compliance are not conditional upon the national designation of bathing waters, a point most clearly demonstrated in case C–59/90 in relation to the bathing areas of Blackpool and of Southport.

Derogations from the obligations under the directive are allowed by the following provisions;

---

[10] Most recent data are found in the Twelfth Report on the quality of bathing waters, EUR 15976.

[11] Amended proposal for a Council Directive amending Directives 80/778 on drinking water, 76/160 on bathing water, 75/440 on surface water, and 79/869 on methods of measurement and frequencies of analysis of surface water, COM(89) 478 final, OJ 1989 No. C 300.

[12] Case C–56/90, *Commission v United Kingdom*, [1994] 1 CMLR 769, ground 36.

- Article 4(3) permits Member States, in exceptional circumstances, to grant derogations in respect of the ten-year period for ensuring that bathing water conforms with the parameters indicated in the annex. The justification for such a derogation must be based on plans for the management of water within the area concerned and be communicated to the Commission not later than six years following the notification of the directive. In case C–59/90 the Court rejected the UK's plea based on the principle of proportionality that a failure by a Member State to comply with the six year time-limit should not deprive it of the right to grant derogations in respect of the ten-year period provided for in Article 4(1).[13]
- Article 5(2) allows deviations from the values referred to in Article 3 not to be taken into consideration in the calculation of the percentages of the samples which must conform to those values, when they are the result of floods, other natural disasters or abnormal weather conditions.
- Article 8 allows derogation in the case of certain physico-chemical parameters in the event of exceptional weather or geographical conditions or when bathing water undergoes natural enrichment in certain substances causing a deviation from the values prescribed in the Annex. However, in no case may the exceptions disregard the requirements essential for public health protection and Member States must always forthwith notify the Commission with the reasons for the derogations and the periods anticipated.

The scope of application of the directive is set forth in Article 1. The directive concerns the quality of bathing water, with the exception of water intended for therapeutic purposes and water used in swimming pools. Of vital importance is the definition of 'bathing water' in Article 1(2)(a) which reads:

> 'bathing water' means all running or still fresh waters of parts thereof and sea water, in which:
> – bathing is explicitly authorized by the competent authority of each Member State, or
> – bathing is not prohibited and is traditionally practised by a large number of bathers.

In Britain such a system of authorization does not exists, so that it initially appeared within the discretion of national authorities to designate those waters which fall within the scope of the second part of the definition. The directive itself provides no indication what constitutes 'a large number of bathers' and whether this criterion should be given a national or a

---

[13] *Ibid.* ground 39.

Community meaning. In July 1979 the Department of the Environment issued guide-lines for the identification of bathing waters which stipulated:

> The Department and the Welsh Office would not expect a stretch of water to be classified as 'bathing water' for the purposes of the directive unless it had been assessed that at some time during the bathing season there were at least 500 people in the water (regardless of the length of the water in question). Any stretch where the number of bathers has been assessed as more than 1,500 per mile will be classified as a bathing water. Where the number of bathers is assessed as between 750 and 1,500 per mile water authorities and district councils should discuss whether the water in question is sufficiently well used to be classified as a bathing water under the terms of the directive.

Under these guide-lines, 27 bathing areas were initially identified. After pressure by the national tourist industry and the European Commission (which issued a Reasoned Opinion) eventually 389 bathing waters were designated by 2 February 1987, the current number totalling 458.

Although the directive hence leaves considerable room for interpretation where the definition of bathing water is concerned it should be noted that, unlike the freshwater fish and shellfish Directives,[14] the bathing water directive does not provide for the 'designation' of bathing waters. Hence, the question whether waters should or should not be regarded 'bathing waters' within for the purposes of the directive is determined by Community law.

In this respect, some guidance was provided by the European Court of Justice in case C–56/90 of 14 July 1993, which focused on bathing water quality at Blackpool, Formby and Southport. After three Reasoned Opinions in 1986 and 1987, the Commission took the case to the European Court of Justice on 7 March 1990. The Court ruled that the definition of bathing water should be interpreted in the light of the directive's underlying objectives as set out in the preamble. It noted:

> Those objectives would not be attained if the waters of bathing resorts equipped with facilities such as changing huts, toilets, markers indicating bathing areas, and supervised by lifeguards, could be excluded from the scope of the directive solely because the number of bathers was below a certain threshold. Such facilities and the presence of lifeguards constitute evidence that the bathing area is frequented by a large number of bathers whose health must be protected.[15]

The effect of this ruling would seem to be that absolute thresholds for numbers of bathers are not acceptable as the sole criterion for determining

---

[14] Directive 78/659 on the quality of fresh waters needing protection in order to support fish life, OJ 1978 No. L 222, and Directive 79/923 on the quality required of shellfish waters, OJ 1979 No. L 281.

[15] Case C–56/90, *Commission of the European Communities v United Kingdom of Great Britain and Northern Ireland*, 14 July 1993, ground 34 (*op. cit.* note 12).

the scope of application of the directive. This, in turn, implies that local authorities are less dependant on central Government guidance than was perhaps previously thought. New bathing waters can be added to the present list providing that local requirements meet the European specification. The NRA advises on any new bathing water proposals.

IV MONITORING AND PRACTICAL IMPLEMENT- ATION EXAMPLES OF OTHER RELEVANT EC WATER DIRECTIVES

1. Freshwater Fisheries Directive (78/659)

With Directive 78/923 on the quality of shellfish waters,[16] Directive 78/659 is the second directive which aims at supporting fish life.[17] It applies to those waters designated by the Member States as needing protection to support fish life with the exception of natural and artificial fish ponds used for intensive fish farming. Waters are divided into salmonid waters (capable of supporting fish life belonging to species such as salmon, trout, grayling and whitefish) and cyprinid waters (capable of supporting cyprinids or other species such as pike, perch and eel). By July 1980, Member States should have designated these waters and the values set for the parameters listed in Annex I should have been attained by July 1985 which is deemed to be the case when 95 per cent of the samples for certain specified parameters conform with the directive's values.

When this directive was implemented during the early 1980s, in the United Kingdom 19,000 km of river were designated and sample points identified. These sample points have to be sampled and analysed each year. The sampling frequency, which is specified in Annex I can vary from 0 to 12 times per year depending on the previous year's quality and the perception of the risk of a polluting discharge being made which will affect the water quality. Thus, Article 7(2) provides that where the quality of the designated waters is appreciably higher than that required by the directive, the frequency of sampling 'may be reduced'. Where there is reduced chemical quality in the rivers, fish populations must be sampled to ensure they are properly protected. All this needs to be planned in advance to ensure adequate data is available. Each Member State has the discretion to identify

---

[16] OJ 1979 No. L 281.
[17] OJ 1978 No. L 222.

any stretch of water under this directive. New stretches can be identified at any time.

2. Dangerous Substances Directive (76/464)

The first environmental action programme contained a commitment to the setting of emission standards prescribing levels of pollutants not to be exceeded in emissions from fixed installations.[18] Following up this commitment, the Commission proposed a system of limit values, adopted at Community level, which emission standards in the national authorizations of discharges of some particularly dangerous substances should not exceed. As is well known the UK, which by that time had joined the Community, strongly favoured a system of emission standards, by reference to quality objectives, thereby linking the emission standards to the characteristics of the receiving waters. Hence the framework directive adopted in May 1976 allowed Member States to choose between the quality and the emission approach, effectively allowing the UK to largely maintain its existing water protection policy.[19]

The 1976 directive is a framework directive establishing the mechanisms for the reduction and elimination of water pollution by dangerous substances, but requiring separate implementing directives for the actual control of individual substances. A distinction is made between List I (black list) and List II (grey-list) substances. Whilst pollution by List I substances which are selected on the basis of their toxicity, persistence and bioaccumulation are to be 'eliminated', pollution by grey-list substances is to be 'reduced'. As said, for the control of List I substances, the UK has opted to comply with the quality objectives laid down by the Council of Ministers. The control of List II substances is based on the quality approach too, the emission standards in the authorizations of discharges of List II substances being based on national or – where they exist – EC quality objectives.

Implementing directives for the control of List I substances where adopted for mercury,[20] cadmium[21] and hexachlorocyclohexane[22] for which both limit values and quality objectives have been adopted in accordance with the compromise reached in Directive 76/464 (e.g. in respect of mercury: the concentration of mercury in a representative sample of fish flesh, the total

---

[18]   OJ 1973 No. C 112.
[19]   OJ 1976 No. L 129.
[20]   Directive 82/176, OJ 1982 No. L 81, Directive 84/156, OJ 1984 No. L 74.
[21]   Directive 83/513 OJ 1983 No L 291.
[22]   Directive 84/491 OJ 1984 No. L 271.

concentration in inland surface waters, the concentration in solution in estuary waters and in territorial waters and internal coastal waters). The NRA must determine the area affected and select from among the quality objectives the ones deemed appropriate, having regard to the use of the area affected, and taking account of the fact that the purpose of the Directive is to eliminate all pollution.

Although the objective of Directive 76/464 is the elimination of pollution by all list I substances, as has been seen, in reality progress has been extremely slow. Directive 86/280 on limit values and quality objectives for discharges of certain dangerous substances included in List I of the Annex to Directive 76/464 was intended to accelerate the implementation of the directive.[23] It has consolidated the so-called 'parallel approach' agreed in Directive 76/464 and agreed a formula for the controversial issue of new plants, to which standards reflecting 'best technical means available' apply. Since adoption of the 1986 directive, carbon tetrachloride, DDT, pentachlorophenol, aldrin, dieldrin, endrin, isodrin, hexachlorobenzene, hexachlorobutadiene, chloroform, 1.2 dichloroethane, TRI, PER and TCB have been added to the Annex II of Directive 86/280 and hence are now subject to the black-list approach.

This is perhaps the most complicated of the directives to implement and enforce. It requires a knowledge of where all trade effluent and sewage discharges are made to the environment and whether one or more of the 18 listed substances are present in the discharge. It requires a knowledge of whether a dangerous substance is discharged to a sewer. Close liaison must be maintained with the sewerage undertaker. The UK having preferred to implement the environmental quality objective option rather than the limit values, this requires a rather more extensive environmental examination programme but it allows each discharger to be treated according to the impact of their discharge on the environment. If a dangerous substance is detected in an effluent then sampling programmes for water and sediment quality downstream of the discharge must be developed. A programme for sampling at sites downstream of the discharge and representing background quality must also be developed. A similar programme to all this must also be developed for environments affected by discharges of 17 less toxic List II substances.

---

[23] OJ 1986 No. L 181.

3. Surface Water Abstraction Directive (75/440)

The directive on the abstraction of surface water for drinking requires samples to be taken from all surface waters which are abstracted for the use of drinking water.[24] The surface water is classified A1, A2 or A3 depending on the extent of the treatment required. The sampling frequency can vary from 1 to 8 samples per annum, depending on the size of the abstraction and the quality of the water. The range of substances analyzed can vary from 13 to 40 depending on the quality of water abstracted. There are over 400 sources in use and careful planning is needed to ensure that the requirements of the directive are met. Virtually all abstractions in UK are A1 or A2, if water was abstracted from an A3 quality source the NRA would require an improvement programme from all upstream dischargers to ensure at least A2 quality was finally attained.

4. Urban Waste Water Treatment Directive (91/271)

As has been seen, within this directive there is a review requirement whereby sensitive areas and less sensitive areas must be reviewed every four years. This requires the NRA to ensure that data for these areas is available well before the review date. Sampling programmes must be completed at least 12 months before the review date. All consented sewage works discharges must have had their consents reviewed before the relevant dates in the directive. Implementation starts in December 1998 and continues until December 2005. Routine sampling programmes must be inspected to ensure the minimum requirements of the directive have been attained.

5. Nitrates Directive (91/676)

The directive concerning the protection of waters against pollution caused by nitrates from agricultural sources seeks to prevent the pollution of water caused by the application and storage of inorganic fertiliser and manure on farmland.[25] The main instrument for the attainment of this objective is the obligation on the part of Member States to designate zones vulnerable to water pollution from nitrogen compounds by December 1993. Vulnerable zones are those areas of land which drain directly or indirectly into one or more of the following waters:

---

[24] OJ 1975 No. L 194.
[25] OJ 1991 No. L 375.

- surface freshwaters, in particular those used or intended for the abstraction of drinking water, contain or could contain more than the concentration of nitrates laid down in accordance with Directive 75/440;
- groundwaters which could contain more than 50 mg/l nitrates;
- natural freshwater lakes, other freshwater bodies, estuaries, coastal waters and marine waters which are found to be eutrophic or in the near future may become eutrophic.

In addition, Action Programmes relating to vulnerable zones were to be established by December 1995 which are revised at least every four years, the mandatory measures of which are specified in Annex III of the directive.

The analysis programmes need to be completed at least 12 months before the review date to ensure that maps and consultations are completed within the timescale. Sampling programmes must be adjusted to the increased levels required by the Government for the review period.

6. Reporting Requirements

Each directive has its own reporting requirements and timetable but the Standardized Reporting Directive (91/692) aims to ensure that all environmental directives are reported to Brussels no less frequently than once every three years. The bathing water directive has an annual reporting requirement. The NRA aims to send the compliance results to DoE within 4 weeks of the end of the bathing season. Work schedules need to be well organized to meet this deadline.

The DoE has also indicated that it would prefer to collect data from the Regulators for all water based directives on an annual basis. This eliminates the risk of missing information at the end of the three year period, but it does place a heavy burden on NRA staff each year at the end of the reporting period.

All data collected for compliance with EC directives is placed on the Water Resources Act public registers and are open for public inspection free of charge.

V CONCLUSIONS

Environmental standard-setting by the European Commission is intended to ensure a comparable and high level of environmental protection throughout the European Union. Therefore, the translation of those standards into national law gives rise to intense local scrutiny to ensure that the spirit and the substance are incorporated properly. Despite the rigour of this process and due to a variety of reasons, a number of practical problems remain.

In the UK a long series of consultations take place before implementing Regulations are drawn up. Once a directive is incorporated into UK law it is up to the 'competent authority' to formulate sampling and analysis programmes which must ensure that the current analytical programmes meet the requirements of the directives. Domestic sampling programmes obviously need to take account of the timetable requirements of the directives. All water quality data is held on public registers at the NRA and is extracted and processed for regular reports to the DoE before it is transmitted onward to the European Commission.

As is illustrated by the case of the Directive on the quality of bathing waters however, despite the careful consideration given to the implementation of EC water directives in the United Kingdom, national interpretations of the obligations imposed by those directives may still differ from those ultimately adopted by the European Court of Justice.

12. The Enforcement of the Wild Birds Directive: A Case Study

David Freestone

I INTRODUCTION

This paper is concerned with two cases heard by the European Court of Justice (ECJ) concerning the enforcement by the Commission of obligations imposed by Directive 79/409 on the conservation of wild birds.[1] The first, *Commission v Germany*,[2] decided in February 1991, the second *Commission v Spain*,[3] decided in August 1993. Both concern the powers of Member States in relation to the designation, and the continued protection, of the 'special protection areas' required by that directive.[4] The implications of the recent *Lappel Bank* or *RSPB*[5] case, the final transcripts of which were not yet available at the time of publication of this chapter, will also be explored briefly.

There are two main groups of reasons which justify such detailed consideration of two cases. The first is ecological and relate to the basic issues of the use of protected areas as a method of nature conservation; the second relate to the issue of the enforcement of environmental directives, particularly the role of the European Court itself, the margins of appreciation, or discretion, left to Member States, as well as the relationship between the EC judicial and legislative processes. In addition, the cases

---

[1] OJ 1979 No. L 103. Reproduced in Freestone and Ijlstra, 1991 pp. 266–75.

[2] Case C–57/89, *The Leybucht Dykes case*, [1991] ECR–I 883; see also Freestone 1991a pp. 152–6.

[3] Case C–355/90, judgment of 2 August 1993, [1993] ECR I–4221. See Somsen 1993 pp. 268–74.

[4] The case study does not look at the issue of controls on hunting – one of the other contemporary areas of controversy under the directive.

[5] Case C-44/95, *Secretary of State for the Environment ex parte Royal Society for the Protection of Birds*, judgment of 11 July 1996, not yet reported.

have been given particular contemporary significance by the fact that the Royal Society for the Protection of Birds has drawn heavily on the two cases in arguments that it has used in its recently instigated action for judicial review against the British Secretary of State for the Environment in relation to his exclusion of an important ornithological habitat (the Lappel Bank) in his designation of a 4681 hectare SPA in the Medway Estuary in Kent, which evetually proved successful after a reference from the House of Lords to the European Court of Justice.

II THE SIGNIFICANCE OF PROTECTED AREAS

The establishment of Protected Areas is a major aspect of conservation strategy at a global, regional and local level. The wild birds Directive itself was introduced to enable EC Member States to meet the obligations of the 1979 Berne Convention,[6] although it is not referred to in the preamble. A considerable number of other international treaties envisage the establishment of protected areas for ecological, historical and cultural reasons.[7] Of late the protection of endangered species and ecosystems has been given particular urgency by the United Nations Conference on Environment and Development (UNCED)[8] and the 1992 Rio Convention on Biological Diversity[9] but the basic strategy of protecting designated areas of land, sea or wetlands has been familiar for many years. In fact, in recent years the very proliferation of instruments envisaging such measures has itself become a problem, in that it has resulted in a parallel proliferation of terminology to describe often identical types of area: protected areas,

---

[6] 1979 Berne Convention on the Conservation of European Wildlife and Natural Habitats, *European Treaty Series* (ETS) No. 104.

[7] Notable is the connection with the Berne Convention, (see note 6), the 1971 Ramsar Convention on Wetlands of International Importance, especially as Waterfowl Habitat, 11 ILM 963, (Lyster 1985 pp. 183–207); 1972 UNESCO Convention Concerning the Protection of the World Cultural and Natural Heritage, 11 ILM 1358 (1972), (Lyster 1985 pp. 208–38); 1979 Bonn Convention on the Conservation of Migratory Species of Wild Animals, 19 ILM 15 (1980), (Lyster 1985 pp. 278–98). Also the UNEP Regional Seas Conventions with protected areas protocols – Barcelona, Nairobi and Cartagena.

[8] The United Nations Conference on Environment and Development, Rio de Janeiro, Brazil, 3–14 June 1992. For documentation of the Conference see *inter alia,* Johnson 1993.

[9] 31 ILM 818 (1992), also reproduced in Johnson 1993 pp 81–102. See Article 8 on in-situ conservation.

specially protected areas,[10] special protection areas,[11] ecologically sensitive areas,[12] special areas of conservation,[13] particularly sensitive sea areas,[14] as well as various national terminology such as particularly sensitive areas, parks, sanctuaries, marine parks, marine sanctuaries, marine protected areas, marine environmental high risk areas,[15] etc.

In the context of EC law, the wild birds Directive and the habitats Directive[16] now provide the framework for nature conservation. The habitats Directive provides that the system of protected areas established under the wild birds directive will now be merged with the new 'Special Areas of Conservation' (SACs) that it requires to be designated so as to produce a network of protected areas to be called Natura 2000.[17] This formal link between the two directives provides additional significance for the cases examined here in that similar language is used in the operative provisions of both directives.[18] In addition, as will be discussed below, it seems clear that important amendments were introduced into the habitats Directive at a late stage, apparently in an attempt by the Council to negate the impacts of the *Leybucht Dykes* case. [19]

---

[10] For a general discussion, see Freestone 1990 p. 362; also Freestone 1991b pp. 579–81.

[11] The term used in Directive 79/409.

[12] Regulation 797/85.

[13] The term used in the habitats directive.

[14] See Guidelines on Particularly Sensitive Sea Areas (PSSAs) in IMO Assembly Resolution A.720(17) of 6 November 1991. These Guidelines were the result of discussions from 1986 onwards and on approving the Resolution the Assembly recalled Resolution 9 of the International Conference on Tanker Safety and Pollution Prevention (1978) concerning particularly sensitive sea areas which had been based on an initiative by Sweden. See *Proceedings of International Seminar on the Protection of Particularly sensitive Sea Areas*, Malmö, Sweden, 25–28 September. See also 'Protection of Particularly Sensitive Sea Areas under International Marine Environmental Law: Report of the International Meeting of Experts.' (1993) 26 *Marine Pollution Bulletin* 9–13. See now, Gjerde and Freestone, 1994.

[15] The term suggested by the Donaldson Report on the wreck of the Braer.

[16] Directive 92/43 on the conservation of natural habitats and of wild flora and fauna, OJ 1992 No. L 206.

[17] *Ibid.,* Article 3.

[18] Compare Article 4(1) last indent of the 1979 directive with Article 3(2) of the 1992 directive. Also Article 4(4) of 1979 with Article 6(2) of 1992 directive, but also note Article 6(4) below.

[19] Note the provision of Article 2 that measures taken under the directive 'shall take account of economic, social and cultural requirements...' and more importantly the provision of Article 6(4) that developments which have a negative impact on protected sites may be carried out for 'imperative reasons of overriding public interest, *including those of a social or economic nature'*. (emphasis added)

III THE ROLE OF THE EUROPEAN COURT

The two cases under investigation also demonstrate some of the working methods of the European Court of Justice. As has already been pointed out by Philippe Sands in Chapter 3 of this book, the ECJ has a distinctive style of work. Not only does this espouse the famous teleological method of interpretation, but as Hartley amongst others has observed, the development of new doctrines or approaches by the Court often follows a similar line.[20] Once a general approach has been established this naturally tends to guide the Court in its later jurisprudence.

It is perhaps excessive to see in these two cases any grandiose new principles, but they do bear some similarities with the general analysis: the first case against Germany was lost by the Commission but the principles laid down in that case, some of them implicit rather than explicit, were developed and clarified in the Spanish case which resulted in an important victory for the Commission. The cases do suggest that the Court regards the ecological policy objectives of the directive as the overriding consideration when assessing cases of failure to designate, or of damage to, SPAs. It is possible that this strong policy approach may well be continued forward into the consideration of cases brought under the habitats Directive despite the amendments introduced into that directive at a late stage – which were obviously intended to reduce the significance of the *Leybucht Dykes* case. Some of the future significance of the important decision in the *Marismas de Santoña* case is reduced by the fact that it was delivered after the amended habitats Directive had been approved.

In any event, whatever the direction taken by the ECJ in any future cases on protected areas, these decisions do add to a growing jurisprudence on the issue of the limits of national Government discretion in the implementation of directives in an area of the law which seems unlikely to be radically affected by the doctrine of subsidiarity.[21] In the meantime they are directly relevant to the RSPB 'Lappel Bank' case because it was initiated before the habitats Directive came into force.

---

[20] Hartley's description of the process by which new principles emerge bears repetition. He suggests that a new principle is often first seen subject to qualifications, perhaps in an innocuous case, or in a case where the principle is not applied, and then 'gradually the qualifications can then be whittled away, and the full extent of the doctrine can be seen', Hartley 1988 pp. 78–9.

[21] See, for example, the discussion in Freestone and Ryland, 1994 pp. 152–76.

IV DIRECTIVE 79/409 ON THE CONSERVATION OF WILD BIRDS

The wild birds Directive has been described by Simon Lyster (Lyster 1985 p. 67) as 'an important step forward' from previous similar international instruments. The directive imposes strict obligations on Member States to maintain populations of wild birds, to protect and maintain their habitats, to regulate hunting and trading and to prohibit certain methods of killing and capture. There is a centralized system of monitoring and the Commission is responsible for enforcement.

The habitat protection provisions are a central part of the philosophy of the directive. The directive requires Member States to take the requisite measures to maintain the populations of 'all species of naturally occurring birds in the wild state' at a level which corresponds 'to ecological, scientific and cultural requirements, while taking account of economic and recreational requirements ... and to preserve, maintain or re-establish a sufficient diversity and area of habitats' for such species. In addition, Annex I of the directive lists certain vulnerable species which 'shall be the subject of special protection measures concerning their habitat in order to ensure their survival and reproduction in their area of distribution.' To this end, Member States:

> shall classify ... the most suitable territories in number and size as special protection areas for the conservation of these species taking into account their protection requirements in the geographical sea and land area where this directive applies (Article 4(1)).

Special protection areas shall also be designated for non listed migratory species 'as regards their breeding, moulting and wintering areas and staging posts along their migration routes' and to this end particular attention should be paid to 'the protection of wetlands and particularly to wetlands of international importance' (Article 4(1)).

Once the Member State has established such 'special protection areas' then Article 4(4) obliges it to 'take all appropriate steps to avoid pollution or deterioration of habitats or any disturbances affecting the birds, in so far as these would be significant having regard to the objectives of this Article'. Thus each Member State has a degree of discretion in the selection of the 'special protection areas' necessary to meet its obligations to species listed in the Annex and to migratory species, but once such an area has been selected and designated the obligation to take all appropriate steps to avoid significant deterioration of habitats or disturbances to birds is a rigorous obligation, although quite how rigorous has perhaps not been fully appreciated until after the judgment was given in the *Leybucht Dykes* case. From subsequent events it seems clear that the uncompromizing approach of the Court took some Member States, particularly the United Kingdom, by surprise.

V THE *LEYBUCHT DYKES* CASE

1. The Facts

The Leybucht is a bay of some five kilometres width in the Wattenmeer in Eastern Friesland in the German sector of the Wadden Sea. Situated on the palearctic flyway, it is a wetland area of established importance for nesting, feeding and staging for a number of species of both sedentary and migratory birds; it is particularly an important breeding site for the avocet (a bird species listed in Annex I of the directive). On 21 December 1985 the Leybucht was placed under special protection by legislation of Lower Saxony which established the 'Niedersaschsisches Wattenmeer' national park. On 6 September 1988 the German Government informed the Commission under Article 4(3) of the wild birds Directive that it had classified the Leybucht as a special protection area.

Meanwhile the regional authority, the 'Bezirksregierung Weser Ems', had on 25 September 1985 after normal planning procedures which involved opportunities for all interested parties to make representations, obtained approval for a coastal defence project involving development of the Leybucht. This major project included the construction of a reservoir enclosed by a dyke to the west of the Leybucht, with locks leading to the sea connecting with a new dyked ship canal to the small fishing port of Greetsiel; the reinforcement, heightening and strengthening of existing dykes, and the enclosure of a new area in the north-eastern part of the bay by a new dyke. Although the purpose of this project was primarily flood defence work to protect the land and its inhabitants from higher storm tides such as those of 1953, 1962 and 1976, environmental groups had expressed concern that a secondary purpose was to open up the region for recreation: there were rumours, subsequently dismissed by the German authorities as unfounded, of plans for large car parks to be built near Greetsiel.

Work started on this project in early 1986. In August 1987 the Commission began proceedings against the German Government for violation of the Treaty under Article 169 EC insofar as the German authorities had failed in their obligation to prohibit the deterioration of habitats or any disturbances affecting the birds in a special protection area as required by Article 4(4) of the directive. It will be recalled that Article

169 EC requires first that the Commission give the defendant State the opportunity to comment on its allegations, followed by a requirement that the Commission issue the State with a reasoned opinion outlining its complaint which usually gives the State concerned a specified time period (commonly in months) in which it must remedy its treaty violation if it wishes to avoid being taken to the European Court. In this case the reasoned opinion was not issued until July 1988 and the Commission lodged proceedings against Germany on 28 February 1989.

2. Application for Interim Relief

In July 1989 the Commission made a further application for interim measures, namely the suspension of the final part of the project until the full case had been heard. Article 186 of the Treaty of Rome empowers the European Court to 'prescribe any necessary interim measures' but the Court's Rules of Procedure[22] put the burden on the applicant to show the circumstances giving rise to urgency and the factual and legal grounds establishing a *prima facie* case for interim relief. The Commission had argued that serious and irreparable damage might be caused by the final phase (stage IV) of the project where the building of the new dyke would result in the disappearance of an important habitat, particularly for the avocet, the white fronted goose and two species of tern (all listed on Annex I of the directive) which might also be driven out by the building work itself. Stage IV would thus directly affect some 10% of the breeding pairs in the Leybucht. These losses could not be made good by a subsequent order of the Court whereas an interim order would, the Commission argued, simply delay completion of the project. The German Government responded that its objection to stopping work was not financial, but related to the threat to human life posed by delaying sea defence structures in the event of storm surges. In its judgment of 16 August 1989[23] the ECJ did not feel that the Commission had made out an urgent case. Not only had the Commission itself taken a long time to bring the case before the Court, but the scheduled work for 1990 did not involve the dyking of substantial new areas, there was no data to support the argument that the avocet population was being driven away by the work, indeed since 1987 the population appeared to be stabilizing after a previous significant decline. Further, the Commission had not been able to substantiate its allegations that the dyking was designed to increase tourism, indeed the Court was satisfied that it was designed to reduce pleasure boat sailing on the Leybucht, rather than increase it.

---

[22] Article 83(2).
[23] Case 57R/89 [1990] 3 CMLR 651.

3. The Judgment of the European Court in the *Leybucht Dykes* Case

Exactly two years to the day after the case was first filed the European Court gave its judgment. Although hailed in some quarters as a defeat for the Commission, a careful reading of the judgment reveals that the Court's interpretation of the obligations of the directive go considerably further than many Member States had anticipated. In an approach which invites some comparison with its interpretation of Member States obligations under the bathing water directive,[24] the Court took the view that although Article 4(1) of the directive conferred a degree of discretion on each Member State in the initial designation of 'special protection areas' the directive did not give an equal discretion to reduce the size and extent of such areas once they had been designated. Such a reduction could only be justified on exceptional grounds, namely a 'general interest superior to the general interest represented by the ecological objectives of the directive.'

Thus, economic and recreational factors, although recognized in Article 2 as valid aspects of the assessment of the ecological, scientific and cultural requirements of certain general wild bird populations, could not justify measures which would reduce the size of an area designated for the special protection of the vulnerable species listed under Annex I. However the protection of human life from the risks of flooding and protection of the coast were legitimate reasons for dyke works and the strengthening of coastal defences so long as these measures were confined to a strict minimum and involved only the smallest possible reduction of a special protection area.

When these tests were applied to the Leybucht project the Court found that there had not been a breach of the directive. Even the building of a new channel to the port of Greetsiel which because of its economic implications appeared *prima-facie* to be incompatible with the obligations of Article 4(4) had a compensatory ecological benefit in that it would allow two existing navigational channels which required constant dredging to be closed and a larger area left undisturbed. Similarly the completion of the dyke would allow the flooding of new areas and thus actually bring about an increase in total wetland available. These benefits the Court thought would offset the likely short term disturbance to the area caused by the building work. Such an interpretation must indeed appear to be justified on the basis of Article 4(4) which seems to permit disturbance which are not significant 'having regard to the objectives of the Article.'

---

[24] Directive 76/160 on the quality of bathing waters, OJ 1976 No. L 281. See in particular case C–56/90, *Commission v United Kingdom*, [1994] 1 CMLR 765.

4. The Legislative Response

The *Leybucht Dykes* decision caused some considerable stir. It will be recalled that the United Kingdom intervened in the case in support of the German Government. Colin Reid has pointed out that in 1987 the UK Government had given its own interpretation of the obligations of the wild birds Directive in relation to SPAs when it had issued advice to planning authorities (Reid 1994 p. 192). The Government had ruled that planning permission could, in some circumstances, be granted in SPAs which had been designated as Sites of Special Scientific Interest (SSSIs). The relevant circumstances were situations where there were economic or recreational requirements which outweighed the conservation interests or where the development would not produce significant effects which threaten the survival or reproduction of birds in the area.[25] Although this indeed was the tenor of the United Kingdom's intervention in the *Leybucht* case, the 1991 judgment demonstrated that this advice was clearly incorrect.

The judgment came at a time when the habitats Directive was making its way through the Community legislative process. Although the deliberations of the Council of Ministers are secret, it seems clear that the United Kingdom led a determined campaign to reverse the effects of the decision by means of a number of amendments to the habitats Directive. Directive 92/43 on the conservation of natural habitats and of wild flora and fauna was approved on 21 May 1992. Late amendments to the directive included the introduction into Article 6(4) of a provision specifically permitting damage to Special Areas of Conservation (SACs) in circumstances which the *Leybucht* case appears to outlaw and Article 7 which appears expressly designed to attempt to reverse the effects of the decision.

Article 6(4) reads:

> If, in spite of a negative assessment of the implications for the site and in the absence of alternative solutions, a plan or project must nevertheless be carried out for imperative reasons of overriding public interest, including those of a social or economic nature, the Member State shall take all compensatory measures necessary to ensure that the overall coherence of Natura 2000 is protected, It shall inform the Commission of the compensatory measures adopted.[26]

---

[25] DoE, circular 27/87; SDD Circular 1/1988.

[26] This exception is not available however where the site concerned hosts a priority natural habitat type and/or a priority species, see Article 6(4) second para. There is also a similar reference in Article 2 (3) which provides that 'Measures taken pursuant to this directive shall take account of economic, social and cultural requirements and regional and local characteristics.' Does the term 'measures' include the actual designation of sites? Probably not, as a similar provision is to be found in the 1979 directive, Article 2.

Even more pointed is the provision in Article 7 which reads:

> Obligations arising under Article 6(2) (3) and (4) of this directive shall replace any
> obligations arising under the first sentence of Article 4(4) of directive 79/409/EEC in
> respect of areas classified pursuant to Article 4(1) or similarly recognized under Article
> 4(2) thereof as from the date of this directive or the date of classification or recognition
> by a Member State under Directive 79/409/EEC, where the latter date is later.

5. The Relationship Between the Wild Birds Directive and the Habitats Directive

In the light of the changes made to the wilds birds Directive by the 1992
habitats Directive, a number of questions remain to be answered about the
exact legal relationship between the two directives which in some respects
appear to have similar spheres of operation.

Under Article 3(1) the birds Directive SPAs will be included into the
Natura 2000 network. There appears to be some uncertainty as to whether
the wild birds Directive SPAs will maintain their own identity (as
interpreted by the Court) or be subsumed within the habitats Directive
SACs.[27] The wording of Article 3(1) together with the fact that bird species
are not reproduced in the Annexes to the habitats Directive suggest the
SPAs and the provisions of the 1979 directive which surround them will
retain their discrete identity within the network. Thus new SPAs can be
declared and the effects of the two cases under consideration may still be of
some relevance.[28]

If on the other hand the wild bird SPAs will simply become habitats
Directive SACs (which is apparently the UK Government view) then the
protection criteria in Article 6(4) would apply. In that case certain aspects of
these cases become significant only as an indication of the importance with
the Court would accord to the maintenance of the ecological integrity of
designated sites should it be called upon (as it surely will be at some point)
to interpret the phrase 'imperative reasons of overriding public interest'
(Article 6(4)).

However, it appears from the Court's judgment of 11 July 1996 in the
Lappel Bank case that Article 6(4) does not produce such retroactive
effects.[29] As regards the House of Lords' question whether Member States
may take account of Article 2 of Directive 79/409 in the classification of

---

[27] This view is taken for example by Reid 1994 p. 190.

[28] Although note Article 7 of the 1992 Directive, above.

[29] Case C-44/95, Regina v Secretary of State for the Environment *ex parte* RSPB, 11
July 1996, not yet reported.

SPAs and/or defining the boundaries of such areas pursuant to Article 4(1) and/or 4(2) of that directive it ruled:

> It is important first to bear in mind that Article 7 of the Habitat Directive provides in particular that the obligations arising under Article 6(4) thereof are to apply, in place of any obligations arising under the first sentence of Article 4(4) of the Birds Directive, to the areas classified under Article 4(1) or similarly recognized under Article 4(2) of that directive as from the date of implementatino of the Habitats Directive or the date of classification or recognition by a Member State under the Birds Directive, whichever is later.[30]

VI THE *MARISMAS DE SANTOÑA* CASE

1. The Facts[31]

The Marismas de Santoña is an estuarine wetland area at the convergence of five rivers on the Cantabrian coast in the north of Spain. The Marismas area provides a habitat for a population of 15–20,000 birds. These include individuals from over 100 species including 20, notably the spoonbill, which are listed in Annex 1 of Directive 79/409. More than 40 species of migratory birds are reported to visit the area annually. Both these issues bring the area within the scope of Article 4 of the directive. However the area had not been designated a special protection area for the purposes of the directive by the Spanish Government.

Complaints had been made to the Commission regarding six matters/activities thought likely to lead to the pollution and deterioration of the Marismas de Santoña area and which would affect the conservation of various bird species. These were as follows:

1. the creation of industrial zones in the Marismas de Santoña at Laredo and Colindres; the reclamation of land bordering these zones and the construction of a dyke surrounding the industrial zone and neighbouring lands;
2. land reclamation of wetlands by the Escalante municipality to create a park and sports fields;
3. the disposal of waste (consisting of building waste from a nearby quarry) on wetlands near Montehano;

---

[30] Ibid. paragraph 36.

[31] These are taken from the translation by Han Somsen of the French text of the report, *op. cit.*

4. the construction of a new road between Argoños and Santoña crossing the wetlands;
5. the granting of permission for a number of aquaculture projects, including a project by an association of fishermen from Santoña to breed clams in a part of the wetlands;
6. the storage and disposal of waste water in the Marismas de Santoña by the municipalities of Santoña, Cicero, Laredo, Colindres, Escalante and Argoños.

On 18 July 1988, the Commission wrote to the Spanish Government commencing formal proceedings against Spain under Article 169 EC, alleging that these activities constituted a violation of Articles 3 and 4 of the directive and giving opportunity for comments. Specifically, the Commission argued that these six matters constituted a breach of Article 3 of the directive, in particular paragraphs (b) and (c). In addition, it was argued that by not classifying the Marismas de Santoña as a special protection area Spain was in breach of Article 4(1) and (2) of the directive and that the six issues also constituted a violation of the obligation in Article 4(4) to 'take appropriate steps to avoid pollution or deterioration of the habitats or any disturbance affecting the birds.'

A reasoned opinion was issued on 27 June 1989 in which Spain was given a further month to comply with the directive. The Spanish Government contested the allegations and the case was brought before the ECJ on 30 November 1990.

2. The Judgment of the European Court in the *Marismas de Santoña* Case

In its judgment of 2 August 1993, the Court considered the question of the temporal application of the directive to Spain before considering each of the three main allegations against Spain in turn.[32]

In relation to the alleged breach of Article 3 of the directive the Court looked at the relationship between Article 3, which lays down certain general obligations in relation to all species, and Article 4 which relates specifically to those species designated in Annex 1. The Commission argued that both Articles provided a schedule of measures which Member

---

[32] Spain had raised a preliminary point that the obligations of the directive should not be imposed immediately from accession upon Spain. In the absence of precise deadlines Spain argued it had the right to implement the directive progressively. The Court found, however, that in accordance with Article 395 of the Act of Accession Spain should have adhered to the directive from the moment of its accession.

States were obliged to take to protect the habitats of wild birds. The Spanish Government in reply however argued that these were obligations of result only – provided that the protection of wild birds was ensured the choice of means was entirely that of the Member State. There had been no reported recent decreases in bird numbers in the area.

The Court disagreed. Drawing upon the directive's 9th preamble, it held that the obligations to preserve, maintain or re-establish habitats were discrete obligations and that these measure should be taken irrespective of whether any deterioration in bird numbers had been observed. The Spanish Government, like the German Government in the *Leybucht* case had argued that the ecological requirements had to be subordinated to other interests such as social and economic factors, or that these factors should at least be weighed against them. The Court invoked the *Leybucht* case to indicate that although the directive referred to such other interests in Article 2, Member States were not permitted to invoke economic and social factors to make derogations at will from the strict obligations of the directive. In relation to Article 4, to be admissible such interest had to correspond to a general interest superior to the ecological objectives of the directives – it will be recalled, for example, that the threat of loss of life had been argued by the German Government in the *Leybucht* case. Economic and recreational factors could not be taken into account.[33]

Second, the Court considered the obligation on the Spanish Government to designate the Marismas de Santoña as a special protection area in accordance with Article 4 (1) and (2). The Spanish Government argued (as did the UK in the bathing water case) that national Governments retained discretion in relation to the choice of, as well as the possible delimitation of, special protection areas, as well as to the time at which they were designated. This view was rejected by the Court. Although some discretion did remain to Member States as to the choice of SPAs, the choice itself had to be based on ornithological criteria set out in the directive. The Marismas de Santoña was one of the most important ecosystems on the Iberian peninsula for water birds and for certain endangered migratory birds such as the spoonbill and it also harboured some 19 other listed species. This meant that by failing to classify the Marismas de Santoña as an SPA the Spanish Government was in breach of Article 4(1) and (2).

It is worth noting that the Spanish Government had argued that it had taken measures to protect the region: the estuary had been declared a bird

---

[33] In case 247/85, *Commission v Belgium*, [1987] ECR 3029 and case 262/85, *Commission v Italy*, [1987] ECR 3073, the Court had ruled that the provision in article 2 relating to economic and recreational factors did not constitute a separate derogation for the protective regime of the directive.

sanctuary and by a law of 27 March 1992 Marismas de Santoña had been classified as a nature reserve (which effectively prohibited hunting in the area). The Court however pointed out that the nature reserve legislation did not satisfy the requirements of the directive either from the point of view of its territorial scope or from its legal status. The territorial designation excluded an important nest-building area of some 40,000 square metres, whilst no management plans had been developed for the reserve.

The third issue on which the Court ruled was the alleged breaches of the obligation to protect the Marismas de Santoña in accordance with Article 4(4) by taking 'appropriate steps to avoid pollution or deterioration of the habitats or any disturbance affecting the birds.' The Court considered each of the six allegations in turn.

a. The industrial zones of Laredo and Colindres

The Commission had argued that these would lead to the disappearance of an important part of the wetlands close to the mouth of the Rió Asón and that land reclamation would adversely affect the water flow in the wetlands in the bay. Despite the fact that the Spanish Government argued that the relevant authorities had abandoned these plans, the Court upheld the complaints as new dykes had been constructed after Spanish accession to the Community, and no action had been taken to destroy these even though their negative impact was recognized.

b. The road between Argoños and Santoña

The building of a new length of the C-629 across the wetlands would, the Commission had argued, not only reduce the area of the wetlands but also create a disturbance to the tranquillity of the area and thus the birds protected by the directive. The Spanish Government had argued that the route chosen involved the least disturbance possible in order to create this important economic link for the city of Santoña, but this argument was rejected by the Court. Drawing on its ruling in the *Leybucht* case in which it had pointed out that although there was a certain degree of discretion in the classification of SPAs, once the areas had been established the same discretion did not exist for changes to such areas. The disturbances could not therefore be justified and the complaint was upheld.

c. The development of aquaculture

In relation to the granting of permits for aquaculture including one grant to a fishermen's association to breed clams in a central part of the wetlands, the Spanish Government had argued that these activities were economically valuable and had a relatively small impact. These arguments too were rejected by the Court. The economic argument for the same reasons as above, but also because it felt that the impact of the activities would not be negligible – the aquaculture infrastructure would result in a loss of wetlands, change the structure of the existing soil and lead to vegetation changes. This complaint was also upheld.

d. Storage of solid waste

It had been alleged that the storage of solid wastes had led to changes in the physical and chemical state of the wetlands. However the Spanish Government claimed this situation had ceased in 1988 and that measures had been taken in the context of a waste management plan. Some illegal storage had taken place, but even this had ceased by 1990. The Court therefore rejected this complaint as inadmissible.

e. The discharge of waste waters

The Commission had alleged that the discharge of untreated water had produced deleterious effects in the bay of Santoña. This was not denied by Spain which argued however that the directive did not oblige Member States to make special provision for waste purification plants so as to prevent damage to SPAs. The Court however upheld the complaint. Bearing in mind the obligation of Article 4(4) and the fundamental importance of water quality for the maintenance of the wetlands ecosystem Spain was required to provide water purification systems to prevent pollution of the area.

f. Land reclamation at Escalante and the impact of the Montehano quarry

The Commission had alleged that land reclamation by the municipality of Escalante and the exploitation of the quarry with consequential storage of waste in the wetlands had led to a reduction in the size of the SPA. The Spanish Government however insisted that these actions related to a period prior to Spanish Accession to the Community the disposal of waste had been made illegal in 1986. The Court was not convinced that these activities had continued after 1986 and therefore dismissed this complaint.

All in all therefore, the Court found that Spain was in breach of the directive for not having designated the Marismas de Santoña as an SPA under the directive and for not taking the appropriate measures to prevent the deterioration of the area as required by Article 4 of the directive.

VII THE *RSPB* CASE

1. The Facts

On 15 December 1993, the Secretary of State decided to designate the Medway Estuary Marshes as an SPA. At the same time, he decided to exclude from it an area of about 22 hectares known as Lappel Bank.

The Medway Estuary and Marshes are an area of wetland of international importance covering 4 681 hectares on the north coast of Kent and listed under the Ramsar Convention. They are used by a number of wildfowl and wader species as a breeding and wintering area and as a staging post during spring and autumn migration. The site also supports breeding populations of the avocet and the little tern, which are listed in Annex I to the Birds Directive.

Lappel Bank is an area of inter-tidal mudflat immediately adjoining, at its northern end, the Port of Sheerness and falling geographically within the bounds of the Medway Estuary and Marshes. Lappel Bank shares several of the important ornithological qualities of the area as a whole. Although it does not support any of the species referred to in Article 4(1) of the Birds Directive, some of the bird species of the area are represented in significantly greater numbers than elsewhere in the Medway SPA. Lappel Bank is an important component of the overall estuarine ecosystem and the loss of that inter-tidal area would probably result in a reduction in the wader and wildfowl populations of the Medway Estuary and Marshes.

The Port of Sheerness is the fifth largest in the United Kingdom for cargo and freight handling. It is a flourishing commercial undertaking, well located for sea traffic and access to its main domestic markets. The Port, which is also a significant employer in an area with a serious unemployment problem, planned extended facilities for car storage and value added activities on vehicles and in the fruit and paper product market, in order better to compete with continental ports offering similar facilities. Lappel bank is the only area into which the Port of Sheerness can realistically envisage expanding.

Taking the view that the need not to inhibit the viability of the port and the significant contribution that expansion into the area of Lappel Bank would make to the local and national economy outweighed its nature conservation value, the Secretary of State decided to exclude that area from the Medway SPA.

The RSPB applied to the Divisional Court of the Queen's Bench Division to have the Secretary of State's decision quashed on the ground that he was not entitled, by virtue of the Birds Directive, to have regard to economic considerations when classifying an SPA. The Divisional Court found against the RSPB. On appeal by the RSPB, the Court of Appeal upheld that judgment. The RSPB therefore appealed to the House of Lord which referred the following questions to the Court of Justice:

1. Is a Member State entitled to take account of the considerations mentioned in Article 2 of Directive 79/409 on the conservation of wild birds in classification of an area as a Special Protection Area and/or in defining the boundaries of such an area pursuant to Article 4(1) and/or 4(2) of that Directive?

2. If the answer to Question 1 is "non", may a Member State nevertheless take account of Article 2 considerations in the classification of the process in so far as:

a)   they amount to a general interest which is superior to the general interest which is represented by the ecological objective of the Directive (i.e. the test which the European Court has laid down in, for example, *Commission v Germany* ("Leybucht Dykes") Case 57/89, for derogation from the requirements of Article 4(4); or

b)   they amount to imperative reasons of overriding public interests such as might be taken into account under Article 6(4) of Directive 92/43 on the conservation of natural habitats and of wild fauna and flora?

2. The Judgment of the European Court in the *RSPB* Case

As for the first question, drawing upon the *Marismas de Santoña* case, the Court rejected the United Kingdom's argument that Article 4(1) and(2) should be read in conjunction with Articles 3 and 2, and ruled that the ecological requirements laid down by Article 4 do not have to be balanced against the interests listed in Article 2, in particular economic requirements. Rather, it re-stated the principle previously articulated in the *Marismas de Santoña* case that the criteria laid down in paragraphs (1) and (2) of Article 4 are to guide Member States in designating and defining the boundaries of SPAs.

  For the first part of the second question the Court that, simply by reiterating its judgments in the *Leybucht and Marismas de Santoña* cases and without having to rule on the possible relevance of the grounds corresponding to a superior interest for the purpose of classifying an SPA, a Member State may not, when designating an SPA and defining its boundaries, take account of economic requirements as constructing a general interest superior to that represented by the ecological objective of that directive.

Finally, the second part of the second question revolving around the relationship between Directive 79/409 and Directive 92/43 was approached by the Court in the way already alluded to above. Hence, Article 4(1) or (2) of Directive 79/409 is to be interpreted as meaning that a Member State may not, when designating an SPA and defining its boundaries, take account of economic requirements which may constitute imperative reasons of overriding interest of the kind referred to in Article 6(4) of Directive 92/43 on the conservation of the natural habitats of wild fauna and flora.

VIII IMPLICATIONS FOR FUTURE CASES

The *RSPB* and *Marismas de Santoña* case confirm the approach which the Court had already adumbrated in the *Leybucht* case. It confirms in particular the fact that the obligations to designate special protection areas and to protect them from pollution and deterioration are discrete strict obligations which are to be assessed and reviewed according to objective criteria established by Community law in the directive itself and not simply discretionary powers to be exercised according to national law. In formal legal terms a number of conclusions can be drawn from these cases. Two conclusions seem clear, two others are more speculative:

First, the classification of an SPA as required by Article 4(1) is to be made in accordance with objective Community law criteria established by the 1979 Directive. This radically reduces the margin of appreciation left to Member States in the establishment of SPAs in that failure to establish a site which meets these criteria as an SPA is a breach of the directive. Certainly, this conclusion appears to have been accepted by the UK which has decided that a site which meets the requirements for SPA designation should for planning purposes be regarded as if it had been designated.[34]

Second, it is arguable whether the requirements of Article 4(1) in this regard are directly effective so as to allow individuals to bring actions based upon it before the national courts. Although both *Leybucht* and *Marismas de Santoña* confirm that some discretion is left to Member States as to the exact delimitation of an SPA, it appears that this discretion does not extend to the exclusion of key or core areas (note the complaint that the Spanish nature reserve designation excluded 40,000 m^2 of key nest building area), nor does it extend to the timing at which designation should be made. While it is obvious that the discretionary element which remains means that it will not always be directly effective, it can, nevertheless, still be argued that in

---

[34] Discussed further below, see also (1993) 3 *Water Law* 89.

those few cases where the Member State has not designated a key site which indisputably meets the objective criteria of the directive, this constitutes a breach of a complete and legally perfect (i.e. directly effective) obligation.

Third, once an area has been classified as an SPA, the obligations imposed by Article 4(4) to 'take appropriate steps to avoid [significant] pollution or deterioration of habitats or any disturbances affecting the birds ...' are strict obligations to be determined according to Community law criteria, namely the objectives of Article 4 of the 1979 Directive. This is not an area of Member State discretion, and activities conducted for economic or recreational purposes will violate the directive. Only activities designed to protect the general interest superior to ecological objectives (such as the protection of human life as in the *Leybucht* case) will be permitted.

Of course the habitats Directive has changed the situation considerably, in that the wider justification in Article 6(4) for activities which have a negative impact on SACs applies. This is not however a *carte blanche* for possibly damaging developments in such areas. 'Imperative reasons of overriding public interest' must be established, and if the project goes ahead the Member State must 'take all compensatory measures to ensure the overall coherence of Natura 2000.' The measures must be compensatory not in mitigation and the term overall presumably applies to the coherence of the network within the Community as a whole.

Finally, it is arguable that once a site has actually been classified as an SPA the requirements of Article 4(4) are sufficiently clear and precise to be directly effective. Therefore, building on the arguments used by the Court in the *Marismas de Santoña* case, could it not be suggested that a directly effective breach of article 4(4) takes place when activities which are obviously contrary to the directive adversely affect sites which may not been designated SPAs but which *should have* been so designated (as argued above) because they clearly meet Community law criteria for classification?

IX IMPLEMENTATION IN THE UNITED KINGDOM: SOME CONCLUSIONS

It was clear that the *Leybucht* case took the UK, as well as a number of other Member States by surprise. The British Government had intervened unsuccessfully in the *Leybucht* case to argue that only activities having significant effects on bird populations were to be avoided. It seems clear that unease at this decision was reflected in the amendment to the text of the 1992 habitats Directive Article 6(4) in an attempt to minimize the impact of the decision. It might be noted that the wording of Article 6(4) bears some resemblance to the instructions given by the UK to planning authorities by circular in 1987 (see Reid 1994 p. 192). It also seems to have been taken aboard to some extent by the UK in its procedures. Those amendments have not however made the *Marismas de Santoña* decision of purely academic interest. The *Santoña* cases should flag up the seriousness with which the ECJ is likely to view future cases involving impingements on 'Special Protection Areas' and possibly also on Special Areas for Conservation (SACs) under the 1992 Directive.

Listed below are a number of issues for consideration and discussion relating to the way in which the wild birds Directive and now the habitats Directive,[35] is being, or is likely to be implemented within the UK.

1. The Method By Which These Areas Are Protected in the UK

The UK strategy for designation of SPA – and it seems SACs[36] – as well as other sites protected by wildlife treaties is essentially based on voluntary compliance. The primary vehicle for this is the planning system together with the designation of Sites of Special Scientific Interests (SSSI),[37] or by the designation of Marine Nature Reserves (for sea areas).[38]

Both processes are extremely lengthy and involve extensive consultation requirements.[39] A number of commentators have doubted whether this procedure – if it ever was properly adequate to meet the international treaty law obligations to which the United Kingdom is a party – meets the requirements of the wild birds Directive, in that SSSI designation, as such, offers no legal protection to such sites.[40] There must be even more doubt

---

[35] Conservation (Natural Habitats etc.) Regulations, 1994, SI 1994/2716.

[36] *Ibid.*

[37] S.28(1) of the 1981 Wild Life and Countryside Act provides:

> Where the Nature Conservancy Council are of the opinion that any area of land is of special interest by reason of any of its flora and fauna or geological or physiographical features, it shall be the duty of the Council to notify that fact:
> (a) to the local planning authority in whose area the land is situated;
> (b) to every owner and occupier of any of the land;
> (c) to the Secretary of State.

[38] Of which there are currently only two, Skomer and Lundy, under the 1981 Act s.36. Other possible means of habitat protection include national nature reserves, local nature reserves (both possibly supported by by-laws), environmentally sensitive areas (established for farming reasons under Regulation 797/85 and 1986 Agriculture Act), and national parks.

[39] See Ball and Bell, 1994, who point out that the re-notification of sites to give them protection under the 1981 Act has only just been completed.

[40] See e.g. Ball and Bell, 1994 p. 421 and Reid 1994 p. 191. It is an offence for an owner or occupier (only) of a notified SSSI to carry out 'without reasonable excuse' a

that it can be simply adapted to meet the requirements of the habitats Directive, without major new primary legislation.

One serious omission is the fact that SSSIs cannot extend beyond low water mark. Hence estuarine and coastal sites or parts of sites are excluded.[41] The limited number of MNRs does not address this defect.

2. The Number of Areas Classified by the UK.

The Second Report of Commission on the Application of Directive 79/409[42] provides information of the numbers of SPAs designated within the UK. Between 1986 and 1991 the number of designated sites rose from 21 to 40. The figure is currently reported to be over 100. However the Nature Conservation Council (now split into the Nature Conservation Agencies of England, Scotland and Wales) has published criteria for SPA designation and in 1990 was of the view that 218 sites met these criteria and was considering a further 43. [43]

A development of interest is that the Government has accepted in its planning policy that a site that meets the criteria for SPA designation should be regarded as if it has been designated.[44] This policy change preceded the *Santoña* case. It is perhaps possible that this change is a direct result of a close reading of the *Leybucht* case.

3. Prevention of Damage to, and the Regulation of Pollution Within, SPAs

As the *Santoña* case indicates, Article 4(4) requires that designated sites be protected from 'pollution or deterioration of habitats or any disturbances affecting the birds.' It is by no means clear that these obligations can be met by the UK system. In relation to SSSIs the NCA must notify 'relevant bodies' of SSSIs that may be affected by their activities.[45] If it is notified such a body must consult the NCA over operations which it intends to carry

---

potentially damaging operation without notifying the NCC or within four months of so notifying them. The maximum penalty is 2,500 pounds.

[41] The evidence suggests these sites are under particular pressure. Between 1986–89, 56 out of 136 estuarine sites suffered damage. *Nature Conservation and Estuaries in Great Britain*, NCC 1991, cited Ball and Bell, 1994, p. 421.

[42] COM(93) 572 final.

[43] *Protecting Internally Important Bird Sites,* NCC, 1990 and see Ball and Bell, 1994.

[44] *Ibid.*, who cite the July 1992 decision of the Secretary of State to refuse permission for developments in North Kent which would affect a candidate SPA, [1993] *Water Law* 89.

[45] For example, the Water Resources Act, 1991 (s.17) and the Water Industry Act (s.4).

out which it thinks might damage or destroy the SSSI. Also the National Rivers Authority (NRA) must consult the NCA before authorizing activities it thinks might damage an SSSI.[46] With the exception of judicial review, there is no remedy for failure to consult.

---

[46] These would include abstraction licences, discharge consents and land drainage consents. The *Code of Practice on Conservation, Access and Recreation*, July 1989, goes further to suggest that all operations be notified to the NCC, rather than simply those which the agency considers may damage an SSSI, see further Ball and Bell, 1994 who point out that there is no remedy for failure to consult.

13. Industry and Access to Information on the Environment

Ian Rose[1]

I INTRODUCTION

1. Policy Background to the Right of Access to Information on the Environment

The right of access to information on the environment is regarded as an essential component of UK and EC policies that the public should know about the state of the environment in which they live and that they should participate in environmental regulation.

In the UK, the Royal Commission on Environmental Pollution has stated that the right of the public to access to information is an important part of the regulatory system. In 1972, the Royal Commission recommended that it was in the public interest that information about waste should be available to research workers and others who made use of it to improve the environment.[2] This lead to provisions for public registers of information being included in the Control of Pollution Act 1974 (Fairley 1993).

In 1984, the UK government accepted a recommendation of the Royal Commission that there:

should be a presumption in favour of unrestricted access for the public to information which the pollution control authorities obtain or receive by virtue of their statutory powers.[3]

---

[1] Please note: This is only a discussion paper. Reliance should not be placed nor decisions taken on the basis of its contents without specific advice.

[2] *Royal Commission on Environmental Pollution Second Report*, Cmnd 4894, March 1972.

[3] Department of the Environment, *Guidance on the Implementation of the Environmental Information Regulations 1992 in Great Britain*, 1992, s. 2.

The government's environmental policy, set out in the 1990 policy paper, *This Common Inheritance*, states that the public should have a right of access to information held by pollution control authorities.

At EC level, the access of the public to environmental information in the Member States is regarded as a key policy objective. When ministers were approving the Fourth Action Programme on the Environment in 1987, they declared that better access to information on the environment was a priority area.[4]

The Fifth Action Programme on the Environment, *Towards Sustainability*, which sets out EC policy and objectives on the environment from 1993 to 2000 and beyond, emphasizes the important role the general public has in ensuring environmental protection.[5] As well as greater awareness of the issues, the Fifth Action Programme states that it is essential for individuals to have good information, in order that they may play their part in the achievement of sustainable economic development.

a. The importance of the right of access to information

The right of access to information on the environment has become essential to the lawyer who advises on commercial transactions. When acting for a party which is buying a manufacturing business, it is essential to be able to find out the history of that business' relationship with the regulatory authorities and details of any past convictions and extra obligations placed on the business. Once the client is operating a manufacturing business, information may be used in negotiations on future compliance and as evidence of good environmental management. Such evidence may be required for customers, consumers and any future buyers of the business.

When acting for the purchaser of any land, including private property, information on the emissions of any industries in the locality may be assessed. Despite the demise of a formal register of land which has been subject to contaminative uses, information may be gleaned to add to the scientific evidence of an environmental audit, to assess the likely contamination of a site or of sites in the vicinity.

The regulatory authorities themselves may use the information held publicly in investigating a business. In exercising their powers generally, the information can help the authority to target prosecutions in the most effective way. Information on previous convictions may be useful also in assessing applications for waste management licences under Part II of the Environmental Protection Act as these may only be granted to 'fit and proper persons'.

---

4   OJ 1987 No. C 328.
5   OJ 1993 No. C 138.

Regulatory authorities are increasingly using public information as an enforcement measure; this is discussed further below.

The right of access to information about industry's effects on the environment may also be used by members of the public and by public interest and pressure groups. Even if the extent of a right of access to justice in environmental matters is questionable, the right of access to information should ensure that the public may at least easily find information with which to argue a case.

The public interest and pressure groups may have access to greater skills and resources actually to enforce environmental regulation in the courts. At the end of June 1993, Friends of the Earth wrote to senior officers in a number of companies enclosing details gleaned from the registers to show that consent limits may have been breached. The officers were threatened personally with prosecution under provisions of UK environmental law which provide for the personal criminal liability of those who control a business which breaches certain environmental laws.

II RIGHTS OF ACCESS TO ENVIRONMENTAL INFORMATION UNDER EXISTING PROVISIONS

UK environmental legislation provides for the keeping of public registers in a large number of areas. These include consents to discharge into the air granted by local authorities and integrated pollution control licences granted by Her Majesty's Inspectorate of Pollution under Part I of the Environmental Protection Act 1990 (the 'EPA'). Details of consents to discharge into water granted by the National Rivers Authority must also be kept on a public register under the Water Resources Act 1991, and waste regulation authorities must keep public registers giving details of the holders of waste management licences and of registered waste carriers under Part II of the EPA.[6]

Some local authorities collate and provide information on the environment in innovative ways, which are useful to researchers and to the public. For example, Lancashire County Council is developing a system whereby the public will have access to a whole range of environmental data kept by the Council, via a computer link in public libraries.[7]

These provisions are often implementation of EC requirements. For example, Directive 84/360 on the combating of air pollution from industrial

---

[6] For UK provisions generally, see Lomas, Payne *et al.*, 1993.
[7] 'Key to a green machine', *The Independent*, 2nd June 1994, p. 30.

plants is the 'framework' directive on air emissions and sets out the requirement that many industrial facilities must obtain an authorization in order to combat air pollution. Article 9(1) of that directive provides as follows:

> Member States shall take the necessary measures to ensure that applications for authorizations and the decisions of the competent authorities are made available to the public concerned in accordance with procedures provided for in national law.

Moreover, under Directive 82/501 on the major accident hazards of certain industrial activities (the 'Seveso Directive'),[8] an operator of a plant falling under the directive must provide information concerning the activities of the plant and accident risks to the relevant authority. The authority must provide that information to the public.

III DIRECTIVE 90/313 ON THE FREEDOM OF ACCESS TO INFORMATION ON THE ENVIRONMENT

1. Development of the Directive

Directive 90/313 on the freedom of access to information on the environment was adopted on 7th June, 1990 and had to be implemented by Member States by 31st December, 1992 at the latest. Although the UK brought in provisions on that date (see below), other Member States did not do so. The European Commission sent Reasoned Opinions under Article 169 of the EC Treaty to Germany, Greece, Ireland, Portugal and Spain concerning the failure of those countries to implement the directive, and in December 1993, Germany, Greece and Italy had still not taken measures to implement it.[9]

As mentioned above, EC environmental policy has for some time considered the importance of the right of the public to information on the environment. The Council of Ministers (now the Council of the European Union) has supported this as an area for the European Commission to develop. Further, the European Parliament resolved as far back as 1984 that information should be published by the European Community, and, when it considered the Fourth Action Programme, the European Parliament stated

---

[8] OJ 1982 No. L 230, as amended.

[9] Answer to Written Question E-2847/93 by Alex Smith MEP to the European Commission, OJ 1994 No. C 300. For discussion of Member States' implementation records, see Wheeler 1995 p. 1.

that 'access to information must be made possible by a specific Community programme' (Haigh 1991).

The directive was first proposed by the European Commission at the end of 1988. At first, the UK considered that the proposal did not add much to domestic proposals which led to the Environmental Protection Act 1990. Together with Spain, the UK were set to vote against the proposal. As the proposal was to be adopted under the pre-Maastricht Article 130s of the EEC Treaty (now the 'EC Treaty'), that is, under the specific basis for environmental legislation introduced by the Single European Act, unanimity of the Council of Ministers was required.

This and other difficulties were however overcome, and after negotiations throughout 1989, which resulted in changes such as an extension of the period in which a response to a request for information was required, the directive was eventually adopted (Haigh 1991).

2. Outline of the Directive

The directive is reproduced as an Annex to this book. Member States must ensure that public authorities, defined in Article 2(a), are required to make available information relating to the environment, defined in Article 2(b), to any natural or legal person at his request and without his having to declare an interest. Further, 'bodies with public responsibilities for the environment and under the control of public authorities' must be required to make the relevant information they hold available to the public.

A request for information may be refused for certain reasons, such as commercial and industrial confidentiality and public security, and the information, or the reasons for a refusal to supply information, must be given within two months. The routes for judicial or administrative review of an act of the public authority in the Member State must be made available to those who are refused information or believe that the information with which they have been provided is inadequate.

Member States must provide general information to the public on the state of the environment and they must report back to the European Commission on the 'experience gained', on the basis of which the European Commission is to make a report to the European Parliament and to the EU Council, together with any appropriate proposal for revision.

3. 'Direct Effect' of the Directive

The principle of 'direct effect' could apply to any of the provisions of Directive 90/313, as it may to the provisions of any directive. Under the principle, laid down by the European Court of Justice , if any provision of a directive is so clear, precise and unconditional that implementation into national law would not affect its substance, then that provision may give rise to rights which an individual may enforce in a national court. This is the case even if the directive has not been implemented by the Member State or if it has been implemented incorrectly.

Whereas not all of the provisions of the directive appear to fulfil the requirements of direct effect, some indeed may. It is reported that the European Commission believes that Article 3 of the directive has direct effect.[10] Moreover, whilst Germany was late in implementing the directive, at least some of the *Länder* were aware of the directive and were giving effect to it.[11]

4. Implementation of the Directive in the United Kingdom – Bodies to Which it Applies

The UK implementing instrument is the Environmental Information Regulations 1992 (S.I. 1992 No. 3240), which came into force on 31st December, 1992.

The Regulations apply to the following:

a) all such Ministers of the Crown, Government departments, local authorities and other persons carrying out functions of public administration at a national, regional or local level as, for the purposes of or in connection with their functions, have responsibilities in relation to the environment; and

b) any body with public responsibilities for the environment which does not fall within subparagraph (a) above but is under the control of a person falling within that sub-paragraph.

It is not, however, easy to interpret from the above precisely which bodies are covered by the Regulations, and particular controversy applies to the question whether the privatized utilities, such as the water and electricity companies, are covered.

The Department of the Environment's guidance on the Regulations is unclear on this issue. It states:[12]

---

[10] European Environmental Bureau, *Your Rights under European Union Environmental Legislation*, 1994, p. 20.

[11] Author's own enquiries.

[12] Department of the Environment, *Guidance on the Implementation of the Environmental Information Regulations 1992 in Great Britain*, 1992, s. 12.

Because circumstances vary and change, the Government is unable to give a definitive list of organizations subject to the requirements of the Regulations. So organizations will need to take a view themselves as to whether they fall into any of the categories and thus become a relevant person. In cases of dispute, it will be for the Courts to decide.

Arguably, this is an example of the UK failing to 'define the practical arrangements' for making information available, under Article 3(1) of the directive (see Friends of the Earth complaint, below).

This is particularly unsatisfactory for the utility companies, many of whom have a responsibility to keep public registers. For example, under the Water Industry Act 1991, the water companies must keep registers of discharges to their sewers. Moreover, directly effective provisions of directives apply to those utilities. In *Griffin v South West Water Services*, which concerned the applicability of an employment law directive, the High Court held that a water company was a 'state authority' under EC law, and therefore the directly effective provisions of directives may be enforced against them by individuals in national courts.

When implementation of the directive was being considered by the Department of the Environment, it did however produce a list of bodies to which the directive applied. This was appended to its consultation paper on the implementation of the directive. The list, whilst including bodies such as British Rail, the Crown Estate (see the *OPAG* case, below) and Nuclear Electric PLC, did not include privatized utilities such as the water companies. Despite the lack of clarity in the Regulations, it is argued that private companies which do exercise a statutory duty to maintain information on the environment should consider that the directive adds to that duty.[13]

An interesting example of the far reaching effect of EC environmental law, or, as some may say, an example of EC law attacking the sovereignty of the Queen herself, is the case of 'Omagh People Against Goldmining' (OPAG).[14] This group applied to the Crown Estate for details of an agreement between the Crown Estate and the lessee from the Crown Estate of mining rights in Northern Ireland. That information having been refused, OPAG has been granted legal aid for an appeal against that decision.

Apart from using the provisions on commercial confidentiality mentioned below, the report states that the Crown Estate claims that the directive does not apply to it, as it operates 'like a private company under private law', and

[13] See Hughes 1992 p.74. It should also be noted that as a single market matter, it would create distortions in conditions of competition if utilities in some Member States, which were not privatized, were held to be bound by the directive and the administrative burden involved, whilst privatized utilities were not so bound.

[14] *Environment Business*, 1st June 1994.

that the information was in any case provided. The Crown Estate has informed the author that although it does comply with the directive, because of its 'Crown status', it is not obliged to do so. Interestingly, the Department of the Environment's list of bodies to which the directive applies, which was appended to its consultation paper (see above), included the Crown Estate.

5. Implementation of the Directive in the United Kingdom – Other Shortcomings

In addition to the lack of clarity as to which bodies are bound, the Regulations also contain other shortcomings. For example, they apply to information on the environment which is held 'in accessible form'; this is not further defined and may mean that information held which has been badly collated or is otherwise difficult to track down need not be given.

Furthermore, there is no provision in the Regulations which would specifically protect a person requesting information from having to express his interest. The importance not merely of keeping the *reasons* for a request from the authority, but also the *identity* of the person requesting the information, can be crucial in the commercial context (see IV below).

6. Action for a Failure to Implement the Directive

Friends of the Earth announced on 20th March 1993, that it had made a formal complaint to the European Commission that the UK had failed to implement the directive properly.[15] This alleged to be in relation to three 'key elements', namely:
  a) the UK had failed to 'define the practical arrangements' under which information should be made effectively available;
  b) there was not an adequate and effective appeal procedure against refusals to supply information; and
  c) the exemptions to the right to information for information relating to 'actual or prospective' legal or other proceedings went beyond the terms of the directive.

The issues raised by Friends of the Earth were discussed at a conference, *Delivering the Right to Know*, in April 1993.[16]

Although the European Commission will not give information on the progress of any complaint except to the complainant and the party

---

[15] Friends of the Earth Press Release, 20th March 1993.
[16] The proceedings of the conference were subsequently published by Friends of the Earth (ISBN 1 85750 212 4).

complained of,[17] it has been reported that the European Commission has sent a letter to the Department of the Environment outlining concerns over the implementation of the directive in the UK, especially with regard to the first of Friends of the Earth's points made above.[18] This is reported to be following complaints not just from Friends of the Earth, but also from others.

IV APPLICATION OF THE DIRECTIVE IN PRACTICE – PUBLIC AUTHORITIES

It is left to the relevant authority to make arrangements for the provision of information under the terms of the Regulations; the complaint that the UK has failed to 'define the practical arrangements' under which information is effectively made available may be well founded here, although the guidance notes mentioned above provide some assistance. In any case, application is patchy across a range of the bodies to which the directive applies.[19]

In general, the local authorities are aware of the implications of the directive and try to give it effect. The main concerns of a commercial lawyer in using the right under the directive are that:

a) the interest of the person making the enquiry should not have to be given;

b) reasonable requests should be granted; and

c) only a reasonable charge should be levied for the information.

Under the directive, a person requesting information does not have to 'prove an interest'. For the lawyer, it can be crucial that his identity should not be given. This is the case, for example, when enquiries are being made into a company with a view to its possible acquisition.

Many local authorities will ask who is requesting the information or on whose behalf the information is being requested; local authorities should not take a blank response as in any way impolite, and they rarely do.[20] This is in contrast to the situation when enquiries are being made of the European Commission. Although the directive does not apply in such cases (see IV(3) below), officials of the European Commission usually ask what interest the lawyer has in requesting information. This can even extend to demanding to know the identity of a client before the information is

---

[17] Author's own enquiries.

[18] *The Independent*, 27th June 1994.

[19] Author's own enquiries.

[20] Author's own enquiries.

released. The spirit of 'openness' required of the European Commission (also discussed below) still needs to filter through its offices.

Reflecting the directive, the Regulations provide that a request for information may be refused if that request 'is manifestly unreasonable or is formulated in too general a manner'. The Department of the Environment's guidance states on this issue:[21]

> Manifestly unreasonable requests could include requests for information that place a substantial and unreasonable burden on the resources of a body. Examples might be where when the amount of information sought is excessive, when extensive scans of historic files prove necessary, or when significant processing of information is necessary before it can be released.... When a request for information is formulated in too general a manner to permit information to be identified and supplied, the body should explain this to the applicant. It is then open to the applicant to reformulate the request in such a way that the required information can be isolated and supplied.

The question whether a request is 'reasonable', whilst being subject to judicial review, can cause difficulties, as what is reasonable to the lawyer may not appear reasonable to the authority.

It is difficult to see, however, that lengthy requests would place an unreasonable burden on the authority, if the information is kept efficiently, such as in a computerized form on Lancashire County Council's model. It would require time and funds to pursue through judicial review whether a request was 'reasonable', and this lack of clarity is a weakness of the directive and of the Regulations.

With regard to costs, these range from free to costs which cover copying. Costs can be related to the amount of work which it takes to gather the information internally, to the copying charge or to both of these. In any event, the cost must not be so great as to discourage the request for information being made.

1. Industry

The right of public access to information on the environment may have both a negative side and a positive side for industry.

Companies need to be secure that information they give to public authorities which is confidential and whose release may damage the company, remains confidential. Conversely, companies which comply with environmental law and operate effective environmental management systems should be rewarded for their investment. The commercial confidentiality of information should in any event be respected by the body

---

[21] Department of the Environment, *Guidance on the Implementation of the Environmental Information Regulations 1992 in Great Britain*, 1992, ss. 41, 42.

receiving it; any breakdown in this regard could lead to a reluctance of companies in the future to provide any information not strictly required to be provided.

'Commercial and industrial confidentiality' is protected by the directive, and the UK implementing Regulations give effect to this. The Department of the Environment's guidance[22] suggests one of two approaches may be taken; information may be classified when it is received or when it is requested. In any event, in order to ensure that confidential information is treated as such, companies must make the fact clear and maintain a good understanding with the relevant public authority.

It should be noted that the other statutory provisions on the commercial confidentiality of furnished information, such as in the EPA, override the provisions of the Regulations.[23]

More and more companies are turning environmental regulation to their advantage. The adoption of an environmental policy, followed up by the implementation of environmental management systems and the publication of environmental reports, can raise the public profile of a company and improve its image, as well as promote efficiency of the operations. The chemical industries have in particular acknowledged the benefits of such actions.

The effects of a company's operations on the environment may be verified by anyone requesting information from the public authorities. This can benefit a company as it strives to convince an often cynical public that it is taking account of environmental management issues.[24]

2. The Public

There is no evidence to suggest that because the directive has taken effect, requests from the public for information have increased. Awareness of the amount of information available and a belief that nothing could be done even with the information must be factors which have caused the directive to have such little effect.

The Fifth Action Programme on the Environment foresees education programmes and other measures to increase public awareness of environmental issues. With some Member States regarding such issues as in their sphere of competence due to the principle of subsidiarity, and with

---

[22] Department of the Environment, *Guidance on the Implementation of the Environmental Information Regulations 1992 in Great Britain*, 1992, s. 55 ff.

[23] Fairley 1993. For provisions on trade secrecy in the USA, see Robbins 1995 p. 26.

[24] This situation will be enhanced when the EC eco-management and audit scheme, set up under Regulation 1836/93 (OJ 1993 No. L 168) comes into effect.

scarce resources at the European Commission, such measures are unlikely to come from a European level, at least not in practical terms.

The Department of the Environment has published some documents explaining rights under the directive generally,[25] and other information is available. This information must in general firstly, however, be requested and is not distributed widely.

3. The European Community Institutions

The directive does not apply to the institutions of the European Community. The European Commission holds information about all kinds of activities or measures which may affect the environment, including information about the implementation by Member States of EC environmental law. Eurostat, the statistical agency, has information about the state of the environment. The European Environment Agency is a gatherer and disseminator of environmental information.

Some information is made available under the pressure towards greater 'transparency' in the institutions, although as noted above, this is far from amounting to a right of access to information under the same terms of the directive.[26] Other information is available under legislative provisions. For example, Regulation 1210/90,[27] which sets up the European Environment Agency, provides in Article 6:

> Environmental data supplied or emanating from the Agency may be published and shall be accessible to the public, subject to compliance with the rules of the Commission and the Member States on the dissemination of information, particularly as regards confidentiality.

There is little argument that the directive itself should not apply to the Community institutions. Indeed, as the directive was being negotiated, the European Commission admitted this as a shortcoming, and the House of Lords' Select Committee on the European Communities urged that the institutions should also be covered by such provisions (Haigh 1991).

At the *Delivering the Right to Know* conference, in April 1993, Denise Juin, a 'consultant' at DGXI of the European Commission stated:

> Community institutions are not yet bound to make environmental information available on terms similar to Member States. The directive is only addressed to Member States.

---

[25] For example, *The Environmental Information Regulations – Your Rights explained*, 92 EP 321.

[26] See the European Commission's Communications to the Council, the Parliament and the Economic and Social Committee, *Public Access to the Institution's Documents* (COM(93) 191 final) and *Openness in the Community* (COM(93) 258 final).

[27] OJ 1990 No. L 120.

This situation might be considered as an anomaly. That will require a separate legal instrument.

The next step as regards freedom of access to information on the environment could consist in extending the principle to the Community institutions.

An extension of the directive to the Community institutions would seem long overdue.

V THE RIGHT OF ACCESS TO INFORMATION AS AN ENFORCEMENT TOOL

The regulators in the United Kingdom have for some time used information covered by the directive as a means to bring about self regulation of industry.

By prosecuting only those cases where the regulator is likely to secure a conviction and by concentrating on a number of representative cases, the regulator compiles a list of polluting companies which can be used to show others how regulatory transgressions may be punished. It is not so much the fines but the bad publicity which is designed to move companies to better environmental management.

Seeing the use of information as a useful tool in regulation, these regulators have become efficient in their dissemination of it. Her Majesty's Inspectorate of Pollution has set up fax 'hotlines', and telephone enquiry lines are available. Whereas these are useful to a practising lawyer, they may also be used by the public. The introduction of these measures is putting pressure on industry to look more carefully at the requirements of environmental law.

The public interest and pressure groups are also using the information available to the public to pursue their campaigns, such as Friends of the Earth's campaign in June 1993 mentioned above.

VI CONCLUSION

This paper has discussed the development of the right of access to environmental information and of Directive 90/313. The effects of the right in general and of the directive in particular on industry have been outlined.

Questions still remain whether the directive has been properly implemented in the UK and how far the directive extends. It also remains questionable whether the public could make greater use of the directive if the rights under it were better explained. The failure to extend the application of the directive to the European Community institutions appears as an anomaly.

Whatever the answers to the above points will be, the directive is part of a major trend towards greater public participation in environmental issues. Aware of this, many in industry are keen to introduce standards of environmental management which will ensure efficiency, create verifiable improvements and lead to a sustainable economy.

14. EC Environmental Law and the Practising Lawyer

Stephen Tromans

I INTRODUCTION

This paper is written from my perspective as a solicitor specializing in Environmental Law in a large City practice, advising predominantly large corporate clients, but also on occasion governmental bodies and non-government organizations of various sizes. Inevitably, therefore, the paper reflects my own perception of the role which EC environmental law plays in practice; undoubtedly there are other perspectives, and others (for example those who act regularly for individual plaintiffs) may have different views as to the issue.

From whatever perspective one views the matter, it seems clear that EC environmental law has moved from an area regarded as of marginal importance, to a central position and an integral part of the work of UK Environmental Lawyers. Indeed, EC environmental law is so much a natural part of the work of the environmental lawyer that it is now difficult to envisage practising environmental law without it; one's work would undoubtedly be much simplified, but would not be nearly so interesting!

However, it was not always thus. There was a time, less than 20 years ago, when EC law generally was regarded as a subject of only marginal interest and importance. When I began learning the law in the mid-1970s, EC law was a new subject, meriting only an optional half paper within the Cambridge Law Tripos. On enquiring as to whether it would be a useful subject to study, I was told that it was of little interest, being essentially concerned 'with the regulation of the size of beetroot'. Even when environmental law began to emerge as a separate subject in the late 1980s, there was a tendency to regard EC law as somehow 'separate', meriting a special (often cursory) chapter in the text books and a separate (often very basic) paper at conferences. It was possible to hold the view that, since the vast majority of EC environmental law is in the form of directives, what is really important is not the words of those directives, but the words of the implementing domestic legislation. This is no longer a credible view, and the environmental lawyer today is likely to be advising his or her client with the UK regulations in one hand, and the relevant EC directives in the other.

What are the reasons for this change? I believe that there are at least four.

First, there is a growing awareness amongst lawyers of the possible applications and uses of EC law. It may well provide a potential remedy, or at least line of argument, where UK law would not. I suspect it was the employment and equal opportunities lawyers who were the first practitioners to realize and exploit these possibilities, but as more cases get decided and reported in these fields, inevitably they suggest exciting possibilities for environmental lawyers. The very flexibility and unpredictability of much of the jurisprudence of the European Court of Justice makes it all the more fertile as a source of new lines of argument.

Secondly, more and more EC environmental measures are of direct relevance to commercial activities. Directives concerned with issues such as drinking and bathing water quality did not impact directly (at least initially) on commercial interests, particularly since at that time privatization of the water industry was just a dim glint in Mrs. Thatcher's eye. If one looks now at the array of actual and proposed EC measures, dealing with issues such as eco-labelling, environmental audit and management systems, packaging waste, environmental impact assessment, landfill and civil liability, it becomes obvious that these measures have the potential to impact very directly upon business activities and balance sheets.

Thirdly, there are increasingly overt references to EC law in UK legislation. A good example is the concept of 'directive waste' introduced by the Waste Management Licensing Regulations 1994, fundamentally recasting the UK definition of waste to correspond (the government hopes) with the definition and requirements contained in the Waste Framework Directive, as amended.[1]

Finally, there is the element of general 'de-mystification' of EC law. As with modern information technology, the proportion of lawyers who grew up with EC law as part of their basic training will increase. So EC law will become generally less intimidating in terms of familiarity with the Treaty, the secondary legislation, institutions and procedures, and the jurisprudence of the European Court.

---

[1]   S.I. 1994 No. 1056, Sched. 4. See DoE Circular 11/94 (Welsh Office 26/94, Scottish Office Environment Department 10/94), Annex 1.

Having said that, it is one thing to be an expert in EC environmental law; it is another thing to build a practice by finding clients who are willing to pay for advice on that subject. So what are the main areas of practice?

I believe that one can discern two strands, which often interweave. One is advice on EC environmental law *per se*, the other is advice on EC law in the context of domestic law.

II EC ENVIRONMENTAL LAW PER SE

Just as there has been an on-going educative process on the part of lawyers in relation to EC law, the same is true for industry. Business managers are now keenly aware that it *does* matter what legislation is enacted in Brussels, whether it be on product or technical standards, employee or consumer safety, or environmental protection; in some cases, industry is aware that it may matter a very great deal.[2] The CBI and other more specific trade associations (for example the Chemical Industries Association, the Packaging Industry Research Association and the Engineering Employers' Federation, to name but three) pay a great deal of attention to EC environmental proposals. At a more specific level, the efforts of the National Association of Waste Disposal Contractors (NAWDC), the trade association for the waste management industry, has made strenuous efforts in relation to the proposed directive on landfill of waste to convince the Commission that co-disposal (the practice of disposing of industrial and municipal waste together under engineered conditions) is an acceptable technique of waste management.[3]

Such interest is not only confined to companies of EC nationality. US and other corporations operating in Europe pay close attention to developments in EC law, as witness the painstaking activities of the American Chamber of Commerce to track and assimilate environmental proposals. Many companies in recent years have taken the step of establishing at least a token presence in Brussels, in order to establish contact with the relevant EC decision makers.

---

[2] For a recent example see the article at ENDS Report No. 233 (June 1994) p. 10, 'Dry Cleaners Panic over CFC Phase-out', referring to the problems of small dry-cleaners who did not belong to trade associations and did not read the environmental press.

[3] Including flying Commission officials over various sites by helicopter: see the oral evidence of NAWDC given to the House of Commons Environment Committee. Session 1990-91, Seventh Report, *The EC Draft Directive on the Landfill of Waste*, HC
263-II, Vol. 2, p. 87, q. 403.

All of this activity represents a source of work for the environmental lawyer. As industry increases in awareness of the need for knowledge of EC proposals, so law firms are putting increasing effort into establishing appropriate monitoring and reporting networks. It is no longer enough to inform a client of a new directive at the time of its adoption; clients wish to be able to look over the horizon at what proposals are likely to be coming forward in the future. In this way, they have an opportunity of influencing those proposals or, at the very least, planning their business strategies for the future around those proposals and in the light of their potential impact.

Lawyers can also be involved in the process of shaping draft proposals, though many would shy away from the label of 'the lobbyist'. At the purely mechanical level, many clients will need advice as to the increasingly complex procedures involved in EC law making, particularly in view of the added complexities introduced by the Maastricht Treaty. Help may also be needed on framing the appropriate arguments on existing drafting, a process which is partly legalistic and partly political in nature. It is possible for lawyers to have a voice before the appropriate institutions considering EC proposals, whether within the EC or the UK. At EC level, bodies such as the European Environmental Law Association, through its working party on civil liability, has played a very active role in relation to the Commission's proposals on civil liability for environmental damage, first in making general representations on the Green Paper, then appearing before the joint hearing of the European Commission and European Parliament on November 3 and 4, 1993, by participation in the series of seminars organized for the Commission by the University of Cambridge, and finally by providing informal drafting advice as to crucial definitions such as 'harm', 'damage', 'owner', etc.[4]

The House of Lords Select Committee on the European Communities, through its relevant sub-committees, frequently hears evidence from lawyers, whether in an independent capacity in the case of bodies such as the UK Environmental Law Association or the Centre for International Environmental Law, or from lawyers in a professional capacity representing trade associations or other interests, such as insurance.[5]

---

[4] European Environmental Law Association, *Repairing Damage to the Environment – A Community System for Civil Liability*, [1994] Env. Liability, Vol. 2, Issue 1, p. 1.

[5] For example, both UKELA and the Centre for International Environmental Law gave written and oral evidence to the Select Committee on its enquiry into the proposed Directive on Civil Liability for Damage Caused by Waste: Session 1989–90, 25th Report, *Paying for Pollution*, HC Paper 84–I and II. UKELA gave written and oral evidence to the Select Committee for its report on implementation and enforcement of environmental legislation: Session 1991–92, 9th Report, HL Paper 53.I and II.

III ADVICE ON EC LAW IN THE CONTEXT OF DOMESTIC LAW

Another extremely important aspect of EC law is its use in the context of advising on domestic primary and secondary legislation. As mentioned above, EC law can give vital indications as to the likely future direction of UK law. However, it also has a very important role to play in the advice given on existing UK law.

It is not always the case that domestic law is transparently clear in its effect; nor is it always the case that it is perfectly accurate in its transposition of EC law. Sound knowledge of the underlying EC legislation is therefore of great relevance to the interpretation of UK law. This may be particularly the case in relation to directives of a general nature, the meaning of which may itself be obscure; one obvious example being the implementation of the Directive on environmental impact assessment.[6] Another good example, referred to by Mr Rose in his paper, is the implementation of the Directive on freedom of access to environmental information, where again there are points of obscurity both in the directive and in the implementing regulations, and where as a result it would seem particularly important to seek to understand the underlying purpose and objectives of the directive.[7]

Attention has tended to focus principally on arguments concerning the possible direct effect of environmental directives;[8] however, consideration of the indirect effect of directives by sympathetic interpretation of domestic law should logically come first and is potentially of much greater importance to everyday legal work. Since its inception,[9] the doctrine of interpreting national law in accordance with Community law has steadily expanded.[10] Unlike the doctrine of direct effect it may, for example, allow the terms of directives to be enforced indirectly against both public bodies and private individuals (O'Neill and Coppel, 1994 p. 37). My suspicion is that indirect effect's potential is as yet little understood and relatively untapped: logically it should mean that any discussion of the meaning of the UK legislation in question should be preceded by consideration of the

---

6   85/337 OJ 1985 No. L 175.
7   90/913 OJ 1990 No. L 158; Environmental Information Regulations 1992 No. 3240.
8   See, for example, the discussion in Krämer 1992 p. 156 et seq.
9   Case 14/83, *Von Colson v Land Nordrhein-Westfalen*, [1984] ECR 1891.
10 For example, the decision in Case C–106/89, *Marleasing v La Commercial*, [1990] ECR I-4153, applying the doctrine to national provisions adopted prior to the directive.

objectives of the relevant Community measures, in the light of the 'essential objective'[11] of environmental protection within Community law.[12] If suggestions that the doctrine is not confined to statutory interpretation, but also applies to case law, are correct then the effect may be far greater yet.[13]

Another important area for attention is the possible use of EC law as a ground for challenge in the public law context as against 'emanations of the State'. Other papers have addressed this issue in depth, and suffice it to say that the practising lawyer must be alert both as to the possibilities of such a challenge on behalf of his or her client, and also the possibility of challenge by others to a decision favourable to the client.[14] Potentially fruitful areas here are (once again) environmental assessment, access to information, and also waste management.

Thirdly, there is the influence of EC law on decision making, the granting of planning permission, waste management licences, the setting of conditions on consents, the formulation of quality objectives and emission limits. Increasingly, domestic law is shaped by the need to comply with EC law, and places explicit duties or powers with the regulatory authorities to achieve those objectives, notable examples being the setting of conditions on authorizations under Part I of the Environmental Protection Act 1990,[15] and the licensing of waste management facilities under Part II of that Act and the Waste Management Licensing Regulations 1994.[16] In this context, quantitative standards or general objectives imposed by specific directives may be relevant; however, equally relevant may well be general principles and objectives arising under the Treaty of Rome. A good example here is the precautionary principle, a tenet of European environmental policy for many years and now enshrined in primary legislation.[17] It is possible to formulate powerful arguments around this principle in the context of administrative proceedings, as is increasingly frequently the case.

---

[11] Case 302/86, *Commission of the European Communities v Denmark (Danish Bottles),* [1988] ECR 4607; see Kromarek [1990] 2 *JEL* 89.

[12] See the excellent analysis of the 'London Lorries Case, *R v London Borough Transport Committee, ex parte Freight Transport Association Ltd'* [1992] 1 *JEL* 121 at p. 134.

[13] *Ibid*, p. 36.

[14] For a powerful recent example, see '*R v Secretary of State for the Environment, HMIP and Ministry of Agriculture, Fisheries and Food'*, *The Independent*, March 8, 1994.

[15] S. 7(2)(b).

[16] S.I. 1994 No. 1056, Schedule 4. Regulations. 14 and 15 are also designed to implement EC directives, dealing respectively with waste oils and the protection of groundwater.

[17] Article 130r(2) EC.

The interaction between EC law and the common law is another fascinating area,[18] and one which may assume increasing importance if the Commission's thoughts on a civil liability regime for environmental damage come to fruition.[19] It is interesting to reflect that the litigation between Cambridge Water Company and Eastern Counties Leather, which resulted in to the leading modern case[20] on nuisance, *Rylands v Fletcher* and groundwater contamination, would never in all likelihood have come to court had it not been for the formulation of quantitative parameters on drinking water by the drinking water Directive.[21] The presence of the relevant organochlorines in the water abstracted from Cambridge Water Company's borehole infringed the implementing domestic regulations, and meant that the water could no longer be lawfully be supplied. In one sense, it was the imposition of those strict standards which led to the water company's loss, as apart from those standards there was no evidence that the water presented a threat to health or was otherwise unfit for consumption:[22]

> There is no evidence in this case that the concentrations of organochlorines in the water taken from Sawston Mill is injurious to health, and I have no doubt that there is an immense margin of safety in the prescribed figures. For all that, Sawston Mill water is now, by reason of the Directive and Regulations and with effect from July 1985, unfit to be supplied for use for one of its primary purposes, human consumption. To my mind it is unimportant that such standards might be thought to be arbitrarily set, or to be variable. It is commonplace that acceptable standards in many fields vary over the years as scientific knowledge enlarges. Sawston Mill water is by today's standards unfit for the purpose for which the plaintiffs wish to use it.

Without being unduly fanciful, it is possible to conceive how future developments under EC law (for example the possible development of soil quality standards in future) might well provide a similar impetus for litigation.

It is also interesting to note that a considerable amount of policy related argument was put forward on both sides in the *Cambridge Water Company* case including reference to developments within the EC, principles such as the polluter

---

[18] See note 13 above.

[19] COM(93)47, (the so-called 'Green Paper').

[20] *Cambridge Water Company Ltd. v Eastern Counties Leather plc* [1994] Env. L.R. 105.

[21] 80/778 OJ 1980 No. L 229, the relevant parameter being a Guide level for organochlorines of 1 microgram per litre (one part per billion). The level set by the UK was 10 micrograms per litre: see The Water Supply (Water Quality) Regulations 1989 No. 1147, Sched. II, Table D, item 10. It should not be overlooked that under the directive, since the figure in question was a Guide level rather than Maximum Admissible Concentration, the UK Government had the discretion whether to set a standard or not.

[22] *Cambridge Water Company v Eastern Counties Leather plc*; *Cambridge Water Company v Hutchings and Harding Ltd* [1992] 1 JEL 81 at p. 90, per Kennedy J.

pays, as well as wider developments such as the Council of Europe Convention on civil liability for environmental damage. The attitude of the House of Lords was to note these developments with interest, but ultimately to refrain from basing any major change in the common law upon them, on the basis that if well informed and carefully structured legislation was being put in place, that was all the more reason why the common law should not seek to interfere[23] – perhaps a debatable conclusion on a number of counts.

IV RELEVANCE IN TRANSACTIONS

It is also possible for EC law to assume importance in the context of commercial transactions, such as corporate sales, asset purchases, property transactions and secured lending.

In this context, it can be relevant in various ways. Mr Rose, in his paper, refers to the importance of the Directive on freedom of access to environmental information in enabling lawyers acting for purchasers to obtain what may be extremely useful information from public authorities. In practice, there is developing an interesting interaction between domestic proposals on contaminated land, and the requirements of EC and UK law on access to information. Before the abandonment of the proposal to create registers of potentially contaminated land under section 143 of the Environmental Protection Act 1990, a number of local authorities had made considerable progress, in anticipation of that section being implemented, towards collating information on land within their area which is or had been put to a contaminative use. Since such information undoubtedly relates to the state of the environment, it may well fall (subject to the relevant exemptions) within the Directive on freedom of access to information, and the implementing regulations.

In transactions relating to certain types of property or business, it may be important to pay close attention to specific pieces of legislation. For example, anyone proposing to acquire a waste company with established landfill operations would be foolish to disregard the likely future onerous requirements stemming from the proposed landfill Directive, and applying both to new and existing sites. Anyone acquiring a power station would be foolhardy not to pay attention to UK's ability to comply with the requirements of the large combustion plants Directive,[24] how that directive

---

23 [1994] Env L.R. 195, at p. 126. In this respect the author is grateful to Mr Phillip Vallance QC, leading counsel for Eastern Counties Leather, for supplying copies of the printed submissions of the appellant and respondent companies.

24 88/609 OJ 1988 No. L 336.

may in future be reviewed in terms of the UK's targets[25] and what non-compliance may mean for the future by way of increasingly stringent emission limits. Similarly, it would be prudent when acquiring a large food processing business to have any regard to likely future expenses involved in complying with the Directive on urban waste water treatment.[26] Acquisition of a pesticides manufacturing or distribution business would merit a long hard look at the Directive on plant protection products[27] and the uniform principles for authorization, contained in its Sixth Annex, just agreed.[28]

At a more general level, it is important to be aware of EC law when considering the drafting of commercial documentation. For example, standard warranties on the acquisition of companies will usually include a warranty as to compliance with environmental law. It may be material whether the definition of 'environmental Law' in this context includes EC directives, and this issue will need careful consideration by the draftsman; it is one thing to warrant that a plant is in compliance with UK legislation, quite another to extend that to compliance with EC law.

Given that property acquired under commercial transactions may be held for many years, there is inevitably an element of looking into the crystal ball as to possible future liabilities. The concern of many purchasers, (particularly in North America) is the possibility of an increasingly onerous liability regime, particularly in relation to contaminated land and old waste sites, driven by EC law. The proposed Directive on civil liability for damage caused by waste,[29] and the apparent willingness to contemplate an EC-wide regime for civil liability,[30] have to some extent fuelled these concerns. Thus there are inevitably arguments as to how this future risk should be treated, and many purchasers will wish to ensure that they have at least limited comfort against being fixed with future clean-up responsibilities under new and more stringent legislation. This perceived risk will need to be allocated.

In practice, many environmental consultants when carrying out due diligence investigations prior to transactions will refer to European Community law in their reports. For example, in one recent corporate transaction involving environmentally sensitive issues where I acted, the purchaser's due diligence report stressed alleged non-compliance with the

---

[25] See Haigh 1992 p. 6.10–7.

[26] 91/271 OJ 1991 No. L 135.

[27] 91/414 OJ 1991 No. L 230.

[28] Directive 94/43 OJ 1994 No. L 227, establishing Annex VI to Directive 91/414 (8107/94, July 11, 1994).

[29] COM(89)282, Proposal for a Council Directive on Civil Liability for Damage Caused by Waste.

[30] See note 19 above.

requirements of the Directives on the quality of surface water abstracted for drinking,[31] the protection of groundwater,[32] and lead in air.[33] Such reliance on E.C. law may be prompted by tactical commercial considerations or by the absence of any clear UK standards or parameters. In any event it is likely to lead to close examination of the actual requirements of the directive – for example, whether the groundwater Directive applies to discharges from old mining tips – and how the directive has been implemented in the U.K.[34] Some consultants when referring to EC directives may well be aware of any quantitative parameters, but may be less familiar with the detailed text, and may have only a hazy idea of the status of EC directives under UK law; therefore the lawyer may have to correct misconceptions which arise from selective reference to EC law.

To summarize, just as employment lawyers advising on transactions need to take account of EC provisions such as the acquired rights Directive[35] and related case-law, so environmental lawyers will need to be familiar with EC law to protect their client's position in the negotiation and drafting of commercial deals. This means not only Community environmental law as it is, but also how it may be developed in the short, medium and (sometimes) long term.

V PROBLEMS AND CONSTRAINTS

So far this paper has been very positive about the role of EC law in the practice of UK environmental lawyers. However, the obstacles to the development of EC law's full potential in this context should not be underestimated. There are a number of such barriers.

First, there is the issue of the resources needed to keep abreast of EC law as it develops. It is easier than it was for non-EC specialists to gain access to the text of environmental directives, through practitioner's books on environmental law. It is more difficult to keep track of the various twists and turns of developing EC measures, and even Her Majesty's Government is not always fully up to date in relation to successive draft proposals.[36]

---

[31] 75/440 OJ 1975 No. L 194.

[32] 80/68 OJ 1980 No. L 20.

[33] 82/884 OJ 1982 No. L 378.

[34] See DoE Circular 4/82 (Welsh Office 7/82), para 11 and Annex B.

[35] 77/187.

[36] See the evidence of the Department of the Environment to the Commons Environment Committee, Session 1990–91, Seventh Report, *The EC Draft Directive on the Landfill of Waste*, HC 263–II, p. 13, qq. 2 and 3.

Secondly, whilst judicial awareness of EC law has increased by leaps and bounds, it may sometimes be a daunting prospect to embark upon a complex explanation of the relevance of a particular measure to a judge, planning inspector or lay bench of magistrates; particularly when it is uncertain how such submissions will be received.[37]

Thirdly, my impression is that with certain notable exceptions, EC law impinges very little on the daily field experience of enforcement officers, such as waste regulation officers. It is difficult enough to know, understand and apply ever more complex domestic legislation, without the added complication of EC law.

Finally, EC law still retains a certain mystique, which can be off-putting. As mentioned earlier much of this mystique is gradually being dispelled, but I suspect many lawyers still feel tentative about advising clients on EC law, or basing possibly risky legal arguments upon it. The inherent uncertainty of much EC case law and issues such as direct and indirect effect may, whilst acting as a stimulus to the bold and creative, deter the unsure or conservative. General tensions regarding centralism or subsidiarity in Europe may also play a part in shaping attitudes here (see Francioni 1994 p. 205).

VI CONCLUSIONS

I have sought to show, from my particular perspective, how EC law occupies a position of equal importance to UK law in the work of environmental lawyers.

Some might go further and argue that it is even more important than UK law in their own experience, particularly those whose work largely involves trying to find new remedies or causes of action which may be lacking in domestic law.

Ultimately, I can only endorse for environmental law what has recently been written about EC law in the context of judicial review:[38]

---

[37] It is still the case that the sort of arguments that would appeal to a national court in a particular case are not necessarily the same as those that would appeal to the ECJ, and vice versa: see O'Neill and Coppel, 1994 p. 24.

[38] Fordham 1994 p. 7.2.

No more is Community law perceived as a separate, specialist discipline. It has become, largely through the self-promoting jurisprudence of the European Court of Justice, an ever-present mainstream legal influence.

Annex I

COUNCIL DIRECTIVE
85/337/EEC of 27 June 1985 on the assessment of the effects of certain public and private projects on the environment (OJ 1985 No. L 175)

THE COUNCIL OF THE EUROPEAN COMMUNITIES,

Having regard to the Treaty establishing the European Economic Community, and in particular Articles 100 and 235 thereof,

Having regard to the proposal from the Commission,[1]

Having regard to the opinion of the European Parliament,[2]

Having regard to the opinion of the Economic and Social Committee,[3]

Whereas the 1973[4] and 1977[5] action programmes of the European Communities on the environment, as well as the 1983[6] action programme, the main outlines of which have been approved by the Council of the European Communities and the representatives of the Governments of the Member States, stress that the best environmental policy consists in preventing the creation of pollution or nuisances at source, rather than subsequently trying to counteract their effects; whereas they affirm the need to take effects on the environment into account at the earliest possible stage in all the technical planning and decision-making processes; whereas to that end, they provide for the implementation of procedures to evaluate such effects;

Whereas the disparities between the laws in force in the various Member States with regard to the assessment of the environmental effects of public and private projects may create unfavourable competitive conditions and thereby directly affect the functioning of the common market; whereas, therefore, it is necessary to approximate national laws in this field pursuant to Article 100 of the Treaty;

---

[1] OJ 1980 No. C 169.
[2] OJ 1982 No. C 66.
[3] OJ 1981 No. C 185.
[4] OJ 1973 No. C 112.
[5] OJ 1977 No. C 139.
[6] OJ 1983 No. C 46.

Whereas, in addition, it is necessary to achieve one of the Community's objectives in the sphere of the protection of the environment and the quality of life; Whereas, since the Treaty has not provided the powers required for this end, recourse should be had to Article 235 of the Treaty;

Whereas general principles for the assessment of environmental effects should be introduced with a view to supplementing and coordinating development consent procedures governing public and private projects likely to have a major effect on the environment;

Whereas development consent for public and private projects which are likely to have significant effects on the environment should be granted only after prior assessment of the likely significant environmental effects of these projects has been carried out; whereas this assessment must be conducted on the basis of the appropriate information supplied by the developer, which may be supplemented by the authorities and by the people who may be concerned by the project in question;

Whereas the principles of the assessment of environmental effects should be harmonized, in particular with reference to the projects which should be subject to assessment, the main obligations of the developers and the content of the assessment;

Whereas projects belonging to certain types have significant effects on the environment and these projects must as a rule be subject to systematic assessment;

Whereas projects of other types may not have significant effects on the environment in every case and whereas these projects should be assessed where the Member States consider that their characteristics so require;

Whereas, for projects which are subject to assessment, a certain minimal amount of information must be supplied, concerning the project and its effects;

Whereas the effects of a project on the environment must be assessed in order to take account of concerns to protect human health, to contribute by means of a better environment to the quality of life, to ensure maintenance of the diversity of species and to maintain the reproductive capacity of the ecosystem as a basic resource for life;

Whereas, however, this Directive should not be applied to projects the details of which are adopted by a specific act of national legislation, since the objectives of this Directive, including that of supplying information, are achieved through the legislative process;

Whereas, furthermore, it may be appropriate in exceptional cases to exempt specific project from the assessment procedures laid down by this Directive, subject to appropriate information being supplied to the Commission,

HAS ADOPTED THIS DIRECTIVE:

Article 1

1. This Directive shall apply to the assessment of the environmental effects of those public and private projects which are likely to have significant effects on the environment.

2. For the purposes of this Directive:

'project' means:
- the execution of construction works or of other installations or schemes,
- other interventions in the natural surroundings and landscape including those involving the extraction of mineral resources;

'developer' means:
- the applicant for authorization for a private project or the public authority which initiates a project;

'development consent' means:
- the decision of the competent authority or authorities which entitles the developer to proceed with the project.

3. The competent authority or authorities shall be that or those which the Member States designate as responsible for performing the duties arising from this Directive.

4. Projects serving national defence purposes are not covered by this Directive.

5. This Directive shall not apply to projects the details of which are adopted by a specific act of national legislation, since the objectives of this Directive, including that of supplying information, are achieved through the legislative process.

Article 2

1. Member States shall adopt all measures necessary to ensure that, before consent is given, projects likely to have significant effects on the environment by virtue *inter alia*, of their nature, size or location are made subject to an assessment with regard to their effects.

These projects are defined in Article 4.

2. The environmental impact assessment may be integrated into the existing procedures for consent to projects in the Member States, or, failing this, into other procedures or into procedures to be established to comply with the aims of this Directive.

3. Member States may, in exceptional cases, exempt a specific project in whole or in part from the provisions laid down in this Directive.

In this event, the Member States shall:
(a) consider whether another form of assessment would be appropriate and whether the information thus collected should be made available to the public;
(b) make available to the public concerned the information relating to the exemption and the reasons for granting it;
(c) inform the Commission, prior to granting consent, of the reasons justifying the exemption granted, and provide it with the information made available, where appropriate, to their own nationals.

The Commission shall immediately forward the documents received to the other Member States.

The Commission shall report annually to the Council on the application of this paragraph.

Article 3

The environmental impact assessment will identify, describe and assess in an appropriate manner, in the light of each individual case and in accordance with the Articles 4 to 11, the direct and indirect effects of a project on the following factors:
- human beings, fauna and flora,
- soil, water, air, climate and the landscape,
- the inter-action between the factors mentioned in the first and second indents,
- material assets and the cultural heritage.

Article 4

1. Subject to Article 2 (3), projects of the classes listed in Annex I shall be made subject to an assessment in accordance with Articles 5 to 10.

2. Projects of the classes listed in Annex II shall be made subject to an assessment, in accordance with Articles 5 to 10, where Member States consider that their characteristics so require. To this end Member States may *inter alia* specify certain types of projects as being subject to an assessment or may establish the criteria and/or thresholds necessary to determine which of the projects of the classes listed in Annex II are to be subject to an assessment in accordance with Articles 5 to 10.

Article 5

1. In the case of projects which, pursuant to Article 4, must be subjected to an environmental impact assessment in accordance with Articles 5 to 10, Member States shall adopt the necessary measures to ensure that the developer supplies in an appropriate form the information specified in Annex III inasmuch as:
(a)   the Member States consider that the information is relevant to a given stage of the consent procedure and to the specific characteristics of a particular project or type of project and of the environmental features likely to be affected;
(b)   the Member States consider that a developer may reasonably be required to compile this information having regard *inter alia* to current knowledge and methods of assessment.

2. The information to be provided by the developer in accordance with paragraph 1 shall include at least:
- a description of the project comprising information on the site, design and size of the project,
- a description of the measures envisaged in order to avoid, reduce and, if possible, remedy significant adverse effects,
- the data required to identify and assess the main effects which the project is likely to have on the environment,
- a non-technical summary of the information mentioned in indents 1 to 3.

3. Where they consider it necessary, Member States shall ensure that any authorities with relevant information in their possession make this information available to the developer.

Article 6

1. Member States shall take the measures necessary to ensure that the authorities likely to be concerned by the project by reason of their specific environmental responsibilities are given an opportunity to express their opinion on the request for

development consent. Member States shall designate the authorities to be consulted for this purpose in general terms or in each case when the request for consent is made. The information gathered pursuant to Article 5 shall be forwarded to these authorities. Detailed arrangements for consultation shall be laid down by the Member States.

2. Member States shall ensure that:
- any request for development consent and any information gathered pursuant to Article 5 are made available to the public,
- the public concerned is given the opportunity to express an opinion before the project is initiated.

3. The detailed arrangements for such information and consultation shall be determined by the Member States, which may in particular, depending on the particular characteristics of the projects or sites concerned:
- determine the public concerned,
- specify the places where the information can be consulted,
- specify the way in which the public may be informed, for example by bill-posting within a certain radius, publication in local newspapers, organization of exhibitions with plans, drawings, tables, graphs, models,
- determine the manner in which the public is to be consulted, for example, by written submissions, by public enquiry,
- fix appropriate time limits for the various stages of the procedure in order to ensure that a decision is taken within a reasonable period.

Article 7
Where a Member State is aware that a project is likely to have significant effects on the environment in another Member State or where a Member State likely to be significantly affected so requests, the Member State in whose territory the project is intended to be carried out shall forward the information gathered pursuant to Article 5 to the other Member State at the same time as it makes it available to its own nationals. Such information shall serve as a basis for any consultations necessary in the framework of the bilateral relations between two Member States on a reciprocal and equivalent basis.

Article 8
Information gathered pursuant to Articles 5, 6 and 7 must be taken into consideration in the development consent procedure.

Article 9
When a decision has been taken, the competent authority or authorities shall inform the public concerned of:
- the content of the decision and any conditions attached thereto,
- the reasons and considerations on which the decision is based where the Member States' legislation so provides.

The detailed arrangements for such information shall be determined by the Member States.

If another Member State has been informed pursuant to Article 7, it will also be informed of the decision in question.

Article 10
The provisions of this Directive shall not affect the obligation on the competent authorities to respect the limitations imposed by national regulations and

administrative provisions and accepted legal practices with regard to industrial and commercial secrecy and the safeguarding of the public interest.

Where Article 7 applies, the transmission of information to another Member State and the reception of information by another Member State shall be subject to the limitations in force in the Member State in which the project is proposed.

Article 11

1. The Member States and the Commission shall exchange information on the experience gained in applying this Directive.

2. In particular, Member States shall inform the Commission of any criteria and/or thresholds adopted for the selection of the projects in question, in accordance with Article 4 (2), or of the types of projects concerned which, pursuant to Article 4 (2), are subject to assessment in accordance with Articles 5 to 10.

3. Five years after notification of this Directive, the Commission shall send the European Parliament and the Council a report on its application and effectiveness. The report shall be based on the aforementioned exchange of information.

4. On the basis of this exchange of information, the Commission shall submit to the Council additional proposals, should this be necessary, with a view to this Directive's being applied in a sufficiently coordinated manner.

Article 12

1. Member States shall take the measures necessary to comply with this Directive within three years of its notification (1).

2. Member States shall communicate to the Commission the texts of the provisions of national law which they adopt in the field covered by this Directive.

Article 13

The provisions of this Directive shall not affect the right of Member States to lay down stricter rules regarding scope and procedure when assessing environmental effects.

Article 14

This Directive is addressed to the Member States.

Done at Luxembourg, 27 June 1985.

For the Council

The President

A. BIONDI

ANNEX I
PROJECTS SUBJECT TO ARTICLE 4 (1)

1. Crude-oil refineries (excluding undertakings manufacturing only lubricants from crude oil) and installations for the gasification and liquefaction of 500 tonnes or more of coal or bituminous shale per day.
2. Thermal power stations and other combustion installations with a heat output of 300 megawatts or more and nuclear power stations and other nuclear reactors (except research installations for the production and conversion of fissionable and fertile materials, whose maximum power does not exceed 1 kilowatt continuous thermal load).
3. Installations solely designed for the permanent storage or final disposal of radioactive waste.
4. Integrated works for the initial melting of cast-iron and steel.
5. Installations for the extraction of asbestos and for the processing and transformation of asbestos and products containing asbestos: for asbestos-cement products, with an annual production of more than 20 000 tonnes of finished products, for friction material, with an annual production of more than 50 tonnes of finished products, and for other uses of asbestos, utilization of more than 200 tonnes per year.
6. Integrated chemical installations.
7. Construction of motorways, express roads[1] and lines for long-distance railway traffic and of airports[2] with a basic runway length of 2 100 m or more.
8. Trading ports and also inland waterways and ports for inland-waterway traffic which permit the passage of vessels of over 1 350 tonnes.
9. Waste-disposal installations for the incineration, chemical treatment or land fill of toxic and dangerous wastes.

---

[1] For the purposes of this Directive, 'express road' means a road which complies with the definition in the European Agreement on main international traffic arteries of 15 November 1975.

[2] For the purposes of this Directive, 'airport' means airports which comply with the definition in the 1944 Chicago Convention setting up the International Civil Aviation Organization (Annex 14).

ANNEX II
PROJECTS SUBJECT TO ARTICLE 4 (2)

1.   Agriculture

(a)   Projects for the restructuring of rural land holdings.
(b)   Projects for the use of uncultivated land or semi-natural areas for intensive agricultural purposes.
(c)   Water-management projects for agriculture.
(d)   Initial afforestation where this may lead to adverse ecological changes and land reclamation for the purposes of conversion to another type of land use.
(e)   Poultry-rearing installations.
(f)   Pig-rearing installations.
(g)   Salmon breeding.
(h)   Reclamation of land from the sea.

1.   Extractive industry

(a)   Extraction of peat.
(b)   Deep drillings with the exception of drillings for investigating the stability of the soil and in particular:
–   geothermal drilling,
–   drilling for the storage of nuclear waste material,
–   drilling for water supplies.
(c)   Extraction of minerals other than metalliferous and energy-producing minerals, such as marble, sand, gravel, shale, salt, phosphates and potash.
(d)   Extraction of coal and lignite by underground mining.
(e)   Extraction of coal and lignite by open-cast mining.
(f)   Extraction of petroleum.
(g)   Extraction of natural gas.
       (h) Extraction of ores.
(h)   Extraction of bituminous shale.
(i)   Extraction of minerals other than metalliferous and energy-producing minerals by open-cast mining.
(j)   Surface industrial installations for the extraction of coal, petroleum, natural gas and ores, as well as bituminous shale.
(k)   Coke ovens (dry coal distillation).
(l)   Installations for the manufacture of cement.

3.   Energy industry

(a)   Industrial installations for the production of electricity, steam and hot water (unless included in Annex I).
(b)   Industrial installations for carrying gas, steam and hot water; transmission of electrical energy by overhead cables.
(c)   Surface storage of natural gas.
(d)   Underground storage of combustible gases.
(e)   Surface storage of fossil fuels.
(f)   Industrial briquetting of coal and lignite.
(g)   Installations for the production or enrichment of nuclear fuels.
(h)   Installations for the reprocessing of irradiated nuclear fuels.

(i)   Installations for the collection and processing of radioactive waste (unless included in Annex I).
(j)   Installations for hydroelectric energy production.

4.   Processing of metals

(a)   Iron and steelworks, including foundries, forges, drawing plants and rolling mills (unless included in Annex I).
(b)   Installations for the production, including smelting, refining, drawing and rolling, of nonferrous metals, excluding precious metals.
(c)   Pressing, drawing and stamping of large castings.
(d)   Surface treatment and coating of metals.
(e)   Boilermaking, manufacture of reservoirs, tanks and other sheet-metal containers.
(f)   Manufacture and assembly of motor vehicles and manufacture of motor-vehicle engines.
(g)   Shipyards.
(h)   Installations for the construction and repair of aircraft.
(i)   Manufacture of railway equipment.
(j)   Swaging by explosives.
(k)   Installations for the roasting and sintering of metallic ores.

5.   Manufacture of glass

6.   Chemical industry

(a)   Treatment of intermediate products and production of chemicals (unless included in Annex I).
(b)   Production of pesticides and pharmaceutical products, paint and varnishes, elastomers and peroxides.
(c)   Storage facilities for petroleum, petrochemical and chemical products.

7.   Food industry

(a)   Manufacture of vegetable and animal oils and fats.
(b)   Packing and canning of animal and vegetable products.
(c)   Manufacture of dairy products.
(d)   Brewing and malting.
(e)   Confectionery and syrup manufacture.
(f)   Installations for the slaughter of animals.
(g)   Industrial starch manufacturing installations.
(h)   Fish-meal and fish-oil factories.
(i)   Sugar factories.

8.   Textile, leather, wood and paper industries

(h)   Wool scouring, degreasing and bleaching factories.
(i)   Manufacture of fibre board, particle board and plywood.
(j)   Manufacture of pulp, paper and board.
(k)   Fibre-dyeing factories.
(l)   Cellulose-processing and production installations.
(m)   Tannery and leather-dressing factories.

9.   Rubber industry

Manufacture and treatment of elastomer-based products.

10.   Infrastructure projects

(a)   Industrial-estate development projects.
(b)   Urban-development projects.
(c)   Ski-lifts and cable-cars.
(d)   Construction of roads, harbours, including fishing harbours, and airfields (projects not listed in Annex I).
(e)   Canalization and flood-relief works.
(f)   Dams and other installations designed to hold water or store it on a long-term basis.
(g)   Tramways, elevated and underground railways, suspended lines or similar lines of a particular type, used exclusively or mainly for passenger transport.
(h)   Oil and gas pipeline installations.
(i)   Installation of long-distance aqueducts.
(j)   Yacht marinas.

11.   Other projects

(a)   Holiday villages, hotel complexes.
(b)   Permanent racing and test tracks for cars and motor cycles.
(c)   Installations for the disposal of industrial and domestic waste (unless
(d)   included in Annex I).
(e)   Waste water treatment plants.
(f)   Sludge-deposition sites.
(g)   Storage of scrap iron.
(h)   Test benches for engines, turbines or reactors.
(i)   Manufacture of artificial mineral fibres.
(j)   Manufacture, packing, loading or placing in cartridges of gunpowder and explosives.
(k)   Knackers' yards.

12.   Modifications to development projects included in Annex I and projects in Annex I undertaken exclusively or mainly for the development and testing of new methods or products and not used for more than one year.

ANNEX III
INFORMATION REFERRED TO IN ARTICLE 5 (1)

1. Description of the project, including in particular:
–   a description of the physical characteristics of the whole project and the land-use requirements during the construction and operational phases,
–   a description of the main characteristics of the production processes, for instance, nature and quantity of the materials used,
–   an estimate, by type and quantity, of expected residues and emissions (water, air and soil pollution, noise, vibration, light, heat, radiation, etc.) resulting from the operation of the proposed project.

2. Where appropriate, an outline of the main alternatives studied by the developer and an indication of the main reasons for his choice, taking into account the environmental effects.

3. A description of the aspects of the environment likely to be significantly affected by the proposed project, including, in particular, population, fauna, flora, soil, water, air, climatic factors, material assets, including the architectural and archaeological heritage, landscape and the inter-relationship between the above factors.

4. A description[3] of the likely significant effects of the proposed project on the environment resulting from:
–   the existence of the project,
–   the use of natural resources,
–   the emission of pollutants, the creation of nuisances and the elimination of waste;
and the description by the developer of the forecasting methods used to assess the effects on the environment.

5. A description of the measures envisaged to prevent, reduce and where possible offset any significant adverse effects on the environment.

6. A non-technical summary of the information provided under the above headings.

7. An indication of any difficulties (technical deficiencies or lack of know-how) encountered by the developer in compiling the required information.

---

[3]   This description should cover the indirect effects and any indirect, secondary, cumulative, short, medium and long-term, permanent and temporary, positive and negative effects of the project.

Annex II

COUNCIL DIRECTIVE
90/313/EEC of 7 June 1990 on the freedom of access to information
on the environment (OJ 1990 No. L 158)

THE COUNCIL OF THE EUROPEAN COMMUNITIES,

Having regard to the Treaty establishing the European Economic Community, and in particular Article 130s thereof,

Having regard to the proposal from the Commission[1],

Having regard to the opinion of the European Parliament[2],

Having regard to the opinion of the Economic and Social Committee[3],

Considering the principles and objectives defined by the action programmes of the European Communities on the environment of 1973[4], 1977[5] and 1983[6], and more particularly the action programme of 1987[7], which calls, in particular, for devising 'ways of improving public access to information held by environmental authorities';

Whereas the Council of the European Communities and the representatives of the Governments of the Member States, meeting within the Council, declared in their resolution of 19 October 1987 on the continuation and implementation of a European Community policy and action programme on the environment (1987 to 1992)[8] that it was important, in compliance with the respective responsibilities of the Community and the Member States, to concentrate Community action on certain priority areas, including better access to information on the environment;

---

[1] OJ 1988 No. C 335.

[2] OJ 1989 No. C 120.

[3] OJ 1989 No. C 139.

[4] OJ 1973 No. C 112.

[5] OJ 1977 No. C 139.

[6] OJ 1983 No. C 46.

[7] OJ 1987 No. C 70.

[8] OJ 1987 No. C 289.

Whereas the European Parliament stressed, in its opinion on the fourth action programme of the European Communities on the environment[9], that 'access to information for all must be made possible by a specific Community programme';

Whereas access to information on the environment held by public authorities will improve environmental protection;

Whereas the disparities between the laws in force in the Member States concerning access to information on the environment held by public authorities can create inequality within the Community as regards access to information and/or as regards conditions of competition;

Whereas it is necessary to guarantee to any natural or legal person throughout the Community free access to avaiblable information on the environment in written, visual, aural or data-base form held by public authorities, concerning the state of the environment, activities or measures adversely affecting, or likely so to affect the environment, and those designed to protect it;

Whereas, in certain specific and clearly defined cases, it may be justified to refuse a request for information relating to the environment;

Whereas a refusal by a public authority to forward the information requested must be justified;

Whereas it must be possible for the applicant to appeal against the public authority's decision;

Whereas access to information relating to the environment held by bodies with public responsibilities for the environment and under the control of public authorities should also be ensured;

Whereas, as part of an overall strategy to disseminate information on the environment, general information should actively be provided to the public on the state of the environment;

Whereas the operation of this Directive should be subject to a review in the light of the experience gained,

HAS ADOPTED THIS DIRECTIVE:

Article 1
The object of this Directive is to ensure freedom of access to, and dissemination of, information on the environment held by public authorities and to set out the basic terms and conditions on which such information should be made available.
Article 2
For the purposes of this Directive:
(a) 'information relating to the environment' shall mean any available information in written, visual, aural or data-base form on the state of water, air, soil, fauna, flora, land and natural sites, and on activities (including those which give rise to nuisances such as noise) or measures adversely affecting, or likely so to affect these, and on activities or measures designed

---

[9] OJ 1987 No. C 138

to protect these, including administrative measures and environmental management programmes;

(b) 'public authorities' shall mean any public administration at national, regional or local level with responsibilities, and possessing information, relating to the environment with the exception of bodies acting in a judicial or legislative capacity.

Article 3

1. Save as provided in this Article, Member States shall ensure that public authorities are required to make available information relating to the environment to any natural or legal person at his request and without his having to prove an interest.
Member States shall define the practical arrangements under which such information is effectively made available.

2. Member States may provide for a request for such information to be refused where it affects:
-    the confidentiality of the proceedings of public authorities, international relations and national defence,
-    public security,
-    matters which are, or have been, sub judice, or under enquiry (including disciplinary enquiries), or which are the subject of preliminary investigation proceedings,
-    commercial and industrial confidentiality, including intellectual property,
-    the confidentiality of personal data and/or files,
-    material supplied by a third party without that party being under a legal obligation to do so,
-    material, the disclosure of which would make it more likely that the environment to which such material related would be damaged.

Information held by public authorities shall be supplied in part where it is possible to separate out information on items concerning the interests referred to above.

3. A request for information may be refused where it would involve the supply of unfinished documents or data or internal communications, or where the request is manifestly unreasonable or formulated in too general a manner.

4. A public authority shall respond to a person requesting information as soon as possible and at the latest within two months. The reasons for a refusal to provide the information requested must be given.

Article 4

A person who considers that his request for information has been unreasonably refused or ignored, or has been inadequately answered by a public authority, may seek a judicial or administrative review of the decision in accordance with the relevant national legal system.

Article 5

Member States may make a charge for supplying the information, but such charge may not exceed a reasonable cost.

Article 6

Member States shall take the necessary steps to ensure that information relating to the environment held by bodies with public responsibilities for the environment and under the control of public authorities is made available on the same terms and conditions as those set out in Articles 3, 4 and 5 either via the competent public authority or directly by the body itself.

Article 7
Member States shall take the necessary steps to provide general information to the public on the state of environment by such means as the periodic publication of descriptive reports.

Article 8
Four years after the date referred to in Article 9 (1), the Member States shall report to the Commission on the experience gained in the light of which the Commission shall make a report to the European Parliament and the Council together with any proposal for revision which it may consider appropriate.

Article 9
1. Member States shall bring into force the laws, regulations and administrative provisions necessary to comply with this Directive by 31 December 1992 at the latest. They shall forthwith inform the Commission thereof.
2. Member States shall communicate to the Commission the main provisions of national law which they adopt in the field governed by this Directive.

Article 10
This Directive is addressed to the Member States.

Done at Luxembourg, 7 June 1990.

For the Council

The President

P. FLYNN

References

Arrowsmith, S. (1992) *Civil Liability and Public Authorities*, Winteringham: Earlsgate Press.

Auby, J. and Fromont M. (1971) *Les Recours contre les Actes Administratifs dans les Pays de la Communauté Européenne*, Paris: Dalloz.

Audretsch, H. (1986) *Supervision in European Community Law*, London: Elsevier.

Axelrod, R. (1994) 'Subsidiarity and Environmental Policy in the European Community', *International Environmental Affairs*, 6:115–132.

Bael van, I. (1994) 'The Role of National Courts' *European Competition Law Review*, 15:3–7.

Ball, S. and Bell, S.(1994) *Environmental Law*, London: Blackstone

Banks, K. (1984) 'National Enforcement of Community Rights – A Boost for Damocles' *Common Market Law Review*, 21:669–674.

Bates, J. (1992) *UK Waste Law*, London: Sweet & Maxwell.

Bebr, G. (1981) *Development of Judicial Control in the European Communities*, The Hague: Martinus Nijhoff

Bebr, G. (1984) 'Direct and Indirect Judicial Control of Community Acts in Practice: the Relation between Articles 173 and 177 of the EEC Treaty', *Michigan Law Review*, 82:1229–1249.

Bebr, G. (1992) 'Joined Cases C–6/90 and C–9/90, Francovich and Bonifaci v. Italy, Judgment of the Court of Justice of 19 November 1991, not yet reported', *Common Market Law Review*, 29:557–584.

Behrens, F. (1976) *Rechtsgrundlagen der Umweltpolitik der Europäischen Gemeinschaften*, Berlin: Erich Schmidt.

Bergères, M. (1989) *Contentieux Communautaire*, Paris: Presses Universitaires de France.

Bethlem, G. and Rood, E. (1992) 'Francovich Aansprakelijkheid' *Nederlands Juristenblad*, 67:250–255.

Bizer, J., Ormond T. and Reidel U. (1990) *Die Verbandsklage im Naturschutzrecht*, Taunusstein: Blottner-Verlag.

Borchardt, G. (1985) 'The Award of Interim Measures by the European Court of Justice', *Common Market Law Review*, 22:203-236.

Bowman, M. and D. Hunter (1992) 'Environmental Reforms in Post-Communist Central Europe: from High Hopes to Hard Reality', *Michigan Journal of International Law*, 13:921–980.

Bradley, K. (1992) 'The European Court and the Legal Basis of Community Legislation', *European Law Review*, 18:379–402.

Brenninkmeijer (1992) 'Het Francovich-arrest', *Nederlands Juristenblad*, 67:256–259.

Bridge, J. (1984) 'Procedural Aspects of the Enforcement of European Community Law through the Legal Systems of the Member States', *European Law Review*, 9:28–42.

Brinkhorst, L. (1993) 'Subsidiarity and European Community Environment Policy: a Panacea or a Pandora's Box?', *European Environmental Law Review*, 2:16–24.

Bronckers, M. (1989) 'Private Enforcement of 1992: Do Trade and Industry Stand A Change against the Member States?', *Common Market Law Review*, 26:513–533.

Bronkhorst, H. (1993) *Deugdelijkheid van EG-regelgeving*, Deventer: Kluwer.

Brown, L. and Jacobs, F. (1994) *The Court of Justice of the European Communities*, London: Sweet & Maxwell.

Buckley, R. (1992) 'Trade and Environment – Will Nafta Improve Gatt?', *Environmental Policy and Law*, 22:327–331.

Buitendijk, G. and Van Schendelen, M. (1995) 'Brussels Advisory Committees: a Channel for Influence?', *European Law Review*, 20:37–56.

Bungarten, H. (1978) *Umweltpolitik in Westeuropa*, Bonn: Europa Union Verlag.

Cappelletti, M. (1981), *Access to Justice and the Welfare State*, Alphen aan de Rijn: Sijthoff.

Cappelletti, M. (1989) *The Judicial Process in Comparative Perspective*, Oxford: Clarendon Press.

Cass, D. (1992) 'The Word that Saves Maastricht? the Principle of Subsidiarity and the Division of Powers within the European Community', *Common Market Law Review*, 29:1107–1136.

Ciririello, M. (1989) 'State and Region in the Enforcement of Community Acts', *Journal of Regional Policy*, 9:153–163.

Close, G. (1978) 'Harmonization of Laws: Use or Abuse of the Powers under the EC Treaty?', *European Law Review*, 3:461–481.

Collins, K. and Earnshaw, D. (1992) 'The Implementation and Enforcement of European Community Environment Legislation', *Environmental Politics*, 1:213–249.

Commission of the European Communities (1993) *Tenth Annual Report to the European Parliament on Commission Monitoring of the Application of Community Law*, OJ (1993) No. C 233.

Commission of the European Communities (1993) *Towards Sustainability*, OJ (1993) No. C 138/5.

Commission of the European Communities (1993) May 5, Communication to the Council, the Parliament and the Economic and Social Committee, *Public Access to the Institutions' Documents*, COM(93) 191 final.

Commission of the European Communities (1993) June 2, Communication to the Council, the Parliament and the Economic and Social Committee, *Openness in the Community*, COM(93) 258 final.

Commission of the European Communities (1994) *Eleventh Annual Report to the European Parliament on Monitoring the Application of Community Law*, OJ (1994) No. C154.

Commission of the European Communities (1995) *Twelfth Annual Report on Monitoring the Application of EC Law - 1994*, OJ (1995) No. C 254

Coppel, J. (1993) *Individual Enforcement of Community Law: The Future of the Francovich Remedy*, EUI Working Paper LAW No. 93/6, Florence: European University Institute.

Corbett, R. (1986) *The 1985 Intergovernmental Conference*, ECRU working paper: Kingston upon Hull.

Crockett, T. and Schultz, C. (1991) 'The Integration of Environmental Policy and the European Community: Recent Problems of Implementation and Enforcement', *Colombia Journal of Transnational Law*, 29:169–191.

Cross, E. (1992) 'Preemption of Member State Law in the European Economic Community: a Framework for Analysis', *Common Market Law Review*, 29:447–472.

Curtin, D. and O'Keeffe D. (eds), (1992) *Constitutional Adjudication in European Community and National Law*, London: Butterworths.

Curtin, D. (1993) 'Gevoegde zaken C–6/90 en C–9/90, Francovich en Bonifaci tegen Italië' *Tijdschrift voor Sociaal en Economisch Recht*, 41:87-101.

Curtin, D and Heukels, T. (eds) (1994), *International Dynamics of European Integration. Liber Amicorum for Henry G. Schermers*, Dordrecht: Martinus Nijhoff.

Dashwood, A. and White R. (1989) 'Enforcement Actions under Articles 169 and 170', *European Law Review*, 14:388-413.

Dehousse, R. (1992) *Does Subsidiarity Really Matter?*, EUI Working Paper LAW no. 92/32, Florence: European University Institute.

Diez-Hochleitner (1994) 'Le Traité de Maastricht et l'Inexécution des Arrêts de la Cour de Justice par les États Members', *Revue du Marché Unique Européen*, 2:111–159.

Dine, J, Douglas-Scott, S and Persaud, I. (1991) *Procedure and the European Court*, London: Chancery.

Editorial Comments (1990) 'The Subsidiarity Principle', *Common Market Law Review*, 27:181–184.

Editorial Comments (1993) 'The Commission's Notice on Cooperation between National Courts and the Commission in applying Articles 85 and 86', *Common Market Law Review*, 30:681–686.

Ehlermann, C. (1984) 'How Flexible is Community Law? an Unusual Approach to the Concept of "Two Speeds"', *Michigan Law Review*, 82:1274–1293.

Ehlermann, C. (1987) 'The Internal Market following the Sinigle European Act', *Common Market Law Review*, 24:361–409.

Emiliou, N. (1992) 'Subsidiarity: an Effective Barrier against the "Enterprises of Ambition"', *European Law Review*, 17:392–410.

Epiney, A. and Furrer A. (1992) 'Umweltschutz nach Maastricht: Ein Europea der drei Geschwindigkeiten?', *Europarecht*, 27:369–408.

European Environmental Bureau (1994) *Your Rights under European Environmental Legislation*, Luxembourg: EC Publication Office.

European Institute of Public Administration (1991) *Subsidiarity: the Challenge of Change*, Maastricht, European Institute of Public Administration.

Everling, U. (1984) 'The Court of Justice as a Decisionmaking Authority', *Michigan Law Review*, 82:1294–1310.

Everling, U. (1984) 'The Member States of the European Community before their Court of Justice', *European Law Review*, pp. 215–241.

Everling, U. (1991) 'Abgrenzung der Rechtsangleichung zur Verwirklichung des Binnenmarktes nach Art. 100a EWGV durch den Gerichtshof', *Europarecht*, 26:179–182.

Fairley, R. (1993) 'Integrated Pollution Control – Public Registers and Commercial Confidentiality', *Environmental Law and Management*, 5:111-114.

Feldmann, D. (1992) 'Public Interest Litigation and Constitutional Theory in Comparative Perspective', *Modern Law Review*, 55:44–72.

Fluck, J. (1994) 'Zum EG-Abfallrecht und seiner Umsetzung in Deutsches Recht', *Europarecht*, 29:71–88.

Flynn, J. (1987) 'How will Article 100A(4) work? A comparison with Article 93', *Common Market Law Review*, 24:689–707.

Freestone, D. (1990) 'Specially Protected Areas and Wildlife in the Caribbean: the 1990 Kingston Protocol to the Cartagena Convention', *International Journal of Estuarine and Coastal Law*, 5:362-382.

Freestone, D. (1991) 'European Community Environmental Policy and Law', *Journal of Law and Society*, 18:135-154.

Freestone, D. (1991) 'Protection of Wildlife and Ecosystems in the Wider Caribbean', *Marine Pollution Bulletin*, 24:579–581.

Freestone, D. (1991) 'The Leybucht Dykes Case: Some Wider Considerations', *Water Law*, 1:152–156.

Freestone, D. (1994) 'The Road from Rio: International Environmental Law after the Earth Summit', *Journal of Environmental Law*, 6:193–218.

Freestone, D. and Ijlstra T. (1991) *The North Sea: Basic Legal Documents on Regional Environmental Co-operation*, London: Graham & Trotman.

Freestone, D. and Ryland D. (1994) 'EC Environmental Law after Maastricht', *Northern Ireland Legal Quarterly*, 45:152–76.

Frowein, J. (ed.), (1993) *Die Kontrolldichte bei der Gerichtlichen Überprüfung von Handlungen der Verwaltung*, Heidelberg: Springer–Verlag.

Fuhr, M. and Roller, G. (eds), (1991) *Participation and Litigation Rights of Environmental Associations in Europe: Current Legal Situations and Practical Experience*, Whitaker:P.Lang

Geddes, A. (1991) 'Locus Standi and EEC Environmental Measures', *Journal of Environmental Law*, 4:29-39

Geelhoed, L. (1991) 'Het Subsidiariteitsbeginsel: een communautair principe?', *Tijdschrift voor Sociaal en Economisch Recht*, 37:422–435.

Gerard, A. (1975) 'Les Limites et les Moyens de l'Intervention des Communautés Européennes en Matière de Protection de l'Environnement', *Cahiers de Droit Européen*, ?:14–30.

Gjerde, K. and Freestone, D. (1994) 'Particularly Sensitive Sea Areas under International Marine Environmental Law', *Special Issue of the International Journal of Marine and Coastal Law*, London: Graham & Trotman, pp. 431–556.

Gordon, R. (1994) 'Servants or Masters? Local Authorities in the European Judicial Review Arena', *Local Authority Law*, 4:7.

Goriely, G. (ed.), (1974) *La Commission Gardienne des Traités*, Brussels: Éditions de l'Université de Bruxelles.

Grabitz, E. and Sasse C. (1977) *Competence of the European Communities for Environmental Policy*, Berlin: Erich Schmidt.

Grabitz, E. and Zacker C. (1989) 'Scope for Action by the EC Member States for the Improvement of Environmental Protection under EC Law: the Example of Environmental Taxes and Subsidies', *Common Market Law Review*, 26:423-447.

Grado, V. (1993) 'Tendenze Evolutive della Comunitaria dell'Ambiente in Relazione al Quinto Programma d'Azione', *Rivista di Diritto Europeo*, 33:17–60.

Green, P. (1994) 'Subsidiarity and European Union: Beyond Ideological Impasse', *Policy and Politics*, 22:287–300.

González et al., (eds), *Hacia un Nuevo Orden Internacional y Europeo*, Madrid: Tecnos.

Grosz, S. (1994) 'Standing to Sue: Who Can Bring a Case?', *Environmental Law and Judicial Review*, IALS, May 13.

Gulmann, C. (1987) 'The Single European Act: Some Remarks from a Danish Perspective', *Common Market Law Review*, 24:31-40.

Haigh, N. (1987) *EC Environmental Policy and Britain*, Essex: Longman.

Haigh, N. (1991) *Manual of Environmental Policy: the EC and Britain*, London: Longman.

Hailbronner, K. (1989) 'Der "Nationale Alleingang" im Gemeinschaftsrecht am Beispiel der Abgasstandards für PkW', *Europäische Grundrechte Zeitschrift*, 16:101–122.

Hanft, K. (1991) 'The Impact of European Policies on Domestic Institutions and Politics: Observations on the Implementation of Community Environmental Directives', *ECPR Joint Sessions' Workshop on National Political Systems and the European Community*, Essex, March.

Hanft, K. (1991) 'Francovich and Bonifaci v Italy: EEC Member State Liability for Failure to Implement Community Directives', *Fordham International Law Journal*, 15:1237–1274.

Hannequart, J. (1993) *Le Droit Europeen des Dechets*, Brussels: Institut Bruxellois pour la Gestion de L'Environnement.

Hartley, T. (1988) *The Foundations of European Community Law*, Cambridge: Clarendon.

Hawkins, K. (1984) *Environment and Enforcement*, Oxford: Clarendon.

Heintzen, M. (1991) 'Subsidiaritätsprinzip und Europäischen Gemeinschaft', *Juristen Zeitung*, 46:317–323.

Hessel, B. and Mortelmans K. (1993) 'Decentralized Government and Community Law: Conflicting Institutional Developments?', *Common Market Law Review*, 30:905–937.

House of Commons Environment Committee (1992) *The EC Draft Directive on Landfill of Waste*, Session (1991–2), 9th Report, London: HMSO.

House of Lords Select Committee (1992) *Implementation and Enforcement of Environmental Legislation*, Session (1991–2), 9th Report, London: HMSO.

Howarth, W. and Somsen, H. (1991) 'The Implication of the Nitrate Directive for UK Law', *Water Law*, 2:149-152.

Howarth, W. (1991) 'Reappraisal of the Bathing Water Directive', *Water Law*, 2:51-56.

Hughes, D. (1992) 'Freedom of Access to Information on the Environment: Directive 90/313/EEC and the DOE Consultation Paper', *Land Management and Environmental Law Report*, 3:74.

Jachtenfuchs, M. (1992) 'Die EG nach Maastricht', *Europa Archiv*, 74:279–287.

Jackson, J. (1992) 'Status of Treaties in Domestic Legal Systems: a Policy Analysis', *The American Journal of International Law*, 86:310–340.

Jacobs, F. (1984) 'Civil Enforcement of EEC Antitrust Law', *Michigan Law Review*, 82:1364–1376.

Jans, J. (1988) 'Article 7 EEC and Non-Discriminatory Transfrontier Environmental Policy', *Legal Issues of European Integration*, 21–33.

Jans, J. (1989) 'Legal Problems Concerning the Implementation of EEC Environmental Directives Regarding Dangerous Substances and The Netherlands' Chemical Substance Act', *Leiden Journal of International Law*, 2:35-47

Jans, J. (1990) 'De Kwaliteit van de Europese Milieuregeling', *Tijdschrift voor Sociaal en Economisch Recht*, 38:503-526.

Johnson, S. (1993) *The Earth Summit*, London: Graham & Trotman.

Johnson, S. and Corcelle, G. (1989) *The Environmental Policy of the European Communities*, London: Graham & Trotman.

Joliet, R. (1981) *Le Droit Institutionnel des Communautés – le Contentieux*, Liège: Faculté de Droit, d'Économie et de Sciences Sociales de Liège.

Kamminga, M. (1991) 'Environmental Provisions of the Treaty on Eurropean Union', *Utilities Law Review*, 2:167–70.

Kapteyn, P. and Verloren van Themaat P. (1989) *Introduction to the Law of the European Communities*, Deventer:Kluwer.

Kindt, J. (1989) 'Dispute Settlement in International Environmental Issues: the Model Provided by the 1982 Convention on the Law of the Sea', *Vanderbilt Journal of Transnational Law*, 22:1097-1118.

Kiss, A. and Shelton D.(1991) *International Environmental Law*, London: Graham&Trotman.

Klinke, U. (1989) *Der Gerichtshof der Europäischen Gemeinschaften*, Baden–Baden: Nomos.

Koskenniemi, M. (1991) 'Peaceful Settlement of Environmental Disputes', *Nordic Journal of International Law*, 60:73.

Krämer, L. and Kromarek P. (1994) 'Droit Communautaire de l'Environnement', *Revue Juridque Revue Juridique d'Environnement*, 209–247.

Krämer, L. (1987) 'The Single European Act and Environmental Protection: Reflections on Several New Provisions in Community Law', Common Market Law Review, 24:659–88.

Krämer, L. (1988) 'Grundrecht auf Umwelt und Gemeinschaftsrecht', *Europääische Grundrechte Zeitschrift* 15:325–549..

Krämer, L. (1990) *EC Treaty and Environmental Protection*, London: Sweet & Maxwell.

Krämer, L. (1990) 'Effect National des Dircctives Communautaires en Matière de l'Environnement', *Revue Juridique d'Environnement*, 325–349.

Krämer, L. (1991) 'The Implementation of Environmental Laws by the European Economic Communities', *German Yearbook of International Law*, 34:9.

Krämer, L. (1992) *Focus on European Environmental Law*, London: Sweet & Maxwell.

Krämer, L. (1993) *European Environmental Law Casebook*, London: Sweet & Maxwell.

Krämer, L. (1994) 'Observations sur le Droit Communautaire de l'Environnement', *Actualité Juridique Droit Administratif*, 9:617–623.

Krämer, L. (1994) 'Um eine Umweltpolitik von Innen Bittend – Das Europäische Parlement und der Umweltschutz', *Zeitschrift für Umweltrecht*, 4:172-177.

Laffan, B. (1987) 'Putting European Law into Practice: the Irish Experience', *Administration*, 37:201–17.

Lane, R. (1993) 'New Community Competences under the Maastrich Treaty', *Common Market Law Review*, 30:939–979.

Leenen, A. (1984) *Gemeenschapsrecht en Volkerenrecht*, Deventer: Kluwer.

Leenen, A. (1984) 'Participation of the EC in International Environmental Agreements', *Legal Issues of European Integration*, 93–111.

Lenaerts, K. (1991) 'Some Reflections on the Separation of Powers in the European Community', *Common Market Law Review*, 28:11–35.

Lenaerts, K. (1992) 'Regulating the Regulatory Process: "Delegation of Powers" in the European Community', *Modern Law Review*, 18:24–49.

Liberatore, A. (1991) 'Problems of Transnational Policy-making: Environmental Policy in the EC', *European Journal of Political Research*, 19:281–305.

Lininger, A. (1995) 'Liberalizing Standing for Environmental Plaintiffs in the European Union', *N.Y.U. Environmental Law Journal* 3:201.

Lomas, O. et al. (1993) *Commercial Environmental Law and Liability*, London: Longman.

Louis, J. and Waelbroeck D. (eds), (1989) *La Commission au Coeur du Système Institutionnel des Communautés Européennes*, Brussels: Éditions de l'Université de Bruxelles.

Lyster, S. (1985) *International Wildlife Law*, Cambridge: Grotius

Macrory, R. (1992) 'The Enforcement of Community Environmental Laws: Some Critical Legal Themes', *Common Market Law Review*, 29:347–369.

Majone, G. (1984) 'Science and trans-science in standard-setting', *Science, Technology and Human Values*, 9:15–22.

Mancini, F. (1989) 'The Making of a Constitution for Europe', *Common Market Law Review*, 26:595–614.

Mancini, F. (1991) 'Attivismo e Autocontrollo nella Giurisprudenza della Corte di Giustizia', *Rivisto di Diritto Europeo*, 30:229-240.

Mazey, S. and Richardson J. (1992) 'Environmental Groups and the EC: Challenges and Opportunities', *Environmental Politics*, 1:109–128.

Mazey, S. and Richardson J. (1993) *Lobbying in the European Community*, Oxford: Oxford University Press.

McGrory, D. (1990) 'Air Pollution Legislation in the United States and the Community', *European Law Review*, 16:298–316.

Mensbrugghe van der, Y. (1989) 'Les Frontières Maritimes de la CEE. Observations à Propo de la Directivie 84/631 sur les Transferts Tranfrontaliers de Déchets Dangereux', *Revue du Marché Commun*, 328:360–373.

Milett, T. (1990) *The Court of First Instance of the European Communities*, London: Butterworths.

Moe, M. (1993) 'Implementation and Enforcement in a Federal System', *Ecology Law Quarterly*, 20:151–164.

Moltke von, K. (1977) 'The Legal Basis for Environmental Policy', *Environmental Policy and Law*, 3:136–140.

Neunreither, K. (1993) 'Subsidiarity as a Guiding Principle for European Community Activities', *Government and Opposition*, 28:206–220.

OKO Institut (Darmstadt) (1993) *Access to Justice in Environmental Matters*.

Oliver, P. (1987) 'Enforcing Community Rights in the English Courts', *Modern Law Review*, 50:881–907.

O'Keeffe, D. and Twomey P. (1994) *Legal Issues of the Maastricht Treaty*, London: Chancery.

O'Neil and Coppel. (1994) *EC Law for UK Lawyers: The Domestic Impact of EC Law within the UK*, London: Butterworth.

Pappas, S. (ed.), (1990) *The Court of First Instance of the European Communities*, Maastricht: European Institute of Public Administration.

Plaza Martin, C. (1994) 'Furthering the Effectiveness of EC Directives and the Judicial Protection of Individual Rights Thereunder', *International and Comparative Law Quarterly*, 43:26–54.

Pollak, C. (1991) *Verhältnismäßigkeitsprinzip und Grundrechtschutz in der Judikatur der Europäischen Gerichtshofs und des Österreichischen Verfassungsgerichtshofs*, Baden-Baden: Nomos.

Poullet, E. and Deprez, G. (1976) *Struktur und Macht der EG-Kommission*, Bonn: Europa Union Verlag.

Rasmussen, H. (1986) *On Law and Policy in the European Court of Justice*, Dordrect: Martinus Nijhoff.

Rehbinder, E. and Stewart R. (1985) *Environmental Protection Policy*, Berlin: De Gruyter.

Rehbinder, E. and Stewart R. (1985) 'Legal Integration in Federal Systems', *American Journal of Comparative Law*, 33:371-446.

Reid, C. (1994) *Nature Conservation Law*, London: Sweet & Maxwell.

Richardson, G., Ogus A. and Burrows P. (1982) *Policing Pollution*, Oxford: Clarendon Press.

Robbins, D. (1995) 'Doing Business in the Sunshine: Public Access to Environmental Information in the United States', *RECIEL*, 3:26.

Roberts, D. (1992) 'European Enforcement', *European Food Law Review*, 3:1–11.

Roberts, D. (1993) 'Food Enforcement in the United Kingdom', *European Food Law Review*, 4:365–374.

Roelants du Vivier, F. and Hannequart, J (1988) 'Une Nouvelle Stratégie Européenne pour l'Environnement dans le cadre de l'Acte Unique Européenne', *Revue du Marché Commun*, 316:225–231.

Ross, M. (1993) 'Beyond Francovich', *Modern Law Review*, 56:55-73.

Sadeleer de, N. (1994) 'La Circulation des Déchets et le Marché Unique Européen', *Revue du Marché Unique Européen*, 71–116.

Saggio, A. (1990) 'Le Basi Guiridiche della Politica Ambientale nell'Ordanmimento Communitario dopo l'Entrata in Vigore dell'Atto Unico Europeo', *Rivista di Diritto Europeo*, 27:39–50.

Sand, P. (1992) *The Effectiveness of International Environmental Agreements*, Cambridge: Grotius.

Sandalow, T. and Stein, E. (1982) *Courts and Free Markets*, Oxford: Clarendon.

Sands, P. and Tarasofsky R. (eds) (1995) *Basic Documents in International Environmental Law: EC Environmental Law*, Manchester: Manchester University Press.

Sands, P. (1990) 'European Community Environmental law: Legislation, the European Court of Justice and Common-Interest Groups', *Modern Law Review*, 53:685-698.

Sands, P. (1995) *Principles of International Environmental Law*, Manchester: Manchester University Press.

Sands, P. (1989) 'The Environment, Community and International Law', *Harvard International Law Journal*, 30:393–420.

Scherer, J. (1993) 'Umwelt-Audit: Instrument zur Durchsetzung des Umweltrechts im europäischen Binnenmarkt?', *Neue Zeitschrift für Verwaltungsrecht*, 12:11–16.

Schermers, G. and Waelbroeck D. (1987) *Judicial Protection in the European Communities*, Deventer: Kluwer.

Scheuer, H. (1975) 'Aspects Juridiques de la Protection de l'Environnement dans le Marché Commun', *Revue du Marché Commun*, 109:441–456.

Scheuning, D. (1989) 'Umweltschutz auf der Grundlage der Einheitlichen Europäischen Akte', *Europarecht*, 24:152–92.

Schimke, M. (1993) 'Zur Haftung der Bundesrepublik Deutschland gegenüber Bürgern der EG-Richtlinie über Pauschalreisen', *Europäische Zeitschrift für Wirtschaftsrecht*, 22:698–702.

Schlemmer-Schulte, S. and Ukrow J. (1992) 'Haftung des Staates gegenüber dem Marktbürger für gemeinschaftsrechtwidriges Verhalten', *Europarecht*, 27:82–95.

Schmitt von Sydow, H. (1980) *Organe der Erweiterten Europäischen Gemeinschaften – Die Kommission*, Baden-Baden: Nomos.

Schockweiler, F. (1993) 'Die Haftung der EG-Mitgliedstaaten gegenüber dem einzelnen bei Verletzung des Gemeinschaftsrechts', *Europarecht*, 28:107–33.

Schroër, Th. (1991) 'Mehr Demokratie Statt Umweltpolitischer Subsidiarität? Anmerkungen zum Titandioxid-Urteil des EuGH', *Europarecht*, 26:356–68.

Schwarze, J. (ed.) (1983) *Der Europäische Gerichtshof als Verfassungsgericht und Rechtsschutzinstanz*, Baden-Baden: Nomos.

Schwarze, J. (1987) *Perspectives for the Development of Judicial Protection in the European Community*, Baden-Baden: Nomos.

Sevenster, H. (1992) *Milieubeleid en Gemeenschapsrecht*, Deventer: Kluwer.

Sharpston, E. (1993) 'Interim and Substantive Relief in Claims under Community Law', *Butterworths Current EU Legal Developments Series*, London: Butterworths.

Siedentopf, H. and J. Ziller (1989) *Making European Policies Work*, Maastricht: Sage.

Smith, H. (1992) 'The Francovich Case: State Liability and the Individual's Right to Damages', *European Competition Law Review*, 13:129–32.

Snoep (1992) 'De nationale rechter, een vooruitgeschoven EG-post', *Nederlands Juristenblad*, 67:260–263.

Somers, E. (1990) 'The Role of Courts in the Enforcement of Environmental Laws', *International Journal of Coastal and Estuarine Law*, 5:193-198.

Somsen, H. (1990) 'EC Water Directives', *Water Law*, 1:93-98.

Somsen, H. (1991) 'The Regionalization of EC Marine Pollution Law: the Example of the Mediterranean', *International Journal of Estuarine and Coastal Law*, 6:229-245.

Somsen, H. (1992) 'Case C–300/89, Commission v Council (Titanium Dioxide)', *Common Market Law Review*, 29:140–51.

Somsen, H. (1993) 'Case C–355/90, Commission v Spain (not yet reported)', *European Environmental Law Review*, 2:152–6.

Somsen, H and Sprokkereef, A. (1995) 'Making Subsidiarity Work for the Environmental Policy of the European Community: the Role of Science',*International Journal of Biosciences and the Law*, 1:37-67.

Steindorff, E. (1990) *Grenzen der EG Kompetenzen*, Heidelberg: Verlag Recht und Wirtschaft.

Steiner, J. (1992) 'From direct effects to Francovich: shifting means of enforcement of Community Law', *European Law Review*, 18:3–22.

Task Force Report (1989) 'The Environment and the Internal Market',

Temmink, H. (1993) 'National Product-Oriented Environmental Policy and EC Law. The Dutch Example', *European Environmental Law Review*, 2:200; 213-217

Temmink, H. (1994) 'Minimumnormen in EG Richtlijnen', *Tijdschrift voor Sociaal en Ekonomisch Recht*, 43:79–106.

Temple Lang, J. (1986) 'The Ozone Layer Convention: a New Problem to the Question of Community Participation in "Mixed Agreements"', *Common Market Law Review*, 23:157–176.

Temple-Lang, J. (1990) 'Community Constitutional Law: Article 5 EEC Treaty', *Common Market Law Review*, 27:645–681.

Temple Lang, J. (1991) 'The Sphere in which Member States are Obliged to Comply with the General Principles of Law and Community Fundamental Rights Principles', *Legal Issues of European Integration*, 23–35.

Thieffry (1992) 'Les Nouveaux Instruments Juridiques de la Politique Communautaire de l'Environnement', *Revue Trimestrielle du Droit Européen*, 28:669–685.

Toth, A. (1986) 'The Legal Status of the Declarations Annexed to the Single European Act', *Common Market Law Review*, 23:803–812.

Van Kersbergen, K. and Verbeek B. (1994) 'The Politics of Subsidiarity in the European Union', *Journal of Common Market Studies*, 32:215–236.

Vandermeersch, D. (1984) 'Het Vrije Verkeer van Afvalstoffen in de Europese Gemeenschap', *Tijdschrift voor Sociaal en Economisch Recht*, 36:315–340.

Vandermeersch, D. (1987) 'The Single European Act and the Environmental Policy of the European Community', *European Law Review*, 12:407–429.

Vandermeersch, D. (1992) 'Twintig Jaar EG-Milieubeleid in Retrospectief: van Causuistiek naar Modern Beleid?', *Tijdschrift voor Sociaal en Economisch Recht*, 41:532–48.

Villeneuve de, C. (1990) 'Les Mouvements Transfrontières des Déchets Dangereux (Convention Bâle et Droit Communautaire)', *Revue du Marché Commun*, 340:568–577.

Vorwerk, A. (1990) *Die Umweltpolitischen Kompetenzen der Europäischen Gemeinschaft under ihrer Mitgliedstaaten nach Inkrafttreten der EEA*, München: Florentz.

Wagenbaur, R. (1990) 'The European Community's Policy on Implementation of Environmental Directives', *Fordham International Law Journal*, 14:455-477.

Ward, A. (1993) 'The Right of an Effective Remedy in EC Law and Environmental Protection', *Journal of Environmental Law*, 5:220-244.

Watson, J. (1991) 'Case 2/88 Imm. JJ Zwarteveld et al., Orders of the Court of 13 July 1990 and of 6 December 1990, not yet reported', *Common Market Law Review*, 2:428–443.

Wheeler, M. (1995) 'The Right to Know in the European Union', *RECIEL*, 3:1.

Whish, R. (1994) 'The Enforcement of EC Competition Law in The Domestic Courts of Member States', *European Business Law Review*, 5:3–9.

Wilke, M. and Wallace H. (1990) *Subsidiarity: Approaches to Power-Sharing in the European Community*, RIIA Discussion Paper No. 27, London.

Wilmowsky von, P. (1993) 'Waste Disposal in the Internal Market: the State of Play after the ECJ's Ruling on the Walloon Import Ban', *Common Market Law Review*, 30:541–570.

Wils, W. (1994) 'Subsidiarity and EC Environmental Policy: Taking People's Concerns Seriously', *Journal of Environmental Law*, 6:85–91.

Zwaan de, J. (1986) 'The Single European Act: Conclusion of a Unique Document', *Common Market Law Review*, 23:747-767.

Index